IFIP Working Conference on
Data Base Architecture
Venice, Italy, 26-29 June 1979

organized by
IFIP Technical Committee 2, Programming
International Federation for Information Processing

NORTH-HOLLAND PUBLISHING COMPANY
AMSTERDAM • NEW YORK • OXFORD

DATA BASE ARCHITECTURE

DATA BASE ARCHITECTURE

Proceedings of the IFIP Working Conference on
Data Base Architecture
Venice, Italy, 26-29 June 1979

edited by

G. BRACCHI
Politecnico di Milano
Italy

G. M. NIJSSEN
Control Data Europe
Brussels
Belgium

1979

NORTH-HOLLAND PUBLISHING COMPANY
AMSTERDAM • NEW YORK • OXFORD

ISBN: 0 444 85384 7

Published by:
NORTH-HOLLAND PUBLISHING COMPANY—AMSTERDAM • NEW YORK • OXFORD

Sole distributors for the U.S.A. and Canada
ELSEVIER NORTH-HOLLAND, INC.
52 Vanderbilt Avenue
New York, N.Y. 10017

PRINTED IN THE NETHERLANDS

IN MEMORIAM

MIKE SENKO

During the Venice 1979 TC 2.6 Working Conference on Database Architecture nobody's absence was more strongly and deeply felt than Mike Senko's.

His totally unexpected death at an almost cruelly young age is to all of a personal bereavement.

He will not be forgotten. One does not forget a man of his exceptional personal warmth and helpfulness, of his brilliant intellectual and professional gifts, and of his tolerance and understanding for ideas other than his own. We have lost a great architect and builder of bridges.

Our thoughts and prayers are with Helen, his wife and with his children.

This volume of proceedings, on a subject so close to his heart, is dedicated to the memory of Mike, in thankful remembrance of all he gave us.

ORGANIZATION

IFIP Working Conference on
Data Base Architecture
Venice, Italy, 26-29 June 1979

organized by
IFIP Technical Committee 2, Programming
International Federation for Information Processing

Co-sponsored by Consiglio Nazionale delle Ricerche
IBM Italia Centri Scientifici
Olivetti Ricerca Applicata Sistemi
Associazione Italiana per il Calcolo Automatico

PROGRAM COMMITTEE

Chairman	G. Bracchi	Italy
Members	F. Bodart	Belgium
	J. Bubenko	Sweden
	A.L. Furtado	Brazil
	M. Hammer	U.S.A.
	P.J.H. King	U.K.
	G. Marini	Italy
	G.M. Nijssen	Belgium
	H.J. Schneider	Fed. Rep. of Germany
	R. Stamper	U.K.
	T.B. Steel	U.S.A.
	R.W. Taylor	U.S.A.
	D. Tsichritzis	Canada

ORGANIZING COMMITTEE

Chairman	R. Marconi	Italy
Treasurer	G. Marini	Italy
Members	G. Bracchi	Italy
	A. Goldmann	Italy

CONTENTS

EDITORS'PREFACE

Data base technology is one of the most rapidly growing fields of computer and information science.

In the recent years data base management systems have come from nothing to be a major area of current interest. The area is not just fashionable, buto also important, since corporations and government agencies are increasingly relying on their data bases for operations, control, and planning.

The need for improved hardware and software tools for managing these data bases is then becoming even more important.

Data base schematics and design solutions ("architectures") are thus becoming complex, while end-user interfaces are becoming increasingly oriented toward the information content of data, and decreasingly concerned with its representational details.

These proceedings of the IFIP Working Conference on Data Base Architecture address the research and development problems related with the organization of data base systems and their interfaces.

Some seventy top-ranking data base professionals from various countries and from various groups such as users, designers, implementors, and researchers, were specially invited participants at the Conference; presentations were given by well-known experts affiliated with the main computer manufacturers, large organizations, and various Universities in Europe, America and Japan.

Their combined efforts have produced a collection of papers that offer a comprehensive and penetrating analysis of the current fundamental issues in data base architecture.

Among these are design and implementation aspects of advanced data base system organizations, design solutions for distributed data bases, access control, integrity, recovery techniques, data models, and high-level languages.

This Conference is a logical successor of the previous IFIP Working Conferences on Data Base Management, that were held in 1974 in Cargese, Corsica, in 1975 in Wepion, Belgium, in 1976 in Freudenstadt, Germany, and in 1977 in Nice, France.

It was a pleasure to observe during this fifth Conference a consolidated maturity in understanding the basic issues in Data Base Management.

Elsewhere the reader will find the names of the Program Committee members and the Organizing Committee members, who fulfilled their role with admirable dedication.

In selecting, over a very wide range of submitted contributions, the papers to be presented at the Conference, the Program Committee had the help of many well known specialists, and we wish to thank all of them for their contributions.

We also want to thank the co-sponsors and supporters who made this conference possible :

Italian National Research Council (C.N.R.)
IBM Scientific Centers of Italy
Olivetti Applied Systems Research
Italian Computing Association (A.I.C.A.)

We hope that this book will be useful to the data base community at large.

June 1979

G. BRACCHI
G.M. NIJSSEN

ARCHITECTURE OF DISTRIBUTED DATA BASE SYSTEMS

Data Base Architecture, Bracchi/Nijssen, eds.
North-Holland Publishing Company

THE EXECUTION KERNEL OF A DISTRIBUTED DATA BASE MANAGEMENT SYSTEM

Georges GARDARIN and Mireille JOUVE
INSTITUT DE PROGRAMMATION
Universite de Paris VI
4 Place Jussieu
75230 PARIS FRANCE
Sponsored by IRIA
78150 LE CHESNAY FRANCE

Continuing improvements in data base management systems have resulted in progressive implementation of relational systems on mini-computers. Given an homogeneous set of such systems, the problem which is studied here is to design a distributed execution kernel which allows reliable communications of data between a user process and remote data bases, but also and in a compatible way, between two user processes. Moreover the kernel insures the concurrency control and the robustness against crashes. In this paper, the basic concepts, the locking algorithm, the commitment procedures, the external interface and the place of the execution kernel are presented. It must be pointed out that the system permits not only the distribution of data but also the distribution of any user transaction.

INTRODUCTION

STARS is a distributed data base management system designed for an homogeneous mini-computer network. It attempts to offer the users a number of features seldom found even in larger distributed data base systems: (1) processes distributed in the network can cooperate in order to accomplish a specific task for the end user; (2) any user process can access in a compatible way to a local or a distant data set or to the input/output of a local or distant process; (3) several external models for distributed data are proposed, among them a relational one with a predicate calculus oriented query language. STARS is constructed upon local data base management systems using the relational model and offering a data manipulation language based on the predicate calculus. The first level of STARS is a distributed execution kernel insuring reliable communications between processes and maintaining the integrity of distributed data bases against concurrent accesses and failures. In the following, the design and nature of the distributed execution kernel is discussed. Then the architecture of the whole system is briefly presented.

The main objectives of the distributed system kernel are the following: (1) to permit one computer to ask another for updating or searching data in its local data base and to deliver the correct answers [20]; (2) to ensure the reliability of operations; when an operation on the distributed data base is started, it will be either correctly completed or totally annulled; consequently it must ever be possible either to stop a computer or to lose the main memory of a computer or to cancel running processes in a computer without destroying the integrity of the data base which will be restored as it was before the beginning of the current processes; (3) to allow compatible interactions with a transaction or a data base portion in order to be able to substitute a program to a data set and vice versa; that is desirable to implement a user task as several cooperating processes distributed in the network and to facilitate the debugging of applications [17]. The principal originality of this paper is to integrate these four objectives and to give a general and detailed solution with relational local data base systems. Moreover the given solutions are compatible with the two

ANSI/X3/SPARC proposals concerning data base management systems [1] and distributed systems [2].

In order to facilitate the comprehension of this paper, some working hypothesis must be formulated. First the distributed kernel assumes that each mini-computer provides a basic local data base management system which permits to describe a local data base at a conceptual level using the relational model [8] and which is able to process high level queries based on the predicate calculus [21]. Moreover a local commitment algorithm allowing the cancellation of updates not yet committed by a process [3,19] must be implemented on each site. Second the mini-computers communicate through point to point lines managed by software communication units which perform the physical control, the link control, the path control and the network control as described in [2]. In addition the network units are supposed to acknowledge every message in a reliable way: that means that a message is considered as sent only when it has been delivered to the addressee. However, a message cannot be sent if the addressee is down. In this case, the send primitive is assumed to return back a down response.

This paper is organized as follows: First, the concepts important to the design of the distributed kernel are introduced. Next, problems to which the kernel is faced up are analyzed. Then, the algorithms and solutions chosen during the design are described. Finally, an overview of the whole system architecture is presented.

CONCEPTS IMPORTANT TO THE DESIGN

Operations

In STARS, users write local programs which can add, modify, delete and retrieve informations located on different sites. These informations are processed by actions specified by statements of a host language derived from ALGOL.68. Because the processors are distributed in the network, the user may wish to interact with distributed application processes. Although this facility is available in STARS, the unit of process which the user programs is executed by a unique processor. It is called an operation. Of course, calls to the distributed data base management system generally entail some amount of remote processing, but this is either system code or actions of another operation.

Each operation is identified through an operation declaration which consists of an operation head and an operation body. The operation head specifies the name of the operation and its input and output parameters. Its general form is as follows:

> <u>Operation</u> op-id (param-1,...,param-k)

where op-id denotes an identifier which is the name of the operation; the parameters appearing within the parentheses may be input or output parameters as defined in the following declaration statements:

> <u>input</u> id1: type, id2: type,...
>
> <u>output</u> id3: type, id4: type,...

where id1, id2, id3, id4 ... denotes identifiers designating the parameters and type denotes their type which must be one of the standard scalar types boolean, integer, character or real.

It is important to remark that the set of input parameters defines a relation, name of which is "op-id-input". Of course, a key attribute which identifies an execution must be added. In the same way, the set of output parameters defines a relation, name of which is "op-id-output". Let us point out that, from an external point of view, the execution of an operation is exactly equivalent to the addition of one tuple in the relation "op-id-input" and a corresponding tuple in the relation "op-id-output". However, an operation can have no input or no output parameters.

Interaction unification

More than in a centralized system [17], in a distributed system it is desirable that the output parameters of every program can be utilized as the input of another. Such a facility allows the coordination of a distributed set of operations in order to accomplish a specific task. Thus, the application administrators are able to choose the best distribution of operations in agreement with the data distribution, the user requirements and the available resources. This is obviously not true in most of the current distributed systems where only one operation can be implemented in order to perform a user task. In such a case, the application administrators must choose one unique computer among the n computers of the network to effect a given task. In STARS, they can choose a set of p computers among the n ones.

Besides, STARS supplies a compatible way to interact with an operation and with a portion of a distributed data base. This feature involves several advantages:

(1) it allows us to realize indifferently connections between operations directly in real time or through the medium of a data set in deferred time;

(2) it permits us to simply replace an operation by a data-set and vice-versa;

(3) it simplifies the user interface by creating a new degree of independence between the tools he manipulates.

Furthermore, it must be emphasized that the possibility to interconnect operations and the compatibility between data manipulations and operation communications greatly simplify the debugging of distributed applications which remains the most important snag against distribution.

In summary, the design of STARS must obey to the general principle that an operation must interact in a compatible way with a data set and another operation. It is called the interaction unification principle.

User process

In STARS, two types of processes exist. The system processes support the execution of system code as usual. The user processes support the execution of user operations. More precisely, in order to have an operation executed by one processor, the system must initiate a user process. The operation code is loaded in main memory during the process initiation. At the end of the process initiation, unless the operation has no input parameters, the process must wait for a tuple of input parameters. When the tuple has been sent by another operation or an operator, the operation is executed and generally delivers a tuple of output parameters. The process is then supposed to wait for another tuple of input parameters which would launch another execution of the operation. Of course, the process can be terminated by another process or an operator using specific commands. Thus a user process can support several successive execution of the unique operation which is linked to it. The main interest of the distinction between user process and operation is to allow several executions of one operation while only one process is initiated. That avoids a costly network overhead due to the fact that it is not necessary to initiate a process several times for executing several times one operation. This is important because users often successively process a lot of identical memoranda [12].

Cluster

In order to accomplish a specific task, a probably distributed set of processes must be initiated and the associated operations must be completed once or several times. Such a set of processes is called a cluster. In a cluster, the cooperation of processes is not totally anarchist. The first process which is initiated, input and output parameters of which are given from/to the operator, must also be the last one which terminates. This process is called the director of the cluster. It generally initiates a set of other processes called employees. Then, it sends input tuples to the associated operations and receives output tuples from them. Every process initiated by the director can in turn initiate a set of other processes. This new processes of the cluster are also employees in regard to the director. The only rule they must follow is that they must be terminated before the director. This rule is automatically enforced by the distributed kernel. Finally a cluster can be seen as a two level hierarchy of processes cooperating in order to achieve a task. The director is the root of the hierarchy and the employees are the leaves.

Commitment unit

It is well known [16] that a distributed data base like a centralized one [10,6] must obey to a set of assertions called integrity constraints. One might think that integrity constraints must be enforced at each execution of an operation, but it is not true. As the execution of an operation is a centralized unit of processing using distributed data, it may need to violate the consistency of the distributed data base while modifying it. Of course, it is necessary that each cluster of processes keeps the integrity of the distributed data base.

Moreover, it is assumed that a cluster can be divided into steps of consistent processing which enforce the integrity constraints. Such a step is called a commitment unit [2]. The first commitment unit of a cluster starts when the director process is started. Of course, the transit of a commitment unit to the next one requires an agreement of all the processes in execution in the cluster. This difficult point will be extensively studied in the following.

Object

In designing, we have attempted to abide by the general principle that operations must interact in the same way with a data set or with the inputs or outputs of another operation. For this purpose we needed to define a notion of object which would be either a relation in a local data base or a set of input parameters or a set of output parameters of an operation. Moreover, it is well known that data independence requires the possibility to define new relations which can be projections, restrictions or joins [8] of the basic relations. In order to allow a maximum amount of local processing when possible and to reduce network transfers, it is necessary to permit the evaluation of projections, restrictions and joins of relations by each local data base system [18,12]. This facility is partially extended to inputs and outputs of operations: one process can read a part of the outputs of another obtained by projection or/and restriction of the whole set of output tuples produced by the second process; one process can also ask the system for controlling and restructuring the tuples it gives as input to another. That allows a smart independence between operations by offering a powerful way to restructure or control the exchanged messages. Moreover, that is consistent with our interaction unification principle.

Finally we define an object as a set of values extracted from tuples satisfying a well formed formula of a predicate calculus interpretation [5]. This interpretation is analogous to that defined in [9] or in the QUEL language [21]. In addition a variable can designate an input or output tuple of an operation. To be valid, a predicate must be composed with homogeneous variables, viz. with variables corresponding to either relations, or operation inputs or outputs. Moreover, operation input and output predicates are so far reduced to monovariable predicates. Thus, there are three types of objects: input one, output one and relation one which can be accessed by an operation. However, an operation does not see its own input and output as objects, but as classical parameters of a procedure.

Session

A session is a connection between a process and an object which basically permits the transmission of data between the process and the object. A session is always initiated by a user process and must be accepted either by another user process if the object is an input or output type one, or by a system process of a local data base management system if the object is a data type one.

Three types of session are distinguished according to the direction of transfers:

- read sessions which permit the transfer of tuples from an object to a transaction,
- write sessions which permit the transfer of tuples from a transaction to an object,
- read/write sessions which permit the transfer of tuples in the two directions.

It is not possible to initiate any type of session with any type of object. Figure 1 gives the possibilities. For example, an operation can read the output and write the input of another.

session / object	READ	WRITE	READ/ WRITE
INPUT	X	OK	X
OUTPUT	OK	X	X
RELATION	OK	OK	OK

FIGURE 1: Possible session types between a process and an object

ANALYSIS OF PROBLEMS

Concurrency

Given two or more independent clusters, an interference is said to have occurred if the results produced by their concurrent execution would not have been obtained by running these clusters one at a time in any order [3]. Interference takes place when data are shared between concurrent processes. Clearly, this situation is not new and interferences can be classified [11] as being either lost operation or inconsistency. A lost operation occurs when the result of an operation is altered by another operation executed at the same time. An inconsistency appears when a temporary inconsistent state of the data base is accessed or modified by a process or when a commitment unit performs two non reproductible reads of the same object.

Moreover, in STARS, the updating of remote objects is impacted by communication overhead so that they remain inconsistent during an important period of time. On the other hand, the degree of parallelism is expected to be greater than in a centralized system. Consequently the frequency of interferences can be expected to be important. Their elimination is then of primary importance. However, as yet STARS does not include an automatic maintenance of multiple copies of the data base or portion thereof. This is in charge of the user which must update all the copies in the same way while executing a commitment unit.

Robustness

The second important problem which must be solved by the kernel is to provide a way to restore a consistent data base when an operation in a cluster fails or when a site crashes. However, the kernel is not concerned by catastrophes which need the restauration of the whole data base from an old copy. Its role is to ensure that either a commitment unit is executed in totality or is not at all executed. As a consequence, during the execution of a cluster, it must always be possible to stop the execution of all the processes of the cluster and to restore the data base as it was at the end of the last commitment unit. Finally, the commitment points of a cluster can be seen as rendez-vous of the composing processes where it is admitted that all the updatings performed by the current commitment unit must be committed or annuled. In order to be able to cancel the updatings without side effect, it is necessary that no other process of another cluster has seen the updated but not confirmed data. Otherwise, if a cluster could read or worst modify uncommitted updatings, it would be necessary to undo the two clusters. Finally, that is another limit to the degree of possible concurrent processing: a cluster cannot process an object modified by an active commitment unit.

Process initiation

When an operation needs access an object, it submits a session initiation request. With the help of the site identification of the object, the local kernel either keeps the request if the object is local or sends it through the communication unit to the concerned kernel. Finally, this kernel must find a process which will act as the correspondent of the operation. It can be:

(i) a database system process if the request is for a relation type object;

(ii) a user process if the request concerns input or output parameters of an operation.

In the first case, a new process must always be activated. In the second one, it is not obvious. Selecting a new process or an existing one depends upon the circumstances and is mainly controlled by the dynamics of the situation as in any distributed system [4].

Tuple transfer

Once a session has been established, tuples can be transferred between the initiating process and its correspondent. The first problem is to control the direction of interaction. Read and write sessions are one way but read/write sessions are two ways alternate. In any case, a process which receives tuples must always be able to stop the flow.

The second problem is to synchronize and control the amount of tuples which is sent by one process and not yet treated by its correspondent. Indeed, this amount critically impacts the performance of distributed processing [12]. For example, one process would like to be activated whenever one tuple is available, another would rather process n tuples at a time, another would prefer to process them when the producer asks for.... In [2], this amount is called the quarantine unit. It is important that the quarantine unit be chosen by the user process.

As a consequence of the two previous problems, STARS must provide a flow control mechanism allowing:

(i) to interrupt a process which sends tuples through a session,

(ii) to quarantine tuples before processing them until a certain amount of tuples is available,

(iii) to quarantine tuples before processing them in such a way that the consumer can be launched when the producer wants.

ALGORITHMS AND SOLUTIONS

Identification and localization of activities

It is assumed that two operations cannot have the same name on a same site and that a user cannot activate simultaneously twice the same operation. Consequently, a user process is identified by a site address, a user identifier and an operation name.

We shall see in the following that data resources are allocated to a cluster. Consequently, it is necessary to get a simple and unique identifier for a cluster. For this purpose, each kernel manages a counter of clusters, the director of which has been initiated locally. When a process is initiated, two cases are possible:

- the process is initiated by an operator; no cluster identifier is known; then the process is associated to the cluster identified by the value of the local counter followed by the local site address; obviously, the local counter is increased;
- the operation is initiated by another process; then the cluster identifier is that of the initiating process.

When a session is established between two active processes, two different cluster identifiers can be available. The smallest one is retained. All the kernels having an activity associated with the old cluster identifier are informed by a special algorithm called the cluster fusion algorithm.

In order to execute the cluster fusion algorithm and some others (see below), it must be easy to find the sites where a cluster has some activities. For this purpose, each time a session is initiated by a transaction with an object located on another site, the site address is entered in a list called the local run list. For every cluster, a local run list is maintained on each site where at least one transaction of the cluster is executed. Let us point out that the activities of a cluster are localized by a union of all the local run lists concerning this cluster. No materialization of this union is permanent in the system.

Locking algorithm

When a session is established with an object, the object is locked. Three modes can be selected:

(i) read mode which allows read operations,

(ii) write mode which allows read and write operations,

(iii) shared mode which allows read and write operations too.

The compatibilities between these modes are defined by the following matrix where 0 means compatibility and 1 incompatibility.

	READ	WRITE	SHARED
READ	1	0	0
WRITE	0	0	0
SHARED	0	0	1

FIGURE 2: Compatibilities between operation modes

In shared mode, the protection is performed at the tuple level. That means that each time a tuple is transmitted on the session, it is locked in exclusive mode.

Locking is performed as follows: Each kernel maintains a lock table of the active objects which are located on it. This table, called the OBJ-LOC, contains for each object its designation, the lock mode and the cluster identifier. If the mode is shared, an additive table called the TUP-LOC, gives the identifiers of the tuples transmitted through the session (see Figure 3).

OBJ-LOC

OBJET	CLUSTER	MODE
p1	4.1	Shared →
p2	5.2	Read
p3	4.1	Write
p4	6.3	Shared →

TUP-LOC

1	212	523	864	1053	
27	59	534	698	1023	2345

FIGURE 3: The lock tables

There are in fact two locking algorithms. The first one works at the object level and is executed at the initiation of each session. If the lock request cannot be granted, it is entered in a wait queue which is examined whenever a process commits. This algorithm which is based on the predicate locking method described in [10] is briefly presented below. Nobj-loc is the number of objects introduced in the OBJ-LOC table.

```
** procedure LOCK1(OBJ,MODE,CLUSTER);

begin
    For i = 1 to Nobj-loc do
        if (OBJ ∧ OBJET(i) ≠ ∅) ∧ (CLUSTER(i) ≠ CLUSTER)
        then if (MODE(i) = Read ∧ MODE = Read)
             then null;
             else if (MODE(i) = Shared ∧ MODE = Shared)
                  then null;
                  else wait;
                  fi;
             fi;
        fi;
    od;
"Insert (OBJ,MODE,CLUSTER) in OBJ-LOC"
Nobj-loc := Nobj-loc + 1;;
end;
```

The second one is executed every time a tuple is transmitted on a session initiated in shared mode. If the lock request cannot be granted, it is entered in the same wait queue as the object level locking requests. Let tid be the tuple identifier and let Ntup-loc(i) be the number of tuples introduced in the TUP-LOC table corresponding to the object i in the OBJ-LOC table. The algorithm can be described as follows:

```
** procedure LOCK2(tid,CLUSTER)

begin
    For i = 1 to Nobj-loc do
        if (tid ∈ OBJET(i)) ∧ (CLUSTER(i) ≠ CLUSTER)
        then For j = 1 to Ntup-loc(i) do
                 if (TUP-LOc(j) = tid) then wait; fi;
             od;
        fi;
    od;
"Insert tid in the correct TUP-LOC(k)"
Ntup-loc(k) := Ntup-loc(k) + 1;
end;
```

Commitment algorithm

As presented above, the commitment is a rendez-vous between all the processes of a cluster where:

(1) the updating must be definitively recorded in each local data base or all aborted;

(2) the locks associated to the cluster must be released.

The principle of our commitment algorithm is based on the two steps commitment protocol [14,7]. Of course, the commitment is coordinated by the director of the cluster. The first step attempts to reverse each kernel which supports an employee in a submitted state (for the considered cluster) which can be defined as a state where the kernel is obliged to obey the orders of the kernel which executes the director and cannot take any local decision concerning the commitment of the cluster. If one kernel whose address is included in the run-lists associated with the considered cluster cannot be submitted because a process of the cluster has failed or because the site is crashed, then the cluster must be backed-up. In the other case, the director initiates the second step which is the commitment and unlocking.

Each time a process of a cluster reaches a commitment point, it executes the primitive COMMIT. When the process which commits is the director, the commitment algorithm is started. In order to improve the performances of the commitment algorithm, the submissions of the employee kernels are accomplished one by one with the help of a circular ring [15]. Three types of messages are introduced (see Figure 4):

- the submission message which includes a submit command, a cluster identifier, a list of kernels and an index in the list indicating the next kernel to submit,
- the commitment message which contains a commit command and a cluster identifier,
- the abort message which contains an abort command and a cluster identifier.

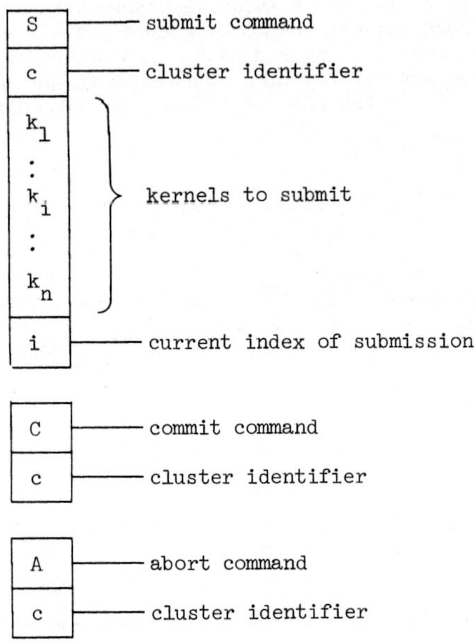

FIGURE 4: Messages utilized by the commitment algorithm

In fact, the commitment algorithm is composed of several procedures. The first one is run when a process calls the COMMIT procedure. If the process is an employee, the number of processes having reached their commitment point is simply increased. When the director commits, if all the local processes of the cluster have committed, a submission message is formed with the local run list completed by the local address as list of kernels. This message is sent to the first kernel in the list. Otherwise, as the director must be the last process which commits in a cluster, there is an abnormal condition and the transaction is aborted. The procedure COMMIT is given below. Status(p) denotes the status of the process p: director or employee. NPROS(c) is the number of processes of the cluster c locally initiated and NCOMIT(c) is the number of local processes of the cluster c which have already executed COMMIT. ABORT is the abort procedure which is described below.

```
** procedure COMMIT;

begin
p := process-identifier;
c := cluster-identifier;
"find the local run-list R(c) = (k1,k2...kn-1)"
    if (status(p) = 'director')
    then if (NCOMIT(c) = NPROS(c))
         then begin
              "Compose the submission message:
              S := ('S',c,R(c),kn,1)"
              send S to k1;
              if "k1 is down" then call ABORT(c); fi;
              end;
         else;
              call ABORT(c);
         fi;
    else NCOMIT(c) := NCOMIT(c) + 1;
    fi;
end;
```

The second one is run when a kernel executing employees receives a submission message $S = ('S', c, k_1, k_2 \ldots k_n, i)$. Then it accepts to commute in submitted state if all the processes of the concerned cluster have reached a commitment point. In this case, the site addresses which are in the local run list and not yet in the submission message are inserted into it before the last site k_n (which is the director address). At last, the index i is increased and the submission message is sent to the next kernel. In the other case where at least one process has not reached its commitment point, an abort message is broadcasted to all the kernels of the local run list because one process at least has not commited before the director process. The procedure which is named SUBMIT is described below. The notation introduced above are used.

```
** procedure SUBMIT(c,k1,k2...kn,i);

begin
"Find the local run list R(c)"
"Extract the director kn from R(c)"
"Let (p1,p2,...pr) the resulting list"
    if (NCOMIT(c) = NPROS(c))
    then begin
         status(s) := 'submitted';
         merge (k1,k2...kn-1) and (p1, p2...pr) into (e1,e2,...em);
         em+1 := kn;
         i := i + 1;
         "Compose the new submission message:
         S := ('S',e1,e2,...em,em+1,i)"
         send S to ei;
         if "ei is down" then call ABORT(c); fi;
         end
    else
         call ABORT(c);
    fi;
end;
```

The third procedure is executed when the kernel which supports the director receives back the submission message. Then, the first step of the commitment algorithm is completed. Consequently, a commit message is broadcasted to all the kernels, addresses of which are in the final submission message. Moreover, the local commitment is performed.

```
** procedure SUBMITTED(c,k1,k2...kn,n);

begin
"Compose a commitment message:
C := ('C',c)"
broadcast C to k1,k2,...kn-1;
"perform the local commitment"
"unlock all the objects and tuples locked for c"
end;
```

When a kernel which executes employees receives a commitment message, it must only perform the local commitment [19,3] by executing the procedure CONSOLIDATE.

```
** procedure CONSOLIDATE(c);

begin
"perform the local commitment"
"unlock all the objects and tuples locked for c"
end;
```

When any kernel receives an abort message or call for the first time, it must broadcast it to all the kernels known in its local run list. This option has been chosen because it is important to make known widely an abortion since some computers are probably crashed and unable to transmit it. Consequently, an abort message or call received when a cluster has already been aborted must be ignored. Of course, the first abort message or call must involve the back-up of every local process of the cluster.

```
** procedure ABORT(c);

begin
    if "c has already been aborted"
    then null;
    else begin
         "Find the local run list (p1,p2...pr)"
         "Compose an abort message:
         A := ('A',c)"
         broadcast A to p1,p2,...pr;
         For "every local process p of c" do
             "back-up p" od;
         end;
    fi;
end;
```

The last procedure must be executed when the director kernel has not received back the submission message or an abort message after a maximum transit time T. In this case, one site have failed in such a way that the submission message is lost. Consequently, the director must abort the cluster.

```
** procedure TIMEOUT(c);

begin
call ABORT(c);
end;
```

A last problem which has not been addressed yet occurs when the director fails during the commitment of a cluster. If the director fails during the first phase, before getting back the submission message, then the kernel which precedes it on the circular ring will fail in sending back the submission message; consequently the transaction will be aborted. If the director fails during the second phase before broadcasting the commitment message, then the employees will hold on to their locks indefinitely; to avoid this situation, every kernel cannot stay in submitted state during a time greater than the maximum transit time T. Consequently, after this time, the procedure TIMEOUT must be executed and the transaction will be aborted. If the director fails during the broadcasting of the commitment message, it could happen that some sites receive this message whereas some others do not receive it. To prevent this situation, it is assumed that a reliable broadcast is implemented: that means that a broadcast command is either thoroughly executed or not at all executed.

Process initiation algorithm

As presented in Section 3, when a request is received to initiate a session, it is not obvious in certain cases if the activation of a new process is necessary or if the session concerns an already existing process. In order to distinguish the two cases, it has been chosen to associate a name to a session. Finally, the general form of the request to initiate a session is:

session-id = INITIATE(user-id,session-name,site-ad,obj-def,session-type,quar-unit)

where:

- session-id is an identification which is given to the process in order to identify the session,
- user-id is the identification of the end user,
- session-name is the name of the session,
- site-ad is the address of the site which manages the requested object,
- obj-def is a predicate which defines the requested object as seen in Section II,
- session-type is the type of the session, i.e. read, write or read/write,
- quar-unit permits to define the chosen quarantine unit (see below).

Of course, like in [4], a session must be accepted by the correspondent process by a special primitive:

session-id = ACCEPT(user-id,session-name,quar-unit)

where the parameters are identical to those defined above.

Consequently, the algorithm to determine if a process must be initiated or not is quite simple: when a request to establish a session with an object is processed by the kernel which manages the object, if the session has already been accepted for the correct user, no new process is created; otherwise, a new process is inititated.

Tuple transfer control

At any moment a session is oriented from one process which is the sender to the other which is the receiver. As proposed in the ANSI/X3/SPARC proposal [2], control may be alternatively passed from one process to the other. The process which does not have the turn may interrupt the other process and demand the turn by executing a special primitive:

status = INTERRUPT(session-id)

where session-id has been defined above and status is a response code.

The amount of tuples that a process must send before its correspondent can be awaked is determined when the session is initiated and accepted. For this purpose, the two parameters quar-unit in INITIATE and ACCEPT are used. The first one specifies the quarantine unit in the direction process initiating the session toward process accepting the session; the second one specifies it in the reverse direction. The possible values of quar-unit are:

- a positive integer n; that means that the quarantine unit is set to n tuples;
- 0; that means that the end of each quarantine unit will be given by the producer of tuples using a special primitive:

status = DELIVER(session-id).

Of course, like in [4], it is always possible to cancel a quarantine unit before its end by the way of the primitive:

status = PURGE(session-id).

Finally, a process can send a tuple on a session with the primitive:

status = PUT(session-id,buffer-ad)

and receive a tuple with the primitive:

status = GET(session-id,buffer-ad).

A session is terminated by the primitive:

status = TERMINATE(session-id).

V. ARCHITECTURE OF THE DISTRIBUTED DATA BASE SYSTEM

General considerations

The STARS architecture is presented here as a distribution of the ANSI/X3/SPARC model [1]. The description and comprehension of the ANSI/X3/SPARC architecture which is used here can be found in [22]. It is assumed that the conceptual schema has been designed in paying regard to the geographical distribution of the data. Consequently, it can be implemented in parts which are not necessarily disjoint on each local site [20]. A more thorough presentation of this architecture can be found in [13].

In order to simplify the presentation, computers in the network are classified in two types:

- data computers which contain data stored in a local data base,
- processing computers which execute the user transactions.

In the last section, an integration will be presented where every host can be simultaneously a data computer and a processing computer.

Place of the distributed kernel

The problem was to distribute the ANSI/X3/SPARC DBMS functional architecture between a data computer and a host computer with the help of a distributed kernel. Of course, a distributed kernel is directly interfaced with the transport units and exchanges data and commands with another distributed kernel by a specific protocol. Consequently, a processing computer can ask a data computer for executing the functions provided by the distributed kernel interface. The main option which had to be chosen was the level of this interface which defines the place of the kernel in the architecture.

Two levels were possible:

- the internal one which would mean that the kernels would be set between the conceptual and the external level.

The choice has been made when the notion of object has been defined. Indeed, the object which has been introduced in Section II is not an internal one but a conceptual one. The first possibility has been rejected for two principal reasons:

(i) the level of interface of the distributed kernel must be far from the internal notions of access path, internal record or file in order to unify the interactions with the transactions and the data sets;

(ii) in order to permit a maximum amount of local processing by the data computers and to reduce network transfers, it is desirable to provide an interface with a high level of functionality.

It must be pointed out that this choice led to some difficulties, particularly for designing the locking algorithm which must use a predicate locking method. But it is a way which gives acceptable performances and data independence.

Distribution of the data dictionary directory

A key point of the ANSI/X3/SPARC DBMS architecture is the data dictionary directory. It can be seen as a meta data base where every DBMS processor fetches the parameters needed during its execution. Of course, it is necessary to distribute the elements of this data dictionary directory. The main elements of interest are:

- the program descriptions,
- the external data base schema object type descriptions,
- the mapping structures relating external and conceptual objects,
- the conceptual data base schema object type descriptions,
- the mapping structures relating internal schema and conceptual schema,
- the internal data base schema object description.

By hypothesis, a program description is located on a processing computer. In the same way, each data computer needs at least an internal schema to describe the internal structure of its local data base. Then, under the assumption that the conceptual schema can be implemented in local parts, it is desirable to implement a part on the data computer which manages the corresponding data base. This is necessary if we want to avoid a duplication of the whole conceptual schema on all the computers [12]. Consequently, mapping structures relating internal and conceptual levels are located on data computers.

The last point to discuss is the place of external schema and mapping structures relating external and conceptual objects. Of course, the external schema must be set on the processing computers. As the mapping structures are strongly dependent on the external model, they are placed next to the external schema associated. Let us point out that an external schema can be mapped on the whole conceptual schema; that means that an external object can be mapped into many conceptual objects of different localization. Consequently, the mapping structures relating external and conceptual objects must include distribution rules and catalogues for external objects.

Presentation of the architecture

Before presenting the architecture, it must be pointed out that the external database schema processor needs accesses to the distributed conceptual schema in order to bind the external objects to objects declared in the conceptual schema. It is performed by consulting the meta data base which contains on each data computer the conceptual schema. For this purpose, the interface of the distributed kernel is used by the external schema processor.

Figure 5 and 6 give the architecture of STARS on a data computer and on a processing computer. Figure 7 gives an overview of the global architecture with two computers which are simultaneously data computers and processing one.

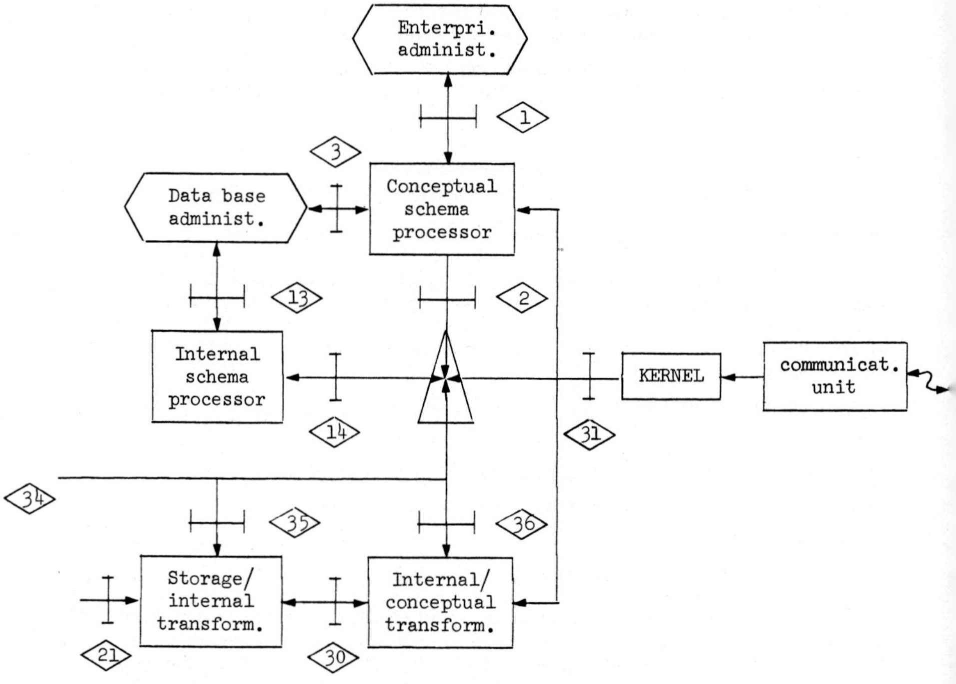

FIGURE 5: Architecture of STARS on a data computer

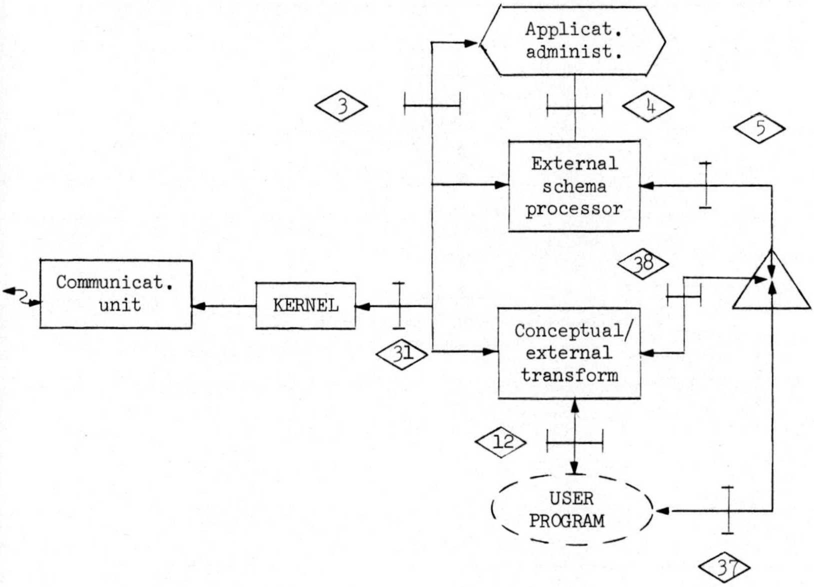

FIGURE 6: Architecture of STARS on a processing computer

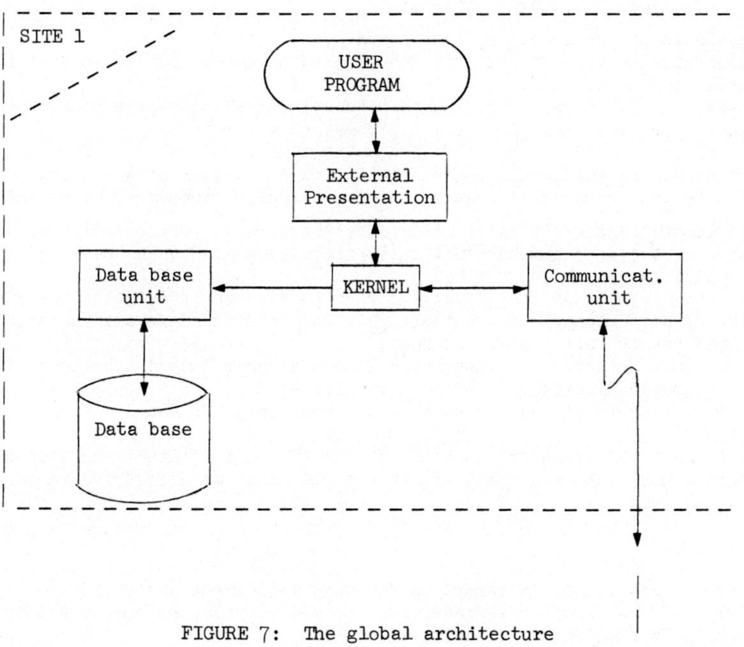

FIGURE 7: The global architecture

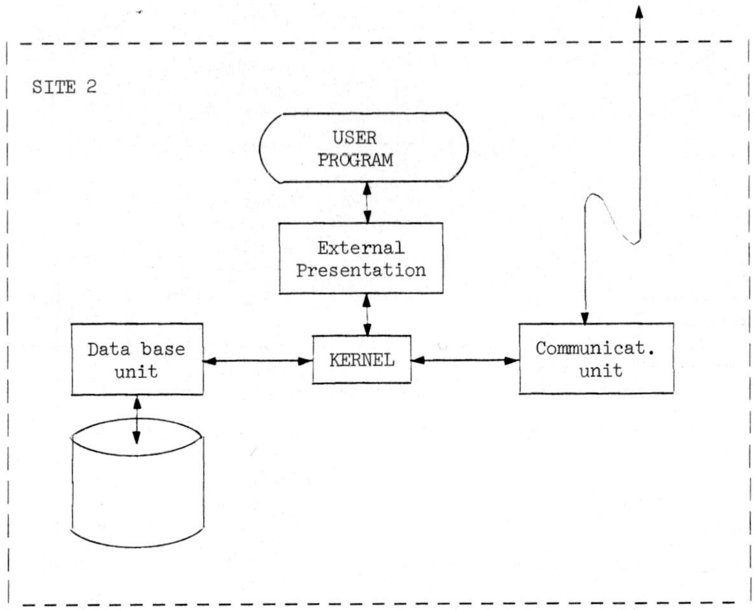

VI. CONCLUSION

In this paper, the distributed execution kernel of an homogeneous distributed data base management system for a mini-computer network has been presented. This kernel insures the following functions:

(1) robustness of the system against crashes,
(2) concurrency control in order to keep the data base integrity against the multi-access conflicts,
(3) initiation of processes to execute a query, an updating or a user operation,
(4) transfer control of tuples from a process to a remote one.

These functions are sufficient to implement a first version of a reliable distributed data base management system, but some problems remain to be solved:

(1) no automatic integrity is maintained by the kernel; particularly, multiple copies of the data base are not automatically updated when the original copy is modified,
(2) no global checkpoint can be set in order to restore in totality the distributed data base after a catastrophe; only states where all the sites are stopped can be restored from a dump;
(3) no deadlock detection is integrated in the kernel; indeed, the cost of such a distributed algorithm is still prohibitive;
(4) security aspects of the system have not been taken in care.

Finally, it must be emphasized that the design of a distributed execution kernel is one of the most important part of the acomplishment of a distributed data base management system.

VII. REFERENCES

[1] ANSI/X3/SPARC, Interim report on database management system, (March 1975).
[2] ANSI/X3/SPARC, Draft reference model on distributed systems, USA contribution to ISO/TC97/SC16, (January 1978).

[3] C. W. Bachman, Advances in database technology, Infotech State of the Art Tutorial, London (December 1977).
[4] C. W. Bachman, What is session control within an open system architecture, American National Standards Committees, (April 1978).
[5] F. Bancilhon, On the completeness of query languages for relational data bases, Lecture Notes in Computer Science, Springer-Verlag N64, (1978) 112-123.
[6] E. Benci, A. Cabanes, F. Bodart and H. Bogaert, Concepts for the design of a conceptual schema, IFIP Conference on Modelling in DBMS, North-Holland (January 1976) 181-200.
[7] M. W. Blasgen, Issues in the design and implementation of DBMS, AICA '77 Proc. Databases (October 1977) 3-21.
[8] E. F. Codd, A relational model of data for large shared data banks, CACM Vol 13/N6 (Juin 1970) 377-387.
[9] E. F. Codd, A data base sublanguage founded on the relational calculus, ACM SIGFIDET WORKSHOP (1971).
[10] K. P. Eswaran, J. N. Gray, R. A. Lorie and I. L. Traiger, The notion of consistency and predicate locks in a database system, CACM Vol 19/N11, (November 1976) 624-633.
[11] G. Gardarin and P. Lebeux, Scheduling algorithms for avoiding inconsistency in large databases, 3rd International Conference on Very Large Data Bases, Tokyo (1977) 501-506.
[12] G. Gardarin, Resolution des conflits d'access simultanes a un ensemble d'informations Application aux bases de donnees repartie, These d'Etat, Universite de Paris VI, (Avril 1978).
[13] G. Gardarin, A unified architecture for data and message management, National Computer Conference, New York (1979) AFIPS Vol 48, pp 681-688.
[14] B. Lampson and H. Sturgis, Crash recovery in a distributed data storage system, Research Report Xerox - Palo Alto, (1976).
[15] G. Le Lann, Algorithms for distributed data-sharing systems which use tickets, 3rd Berkeley Workshop on Distributed Data Management and Computer Networks, (August 1978) 259-272.
[16] C. Parent, Integrity in distributed data bases, AICA 1977, Pisa (October 1977) 187-198.
[17] D. M. Ritchie and K. Thompson, The unix time-sharing system, CACM Vol 17/7, (July 1974) 365-375.
[18] J. B. Rothnie, A survey of research and development in distributed data management, 3rd International Conference on Very Large Data Bases, Tokyo (1977).
[19] D. G. Severance and G. M. Lohman, Differential files: Their application to the maintenance of large databases, ACM TODS Vol 1/3, (September 1976) 256-267.
[20] S. Spaccapietra, Problematique de conception d'un systeme de gestion de bases de donnees reparties, These d'Etat, Universite de Paris VI, (Novembre 1978).
[21] M. Stonebracker et al, The design and implementation of INGRES, ACM TODS Vol 1/3, (September 1976) 189-222.
[22] D. Tsichritzis and A. Klug, The ANSI/X3/SPARC DBMS Framework, Technical note 12, University of Toronto, (July 1977).

Data Base Architecture, Bracchi/Nijssen, eds.
North-Holland Publishing Company

GROSS ARCHITECTURE OF THE DISTRIBUTED DATABASE SYSTEM VDN

Rudolf Munz

Technische Universität Berlin
Fachbereich Informatik

Abstract:

This paper tries to give an argumentation for distributed database systems in contrast to distributed file systems. The gross architecture of the distributed database system VDN and the key decisions of its design are outlined. Selected topics of the problems of concurrency control in a distributed database environment and our solution ideas are sketched.

1. Filesystems versus database systems

For reasons of clarity we will start with working definitions of the terms "file system" and "database system".

File system:

A file system handles records. The composition of a record out of different fields is irrelevant for the file system, that is, the access to a particular record field and the relations between different record types are hidden in the logic of application programs. Depending on the physical organization of the file, records are identified by their position or by a unique record key. Only single record accesses are possible. The lock unit is usually the entire file. By this, only one user can update a file at a particular point of time.

Database system:

A database system handles record fields. The structure of a record, that is the record fields, and the relations between different record types are known by the database system (schema definition). Records are identified by unique record keys. Secondary keys can be used to specify the access to sets of records. The lock unit is usually an individual record, that is, update requests collide only at the record level. The user can specify update transactions (consisting out of several dependent updates) which are performed as an atomic action by the database system.

These two definitions form the end points of a scale. A large number of commercially available software systems lay in-between. These definitions also show the well-known advantages of database systems:

- Independence of the physical data organization.
- Less redundancy, as contrary to file systems no processing restrictions exist which are caused by particular physical file organizations.
- Programs depend only on those record fields which they use. They do not depend on the sequence or number of fields in a particular record type.
- Sets of records can be selected based on the contents of particular record fields.
- Several users can update simultaneously records of the same type.
- Update transactions produce all intended effects or, in case of a failure have no effect at all.

2. Why systems for distributed data management?

A system for distributed data management is a software system which administers in an uniform manner data stored on different nodes of a computer network. For a user of such a system, the physical distribution of data is transparent, that is the system for distributed data management realizes a logically centralized view of physically distributed data. Out of the user's view, a system for distributed data management is not different from a system for centralized data management.

There are several reasons for the use of systems for distributed data management:

- Integration of data which exist for historical reasons at different locations and have been administered separately.
- The new technology of systems for distributed data management allows better and more problem adequate solutions. Tasks with a decentral nature must no longer be centralized if they should be done by computers. This has consequences for the following areas of computer applications:

    o Branches of bank and assurance companies

    o Inventory and manufactoring control systems in multi-plant companies

    o Personnel systems in multi-site, multi-division companies

  These applications form a large part of "classical" edp applications. With todays technology, these applications are usually implemented on big, central computers. If the locality behaviour (see /3 /) of these applications (data are created, updated and used mainly at the same location) and the cost of data transmission is taken into account, this centralization does not make sense. For these application classes, the communication costs can be lowered by storing and processing the data there, where they are used. For this, the processing capabilities of minicomputers are usually sufficient and their use results in a better price/performance ratio than a comparable main frame. The interconnection of several minicomputers by a communication facility makes a system for distributed data management possible. By an access possibility to nonlocal data, this system can provide a logically centralized view of data if needed. This decentralized approach has the following advantages:

- Line costs will be saved because the data are there where they are needed.
- The data are more up to date because they are entered into the system where they are created.
- Such a system provides better communications because all users can access the most actual data.
- Because of the inherent parallelity of a computer network, response times are expected to be better compared to central, mostly overloaded main frame.
- Departments, divisions or plants with "own" data feel responsible for them and can process them autonomously.
- Organizations based on the division of labor can be supported quite naturally with computing power by a corresponding distribution of data.
- The breakdown of a local computer and the resulting unaccessibility of its data have not the same disastrous effects as the breakdown of a single, central computer.
- It is easy to upgrade the computer performance of a minicomputer network by adding a further minicomputer where it is needed. Central mainframes are not as flexible with respect to their upgrading.
- Because of the price/performance trends for minicomputers and main frames we expect a network of minicomputers to be cheaper than a comparable main frame.

As mentioned above, for us, decentralized processing should be based on a strong locality behaviour of applications. That is, most accesses should address locally available data. Accesses to non-local data should be exceptions.

- Process control and military command and control applications have another primary requirement: high security and availability. Systems for distributed data management can meet these requirements better than central systems. In a distributed system copies of local data can be kept and maintained elsewhere. Depending on the degree of this redundancy, all data remain available even after the breakdown of one or more computers. Of course, a price must be paid for the simultaneous updating of these copies.

3. Distributed file systems versus distributed database systems

Distributed file systems are already available from several edp manufacturers. Out of a user's view they make the location of a particular file in a computer network transparent. That is, local and nonlocal files can be treated in the same manner. The units of data distribution are files, although this is a somewhat arbitrary decision. All distributed file systems provide single record accesses via the record key.

If one intends to implement a distributed database system one has to investigate whether it makes sense to put this system on top of a distributed file system. By this, all problems of data distribution would be solved by the underlying distributed file system. Therefore the internal logic of the distributed database system would not be different from a central one. However, this bottom-up approach has the disadvantage that, in certain situations, accesses to record sets (e.g. "Find all persons living in a particular city") must be processed very inefficiently. If the existing secondary key indexes are not sufficient for the processing of such a query, a large number of records must be checked sequentially. If a distributed file system is used, each one of these checks can result in the transport of a record. By this, a large amount of unnecessary communication is generated, which is very time-consuming because of the low transmission rates of present day communication lines.

In the design of a system for distributed data management we therefore follow the rule, that it makes more sense to bring the operations to the data than to bring the data to the operations.

For accesses to sets of records this means, that the corresponding node gets the whole query (e.g. "Find all persons living in a particular city"). That is, two computers cannot only communicate at the level of single record accesses but also at the level of accesses to sets of records. Consequently, the distributed database system is aware of the data distribution and has to solve the resulting problems. However, this top-down approach has the advantage that it minimizes the communications within the computer network. The principal guideline is that all tasks which can be performed at one location result in one command at the communication level which is processed at the addressed location.

4. The distributed database system VDN

4.1 The datamodel

Records consist out of a linear sequence of fields. Fields may be optional. Integers, reals, packed decimals and character strings are possible as field values. One or more key fields must be specified for each record type. For record fields simple integrity constraints can be formulated by an enumeration or by an interval of possible field values. New fields can be defined "on the fly" for already existing record types.

A dynamic subtype construct is provided similar to the one proposed in /10/. It allows the definition of subsets of a record type by specifying a qualification which must hold for all records of this subset.

Examples of subset definitions are:

```
DEF SUBSET VIP OF PERSON WHERE SALARY > 5000

DEF SUBSET GERMAN_EMP OF PERSON
                    WHERE NATIONALITY = 'GERMAN'
                    AND   STATUS = 'EMPLOYEE'
```

Subsets can overlap. They serve as an abbreviation for the qualification of a certain subset of a record type. In addition to this, the access to records of a subset can be supported. Subsets play also an important role for the distribution of data.

Associations between records must be expressed in the relational sense. That is, different record types (or restrictions of record types) can be joined according to a particular join expression. Associations between records can be named and are then called links. Linknames serve as abbreviations for the join expressions by which they are defined.

Examples of link definitions are:

```
DEF LINK WORKS_IN FROM PERSON TO DEPARTMENT
                  WHERE PERSON.DEP# = DEPARTMENT.DEP#

DEF LINK SUPPLIES FROM SUPPLIER TO PART
                  WHERE SUPPLIER.SUP# = PART.SUP#
```

Links can also be supported to achieve a more efficient realization of the corresponding join.

The operations on these data structures consist out of commands for the selection of record sets and commands for the update of individual records. The selection of a set of result "records" is provided where this result record can contain fields of out of different record types. Such a result set can be reused in subsequent queries like an ordinary record type. The elements of a result set can be accessed in a pipelined mode, that is record by record. Subsets and record types can be used in the same manner in all operations. Update operations (add, delete and replace) are only possible for individual records.

Update transactions with read and write locks are provided. Preclaiming of all locks is used to avoid deadlocks. The finest lock granules are records. Data privacy is assured by a proper user identification and a capability list for each user. Privileges for a user with respect to particular operations can be granted at the record field level.

A large degree of data independency is achieved by allowing user operations only for record fields. That is, the user addresses record fields by their names and has no possibility to handle an entire record and to get dependent of its internal structure of length. For the same reasons, subsets and links can exist at a "define" and at a "create" level. The access path support they provide at the "create" level can therefore be switched off without implications for application programs. If subsets or links are still defined, their names in the application programs play only the role of abbreviations and are simply expanded by their definitions.

4.2 Units of data distribution

A distributed database system adds another degree of freedom and by this a new problem area to the data base design. If a data base schema is defined, there must also be stated at what locations of the computer network which portions of the database are to be stored. Thus, the database administrator gets a new task in a distributed database environment.

To be able to specify the data distribution, suitable units of data distribution must be identified. In the VDN system we use the above mentioned subsets of record types as units of data distribution. A special case of such a subset is the actual record type. Different approaches are to use disjoint subsets (see /5/) or disjoint fragments (see /6/) of a record type as units of data distribution. Subsets are allowed to overlap, by this we get an implicit copy mechanism. Copies of the same subset can also be installed explicitly at different locations. The data distribution can also be redefined "on the fly".

The data distribution defined by suitable subsets is invisible for the application programmer if he uses the corresponding record type names. If the application programmer uses the names of those subsets by which the data distribution is defined he can be aware of the data distribution. In certain applications this might be desirable. However, the resulting application programs are not dependent on the data distribution.

Subset names can exist at the "define"-level where they are only abbreviations and at the "create"-level where they are used for the definition of the data distribution. Subsets must be defined before they can be created. If the data distribution is altered and a subset name is no longer used at the "create"-level, it still exists at the "define"-level. Therefore all application programs which use this subset name are unaffected from this change.

Although it is desirable to shift the task of defining the data distribution from the database administrator to the system, this is in our opinion not possible within the present state-of-the-art. We have outlined several of the intrinsic problems in /3/.

4.3 Gross architecture

Like the definitions of record types, subsets and links, the assignation of subsets to particular locations is known by all computers of the network. This means, schema information is kept redundant at each location. As the schema description is relatively small and the most static part of the database, this does not cause problems. The distributed database system VDN at each location of the network can be split into two parts:

global module

local module

The global module knows the schema definition and the global data distribution at the level of subset definitions. If a user task enters the system, each global module can decide, which locations are involved in the processing of this task.

A local module at a particular location only knows the data which are locally available and processes incoming queries or updates with respect to the local data base.

The processing of a user task is controlled by the global module at the location where this task is entered. This global module generates subtasks for the involved local modules at other locations. This results in the following communication structure:

global module i

local module k ... local module i ... local module n

The generation of subtasks is based on a suitable representation of data distribution definitions and user tasks by sets of intervals (see /7/, /9/). The generated subtasks are processed autonomously by the addressed local module. The returned subresults must be assembled to the final result by the global module. As we assume a strong locality behaviour of data for our applications, in most cases only the local module at the same location will be involved.

A more detailed description of the system architecture and the division of labor between different system layers is expressed in figure 1.

We will explain these layers in a bottom-up manner. The system is based on direct addressable files of fixed-sized blocks provided by the underlying operating system. With the help of these files a B*-tree like record access organization with variable length records and variable length keys is implemented. Records at this layer correspond to user records. To support accesses to record sets, the system uses index lists for secondary keys. These index lists are treated as special records within this layer. For each record type and for each inverted record field there exists such a B*-tree-like construct which contains the records or the index lists, respectively.

------------------------------------ application programmer interface

parser:

syntax-checking, check of data privacy privileges, internal representation

------------------------------------ parser interface

task distribution and administration:

generation of subtasks, determining the communication partners, sending of subtasks, administration of received subresults, processing of joins

------------------------------------ communication interface

local dbs:

processing of queries per record type, administration of index lists, administration of lock lists, logging

------------------------------------ file system interface

local file system:

single record accesses and updates via the record key, operations on record fields, operations on index-lists

------------------------------------ operating system interface

local operating system:

direct addressable files with blocks of a fixed size

Figure 1: System layers of VDN

At the communication interface there exists a local database system which is able to answer one variable queries, that is queries which concern only one record type. By this, join evaluation has to take place in the next higher layer. The local database system also handles updates for the locally available data and administers the related index lists. Synchronization of concurrent updates for local records is also done at this layer. These design decisions are based on the philosophy that each location should only administer locally available objects. That is, index lists are kept only for local data and data has to be locked at all locations where it exists (distributed locking). The next higher level covers the organizational aspects of data distribution, generating of subtasks according to the data distribution and assembling of subresults. Queries which imply joins are decomposed into several queries concerning a single record type, even if they can be answered locally.

The output of the parser has a direct correspondence to the commands available at the application programmer interface. However, beside the syntax-checking, most of the data privacy privileges are checked and data dependent privacy conditions can be satisfied by a corresponding manipulation of the query.

4.4 Uniqueness of record keys

If the units of data distribution are not only entire record types but also subsets of a record type, it is relatively difficult to provide the uniqueness of record keys. The resulting problems are illustrated by the following example.

Let us assume that record of type "person" are to be distributed. The record key is a personnel number, the distribution criteria the place-of-living. If a new record is added to the database with a personnel number "1000" and a place-of-living "London", the given distribution definitions determine at what locations this record is to be stored. However, it is not known whether there already exists a record with the same personnel number but with another place-of-living. If the distributed database system should guarantee key uniqueness like a central database system, then at all locations where records of this type exist there must be checked whether there already is a personnel record with the same personnel number. As this causes a lot of communication, guaranteeing key uniqueness in a distributed database system is relatively expensive. This is true for all semantic integrity constraints which depend on all records of a particular type. Key uniqueness seems to be the most important constraint of this type.

Things are much simpler if the record key is used as a distribution criteria. Other solutions to this problem are a special treatment of mass additions by the use of a global key index or suitable organizational measures. However, a global key index is not convincing for a permanent use because of its maintenance overhead.

4.5 Consistency of subset copies

Copies of a subset at different locations of the network should be in the same updating state at each point of time. This requirement can be approximated by the strategies of "distributed locking", "primary copies" (see /8/ or "time stamping" (see /1/) if a failure-free behaviour of computers and lines is assumed.

With respect to "distributed locking" which is used in VDN this means that all subset copies must be locked by the database system before a user transaction which intends to alter this subset is allowed to start. In the same manner all nodes where copies of a subset are held must be informed of the end of an update transaction.

In reality, however, we have also to cope with possible breakdowns of computers and lines. After such a breakdown has occured, the distributed database system has to guarantee the consistency of subset copies. One reason for keeping copies of subsets is a higher availability in case of such a breakdown. Therefore it must be allowed to update the subset copies which are still up.

If a down node is up again it has to take measures to get informed about the changes of subset copies it missed during its downtime. That is, beside its local restart measures, the restarting node has to contact all relevant "copy locations" to get these changes.

At all nodes of network a log of all changes of the database is kept. Therefore the restarting node can re-establish its local database up to the point of the breakdown. With the help of its global knowledge of the schema and the data distribution, this node is able to determine where copies of its subset are held. These "copy locations" must be contacted to get informed about the newest state of this subset. The missing updates can be simply determined if the restarting node transmits the identification of the last update transaction it has performed on the regarded subset.

The restarting node is therefore fully responsible for the consistency of its subset copies. Note that the usual communication structure global module - local module - global module must be violated for restart purposes where a direct interaction of local modules is required.

4.6 Update transactions in a distributed environment

Out of the view of an application programmer, an update transaction is a sequence of dependent operations on the database. This sequence should be treated as an atomic action by the database system, that is in case of a failure an update transaction should produce all of its intended effects or none of them.

A typical example of an update transaction is a bank transfer:

$$A := A - 10$$

$$B := B + 10$$

These two updates should be performed completely or not at all. It may not happen, even in case of a line or node breakdown, that for example the first update is the only one which is performed.

Such a transaction concept can be realized for central database systems by working on copies of data (see /2/) or by keeping a log file. Both methods allow the backout of an update transaction in case of a failure. The same methods for the realization of update transactions are possible for a distributed database system. The situation gets however more complicated by the fact, that several nodes can be involved in the execution of an update transaction.

In VDN we use some sort of a differential file concept and we keep a log file to eliminate the influence of buffering and for reasons of data security. An update transaction is controlled by the global module of the node where the transaction is entered.

Minor problems are caused if a node participating in an update transaction breaks down. If this is detected by the controlling global module, this update transaction is backed out at all involved locations.

The breakdown of the node at which the global module is situated can be more critical. Especially if the global module has signaled the end of an update transaction to some but, because of its breakdown, not to all of the involved nodes. To solve this situation, these nodes autonomously decide what to do with a pending update transaction. To be able to do this, they must know their "transaction partners", that is the nodes which participate in this update transaction. If a node detects a pending update transaction due to a breakdown of the global module, it contacts a transaction partner to get informed about what to do with this transaction. Again, for this purpose the usual communication structure has to be violated to allow a direct interaction of local modules. An elaborated treatment of the aspects of concurrency control in the distributed database system VDN is given in /4/.

5. Final remarks

The VDN project has finished its design phase which took from the midth of 1977 to the end of 1978. With a project team of seven members we are now in the implementation phase and expect to have a first version of an operational system at the end of 1979.

Acknowledgements

The author wishes to acknowledge helpful discussions with H.-J. Schneider, J. Bieber, B. Freier, F. Steyer, F. Schiele and H. Schweppe.

This work is part of the project "Distributed Databases" at Technical University of Berlin, sponsored by the Federal Ministery of Research and Technology under grant FKZ 081 5011 A.

References:

/1/ P.A. Bernstein, D.W. Shipman, J.B. Rothnie, N. Goodman: The concurrency control mechanism of SDD-1: a system for distributed databases, Technical Report CCA-77-09, Computer Corporation of America

/2/ R.A. Lorie: Physical integrity in a large segmented database, ACM TODS, Vol.2, No.1, March 1977

/3/ R. Munz: System architectures for managing distributed databases, in: "Datenbanken in Rechnernetzen mit Kleinrechnern", Informatik-Fachberichte 14, Springer, 1978

/4/ R. Munz, H.F. Schweppe: Concurrency control in the distributed database system VDN, VDN-Report 16/78, Project "Distributed Database", Technical University Berlin

/5/ E.J. Neuhold, H. Biller: POREL: a distributed data base on an inhomogeneous computer network, Proc. Third VLDB, Tokyo, 1977

/6/ J.B. Rothnie, N. Goodman: An overview of the preliminary design of SDD-1: a system for distributed databases, Technical Report CCA-77-04, Computer Corporation of America

/7/ F. Steyer: Processing of queries in distributed database systems, VDN-Report 3/77, Project "Distributed Databases", Technical University Berlin

/8/ M. Stonebraker, E.J. Neuhold: A distributed database version of INGRES, 1977 Berkeley Workshop on Distributed Data Management and Computer Networks

/9/ H. F. Schweppe: On different classes of predicates for distributing data, in: "Datenbanken in Rechnernetzen mit Kleinrechnern", Informatik-Fachberichte 14, Springer, 1978

/10/ D. Tsichritzis: LSL: a link and selector language, Proc. ACM SIGMOD Conf. 1976

Data Base Architecture, Bracchi/Nijssen, eds.
North-Holland Publishing Company
© IFIP (1979)

Distributed Database Partitioning and Query Processing

S.A. Mahmoud, J.S. Riordon, and K.C. Toth

Department of Systems Engineering and Computing Science
Carleton University
Ottawa, Canada.

ABSTRACT: An architecture for distributed databases is presented, and the problem of data distribution and directory structure for a distributed DBMS is examined. As an aid to the design of a query processing strategy, the concept of a query graph is introduced. Nodes correspond to subsets of database relations, while arcs represent qualification terms linking relations. A simple example is shown in which the object is to minimize network communications associated with query processing. Finally, a distributed file access coordination procedure is presented.

1. Introduction

This paper describes the architecture and operational concepts of a distributed database (DDB) in an interactive transaction processing system. The distributed database is formed based on two types of data distribution. The first type characterizes the requirements of many large organizations having distributed operations spread over a wide geographic region. Transactions processed against the databases of such organizations are expected to originate (and/or terminate) from the various districts of operation. The database can be seen in this case as a collection of several segments, each segment containing the set of data elements accessed most frequently by a particular region. When the database segments are allocated to different processors, a distributed database results. The second type of data distribution is a result of functional (processing) specialization in which segments of the database are allocated to certain processing sites because special processing capabilities exist at these sites. The allocation of certain segments of the database in this type of distribution may also be based on administrative or security considerations.

In interactive processing systems, terminal users connected to a nodal processor invoke interactive application programs which are resident in their local processor. The application programs issue one or more of the following types of transactions to the information network:

a) transactions which invoke direct data access (update or query) on database segments in the local and remote processing sites (nodes) of the information network.
b) transactions which cause the transmission of entire database files (possibly with directories or logical access paths) to the host node of the application program.
c) transactions which cause the transmission of spawned application programs to remote nodes to execute against database segments which are stored in these nodes.

The database architecture described in this paper is general in the sense that it allows the processing of the three types of transactions described above.

However, the operational concepts described here are particularly suited for the first type of transaction, i.e., those involving retrieval and/or update operations on local and remote data segments.

The distributed database architecture described in this paper offers several advantages over physically centralized database systems:

1) Availability: By providing redundent storage of critical data segments in two or more sites, the overall availability of these data segments will be substantially enhanced, especially for retrieval purposes [1].
2) Fast Response Time: By proper allocation of the data segments so that they are stored close to where they are most frequently accessed, fast response times can be attained [1], [2].
3) Modularity and Upward Scaling: The distributed database can be implemented initially on a small number of processing sites. As the size and usage of the database grow over time and geographical space, new sites can be added without disrupting or substantially altering existing operations. By comparison, upgrading of centralized systems is difficult to achieve without major service disruption.
4) Cost Reduction: The DDB architecture presented here is particularly suited for moderate size computers. The increasing power and complexity of these computers enable them to handle efficiently direct data access operations in addition to simple computational functions. The decreasing cost of moderate size computers and telecommunications services, coupled with the upward scaling potential, is expected to decrease the cost of distributed database systems below the cost of a functionally equivalent centralized (main-frame supported) database system.

The realization of a DDB system which attains all or some of the above advantages is currently an active research area. Several problems have been identified in this research area and have been classified into three main categories [3].

1) Database structure and organization
2) Operation and control (query processing strategies, access control and synchronization, integrity preservation, etc.)
3) Allocation of database segments, programs, communications resources, etc.

The system presented in this paper and referred to as "An Architecture for a Distributed Database", or ADD, represents an on-going research whose objective is to realize a DDB that offers the aforementioned advantages. The general architecture of ADD has been described in [4] and will be summarized in this paper to facilitate its reading. The main emphasis of this paper, however, will be placed on the operational and control concepts in ADD. The interrelationship among the problems of database structure, data allocation, and access control to distributed data segments is also emphasized.

The remainder of this paper is organized as follows: Section 2 presents briefly the general architecture of the ADD system. Section 3 describes the logical and physical partitioning of the database and the structure of the directory which provides logical access paths to the partitioned database. Section 4 outlines general query processing strategies and states the criteria used to determine these strategies. Section 5 describes the protocols used to control concurrent accesses to distributed database partitions and to preserve internal database consistency. Section 5 describes also the interrelationship between query processing strategies and the approaches used in controlling concurrent access to database partitions.

2. The General Architecture

The structure of the ADD system and its implementation in each network node is based on a layered approach. The underlying concept is that transactions enter the network from any processing node and progress from one layer to the next within that node. At some point in thelayered structure a transaction may be split into subtransactions that are in turn routed to other nodes to access remote data segments. Each layer in the hierarchy is completely defined by its processing functions and the input and output parameters associated with the transactions entering the layer and leaving it. The remainder of this section explains briefly components of the architecture and serves as a basis for the material contained in the following sections. Detailed description of the architecture is available in [4].

Figure 1 illustrates layers of the ADD system. A total of seven layers exists in general, with the outermost layer serving as the interface between the user and the DDB, and the innermost layer representing the physical (file) access controller. At any network node, the functions associated with a given level may be grouped together and assumed to run on a virtual view processor. Thus each layer, while representing a view or a "schema" of the database, can be represented by a virtual processor which embodies all the functions of the layer.

The outermost layer of the architecture shown in Figure 1 represents the external (user) view of the integrated database and is termed the Users Views Processor (UVP).

This is followed by the System View Processor (SVP) which embodies the global logical model of the database. To allow distribution of data segments to nodes, two additional levels are introduced. First the Partitioned View Processor (PVP) which carries the definition of a logical decomposition of the System View. Second is the Distributed View Processor (DVP) which carries the information concerning the physical (geographic) allocation of data segments to network nodes. Transactions enter the node and are passed from the UVP to the SVP and then to the PVP and DVP where they may be split into subtransactions that are routed to the DVP's of other nodes. A common network access language is used and for this reason the top four layers (UVP, SVP, PVP and DVP) are generally similar in all processing nodes.

The internal and physical access paths [5] are collocated with their database segments in each network node and are defined in the two innermost layers: (1) the Access and Association View Processor (AVP) and, (2) the Physical (File) View Processor (FVP). The Nodal View Processor (NVP) is introduced to translate between the common access language (in which subtransactions received from DVP are expressed) and the local access language, if they differ. Thus heterogeneous database structures can exist in the network.

Using a conventional database terminology, it is possible to explain how the ADD structure generates a physically distributed but logically integrated database. For this purpose we consider the ANSI/X3/SPARC model [6] in which four levels are identified:

1) The external model level: User View
2) The conceptual model level: Logical System View
3) The internal model level: Internal System View
4) The file model level: File View

In the ADD structure, the external model isbuilt into the UVP layer and the conceptual model level is built into the SVP. These two layers isolate the users completely from the distribution aspects of the data. The PVP and DVP layers are introduced in ADD to handle the logical partitioning and the data distribution related functions. To this extent, the telecommunications (networking) functions are treated as part of the DVP. The internal model of the ANSI proposal is

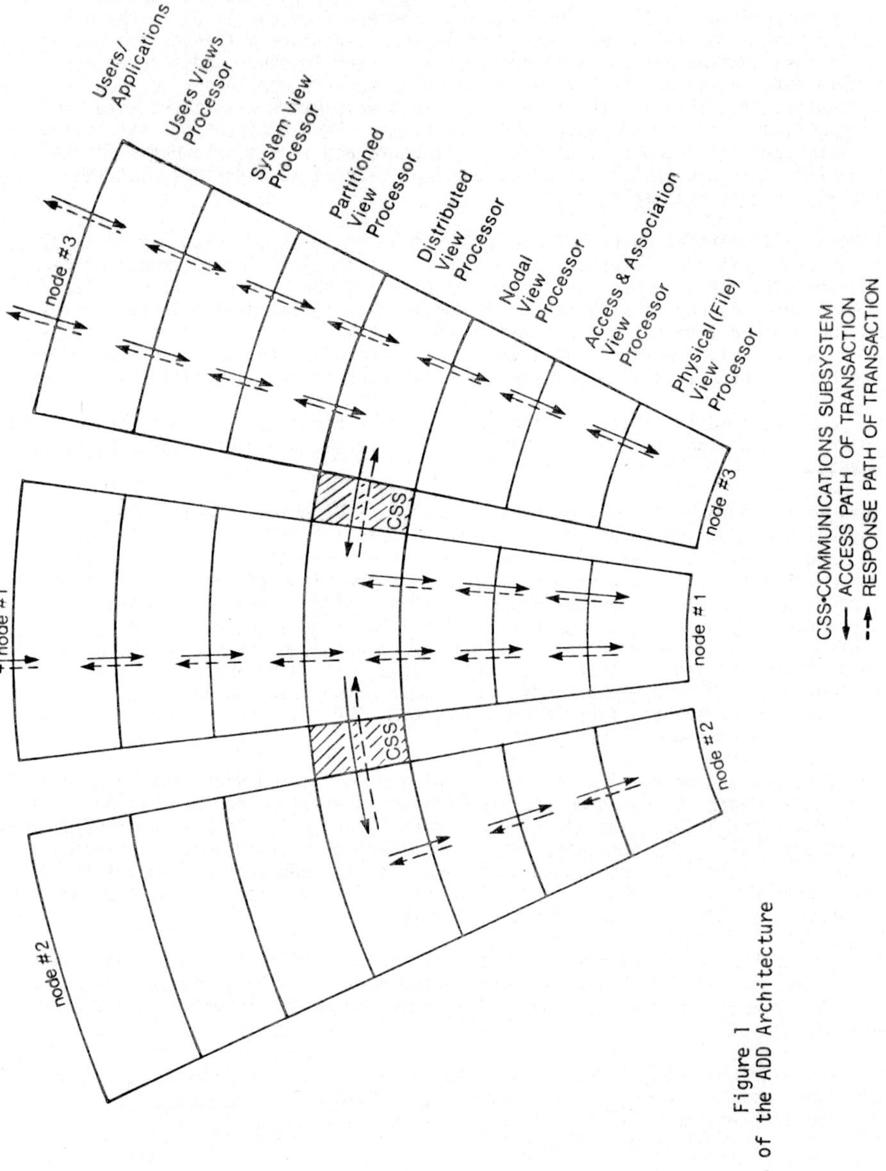

Figure 1
Layers of the ADD Architecture

represented in ADD by the AVP while the file model is represented by the FVP. The NVP layer is introduced to allow each node to retain its local data access language eventhough network users interact with the distributed data through a common access language.

3. Data Distribution and Directory Structure

As explained in the previous section, a common access language is used by all distributed database users in ADD. For reasons of efficiency and simplicity of implementation, it is important that the flow of transaction parameters in the first four layers of the ADD system (UVP, SVP, PVP and DVP) be based on data structures compatible with the common access language. A relational data model has been adopted in ADD for the following reasons:

1) Flexibility and generality of the relational model in describing external and conceptual schemas.
2) Completeness and compactness of the relational calculus.
3) The relational model lends itself readily to partitioning both logically and physically while maintaining the same properties, as will be explained in this section.

Clearly, there is a need to extend the relational model so that partitioning and distribution of the database can be defined. To realize this objective, a decomposition approach developed by Chang and Cheng [7] is adopted in the ADD system. The decomposition approach is summarized in Section 3.1.

3.1 Data Distribution

A relation can be divided into subrelations or partitions by means of a number of operators. The reverse operation is also valid, i.e., it is possible to define operators which combine subrelations or partitions to form a relation. Two partitioning operators are significant:

1) The horizontal partitioning operator which divides a relation into subrelations with the property that the set of non-key attributes in any subrelation is mutually exclusive with the set of non-key attributes in other subrelations. Each subrelation in this case is known as a horizontal partition.
2) The vertical partitioning operator which divides a relation, or a horizontal partition into subrelations according to the value of one key (referred to as the partitioning key) or a combination of keys. The resulting subrelations have the same attribute set but have mutually exclusive values in the partitioning key attribute. Each subrelation in this case is called a vertical partition.

In the ADD system, a relation can exist physically in the network in one of the following forms:

1) The relation is not partitioned and exists as a single copy in one node or as duplicate copies in several nodes.
2) The relation is vertically partitioned with the vertical partitions distributed among network nodes. The vertical partitions may also be redundantely stored.
3) The relation is horizontally partitioned with the horizontal partitions broken further into vertical partitions using the same or different partitioning key.

A partition which is not divided any further, i.e. which is stored physically as one unit is referred to as an elementary relation. The distribution of the various partitions among network nodes can be done according to the model described in [1] after modifying the communications cost function to model the communications subsystem of ADD [4].

3.2 Directory Structure

In general, the processing of a transaction in a distributed database environment involves traversing two types of access paths:
1) Network level access paths which direct the transaction to the set of nodes containing the target data of the transaction.
2) Internal (logical) access paths which are associated with the data partitions (files) within a given node.

Allocation of these access paths to network nodes can very depending on system requirements and other operational factors. The two most important operational factors are:

1. Efficiency of Transaction Processing:

When a transaction is originated in a given node by a user or an application program, it is analyzed first to determine the set of elementary relations the transaction needs to access. The existence of some parts of the directory in every processing node will make it possible for the node to execute a query processing strategy without initially consulting other network nodes.

2. The Overhead Associated with Directory Updates:

Duplication of directory parts in the network will lead to an increase in the overhead traffic required to coordinate and apply the updates to each copy of the directory in the network.

The trade-offs associated with various degrees of directory distribution have been analyzed in [8]. The design of the directory in the ADD system attempts to strike a balance between the two opposing factors mentioned above. This is accomplished by storing the directory of the network access paths as a fully redundant resource, i.e. one copy is placed in each processing node. Internal (logical) access paths are collocated with their data partitions in various network nodes. Table 1 gives a summary of directory components and their distributions in ADD.

Directory Component	Responsible ADD Level	Distribution
- Relations (names, syntactical details, domain names, etc.)	UVP & SVP	fully redundant
- Horizontal partitions (names, syntactical details, etc.) - Indices of vertical partitioning keys	PVP	fully redundant
- Locations of vertical partitions and statistical data	DVP	fully redundant
- Internal access paths (inverted lists, etc.)	AVP	collocated with data partitions

Table 1
Allocation of Directory Components

The directory allocation sheme given in Table 1 has the following advantages:

1) The rate of updating fully redundant components is relatively small. Such updates fall into one of two categories (i) updates that must be synchronized, i.e. applied concurrently to all directory copies; these include changing the structure of a relation, reallocating elementary relations in the network, redefining the partitioning of a relation or deleting elementary relations from the database; (ii) updates that can be applied without synchronization; these include creation of new relations or data partitions. Only the updates of category (i) require invoking the full power of synchronization protocols (Section 5) and thus incur overhead traffic in the network.
2) Query processing strategies can be executed in any processing node which has a copy of the fully redundant parts of the directory. This significantly reduces the delays associated with processing most network user queries (Section 4).
3) Since internal access paths are collocated with their database partitions, it is possible for any node to implement local consistency protocols which are independent of the synchronization protocols executed at the network level. Thus each node can run a consistency subsystem which provides maximum efficiency with respect to the parameters of the database operation within the node. This feature of the ADD system will be explained in detail in Section 5.
4) Interference among transactions originated at different nodes can be determined at run time. This feature plays an important role in the way the synchronization protocols function. The interference is determined at the elementary relations level, rather than at the data item level to avoid the need for an off-line (a priori) analysis of the interrelationship among expected user transactions.

4. Query Processing Strategies

An optimal solution to the data segment allocation problem results in a configuration in which a large number of user transactions can be processed locally to completion. However, there will remain a number of user transactions that require access to data partitions stored at remote nodes. In general, a transaction can access data partitions distributed among several nodes, extract certain data at each node, merge certain interrelated data (e.g. by a tuple substitution process) and ship the final results to a given destination as output. The processing of such transactions requires a clearly defined strategy. As will be explained in this section, certain performance aspects are highly sensitive to the query processing strategy and an attempt to design the strategy to improve a given performance measure is bound to worsen other performance aspects. For example, a strategy that attempts to minimize the communications traffic associated with transaction processing may lead to excessive delays in obtaining the target data. For this reason, it is essential that the number of transactions that span several nodes be kept to a minimum. Such pathological cases will be handled by invoking the full power of the query processing strategy. However, in an optimally designed system, most transactions involve relatively simple interactions. In the ADD system, the execution of each transaction, from initiation to termination will be the responsibility of a single node in the network. This means that all data access and processing operations associated with the transactions in the network will be performed in response to commands from the node responsible for that transaction. Thus for each transaction entering the network there will be a "supervisor" node which monitors all of its operations until it exits from the node. The responsibilities of the "supervisor node" can be summarized as follows:

1) Checking the logical and syntactical validity of the query (these are functions built into the UVP and SVP layers).

2) Execution of a query processing strategy. This involves:
(i) Division of the query into a set of subqueries
(ii) Association of the subqueries with their target data partitions
(iii) Determination of a routing strategy for commands and data.
Part (i) is exuceted in the SVP layer, part (ii) is executed in the PVP layer and part (iii) is executed in the DVP layer.
3) Initiation of the synchronization protocols (Section 5). The synchronization protocols are implemented as part of the DVP.

Several query processing strategies have been proposed in [9], [10] and [11]. These strategies are based onoptimizing one of the performance parameters (e.g. response time, total transmitted data, total processing time, etc.). Unfortunately, in most instances the values of the assumed fixed parameters are not known a priori and can be obtained only after executing parts of the non-optimal alternative strategies, which obviously defeats the purpose the strategy is intended for.

Three factors were taken into consideration in designing a query processing strategy for ADD:

1) Most processing sites are mini-computers with limited processing power. Thus it is essential to use simple query strategies.
2) The volume of statistical data that will be stored and used in determining strategy phases must be kept to a minimum. In addition, the statistical data needed for the strategy should not be of the type whose accuracy is sensitive to database modifications resulting from updates. This is to avoid extensive overhead costs which would be needed to update the redundantly stored statistical data frequently.
3) The strategy must be compatible with the access synchronization protocols. As will be explained in Section 5, the access synchronization protocols are invoked when the first phase of the query strategy protocols are executed and certain interdependencies exist between the two types of protocols.

In the remainder of this section, an attempt to formalize the query processing strategy problem is presented. This will be followed by a description of the strategy adopted in ADD.

In general, relational query can be written in the conjunctive normal form [12]:

$$\Phi : W \leftarrow T \ni E$$

Where Φ refers to the query, W refers to the user's work space, $T=\{R_1, R_2, \ldots R_n\}$ which form the database and E is the qualification list. The qualification list, E, is a set of variable query terms which consists of two mutually exclusive subsets:

1) The subset $E_1 \subset E$ which contains all single variable qualification terms
2) The subset $E_2 \subset E$ which contains all two variable qualification terms.

A single variable qualification term is expressed in the following form:

$$(R.a*v)$$

where R denotes a relation, a denotes an attribute in relation R, v denotes a value taken from the domain of attribute a, and * is a binary relational operator (e.g., =, $\neq$, $\leq$, $\geq$, <, >,, etc.). The term itself corresponds to all tuples in relation R such that a*v (for example all tuples in which $a \leq v$). A two variable qualification term is expressed in the following form:

$$(R_i.a_k*R_j.a_\ell)$$

This term associates with each tuple in relation R_i a subset of tuples in relation R_j such that a_k in the tuple satisfies $a_k * a_\ell$ in each of its associated tuples.

The relational query can be represented by a graph structure as follows. Let G=(N,A) be graph consisting of a set of nodes N and a set of undirected arcs A. Also let $E_{1i} \subset E_1$ be the subset of single variable qualification terms defined over relation R_i. Thus E_1 is partitioned into subsets and each of these subsets corresponds to a relation. We assign each subset E_{1i} to a node in N. It follows that each relation appearing in the terms of E_1 will correspond to a node in N. Since each two variable qualification term links two relations, it is possible to represent each such term by an arc in graph G. Thus an arc will exist in graph G betwen two nodes n_i and n_j if a two variable term exists in E_2 which contains relations R_i (represented by node n_i) and relation R_j (represented by node n_j). Modelling the qualification set E by a graph structure can be done at the SVP layer. In Figure 2(a), a graph is shown which represents a set E consisting of four single variable qualification terms that access four relations R_1, R_2, R_3 and R_4, and four two variable qualification terms that relate pairs of relations (R_1, R_2), (R_2, R_3), (R_3, R_4) and (R_2, R_4). Each two variable qualification term is represented by an undirected arc in the graph. We refer to this graph as the System View Query Graph since it is formed at the SVP layer level.

The System View Query Graph is expanded by the PVP to reflect the logical partitioning of the relations into horizontal and vertical partitions. The PVP determines which partitions will be accessed by the query by inspecting the terms in E_1 (single variable qualification terms). As an illustration, assume that relation R_3 in the above consists of two horizontal partitions R_3' and R_3'', and that the single variable qualification terms on R_3 are equivalent to a two variable qualification term on the partitions R_3' and R_3''. Node R_3 will be split in this case into two nodes with an arc connecting them. Also assume that relation R_4 consists of two vertical partitions $R_{4,1}$ and $R_{4,2}$. The node representing R_4 will be split into two nodes each representing a vertical partition. The transformation of the System View Query Graph shown in Figure 2(a) at the PVP level results in the graph shown in Figure 2(b) which is called the Partitioned View Query Graph. The complete set of rules for transforming the System View Query Graph to the equivalent Partitioned View Query Graph is presented in [13].

The location at which each database partition is stored can be determined at the DVP level. Assume that the data partitions in the previous example are distributed among three network nodes as follows:

node 1: R_1

node 2: R_2, R_3', $R_{4,1}$

node 3: R_3'', $R_{4,2}$

The distribution information can be used to transform the Partitioned View Query Graph to a new graph which reflects the physical locations of the data partitions. The transformation is done at the DVP level and the resultant graph is named the Distributed View Query Graph. This graph has the same structure as the Partitioned View Query Graph and it reflects merely the clustering of partitions at different network nodes. The graph shown in Figure 2(c) is a transformation of the graph shown in Figure 2(b).

As a first step in the processing of the queries, each network node will execute, upon receiving a command from the supervisor node, parts of the query that are shown in the Distributed View Query Graph to fall within the node. The result is stored in one or more temporary relations within the node. For example node 1 can execute a subquery on R_1 and store the result in T_1. Node 2 can execute a

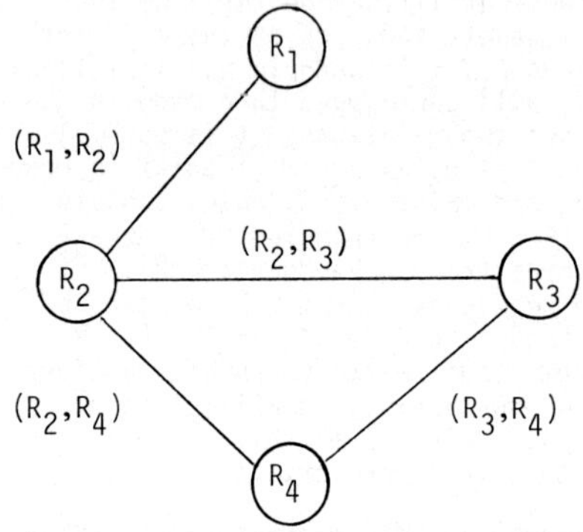

Figure 2(a)

An Example of System View Query Graph

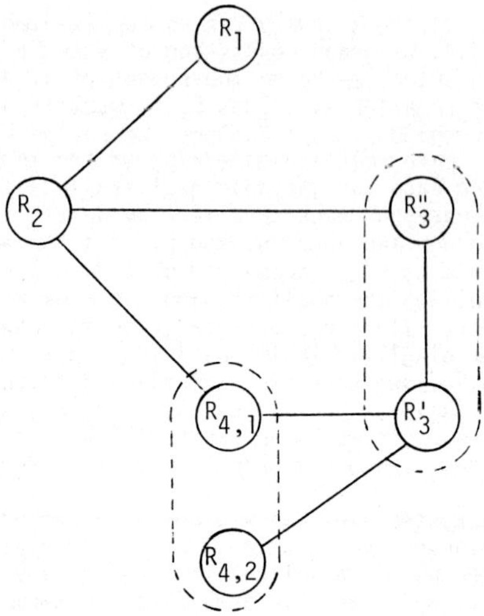

Figure 2(b)

Partitioned View Query Graph

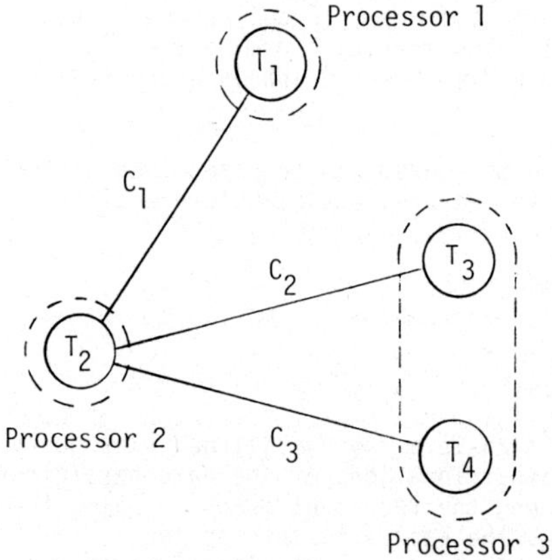

Figure 2(d)

Coalesced Query Graph (C_1, C_2 and C_3 are two variable qualification term definitions)

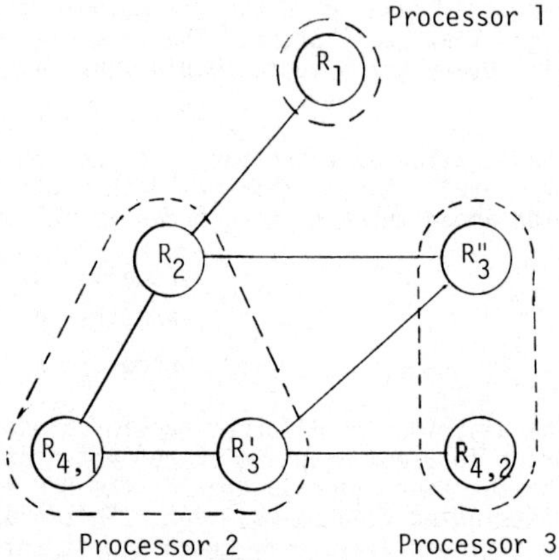

Figure 2(c)

Distributed View Query Graph

subquery on R_2, $R_{4,1}$ and R_3' and store the result in T_2. Node 3 will execute the subquery separately on R_3'' and $R_{4,2}$ (since no association exists between the two partitions, and the results will be stored in T_3 and T_4. This process coalesces the subgraphs, whenever possible, within each network node. The resultant graph is called the Coalesced Query Graph and preserves the associations expressed by the arcs of the Distributed View Query Graph. The Coalesced Query Graph for our example is shown in Figure 2(d).

Continuation of the query processing beyond the Coalesced Query Graph necessitates movement of data (the temporary relations T_1, T_2, T_3 and T_4) between network nodes. Several alternatives exist, and the objective of the query processing strategy is to select the one which optimizes a given cost or performance measure. To examine this problem, we extend our definitions to express the steps of the strategy.

The query processing strategy as applied to the Coalesced Query Graph consists of a series of data moves with certain local processing to be performed between successive moves. For example, a strategy for the graph shown in Figure 2(d) may consist of the following steps:

1) Move T_3 and T_4 from node 3 to node 2.
2) Peform local processing on T_2, T_3 and T_4 at node 2.
3) Move the result from node 2 to node 1.
4) Perform local processing in node 1 to obtain the final result.
5) Move the final result to the destination node.

The set of moves preceding or succeeding each local processing constitute a 'phase'. The set of phases together with the local processing that takes place form a 'strategy' for processing the query. Each phase will involve the movement of traffic over the communications network. The total traffic volume of a strategy will be the sum of the traffic moved over all phases of the strategy. Three cost functions can be considered in the design of query processing strategies:

1) Total traffic volume: the sum of the total traffic transmitted over all strategy phases.
2) Total processing time: the sum of the local processing time is all network nodes involved in processing the query.
3) Response time to query: the response time is defined to be the time elapsed between the moment the query is entered and the time the response to the query is received at the destination node.

To select an optimal strategy based on any of the above three cost functions, it is essential to determine a priori the cost involved in executing different sequences of phases and local processing. This is extremely difficult to determine because the sizes of the temporary relations formed at different nodes are not known at the beginning of each phase before completing the local processing preceding the phase at each participating node. Future research in this area may make it possible to predict with a high degree of accuracy the sizes of the data segments formed at the beginning of each phase by employing extensive statistical analysis of the contents of the distributed database. However, the cost of maintaining, updating and utilizing such statistical data, if it exists at all, will be prohibitive in a practically oriented system like ADD.

The query processing strategy adopted in ADD is based on a practical approach which attempts to reduce the response time of the query while reducing the total transmited traffic volume as much as possible. The concept underlying the approach can be explained as follows. Using the Coalesced Query Graph it is possible to define a strategy as a series of reductions of the graph in which the nodes are collapsed until the graph is reduced to a single node. As an example, the following strategy can be defined on the graph of Figure 2(d):

phase 1: move temporary relations T_3 and T_4 from node 3 to node 2.
local processing: merge T_2, T_3 and T_4 in node 2 and generate the result T_5.
phase 2: move T_5 (the result of the local processing) from node 2 to node 1.
local processing: merge the relations T_5 and T_1 to generate the target data (the response to the query).

The above described strategy contains two phases. We define also for each query processing phase a 'block threshold' which is a certain traffic volume level used by each node to decide whether to transmit or to hold temporary relations. If the temporary relation size exceeds the threshold, the relation is held, otherwise it may be transmitted. The use of the block threshold will be explained in the following analysis.

For the processing of a query in ADD, the strategy to be selected is the one that has the minimum number of phases and at the same time meets certain threshold constraints. The following steps explain the procedure followed to determine the strategy and also to execute it.

1) The node supervising the query performs all the required processing until the formation of the Distributed View Query Graph and the corresponding Coalesced Query Graph.
2) The supervisor node determines a threshold value by consulting special tables which have been prepared based on off-line analysis of the distributed database. The supervisor node can also extract from these tables estimates of the sizes of some of the temporary relations that are formed remotely. As for the remaining temporary relations, the supervisor node assumes at this stage that their sizes are below the threshold level.
3) The supervisor node determines a strategy based on the estimates made in step 2 such that the strategy has a minimum number of phases while meeting the threshold level.
4) The supervisor node sends commands to the remote nodes to execute the subqueries. The commands include the threshold value and the location(s) to which the results should be moved.
5) Following the execution of the subquery, each participating node will either: (i) move the results if their volume is below the threshold, or (ii) hold the results if their volume is greater than the threshold level, and inform the supervisor node of the size of the temporary relations formed.
6) The supervisor node forms the new coalesced graph, following the moves in step 5 and updates the threshold value based on the information received from other nodes. The supervisor node determines a strategy of moves based on the new values of the threshold level and temporary relation sizes. The processing continues by executing step 4.

Steps 4 to 6 are executed iteratively until the query is completely processed. As an example, consider the Distributed View Query Graph of Figure 2(c) and assume that node 3 is the query supervisor node. Also assume the size of T_3 to be 30 units and the size of T_4 to be 40 units and no estimates of the sizes of T_1 and T_2 are available (the sizes of T_3 and T_4 are found after node 3 completes its local processing). The strategy of query processing in this case can be summarized in the following steps:

1) The two graphs of Figures 2(c) and 2(d) are formed.
2) The threshold value is estimated to be 70 (the sum of T_3 and T_4).
3) Assuming node 2 to be the destination node, the strategy adopted at this stage will consist of one phase: the transmission of relations T_1, T_3 and T_4 to node 2.

4) Node 3 sends commands to nodes 1 and 2 to execute their subqueries, the results of which will be relation T_1 in node 1 and relation T_2 in node 2. The commands also request node 1 to transmit T_1 to node 2. Node 3 also sends T_3 and T_4 to node 2.
5) If the size of T_1 is less than 70 units, it will be transmitted to node 2 and the final stage of query processing will take place in node 2 by merging T_1, T_2, T_3 and T_4. Otherwise T_1 will be held in node 1, and node 3 will be notified of the actual size of T_1 (which must in this case be greater than 70 units). In the latter case, node 3 will base the final stage of the strategy on the relative sizes of T_1 and the size of the relation resulting from processing T_2, T_3 and T_4 in node 2.

5. The Synchronization Procedure

Concurrent access to any centralized data base requires the existence of certain mechanisms to coordinate the access requirements of various transactions and thus preserve the consistency of the database. In a database which is logically integrated but physically distributed, the access coordination problem is complicated by the existence of random network delays and possible failures of independently functioning elements (links, processing nodes, etc.). Because of the logical dependence among the distributed partitions of the database and the requirement of some transactions to access data at multiple sites, the existence of coordination mechanisms at each site is not sufficient by itself to guarantee the consistency of the entire database. For example, two transactions attempting to update a multiple copy file can violate the consistency rules if they update the copies in different sequences at different nodes. The same thing can happen if two or more transactions are accessing a common set of data partitions at multiple sites. It is necessary then to augment the coordination mechanisms within each node by a global coordination mechanism which will be responsible for coordinating the processing of all transactions that access data at remote sites.

The global coordination mechanism executes most of its functions by means of a set of coordination protocols. A coordination protocol is a set of messages exchanged between the processing sites. Within each site, all access to local partitions will be executed under a local coordinator which follows certain consistency rules.

In practice, the global coordination mechanism must have the following properties:

a) Correctness of Operation: the mechanism must prevent and/or detect and recover from deadlock situations that involve resources at two or more sites.
b) Robustness: The protocol must function correctly during the failure and recovery of any system component (processing site or communications links).
c) Acceptable Performance: Operation of the protocol introduces certain traffic and processing overhead. It is essential that this overhead does not degrade the performance of the distributed system. Thus the overhead cost must remain within certain acceptable limits which are defined in relation to the requirements of the system.
d) Integration with local consistency mechanisms: It is essential that the global coordination mechanism can be integrated with thelocal consistency mechanisms within each network node after minor modifications to these local mechanisms.

In the remainder of this section, we present a global coordination mechanism which has been designed for the ADD system. The coordination mechanism satisfies properties a, b, and d above. Preliminary analysis and simulation work indicate that the technique is efficient in performance for many practical situations. More detailed simulation work is currently underway to examine the performance of this technique under various operational environments. This section also includes a brief survey of other synchronization techniques that have been proposed in the literature.

To explain the concept underlying the proposed coordination protocol, we introduce the following notions:

1) Each processing node in the network has a local concurrency coordination unit, referred to as 'local coordinator', which coordinates access to all data partitions within the node. In ADD, the 'local coordinator' executes a procedure based on the predicate locking approach [14]. Transactions accessing the resources of the node under the local coordinator's control arrive from two sources:

i) Transactions originated locally to access partitions that exist exclusively within the node. These transactions are handled directly by the local coordinator.

ii) Transactions originated locally and requiring concurrent access to partitions in two or more nodes in the network. These transactions together with other transactions that arrive from remote sites are handled by the 'global coordinator' which exists within the node and communicates with other global coordinators in the network.

2) Transactions arriving directly to the local coordinator and other transactions arriving through the global coordinator (subqueries) are handled by the local coordinator uniformly as atomic units. Thus the query processing strategy in the network is transparent to the local coordinator which handles the incoming ransactions uniformly on a first-come-first-serve basis by placing them on the resource queue tables of the lock graph which represents the local resources [14].

3) By executing the global coordination protocol (described next), each global coordinator presents its co-resident local coordinator with the transactions (subqueries) arranged in a time sequence. The order of this sequence is crucial to the correct operation of the global consistency protocols as will be explained later.

4) It is obvious then that no global locking requests exist since local coordinators control their lock graphs much the same as in centralized database systems. It follows that no global deadlock conditions take place. The responsibility of the global coordination protocol will be to select global transaction sequences that provide a level of consistency for the entire database which is as strong as the level of consistency provided by the local coordination procedures.

Figure (3) illustrates the interaction between the local and the global coordinators within each node. In the ADD system, the global coordinator is implemented at the DVP level within each node. The decisions made by the global coordinator is dependent on the strategy followed for processing the transaction (the query processing strategy). The local coordinator is implemented at the AVP level and executes a set of predicate locking protocols in a similar way to centralized databases [14] with some minor modifications. These modifications are related primarily to lock releases at the end of the transactions (Subquery) processing and are explained in the synchronization procedure.

5.1 The Synchronization Protocol

The synchronization procedure presented here is based on the following two assumptions: (1) Messages between any two nodes i and j are pipe-lined, i.e., messages originating from node i arrive at node j in the same order of the generated sequence, and (2) the system of message delivery is fully reliable. The practical case of an unreliable system is handled in [13].

The global coordinator of the supervisor node of each generated transaction will be responsible for synchronizing its activities with other global coordinators in the network. The global coordinator of each node maintains an up-to-date resource access table which contains the following (constantly up-dated) information:

- All transactions (subqueries) being synchronized and which are demanding access to resources within the node. Associated with each transaction are two sets: (1) the set of elementary relations to be accessed, and (2) the set of network nodes containing these relations. Associated with each transaction there will be also a unique identifier and a time-stamp assigned to it at generation time by its supervisor node. The transaction time-stamp is unique throughout the network (this is made possible by adding the originating processor number as the least significant bits of the time stamp).
- Names and locations of all elementary relations within the network. The global coordinator associates with each elementary relation a time field. The value of this field will be assigned as explained later in the steps of the synchronization procedure.

To facilitate the presentation of the synchronization procedure, we introduce the following definitions for each generated transaction T in the network:

R(T): The set of elementary relations to be accessed by transaction T - copies of a relation are represented as different elements in R(T).

N(T): The set of nodes containing the elementary relations in R(T).

t(T): The value of the time-stamp of transaction T. A transaction T_1 is said to have higher priority than another transaction T_2 if $t(T_1) > t(T_2)$, which implies T_1 is generated earlier than T_2.

$X_i(T)$: The set of all transactions in the resource table of node i such that for each $T_j \varepsilon X_i(T)$ we have:

$$R(T_j) \cap R(T) \neq \emptyset$$

we refer to $X_i(T)$ as the interference set of T in node i.

The synchronization procedure can be summarized in the following steps:

(1) When transaction T is generated in a given node, it is decomposed into subqueries and the two sets R(T) and N(T) are defined. Queries messages are transmitted to the nodes of the set N(T). Each query message contains the identification number of T, its time stamp t(T), the two sets R(T) and N(T), and the subquery statement which will be executed in the recipient node, as explained previously in the query processing strategy.

(2) When the global coordinator of each node in N(T) receives the message, it compares the time-stamp t(T) with the time fields of all elementary relations in R(T) - one of two actions is taken based on this comparison:
- If t(T) is less than the value of all the time fields of the relations of R(T) (i.e. t(T) is newer), then T is entered in the resource table where it waits until acknowledgements are received from all other nodes in N(T).
- Otherwise, a rejection message is sent to the supervisor node of T which must give T a new time-stamp value and retransmits this new value to all nodes in N(T).

(3) The transaction T waits in the resource table until acknowledgements are received from all the nodes in N(T). A transaction in the resource table is given to the local coordinator, and in turn erased from the resource table, only if:
i) acknowledgements have been received from all other nodes in N(T), and
ii) its time-stamp is greater than the time stamps of all transactions in $X_i(T)$.

If Condition (i) is satisfied but not condition (ii), the transaction waits in the resource table until all transactions with higher priority in $X_i(T)$ are sent to the local coordinator or given a new time stamp value, so that the priority of T will become higher than all transactions in $X_i(T)$.

(4) When transaction T is sent to the local coordinator, its time-stamp value is assigned to the time field of each relation in R(T).

(5) If the supervisor node of T receives a rejection message from one or more of the nodes of N(T), it assigns T a new (future) time stamp and transmits a short message containing the new time stamp along with the identification of T. The new time stamp replaces the old one in all of the nodes of N(T).

The processors of the network don't have to be perfectly synchronized in time. A scheme in which each processor increments its time stamp to the newest value received from any other processor will be sufficient for the correct operation of the above procedure. This is similar to the time-stamp scheme adopted in SDD-1 [18].

In [13] a formal proof is presented which shows that the above procedure provides a consistency degree for the entire database which is as strong as the consistency degree provided by the local consistency mechanism in each node. The average number of messages needed to synchronize a given transaction is n(n-1) where n is the average size of the set of nodes N(T) involved in processing the transaction. It should be noted, however, that in practical operational environments, a large number of messages do not require the application of the synchronization procedures. Examples include: (1) transactions retrieving data from a single elementary relation, (2) transactions updating a single copy relation and (3) transactions whose target relations exist all within one node. In the applications for which the ADD system is considered, the average value of n is between 2 and 3, which means that the synchronization procedure incurs an average of two to six overhead messages when it is executed.

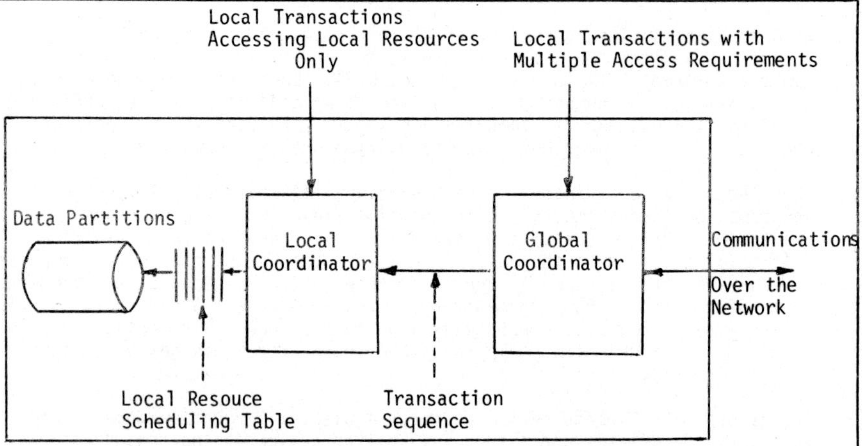

Figure 3

Interaction Between the Global and Local Coordinators

5.2 Alternative Coordination Procedures

In this section, a brief survey of other access coordination procedures that have been reported in the literature is presented. The similarities and differences between these coordination procedures and the coordination mechanism presented here are indicated whenever they exist.

In [15], two file access coordination approaches are proposed and compared. The first approach is centralized in which all file access requests are sent first to a certain node which controls all resource tables and thus controls access authorization to all segments of the database. In the second approach, the coordination mechanism is distributed and all nodes participate in controlling access to database segments. The nodes exchange information regarding their resource tables status periodically, i.e. at the onset of synchronized clock intervals. The exchanged information concerns all transactions that are requesting access to resources at more than one node. Unlike the coordination mechanism discussed here, the distributed control scheme proposed in [15] requires perfect synchronization of the timers at all nodes, a rather difficult task to achieve in practice.

In [16], a file access coordination protocol based on a centralized approach is presented. In this protocol, one node assumes the responsibility of a central controller and is backed up by one or more nodes which will assume its duty when it fails. The protocol is shown to require overhead traffic proportional to the number of nodes, n, in the network. Using an informal proof, the protocol is shown to function correctly in the face of failure of the controlling (central) node as the control is switched over to another node.

In [17], two approaches are proposed for synchronization of update requests to multiple copy files. In the first approach, a network wide semaphore scheme is developed into a protocol which ensures that only a single user can apply his updates to a copy of the file; other copies will be locked until the updates are applied to them. This approval requires precise synchronization of the clocks at multiple sites and generates overhead traffic in the order of n^2 messages per update request, where n in this case represents the number of file copies. It is not clear how the approach can be extended to handle requests involving access to a set of different files simultaneously. The second approach proposed in [17] is asynchronous, i.e., it does not require synchronization of the clocks of the different nodes. Instead, a 'permit' is associated with each multiple-copy file in the network. The permit is passed from one node to another in a predefined deterministic chain. Each node will queue up update requests and executes them only when the file 'permit' is passed to it from the previous node on the chain. Excessive delays (waiting times) may be encountered by file update requests in this scheme due to the time required in passing the 'permit' serially along the chain. As pointed out in [17], failure of nodes along the chain leads also to confusing situations, some of which are difficult to detect and identify even with time-out schemes.

Synchronization procedure in SDD-1 [18] is handled by several different protocols designed to co-exist with one another. The protocols vary in complexity with the simpler ones used for certain restricted classes of transactions determined in advance of system generation by means of extensive analysis of the database and the behaviour of expected transactions. This analysis groups all transactions that are bound to interfere with each other into a class; each class is treated by a designated synchronization protocol. In systems where the number of transactions treated by the simpler protocols is large, significant improvements in cost and delay over general protocols result. Unlike the SDD-1 synchronization procedure, the one suggested here does not require prior (off-line) analysis of transaction classes. The procedure suggested here, however, shares with the

SDD-1 protocols the property that no global locking of database partitions is required.

In [19], a general resource access control procedure is described in which each request for access is communicated to all network nodes. Upon receiving the request, each node transmits an acknowledgement message to all other network nodes. A priority scheme allows the nodes to allocate the resources in a consistent way to all (asynchronous) requesting processes. A similar procedure is followed when the resource is released. Thus a total of $2(n-1)^2$ messages are exchanged for each request in a network of n nodes. The procedure is also extended in [19] to handle cases of node or link failures in the network. This technique is applied in [20] to handle accesses to distributed files and directories. Through the use of a hybrid technique of deadlock prevention and deadlock detection and recovery, the performance of the synchronization procedure can be improved to an average number of coordination messages per request which is considerably less than $2(n-1)^2$.

6. Summary

A general distributed database architecture for a mini-computer network has been presented together with approaches to solving two of the most critical problems in the operation of the distributed database. These are the query processing strategy and the coordination procedures employed to synchronize concurrent transaction accesses to distributed database partitions.

The architecture of the distributed database is based on a hierarchical structure with several layers. Each layer embodies a set of functions and passes partially processed transactions to the adjacent layers in the hierarchy. The distributed aspects of the database are totally transparent to the users as the first two layers of the hierarchy (UVP and SVP) present a logical view of the database independent of its distribution. The next two layers in the hierarchy (PVP and DVP) contain all the logical partitioning and physical distribution information of the database and have the responsibility of determining and monitoring query processing details as well as the responsibility of coordinating the processing of the query with other network queries to maintain database consistency.

The lower level layers of the hierarchy represent the local database management system within each node. The design allows each local processing system to run independently and process simultaneously local and remote (network) queries uniformly.

The difficulties associated with query processing at the network level have been discussed. These difficulties stem from the lack of a priori information which is needed to determine an optimal strategy. An approach is presented in which a search is conducted to determine a strategy for processing the query in a minimum number of phases subject to a traffic threshold constraint. The approach requires the storage of small amounts of statistical data as it modifies the strategy when more information is obtained in the intermediate steps. Simulation work is curently underway to examine the performance of the strategy for different operational conditions.

A synchronization procedure which is consistent with the query processing strategy and with local consistency procedures has been presented. The procedure does not require a priori analysis of transaction classes and no global locks are applied during the synchronization process. The performance of the synchronization procedure and the query processing strategy which forms its core is heavily dependent on the partitioning and allocation of the database in the network. To obtain reasonable performance, it is essential to keep the number of transactions with concurrent accesses at multiple sites to a minimum.

7. References

[1] S.A. Mahmoud and J.S. Riordon, "Optimal Allocation of Resources in Distributed Information Networks", ACM Trans. on Data Base Systems, Vol. 1, No. 1, March 1976, pp. 66-78.

[2] W.W. Chu, "Optimal File Allocation in a Computer Network", in Computer Communications Networks, F.F. Kuo, Ed. Englewood Cliffs, N.J.: Prentice Hall, Computer Applications in Electrical Engineering Series, 1973.

[3] J.B. Rothnie, "A Survey of research and development in distributed data base management", Proc. of the International Conference on Very Large Data Bases, TOKYO, October 1977, pp. 48-62.

[4] K.C. Toth, S.A. Mahmoud, J.S. Riordon and O. Sherif, "The ADD System, An Architecture for Distributed Data Bases", Proc. of the International Conference on Very Large Data Bases, West-Berlin, Germany, September 13-15, 1978, pp. 462-471.

[5] M.M. Astrahan, E.B. Altman, P.L. Fehder, M.E. Senko, "Concepts of a Data Independent Accessing Model", Proc. ACM-SIGFIDET Conference, pp. 349-362, Denver, November 1972.

[6] D. Tsichritzis and A. Klug, editors, "The ANSI/X3/SPARC DRMS Framework", Technical Note 12, CSRG, University of Toronto, 1977.

[7] S.K. Chang, W.H. Cheng, "Structured Database Decomposition in the Medical Information System Environment", Proc. IEEE Computer Software and Applications Conf. pp. 71-79, Chicago, November 1977.

[8] W.W. Chu, "Performance of Directory Systems for Data Bases in Star and Distributed Networks", AFIPS Conference Proceedings, Vol. 45, June 1976, pp. 577-587.

[9] R. Epstein, M. Stonebraker and E. Wong, "Distributed Query Processing in a Relational Data Base System", ACM International Data Base Conference, Austin, Texas, June 1968.

[10] E. Wong, "Retrieving Dispersed Data from SDD-1: A System for Distributed Databases", 1977 Berkeley Workshop on Distributed Data Management and Computer Networks, Lawrence Berkeley Laboratory, May 1977.

[11] M. Stonebraker, E.J. Neuhold, "A Distributed Data Base Version of Ingres", Electrical Research Lab. University of California, Berkeley, Memo No. ERL612, 1976.

[12] E. Wong and K. Youssafi, "Decomposition - A Strategy for Query Processing", ACM Transactions on Data base Systems, Vol. 1, No. 3, pp. 223-241, September 1976.

[13] S. Mahmoud, K.C. Toth and J.S. Riordon, "On the implementation of a Query Processing Strategy and Synchronization Protocols in the ADD System, Technical Report in Preparation, Department of Systems Engineering and Computing Science, Carleton University, Ottawa, Canada.

[14] K.P. Eswaran, J.N. Gray, R.A. Lorie and I.L. Traiger, "The Notions of Consistency and Predicate Locks in a Database System", Communications of the ACM, Volume 19, Number 11, November 1976.

[15] S.A. Mahmoud and J.S. Riordon, "Protocol Considerations for Software Controlled Access Methods in Distributed Data Bases", Proceedings of the ACM International Conference on Computer Performance, Modelling, Measurement and Evaluation, pp. 241-263, Boston, March 1976.

[16] D.A. Menasce, G.J. Popek and R.R. Muntz, "A Locking Protocol for Resource Coordination in Distributed Data Bases", ACM International Database Conference, Austin, Texas, June 1968 (to appear also in the ACM Transactions on Data Base Systems).

[17] C.H. Lee, R. Shastri and R. Metzger, "Distributed Control Schemes for Multiple Copies File Access in a Network Environment", Proceedings of COMPSAC 77, pp. 722-728, Chicago, November 1977.

[18] P. Bernstein, J.B. Rothnie, N. Goodman and C.A. Papadimitriou, "The Concurrently Control Mechanism of SDD-1: A System for Distributed Databases (The Fully Redundant Case", IEEE Transactions on Software Engineering, Vol. SE-4, No. 3, pp. 154-168, May 1978.

[19] O. Drobnik, "Verfahren Zur Sicherung Der Operationalen Integrität In Verteilten DatenBasen Bei Dezentraler Kontrollstruktur", Ph.D. Dissertation, Karlsruhe University, W. Germany, July 1977 (In German).

[20] S. Mahmoud, O. Drobnik and E. Holler, "Directory Management and Access Coordination in Data Bases", In preparation.

Data Base Architecture, Bracchi/Nijssen, eds.
North-Holland Publishing Company

A MODEL OF AN ACCESS STRATEGY IN A DISTRIBUTED DATABASE

by

G. Pelagatti F.A. Schreiber

Istituto di Elettrotecnica ed Elettronica
Politecnico di Milano
P.za L. da Vinci, 32- I 20133 Milano - Italy

Abstract

The CADDAS project deals with the problem of designing an efficient access strategy to a Distributed Database. The problem is approached from the point of view of a system analyst having to design a global application function. An overview of the CADDAS project is presented, together with a precise definition of the model which is used as a unified framework for the analysis of relevant design sybproblems.

Key words

Analysis of Data, Computer Networks, Distributed Access, Distributed Application Design, Distributed Databases, Distribution Constraints, Distribution Strategy, Operator Tree, Transmission strategy Optimization.

1. Introduction

A distributed database is a collection of data which belong logically to the same system but are spread over different nodes of a computer network. One of the main advantages of distributed databases over centralized ones is the fact that data are stored at the places where they are mainly used by local applications, but the distinguishing feature of a distributed database with respect to a set of local databases is the existence of several global functions which need data stored at different sites.

The problems of global functions in distributed databases are receiving increasing interest, expecially in two distinct areas: update of redundant copies of data in presence of concurrency /1,2/ and retrieval of data answering complex queries /3, 4, 5/.

The CADDAS project deals with the problem of designing an efficient access strategy to a distributed database for the retrieval of data needed by a global application, and is therefore related to other works in the field of query optimization. Nevertheless, many assumptions are rather different from those works, which are devoted to the dynamic optimization that can be done automatically by a query-processor; in CADDAS the design of a global application which is done by a system analyst is considered.

Of course, the designer of an application which has to access data spread over a computer network is faced with a very complex optimization problem. As it will be shown, a complete automation of this problem does not seem computationally feasible; therefore, the CADDAS project aims at the development of tools which can be used to improve current design practice by supporting the application designer in several design subproblems. This support is given mainly in the following forms:

a) A model which permits the precise definition of the relevant subproblems involved in the design of an access strategy;
b) A methodology for conceiving and expressing alternative solutions;
c) Automated procedures for the quantitative evaluation of alternatives;
d) Automated procedures which allow optimization in restricted subproblem areas;
e) An interactive system which helps the designer in developing and recording alternative solutions.

This paper presents an overview of the CADDAS project, a precise definition of the model which is used as a unified framework for the development of automated tools, and a short description of the mathematical models on which the automated procedures which have been or are being developed are based.

Section 2 describes the different levels at which the design process can be considered.

In Section 3 a formal definition of the model is given. Sections 4 and 5 are devoted to the analysis of some main subproblem areas.

2. Levels of Access Strategy Design

In figure 1 the overall design process is shown together with the inputs which are needed at each design level.

The first Input is a statement which specifies the application in terms of functions to be applied to the data. From the viewpoint of a global application, the distributed database can be considered consisting of a set of logical relations, and the functions that have to be performed on it can be expressed through a query in some high-level query language operating on them.

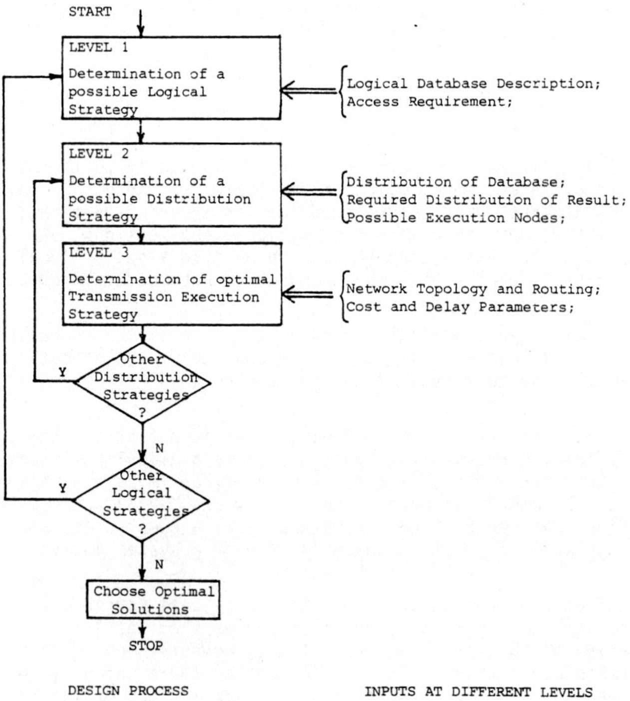

Fig.1-The Design Process

2.1 Logical Strategy

A Logical Strategy is a sequence of operations which extracts the required result from the database. This strategy does not consider the distribution of the database at all, therefore the usual concepts of a centralized database can be applied to the problem of generating possible Logical Strategies from an Access Requirement. A Logical Strategy will be represented by an Operator Tree, its nodes being the operations themselves and the arcs being the relations /6/.

Example

Consider a database consisting of two relations having the following domains:

Population (Name, SSN, Address, City, Other items)
Transaction (Trans##, Location, Name, Amount)

A global application has to be designed which satisfies the following requirement: "Find the SSN of persons having a Total Amount>100.000, where Total Amount is the sum of all the amounts of transactions referring to the same person". This requirement can be stated more formally in the following way:

GET(Population. SSN): Population Name = Transaction.Name
AND IMAGE-TOTAL (Name, Amount)> 100.000

(IMAGE-TOTAL(x,y)returns for each different value of x the sum of the associated values of y).

Many different Logical Access Strategies can be found to perform the above function, but this problem is not discussed here. A possible strategy is the one which is represented by the Operator Tree of figure 2. The Operator Tree shows explicitely each operation, although it may be convenient to perform some of them simultaneously.

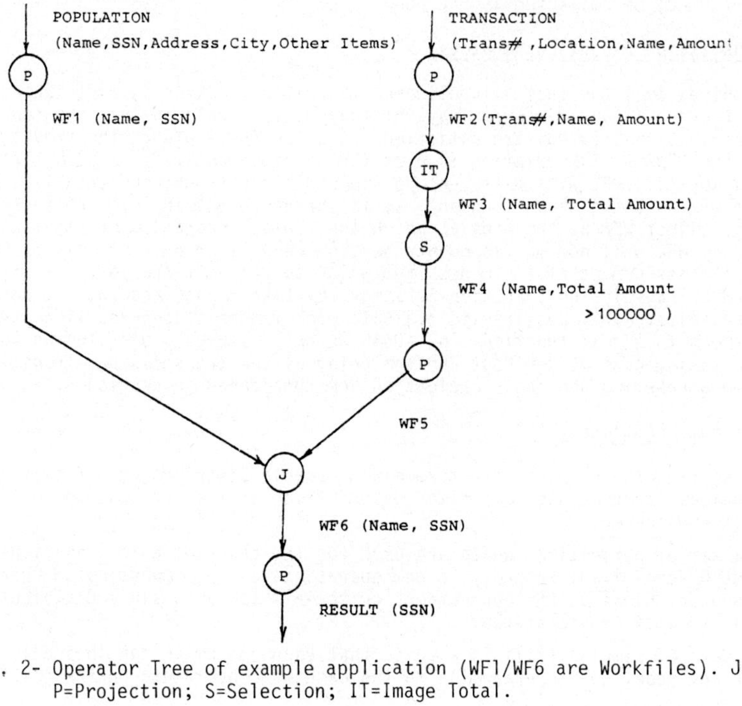

Fig. 2- Operator Tree of example application (WF1/WF6 are Workfiles). J=Join; P=Projection; S=Selection; IT=Image Total.

2.2 Distribution Strategy

At the second level the distribution of the DB is taken into account. The "Distribution of the data involved in operations" and the "Required Distribution of the Result", together with the fact that operations can be executed only at some nodes, cause the necessity of transmitting data between nodes. A Distribution Strategy adds to a Logical Strategy a determination of the nodes at which each operation is performed; as a consequence, also the allocation of the intermediate workfiles is fixed. The determination of a Distribution Strategy has to take care also of the fact that each operation constrains the distribution of the relations on which it operates. The need of transmitting relations stems for the necessity of fitting the distribution of the relations themselves to the operations requirements.

In general, there are many different Distribution strategies for a Logical Strategy. A model of distribution will be developed in section 3.

Example

Consider the Logical Strategy represented by the Operator Tree of figure 2. A description of the distribution of the POPULATION, TRANSACTION and RESULT relations is given as an input to this level of design. Suppose that the TRANSACTION relation is distributed in some way over different nodes. The "projection" operation can be performed in a distributed way, i.e. all parts of the TRANSACTION relation are projected at the nodes at which they reside. As a result, also the workfile WF2 is distributed in a similar way. Now the "total" operation must be performed on WF2. This requires WF2 to be collected at one node. However, a more efficient strategy would be to perform partial totals in a distributed way and then to collect them. A Distribution Strategy is an assignment of the nodes at which the Projection and the Total operations as well as all the other operations, have to be performed. An example of the need of transmission is the requirement that the workfile WF2, which is distributed, be collected at one node.

2.3 Transmission Execution Strategy

At the third level the fact is considered that if a relation is distributed redundantly, there are many different ways of transmitting data so that the constraints of a Distribution Strategy are satisfied. Consider for instance the previous example. If the TRANSACTION relation is distributed redundantly it is possible to obtain the workfile WF2 with different possible distributions; conceptually, we can think of WF2 as being also redundant. It is therefore possible to choose from which nodes to collect WF2 at the node at which the "Total" operation has to take place (of course, WF2 will not be redundant, because we will produce it only at these nodes). The assignment of the nodes from which to transmit the parts of a relation is called a Transmission Execution Strategy. By taking into account the network's characteristics, it is possible to evaluate each Transmission Execution Strategy with respect to a goal function. In CADDAS we have assumed a bicriterion goal function taking care of the Cost and the Delay of the transmission. Transmission Execution Strategies and their evaluation are considered in section 5.

3. Distribution Strategy

In this section the problem of determining possible Distribution Strategies for a given Logical Strategy and some fixed Distribution of the Database and of the Result is considered.

First, a set of definitions which are used for the description of relations distribution are given. Secondly, a new operation, called Transmission Operation, is introduced. Finally, the correctness criteria which a possible Distribution Strategy has to satisfy are stated.

For the sake of simplicity it is assumed that each operation can logically take place at any node, but an extension to the case of constraints on the possible execution nodes is straight forward.

3.1 Distribution of a relation

1. The Cardinality C_F of the relation F is the number of tuples of F.
2. The Projection Schema of the relation is a list of the domains of the relation and their length: I_{F1}, l_{F1}, I_{F2}, l_{F2},..., I_{Fn}, l_{Fn}.
3. A relation F can be logically partitioned into p_F disjoint subsets of tuples called fragments. The fraction of the complete relation contained in each fragment is given by a Fragmentation Vector:

   $$FV_F = |f_{Fi}|,\ 1 \leq i \leq p_F:\ f_{Fi} = \frac{\text{Number of tuples of the } i^{th} \text{ fragment}}{C_F}$$

   Of course $\sum_{i=1}^{p_F} f_{Fi} = 1$

4. The fragments of a relation can be distributed redundantly over the n nodes of the Network. The Allocation Matrix AM_F of F describes how the fragments are distributed:

   $$AM_F \equiv |a_{Fij}|,\ 1 \leq i \leq n,\ \ 1 \leq j \leq p_F:$$

   a_{Fij} = 1 if the jth fragment exists at node i

   a_{Fij} = 0 otherwise.

The Fragmentation Vector and the Allocation Matrix describe quantitatively the Distribution of a relation.

Particular forms of distribution are of special interest. In the following definitions N is the set of the nodes of the Network and D is an arbitrary subset $D \subseteq N$.

5. A relation F is completely duplicated on D iff $\forall i \in D \wedge \forall j,\ 1 \leq j \leq p_F \Rightarrow a_{Fij} = 1$, i.e. at each node of D there is a complete copy of F.
   Notation: F cdu (D).
6. A relation F is completely distributed on D iff $\forall j,\ 1 \leq j \leq p_F, \exists i \in D: a_{Fij} = 1$, i.e. a complete copy of the relation exists partitioned on the nodes of D.
   Notation: F cdi (D)
7. If D contains only one node d, then definition 5. and 6. are equivalent. A relation F is collected at node d iff

   $\forall j,\ 1 \leq j \leq p_F \Rightarrow a_{Fdj} = 1$. Notation: F col (d). Of course, $D \equiv \{d\} \wedge F cdu\ (D) \Rightarrow F\ col(d)$

8. A relation F1 is completely duplicated with respect to a relation F2 if there exists a subset of nodes D such that F1 cdu $(D) \wedge$ F2 cdi(D). Notation F1cdu(F2). Of course, F1 col(d)$\wedge$ F2 col (d) F1 cdu(F2), F2 cdu(F1)

3.2 Correctness of a Distribution Strategy and necessity of Transmission

The Distribution of the Database determines the Fragmentation Vectors and the Allocation Matrices which are associated with the Input arcs of the Operator Tree. In a similar way, the Required Distribution of the Results is represented by a Fragmentation Vector and an Allocation Matrix.

Each node of the Operator Tree imposes particular conditions on the Allocation Matrices of the entering arcs (node constraints), and generates the Allocation Matrix of the exiting arc (node effect). Both node constraints and node effect depend on the type of node (type of operation) and will be analysed in section 3.3.

Consider for example the generic node of an Operator Tree shown in figure 3. The type of operation Op determines which are the permitted configurations of the Allocation Matrices AM_A and AM_B. An assignment of a configuration of AM_A and AM_B defines implicitely also at which nodes of the Network the operation Op will be executed. The effect of this assignment is also an assignment of AM_C.

A Distribution Strategy is correct if it is possible to assign to each arc of the Operator Tree one Allocation Matrix such that

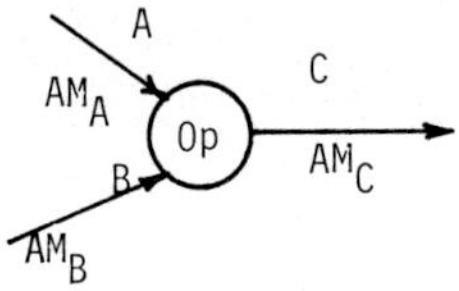

Fig. 3

1. The Allocation Matrices of the entering and exiting arcs of the whole Operator Tree are those which are imposed by the Distribution of the Database and by the Required Distribution of the Result (Boundary Conditions);
2. For each node, the Allocation Matrices of the entering and exiting arcs are such that the constraints and effect of the operation are satisfied (Node Conditions).

Often, Boundary and Node Conditions are such that it is impossible to find a correct distribution strategy without transmitting files, i.e. without changing the Allocation Matrix of an arc. Therefore a new type of operation, called Transmission Operation must be introduced:

A Transmission Operation of a relation R is a transformation of its Allocation Matrix, $TR: AM_R \rightarrow AM'_R$.

Through the insertion of Transmission Operations on the arcs of an Operator Tree it is possible to generate many different Distribution Strategies. The Transmission Operations express the need of transmission of a Distribution Strategy and are therefore the basis for an evaluation of the Cost and Delay of that Strategy.

3.3 Node Conditions

A logical operation generates a new output relation from one or more input relations, i.e. its Cardinality, Projection Scheme, Fragmentation Vector and Allocation Matrix, are generally different from those of the input ones.

With respect to node conditions, only the Allocation Matrix is relevant, but the Allocation Matrix is tightly bound to the Fragmentation Vector. We will assume in this subsection that the Fragmentation Vector of the output relation has the same number of elements Po as the Fragmentation Vector of one of the Input relations P_I; the limits of this assumption will be discussed in the next section together with the quantitative changes of Cardinality and Fragmentation Vector.

Node conditions can be defined for any type of logical manipulation of relations. A discussion of node conditions for several relational and arithmetic operators can be found in /7/. A summary of node conditions is given in Table 1, where some operations, like Total and Projection, have been splitted in two suboperations, the first of which can be performed in a distributed way while the second has to be performed on a single node (therefore the input relation has to be of the collected type).

Consider for instance the operation "Total".

Operation Type	Constraints on Input	Effect on Output	Assumption on Structure of Fragmentation Vector of Output
Selection	None	$AM_O=AM_I$	$P_O = P_I$
DProjection	None	$AM_O=AM_I$	$P_O = P_I$
GProjection	$\exists x \in N$:Icol(x)	$AM_O=AM_I$	
Join	I_1cdu (I_2)	$AM_O=AM_{I2}$	$P_O=P_{I2}$
DTotal	None	$AM_O=AM_I$	$P_O=P_I$
GTotal	$\exists x \in N$:Icol(x)	$AM_O=AM_I$	

I, I_1, I_2 are Input Relations, O is the Output Relations.

Table I

We can consider this operation as splitted in 2 suboperations: DTotal, and GTotal the first one consisting in building the subtotals at each node and the second one consisting in building the global amount on the whole file.

As an example of node conditions on an operation with two input relations, consider the Join operation.

In order to perform a Join on two relations I_1 and I_2 one of the two relations has to be completely duplicated with respect to the other one, for instance I_1cdu(I_2). In this case, if the Fragmentation Vector of the Output has the same number of elements as the Fragmentation Vector of I_2, then the Allocation Matrix of the Output is equal to the Allocation Matrix of I_2.

Remark: a special case is constituted by both Input relations beeing collected at the same node.

The node conditions represented in Table 1 together with the logical conditions on the possible sequences of logical operations (for instance, for a Total operation, DTotal must precede GTotal) are a set of constraints on the tree transformations that are possible in the design of a good access strategy /7/.

3.4 Example of Distribution Strategies

In figure 4 a possible Distribution Strategy for the Operator Tree of figure 2 is shown, assuming that the POPULATION and TRANSACTION relations are arbitrarily distributed and the RESULT has to be collected at node 5. This solution is perhaps the simplest one and it consists in performing locally the operations that can be performed in a distributed way, then to collect all the workfiles directly at the node where the result is required.

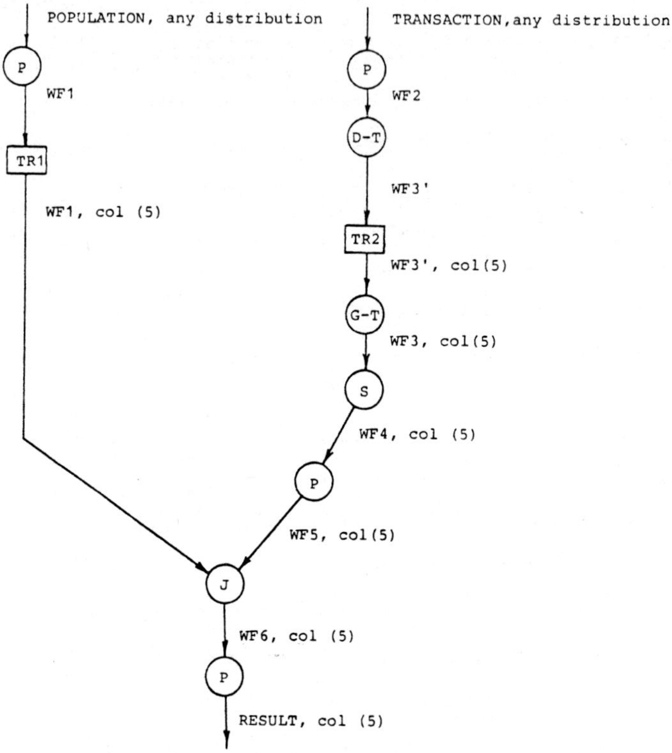

Fig. 4- Distributed Access Graph for the Example (Solution 1)

Many other different Distribution Strategies are possible. For instance, let us suppose that at node 3 of the network there is a global copy of the POPULATION relation, i.e. the Allocation Matrix of this relation has a row of all 1s corresponding to this node. In this case, the projection operation which produces WF1 can be performed at node 3 and WF1 would be collected at node 3. A Distribution Strategy which takes advantage of this fact is shown in figure 5. This solution could be better than the previous one if the transmission of the result from node 3 to node 5 and the collection of WF3' at node 2 were cheaper (with respect to the parameter which will be considered in section 4) than the collection of WF1 and of WF3' at node 5.

A still different solution could be to perform the Join distributedly, but it is impossible to show further examples, without considering the network structure and the quantitative parameters of the relations. In fact, as we saw above, the execution of a join operation between two relations requires duplication of one relation with respect to the other one. This can be obtained by moving fragments of both relations - making partial collections - between the network nodes and this can be made in many different ways which must be evaluated on the basis of the chosen merit factors.

4. Quantitative Parameters

In order to evaluate different Distribution Strategies, it is necessary to know also the quantitative parameters of the relations and workfiles which are affect-

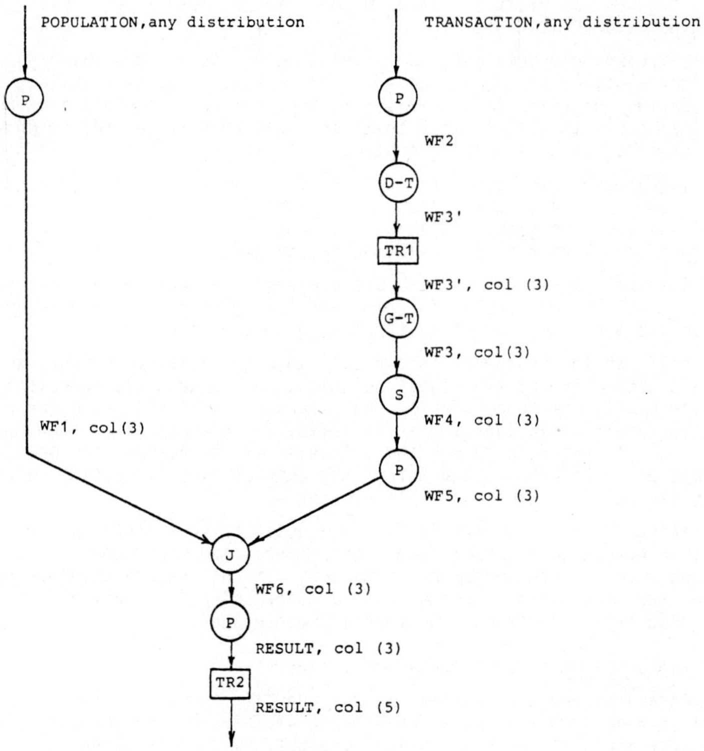

Fig. 5 - Distributed Access Graph of Example (Solution 2)

ed by transmission operations, since they are needed in determining the amount of information to be exchanged among the network nodes, as we shall see in the next section. These parameters are determined by the logical operations and depend on statistical properties of data.

For some parameters, like Cardinality, the same considerations apply as for centralized databases. The fact that relations are physically fragmented, however introduces difficulties as to the evaluation of the Fragmentation Vector of the output relations. In fact we cannot say "a priori" that changes in the Cardinality of the global relation are reflected in the same way on the Cardinalities of all the relation fragments. It suffices that some sort of correlation exists between the domain on which the operation is made and the Fragmentation Criterion (i.e. the logical property determining how a relation is fragmented and where the fragments are allocated) for introducing strong inhomogeneities between the Fragmentation Vectors of the input and of the output relations. In the general case this observation entails that a thorough analysis of data has to be made with the aid of well established statistical methods.

A way to estimate correlation between a value of a domain and the Fragmentation Criterion can be the observation of a relative frequency plot of the considered value against the values of the Fragmentation Criterion itself. As an example we can consider the transactions made by Mr. X in different cities, when the city is the Fragmentation Criterion for the relation TRANSACTION. The ratio of the number of transactions made by Mr. X in each city to the total number of transactions made by Mr. X gives the relative frequency of transactions of Mr. X with respect to the Fragmentation Criterion.

If the ratio is sensibly constant, no correlation exists. If the ratio is highly variable a correlation is present. Generally speaking, these plots belong to the class of frequency distributions of discrete qualitative parameters and there are few analytical tools to operate with them. We shall show in the following how particular statistical tests can be applied to obtain synthetic quantitative data.

In any case, whichever way we quantify correlation, we can classify the quantitative effect of logical operations in two major ways:
- the Cardinality of the global relation is changed;
- the Fragmentation Vector of the relation is changed;

We must notice that, when both effects are present, some entries in the Fragmentation Vector might become zeroes. In this case the hypothesis stated in section 3.3 could be violated. However we must distinguish two cases:

a) The vanishing of the fragments is due only to a quantitative effect, such as a Cardinality reduction of the global relation, and no sensible correlation is present to modify the fragmentation characteristics. In this case, we can assume that the general conclusions are still valid. The dimensions of the Fragmentation Vector remain the same, although the values in it can be modified and the null value must be considered in the set of the entries. The Allocation Matrix will consider the null fragments as still present.

b) the vanishing of the fragments is due to a qualitative effect, such as a strong correlation effect (e.g. a selection operation is made on a domain which is coincident with the Fragmentation Criterion). In this case a complete reorganization of the Fragmentation Vector must be made, since the vanishing is essential and the Allocation Matrix must be modified consequently.

4.1) Quantitative Parameters without Correlation

As to the changes in the Cardinality, we can quantify them, when correlation is absent, as the mean number of tuples which are affected by the logical operation. Let us consider the simplest case: values are uniformly distributed in the domain (i.e. their p.d.f. is rectangular the same number of elements of each value being present) and no correlation exists with the Fragmentation Criterion (i.e. they can be considered uniformly distributed at every local site).

In this case, be C_I the cardinality of the file and n the number of different values of the domain a simple selection operation on this domain will produce a result relation having a cardinality $C_O=C_I/n$ and the same Fragmentation Vector $FV_O=FV_I$ since the probability of finding the required value is proportional to the percentage of the relation stored at a given node. If the selection clause is a complex one among several domains which are not correlated (statistically independent) we can apply the results of the probability theory to the selectivities of these domains. For example, be n_A and n_B the number of different values os two domains and be $S_A=1/n_A$ and $S_B=1/n_B$ their selectivities. If the selection clause spans the two domains, the selectivity of the result will be:

-AND clause $S_R = S_A \cdot S_B$;
-OR clause $S_R = S_A + S_B - S_A.S_B$;

and the cardinality of the output relation will be $C_O=C_I.S_R$

Similar arguments can be applied to the compression of records in the projection operation. A more complex situation arises if a selection is made on a domain, followed by a projection of the result on another domain which has not been object of the selection and which is not a key. It has been demonstrated /8/ that, in the hypothesis of uniformly distributed values and no correlation with the Fragmentation Criterion, the problem is analogous to that of finding which is the mean number of different colours $E_{(K)}$ we can find by drawing K balls out of an urn containing C_I balls uniformly distributed over n colours. The result is

$$C_O = E_{(k+1)} = \frac{\bar{C}_I}{C_I - K} + \frac{C_I(1-1/n)-K}{C_I - K} E(K); \qquad E(\emptyset) = 0 \tag{4.1}$$

This function can be approximated by a family of two segments piecewise linear curves (one for each value of n). At lower values of k, $C_O = k$, at higher values of k, $C_O = n$. (See fig. 6);

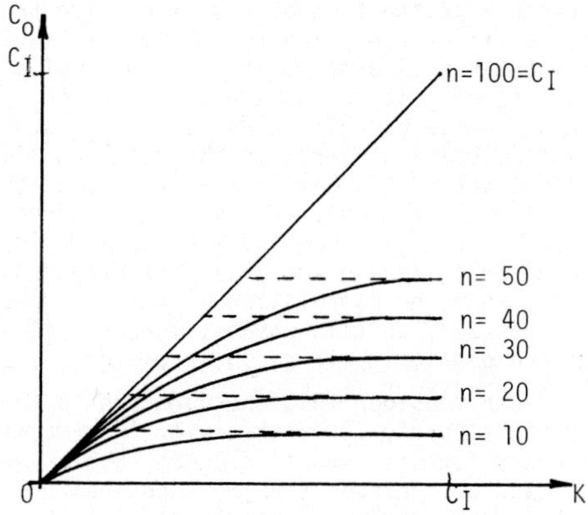

Fig. 6

This behaviour can be found in similar problems such as the evaluation of Block Accesses in conventional Databases /9/.

Starting from this result, a slightly more complex case has been treated in /10/. In this case the hypothesis of no correlation with the Fragmentation Criterion is maintained (i.e. the histogram representing the frequencies of values in the domain is the same everywhere) however the domain values are no more uniformly distributed, but it is enough that their distribution can be brought back to a monotone non-growing unimodal histogram.

In this case an excess approximated value can be found by splitting the histogram into two parts. Be n' and n" and C_I' and C_I'' the number of different colours and the number of balls in the first and in the second part so that

$$n' + n'' = n \qquad \text{and} \qquad C_I' + C_I'' = C_I$$

an excess value of the output Cardinality can be evaluated as follows:

$$C_O \leq \bar{C}_O = n' + (C_I''/C_I) * k$$

Considering all the possible splittings of the histogram and their associated $\bar{C}_O$:

$$C_O \leq \min \{\bar{C}_O\}$$

4.2) Effect of Correlation on the Fragmentation Vector

As we saw, unitl the no-correlation hypothesis is maintained, only the cardinality of the global relation is affected by relation manipulation operations, while the Fragmentation Vector remains unchanged.

To introduce the effect of a correlation among a domain or among some of its values, and the Fragmentation Criterion, let us use a simple example for the selection operation. Let us specify two domains among the "other items" in the POPULATION relation of the example (Fig. 2): a domain "disease" and a domain "disease date". With this information added we can do epidemiological analysis. For example we could ask, from the Regional Health Office, the dates and the places of all the cases of a certain disease. Moreover we could ask also the birthplaces of the people affected by the disease. The first operation to be made in replying this questions is a selection on the domain "disease" in the POPULATION relation. Let us think the disease we are enquiring about is FLU. We can think that flu is not bounded to a particular town or region in the area domain of our information system, but it hits people in the same way all over the area. Therefore we can say that FLU is uniformly distributed in the area and it has no correlation with the Fragmentation Criterion, which in our example is the town of residence. The Fragmentation Vector of the relation after the selection operation for the value FLU will be unchanged. Let us now enquire about MALARIA a disease which is endemic of a rather small area. In this case the greatest part of malaria cases will belong to tuples stored at the node placed in that area, while a negligible number of cases will be found at other nodes of the DDB. The Allocation Matrix of the relation after the selection for the value MALARIA will be very different from that of the POPULATION relation since, in the limit case, it will have only a 1 in correspondence with the affected area, while all the other values will be Ø' s. The same would happen if we should enquire about people living in a given area (the Fragmentation Criterion itself).Therefore we can say that the correlation with the Fragmentation Criterion property belongs to the values of a certain domain; moreover if all the values are uncorrelated, we say that the domain itself is uncorrelated.

However in certain cases we can consider that the domain as a whole is uncorrelated even if each of its values is strongly correlated with the Fragmentation Criterion In fact when a universal quantifier is used in a query such as "give me all the cases of whatever disease" and we consider the smoothness of the relative frequency plot of the morbidity (i.e. of the domain disease), it will be greatly increased with respect to the smoothness of the relative frequency plot of each value, therefore the effect of the correlation with the town of residence will be much less aperceivable.

It follows from the above examples that to obtain the Fragmentation Vector for every possible kind of query we should store in a Data Dictionary the relative frequency plots of each value of each domain with respect to the Fragmentation Criterion. This would result in an enormous amount of data, which would be hardly bearable for whatever information system.

However there are some methods, such as the analysis of correspondences, which allow both the analysis of the possible correlation between two sets of data, and the reconstruction, with some degree of approximation, of the original plots, starting from a much smaller subset of data /11, 17/.

Ad an index of the amount of correlation we have chosen Pearson's index, widely known as χ^2. This index allows to decide whether samples drawn from a given population (e.g. the values of a domain), conforms to a predefined hypothesis, which in our case is the independence of the values from the Fragmentation Criterion. High values of χ^2 mean that a significant difference exists between the expected values, under the stated hypothesis, and the actual values found in the samples. A zero value of χ^2 means that the hypothesis is exactly confirmed.

Data to be analyzed are partitioned in a 2 x N contingency table in which the N columns represent the values corresponding to the Fragmentation Criterion, and the two rows represent, respectively, the number of cases the value is present and the number of cases the value is absent. Fig. 7 shows a 2x4 table with associated derived values

	A	B	C	D	
X	x_A	x_B	x_C	x_D	$T_x = x_i$
non X = $\bar{X}$	$\bar{x}_A$	$\bar{x}_B$	$\bar{x}_C$	$\bar{x}_D$	$\bar{T}_x = \bar{x}_i$
$T_i = x_i + \bar{x}_i$	T_A	T_B	T_C	T_D	$T = T_x + \bar{T}_x$
proportion of x $p_i = x_i/T_i$	p_A	p_B	p_C	p_D	$\hat{p} = T_x/T$

A,B,C,D = values of the Fragmentation Criterion;
x = value of the analysed domain.

Fig. 7

For data organized in such a way a useful formula to calculate χ^2 is the following:

$$\chi^2 = \frac{\sum_1^N x_i p_i - \hat{p} T_x}{\hat{p}(1-\hat{p})}$$

with (N-1) degrees of freedom /13/.

The underlying hypothesis to be tested is that occurrencies of X are independent (not correlated) with the values of the domain acting as Fragmentation Criterion.

However, determining the χ^2 value on the whole table can give only a first index of the existence of correlation. This information is not yet enough to calculate the new values of the Fragmentation Vector; once we know that a significant cor - relation exists, we must determine how it behaves with respect to each value of the domain on which the Fragmentation Criterion is based. This requires a partitioning of the total χ^2_T into several fractions expressing the contribution of each column, or set of columns, to χ^2_T.

A very detailed analysis of this kind can be made using Kimball's formulae for N-1 degrees of freedom. The general form of Kimball's formulae is /13/.

$$\chi^2_j = \frac{T^2[\bar{x}_{j+1} \cdot S_j^{(x)} - x_{j+1} \cdot S_j^{(\bar{x})}]^2}{T_x \cdot T_{\bar{x}} \cdot T_{j+1} \cdot S_j^{(T)} \cdot S_{j+1}^{(T)}}$$

where

$$S_j^{(x)} = \sum_{i=1}^{j} x_i, \quad S_j^{(\bar{x})} = \sum_{i=1}^{j} \bar{x}_i, \quad S_j^{(T)} = \sum_{i=1}^{j} T_i$$

for

$$1 \leq j \leq N-1$$

A check on the correctness of the calculation can be made by the relation

$$\chi^2_T = \sum_{j=1}^{N-1} \chi^2_j$$

Further researches are in progress to relate the values of χ^2_j determined by this method to the values of the Fragmentation Vectors, and to determine the minimum amount of information to be stored in a Data Dictionary for a fast evaluation of the correlation properties.

5. Subproblems and Optimization

The model which has been presented in the previous sections shows that the choice of a distributed access strategy represents a complex optimization problem. In this section two partial subproblems are formulated in the form of integer programs for which well known algorithms exist. A basic assumption is that the quantitative parameters of the involved relations can be known.

5.1 Choice of a Transmission Strategy

Each Transmission Operation required by an access strategy is characterized by the Allocation Matrices of the relation before and after transmission. Different Transmission Strategies exist because:

a) some fragments of the relation can be duplicated, giving rise to a need of choosing among different sources of data;

b) the distribution of the relation after the transmission operation is not always completely determined. In fact the set D of destination nodes might be specified without specifying the assignment of which fragment to which node. This is the case of some logical operation followed by a join in the operator tree. We saw in section 3 that node conditions for a Join require that one of the relations be completely duplicated with respect to the other one. Fig. 8 shows the case of relation F1 being completely duplicated on the set D.

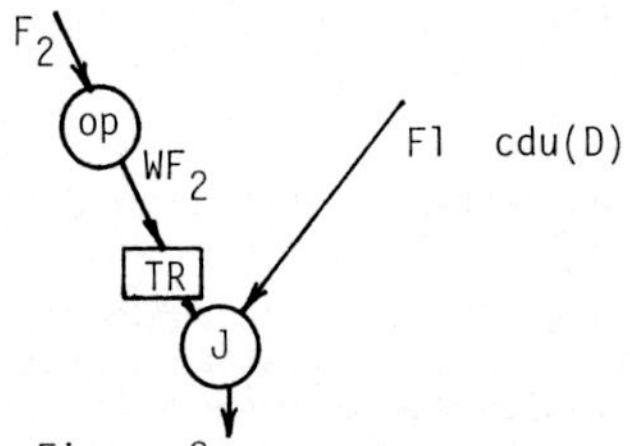

Fig. 8

It is clear that the type of WF_2 after transmission should be cdi (D). This solution gives the designer the most of freedom degrees, since he can optimally choose the transmission strategy for distributing fragments on the set of nodes D.

An inspection of Table 1 of section 3 shows that the general transmission operation TR : $AM_F \rightarrow AM_F'$ with AM_F and AM_F' beeing completely free is not needed, because, as a result of transmission, only particular distributions of the relation are required, i.e. either the relation is completely duplicated or it is completely distributed on a set D of destination nodes. Therefore a simpler form of Transmission Operation will be considered, having the result allocation AM_F' defined by the couple $<D_F, t_F>$, where D_F is the set of destination nodes and t_F is the type, i. e. either "completely duplicated" or "completely distributed". If t_F is "completely distributed", then $<D_F, t_F>$ represents not only one Allocation Matrix, but a whole class of them, each member of which corresponds to a particular permutation of the fragments on the nodes, and the previous considerations apply.

Problem Statement

A transmission strategy is defined by a set of boolean variables

$$x_{ijk}, \quad 1 \le i \le p_R, \quad 1 \le j \le N, \quad k \in D$$

x_{ijk} =1 if the ith fragment is transmitted from node j to destination k

x_{ijk} =∅ otherwise

The problem consists in finding an optimal assignment of the x_{ijk} in order to minimize both Cost and Delay. In general such a bi-criterion optimization does not have a unique solution but a set of solutions which lie on the indifference curve in the Cost/Delay plane. This happens even in the case that the unit cost and unit delay of the arcs of the network are proportional, because the intrinsic nature of the delay function is such that it tries to maximize transmission parallelism, while the cost function is completely unsensitive with respect to parallelism.

There are two possible ways of dealing with a bi-criterion optimization, either to find some α such that a new criterion can be defined

$$z = \min |(\alpha . \text{Cost}) + (1 - \alpha). (\text{Delay})|$$

or to solve the problem with respect to one criterion and fixing a maximum value for the other one, thus obtaining a set of new constraints. The second approach has been followed, thus obtaining an integer program which minimizes the total cost of a transmission operation with a total delay less than a fixed value $\bar{d}$. By starting from the optimal solution providing the minimal cost with no concern for the delay (i.e. $\bar{d}=\infty$), we can build the indifference curve by evaluating the minimal cost for decreasing values of $\bar{d}$.

In order to build the integer program, the linear functions $n_{lm}(X_{ijk})$, which express the number of bytes that have to be transmitted on each arc, have to be determined. The integer program becomes then for the "completely duplicated" case

$$z = \min \sum_{\text{all arcs}} C_{lm}\, n_{lm}\, (X_{ijk}) \tag{1}$$

$$d_{lm}\, n_{lm}\, (x_{ijk}) \leq \bar{d} \tag{2}$$

$$\sum_{1j}^{N} x_{ijk} = 1,\ 1 \leq i \leq p_k,\ k \epsilon D \tag{3}$$

$$x_{ijk} \text{ integer, } \emptyset \text{ or } 1 \tag{4}$$

For the "completely distributed" case, constraint (3) becomes

$$\sum_{1j}^{N} \sum_{k \epsilon D} x_{ijk} = 1$$

where:

C_{lm} is the unit cost of transmitting one byte on link l,m
d_{lm} is the unit delay of transmitting one byte on link l,m

Constraints (2) are based on the assumption that the total delay of the operation is the following:

$$\text{Total Delay} = \max_{\text{all arcs}} \{n_{lm}\, d_{lm}\}$$

5.2 Distribution of Operations

This subproblem consists in determining at which nodes to perform the logical operations in order to minimize transmission Costs and/or Delays. By inspection of Table 1 of section 3 it can be seen that transmission requirements are determined mainly by Join operations and by operations that require that the Input relation be collected at a single node.

The general treatment of this subproblem is extremely complex since it requires the solution of the Tranmsission Strategy subproblem for the evaluation of each possible distribution. However, the Transmission Strategy subproblem becomes trivial if the "Delay type" constraints are relaxed; therefore, it seems reasonble to solve the distribution subproblem under the assumption that only Cost is considered without taking care of Delays.

Let us consider for example an operator tree consisting of a single Join Operation (Figure 9). The two Transmission Operations TR1 e TR2 are needed in order to satisfy the condition I'_1 cdu(I'_2), while TR3 is needed in order to obtain the result with the required allocation. Under the simplifying assumptions that the delay is not considered and that I_2 has no duplication, it is possible to formulate the problem of choosing an optimal distribution of the Join (thus implicitely defining an

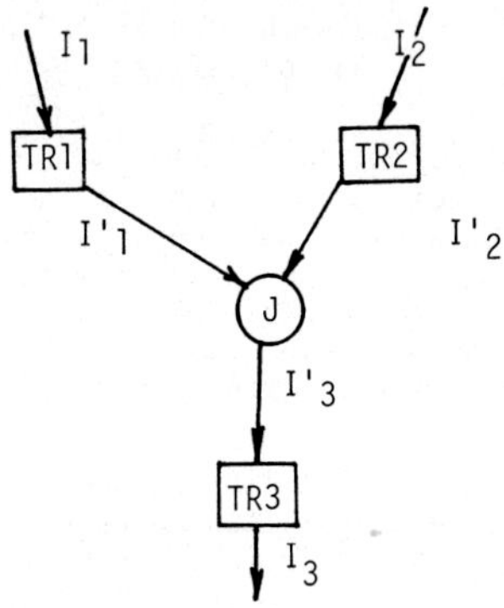

Fig. 9

optimal distribution for I'_1, I'_2 and I'_3) as an "Uncapacitated Plant Allocation" problem, in which the "plant sites" which have to be determined are the nodes at which to perform the Join.

The general form of these problems is the following:

$$z = \min \sum_{i\in I} \sum_{j\in J} c_{ij}x_{ij} + \sum_{j\in J} d_j y_j$$

$$\sum x_{ij} = 1, \quad i\in I,$$

$$1 \leq \sum_{j\in J} y_j \leq N,$$

$$0 \leq x_{ij} \leq y_j \leq 1 \qquad i\in I,\ j\in J$$

x_{ij} and y_j integers, $i\in I$, $j\in J$.

In order to apply this formulation to the distribution of operations problem, I=J are the nodes of the network, N is the number of nodes, $c_{ij}\ x_{ij}$ take care of the cost associated with the distributed file and $d_j y_j$ take care of the cost associated with the duplicated file and the result file. This class of allocation problem has been studied by several authors /14, 15/.

Further research is needed in order to extend the above result to an arbitrarily complex operator tree.

6. Conclusions

A model which permits the precise definition of the main subproblems involved in the design of an access strategy to a distributed database has been presented. Two restricted optimization subproblems have been defined and the possibility of applying already known mathematical tools to them has been shown. Further research is needed in order to extend these results to less restricted subproblems. However, the model itself and the partial results that have been obtained represent al -

ready a useful tool for a designer.

Bibliography

/1/ Bernstein P.A., Shipman D.W., "A Formal Model of Concurrency Control Mechanisms for Database Systems" Proc. 3rd Berkeley WS on Distrib. Data Manag. August 78.

/2/ Menasce D.A., Muntz R.R., "Locking and Deadlock Detection in Distributed Databases", Proc. 3rd Berkeley WS on Distrib. Data Manag., August 78.

/3/ Hevner A.R., Jao S.B., "Query Processing on a Distributed Database", Proc. 3rd Berkely WS on Distr. Data Manag. August 78.

/4/ Wong E., "Retrieving Dispersed Data From SDD-1", Proc. 2nd Berkeley WS on Distr. Data Manag. May 77.

/5/ Stonebraker N., Neuhold E., "A Distributed Database Version of Ingres", Proc. 2nd Berkeley WS on Distrib. Data Manag. May 77.

/6/ Smith J.M., Chang P.J., "Optimizing the Performance of a Relational Algebra Database Interface", Communications of the ACM, Vol. 18, n. 10, 1975.

/7/ Pelagatti G., Schreiber F.A., "Evaluation of transmission requirements in Distributed Database Access", Proc. ACM-SIGMOD 1979 Conference, Boston, May 1979.

/8/ Pelagatti G., Schreiber F.A.,"Comparison of Different Access Strategies in a Distributed Database", in B.Schneidermann (Ed.) "Database: Improving Usability and Responsiveness", Academic Press, Aug. 1978.

/9/ Yao S.B., "Approximating Block Accesses in Database Organizations", Communications of the ACM, Vol. 20, n. 4, April 1977.

/10/ Baldissera C., Bracchi G., Ceri S., "An algorithm for optimal processing of queries on a distributed Database", Internal Report IEEPM - LC n. 78-14, 1978.

/11/ Lebart L. et al., "Techniques de la description statistique", Dunod, Paris 1977.

/12/ Benzecri J.P., "L'Analyse de données", Voll. 1 & 2, Dunod, Paris 1976.

/13/ Maxwell A.E., "Analysing Qualitative Data", Methuen & Co. Ltd.

/14/ Cornuejols G., Fisher M., Nemhauser G., "Location of Bank Accounts to Optimize Float: an Analytic Study of Exact and Approximate Algorithm", Management Science, Vol. 23, N. 8, 1977.

/15/ Effroymson M.A., Ray T.L., "A Branch-Bound Algorithm for Plant Location", Opns. Res. Vol. 14, pp. 361-368, 1966.

INTEGRITY

Data Base Architecture, Bracchi/Nijssen, eds.
North-Holland Publishing Company

OBSERVATIONS ON SHARING IN DATA BASE SYSTEMS

John S. Nauman

International Business Machines Corporation
General Products Division
Santa Teresa Laboratory
550 Bailey Avenue
San Jose, California 95150

ABSTRACT: This paper explores the concept of data sharing in a data base environment. It describes the need for a data base lock facility and the functions such a facility would provide. In addition it shows how various functions provided by the data base system would utilize the lock facility. The paper is intended to provide a starting point for the data base designer when considering data sharing.

INTRODUCTION

The sharing of data in a data base system has been the subject of several works referred to in this paper (Ref. 1-5, 7, 9, 10). It is assumed that the reader is aquainted with the concepts presented in those works. Working from those concepts, the practical problems concerning the nature of sharing in a data base environment are explored. Practical, in this sense, denotes problems which must be addressed by the designer of a data base manager that will provide and support shared data.

Before proceeding with the discussion, a few concepts and terms will be described. A transaction is the entity which does work within the system. The author assumes a transaction-processing data base system in which interactive (short-running fast response); batch (long-running medium response); and background (very-long-running slow response) transactions are all allowed to access and process the data. It is assumed that any reasonable number of these transactions may be operating against the data concurrently. This desire for concurrency implies the need to share data among them.

Transactions are one of two types, based on their interaction with the data on which they operate: those which only read data, and those which both read and update data ("update" as used here includes deletion, insertion, and modification). The levels of data on which the transaction may operate are fields, which make up records. The records exist in pages or buffers, which in turn make up files, and the files are finally gathered into data bases. The actual structure is less important than the concept of varying granularites of data. The remainder of this paper will address only data bases, buffers, and records in order to simplify the discussion. However, the reader should keep in mind that other levels of resources are involved and may or may not be directly supported by the data base manager. All relationships among records are assumed to be contained within one data base (i.e., a data base is a complete entity). This means that the affect of any update of the data (and hence the locking considerations) can be contained within a single data base.

Allocation is the process of granting requests made by transactions for high-level resources (e.g., data bases, storage, devices). As used in this paper, the term allocation will refer to the granting of requests for data bases only. The transaction processes the data, performing whatever retrieval or update activity is dictated by the type of work being done. A transaction is assumed to either complete successfully (in which case all its updates to the data are exposed) or fail (in which case all its updates are assumed to be backed out). Data for which this assumption is not true is called "nonrecoverable data". The problems associated with this kind of data will not be addressed in this paper.

The data base manager is the set of processes and programs which control the data contained in the data base. The manager allocates data to the transactions and insures that sharing and recovery protocols defined over the data are enforced. The data base manager is composed of several internal functional areas, including:

- A record manager - which understands a transaction request for a data record and produces the record that the transaction expects to see.
- A buffer manager - which understands the relation among 1) the data, 2) the external media on which the data resides, and 3) the buffers through which the data is transmitted.
- A lock manager - which allows other functions of the data base manager to lock resources (i.e., data).
- A transaction processing manager - which acquires and releases resources to be used by the transaction, schedules transactions, and insures that transactions complete in one of two ways (success or failure).
- Several other components which provide other services performed by the data base manager (e.g., terminal control, data communications, logging, and recovery control).

In this paper it will be useful to describe transactions and the data resources that they hold in a shorthand form. Thus, T(n) denotes transaction instance n, and R(m) denotes data resource instance m. Other terms used are either self-explanatory or described when they first appear.

Occasionally, mention will be made of techniques employed by existing data base managers. This is done for expository purposes and should not be considered an endorsement of the data manager as a whole. It is likely that there are data base managers which implement many of the techniques described here. Failure to mention these products should be viewed as ignorance of them rather than a deliberate slight.

It is assumed that, for a variety of reasons, the installation wishes to execute transactions concurrently. However, if transactions executing concurrently are allowed to process the same data, a potential for lost update exists (Ref. 1). (Two transactions which update the same record concurrently may result in two writes back to the data base. Neither will reflect the changes of the other, and only the last will persist.) Therefore, the transactions must be protected from concurrently updating the same data. This protection is the responsibility of the data base manager.
The protection can take the form of:

- interpreting the concurrent changes and performing the desired actions in a consistent fashion, or

- serializing the changes such that one is complete before the next is performed.

Because of the complexity of determining the eventual result inherent in the first approach, most data base managers implement the second. The serialization approach is the only one addressed in this paper. The level at which this serialization is to take place is the first decision that the designer of the data base manager must make. Concurrency may be controlled at any level between the data base and the record (field serialization, while possible, is usually considered unnecessary).

If the serialization is done on a data base, only one transaction at a time may process a data base. With this approach, the transaction runs to completion (success or failure) and the data base is changed to reflect the modifications made by the transaction. The next transaction which wishes to process the data base is then permitted to run. Some transactions will need the entire data base to themselves in order to perform their function (e.g., reorganization utilities), but these are the exception. Most transactions will need only a small part of the data base to complete their processing. It is unnecessary to force these transactions to serialize each other unless they try to process the same data at a lower level (e.g., record). It therefore seems worthwhile to provide various granularities of sharing, from the data base down to the record. This allows the transaction to select the granularity of sharing which best supports its usage of the data.

In the preceeding discussion it was assumed that the transaction must have exclusive control of the data which it is processing. This is only necessary if the transaction updates the data. If several transactions need only read access to the same data, there is no reason why they cannot be allowed to run concurrently. Transactions requiring update access to the data would still need to be granted sole control of the data.

Reading transactions, while allowed to run concurrently with other readers, must usually be prevented from running concurrently with an updater. Allowing readers and updaters to run concurrently on the same data exposes the readers to "dirty" data. "Dirty" data is data which has been updated by a transaction whose fate has not yet been decided. The problems which exist when transactions are allowed to read "dirty" data are described in References 1 and 4. These problems revolve around the fact that the reading transactions may see the data in a temporary, inconsistent state. They may read some records which the updater has modified and some that remain to be modified, or they may see changes which will be removed if the updater fails. In general, most reading transactions need to be protected from seeing "dirty" data; however, some transactions (e.g., sampling programs which are not concerned about exact values) may not be sensitive to minor inconsistencies.

The remainder of this paper is divided into a discussion of locking management and sharing of data within one data base manager. The additional topic of sharing data among data base managers (in the same or different processors) will not be covered here because of its complexity and the fact that the entire area of distribution of data among data base managers is a current research topic.

The discussion of lock management consists of identifying the functions of a data base lock manager and the problems of its operation. The discussion of sharing of data within one data base manager includes the problems of the transaction processing manager, the record manager, and the buffer manager functions of the data base manager.

LOCK MANAGEMENT

The lock management function of a data base manager is responsible for providing a basic serialization mechanism for the other functions of the data base manager. This includes providing a granting and queueing mechanism for resources and a means of suspending and resuming transactions if the resources cannot be immediately granted. The lock manager would typically be invoked via a LOCK or UNLOCK request for a resource or at transaction COMMIT (see below). Requests for resources could be expected to take one of two forms. A request for exclusive control of the resource (X) if an update is to be performed, prevents any other transaction from seeing the resource while it is being processed. A request for shared use of the resource (S), if the data is only to be read, prevents concurrency with updaters but allows concurrent use among readers while the data is being processed. Additional functions which would be extremely useful include:

- Allowing the different levels of resources to be locked with different protocols (see intent locking below).
- Providing support for various kinds of resources (data bases, records).
- Providing a variable and extensible approach for determing the grantability of resource requests.
- Providing categories of lock requests to enhance the capabilities of the data base manager.
- Handling the problem of deadlock.

LOCKING HIERARCHY

As outlined in the introduction to this paper, levels of granularity need to be specified when locking a resource. This may lead to a problem if the same level is not specified consistently (e.g., one transaction decides to use data base locks and another decides to use record locks). The problem occurs because each transaction functions as if it were processing its resource in the absence of the other (which has been blocked by the lock). This problem may be solved by viewing the resources as a hierarchy in which resources must be acquired in a hierarchical order (Figure 1). At the highest level is the data base. At intermediate levels are resources of a finer granularity than the data base, and at the lowest level are the records, which make up the data base and the intermediate constructs. Such a hierarchy allows the locking at any level to dictate the potential sharing of data at that and all lower levels.

```
Data Base
    |
   File
    .
    .
    .
  Buffer
    |
  Record
```

Figure 1. Hierarchy of Data Resources

INTENT LOCKING

The concept of hierarchical resource acquisition makes it necessary to introduce a new mode of locking resources in a hierarchy so that intent to lock at a lower level is communicated. If only shared (S) and exclusive (X) modes are supported, no lower-level locks will have meaning once a lock is acquired at the data base level.

To solve this problem Gray, et al (Ref. 4) introduced the notion of intent locks. If locking is to take place at lower levels in the resource hierarchy, an intent lock is acquired on the resources at all higher levels, and only the lowest level of the hierarchy to be locked is locked in non-intent state. For example, to maximize concurrency by locking at the record level, the data manager would lock all elements above records in the hierarchy (data base, ...) in intent mode and the records themselves in non-intent mode. In his concept of intent locking, Gray distinguishes between the intent to read data (IS) and the intent to update it (IX). A transaction with only read intent will never request an exclusive lock at a lower level of the hierarchy. A further refinement is the notion of a shared and intent exclusive (SIX) state of a higher-level lock. This state would be used by a transaction which required exclusive update control at lower levels of the hierarchy but could share with readers at these lower levels (and lock the lower levels exclusively when updating them).

Example 1. Assume that T(1) is an interactive transaction which is updating many records within a data base, but that the installation wishes to enhance concurrency by having T(1) lock at the record level. During the allocation (setup) phase for T(1), the data base manager would acquire the locks needed by T(1) for processing. This would be done by acquiring the data bases in which T(1) was allowed to process and locking them in intent exclusive (IX) mode. Any intermediate levels of the data bases would also be locked in IX mode. Each time T(1) referenced a record for update, the data base manager would lock that record in exclusive (X) mode.

Example 2. If transaction T(2) were now initiated to perform an interactive query function on the data base, it could be in conflict with T(1). The setup phase for T(2) would consist of acquiring data base locks in intent shared (IS) mode. Each time T(2) referenced a record, the data base manager would lock the record in shared (S) mode.

Example 3. Now assume that while transactions T(1) and T(2) are processing the data base as described above, transaction T(3), a reorganization utility, is to be run against the data base. The data base manager must acquire an exclusive lock on the data base to allow T(3) to proceed. However, T(3) will not be allowed to process the file while T(1) and T(2) are active (since the data base manager cannot acquire the data base lock and allow T(3) to continue).

The approach, then, is to support two types of locking. High-level locks may be acquired in exclusive, shared, or intent states, depending on the desire of the user to permit sharing at a lower level. Low-level locks, on the other hand, are always acquired in shared or exclusive states, since they represent the lowest level of the data hierarchy. All data are potentially shareable among transactions running concurrently. The actual shareability of the data is dependent on the state in which the various levels are locked by the data base manager on behalf of a transaction.

POSSIBLE LOCK MANAGER APPROACHES

In supporting locking for different levels, the lock manager may be aware of the hierarchy of data itself, or it may view the data only as named resources, allowing the other areas of the data base manager to understand the relationships in more detail. The first approach leads to a lock manager which knows both the name of the resource and the level it occupies in the hierarchy. This dual knowledge allows the lock manager to make certain optimizations in processing data which are related in some fashion. For example, knowledge that a given transaction has locked a data base and that no other transaction has locked that data base would permit the lock manager to simplify any locking done at a lower level on behalf of the transaction. Since this transaction would be the sole user of the data base, no contention could exist at the record level; hence, the normal search for a contention on record requests could be avoided. While this may seem to be a desirable characteristic of the lock manager, the added complexity of the lock manager may outweigh the potential savings.

The second approach forces the individual data base manager functions to remember and/or understand the relations between data, but allows a much simpler lock manager implementation. In this case, the lock manager is unable to optimize the related data requests and so would have to search for contention on each lock request. A second result of this approach would be that the data base manager functions that used the lock manager would have to present fully qualified resource names. The name of the data item to be locked would have to be sufficient to insure that the data to be locked is not confused with a data item from another hierarchy. For example, if the name of the record to be locked were the relative record number in the data base, the fully qualified resource name might be the data base name concatenated with the record number to avoid conflicts which would occur if only the record number were used. (This, of course, assumes that data base names are unique.)

LOCK MATRICES FOR GRANTING LOCKS

It is desirable that the lock manager allow for expansion of request states as well as new levels of compatibility. This requirement can be seen in the previous discussion on locking at various levels of the hierarchy. Some levels need a five-state lock and some only a two-state lock. The lock manager should be flexible enough to tolerate a change in the number of states which can be specified and the compatibility among these states. A nice method of providing this flexibility is that used by System R as outlined in Reference 4. The System R lock manager uses a set of matrices to determine the grantability of requests, given the current state of the requested resource.

If a resource is not held by any transaction, a request for the resource R(i) by transaction T(1) may be immediately granted. A request for R(i) by T(2) will be granted only if it is in a state which is compatible with the state which is held by T(1). If the request is compatible, T(2) is also granted the resource lock. Subsequent requests for R(i) must now be in states compatible with those in which both T(1) and T(2) hold the lock.

If R(i) is requested by T(3) in a state which is not compatible with those of both T(1) and T(2), then T(3) cannot be granted the resource. This could occur because T(3) has suddenly become interested in R(i) or because T(3) has changed its intent with respect to R(i) and therefore wishes to change the state in which it has R(i) locked. The first type is the case in Example 3, above. Several options are available to the lock manager at this point. The lock manager may allow conditional and unconditional requests, in which case T(3) will either be told that the lock is not available in the state requested or it will wait for the resource lock to become available. The option chosen will depend on the ability of the data base manager process requesting the data lock to continue processing without the data. If the data base manager process cannot continue until the data becomes available, then the lock will be requested unconditionally and the transaction will wait for the data lock to become available. If the requesting data base manager process can continue with other processing, then the data lock will be requested conditionally. If the lock is not acquired, control will be returned to the process with an indication that this is the case. If the lock manager chooses to allow unconditional (wait for the lock) requests, several additional issues must be addressed.

What happens if T(4) makes a request for R(i) in a state which is compatible with those in which T(1) and T(2) currently hold the resource, but T(3) is waiting for the resource? If the resource is granted to T(4), then T(3) must now wait for T(4)'s request, which was made after its own request. In the extreme, T(3) might never be granted the resource. On the other hand, if T(4) is forced to wait behind T(3) (strict FIFO order of granting), then T(4) is being forced to wait when it is not really necessary. The easiest solution, from the standpoint of the lock manager, is to grant the requests in FIFO ordering (to avoid having to check for a never-granted request). A second problem introduced by allowing T(3) to wait for R(i) is the possibility of deadlock, which will be discussed later.

Compatibility Matrix

Figure 2 illustrates the concept of a compatibility matrix. As discussed previously, a transaction's request for a resource lock must be in a state compatible with the states in which other transactions currently hold the resource lock. The matrix indicates whether or not the requested states listed at the top of the matrix are compatible with the "held" states listed at the left.

HELD \ REQ	IS	IX	S	SIX	X
NOT HELD	ok	ok	ok	ok	ok
IS	ok	ok	ok	ok	no
IX	ok	ok	no	no	no
S	ok	no	ok	no	no
SIX	ok	no	no	no	no
X	no	no	no	no	no

ok - indicates that request can be granted
no - indicates that request cannot be granted

Figure 2. Compatibility Matrix

A lock manager using this approach may be modified to handle larger or different sets of lock states and compatibility with much more ease than one which has been designed around a specific set of states and compatibilities.

Maximum Matrix

Since the lock manager tracks all lock requests made by a transaction, it is unnecessary for any other area of the data base manager to track such requests. Another data base manager process (the record manager, for instance) may not know that there is already a lock on a specific record. This could occur if the record were left locked after an update in order to protect readers from "dirty" data or because the record manager supports multiple cursors against the data base. In any case, the lock manager should allow multiple requests for a resource lock from the transaction. This implies that the lock manager must keep track of the number of times that a given transaction has locked a resource and may also need to remember the state requested each time.

Keeping a count of requests does not present a serious problem, but tracking the state of <u>each</u> request is costly. Instead of doing this, the lock manager may remember <u>only</u> the maximum (summary) state in which the transaction has locked the resource (i.e., if the resource is locked both S and X by a transaction, only the fact that the transaction holds the resource in the X state will be remembered). This implies that some partial ordering is defined over the lock states and known to the lock manager. As with compatibility determination, discussed previously, this information may be conceptualized as a matrix (Figure 3). A request for a resource lock by a transaction which already holds the resource must first be in a state compatible with the state in which any other transactions hold the resource lock. If this is the case, the current state and the requested new state are compared to determine the state in which the transaction will now hold the resource (the maximum of the two states). The matrix indicates what the resultant state will be for the transaction request state listed at the top of the matrix versus the "held" state listed at the left.

HELD \ REQ	IS	IX	S	SIX	X
IS	IS	IX	S	SIX	X
IX	IX	IX	IX	SIX	X
S	S	IX	S	SIX	X
SIX	SIX	SIX	SIX	SIX	X
X	X	X	X	X	X

Figure 3. Maximum Matrix

The matrix in Figure 3 is derived from the linear ordering among states, as shown in Figure 4.

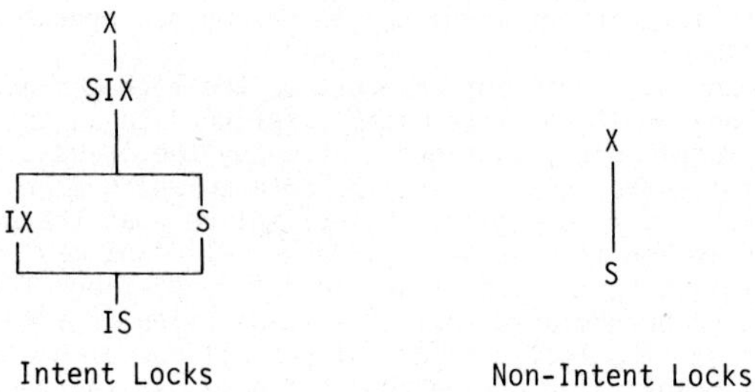

Figure 4. State Ordering

LOCK CLASSES AND TRANSACTION SUPPORT

Beyond the basic granting and queueing services provided, the lock manager can support the data base manager in more subtle ways. Lock managers in existing data base management systems as well as those incorporating the proposed standards enable the data base manager to collect locks into classes for later processing as a group (IMS/VS *Q, System R lock classes, CODASYL keep lists). This group processing usually consists of freeing the locked data with a single call to the lock manager, rather than with several individual calls, when processing of the data is complete. Such a lock manager would support some number of classes into which the locks could be placed. It could allow a requestor to have the lock classified either when acquired or at some time during processing and could allow the record to be a member of more than one class simultaneously.

The lock manager could also directly support certain processing points of a transaction. As outlined above, a transaction is the processing unit of the data base system and has certain well-defined points in its life. Transaction initiation, the first of these points, includes the allocation of many of the resources which the transaction needs to process. The type of transaction being initiated will dictate the extent to which the resources can be allocated before initiation. For example, a background transaction can probably make known at initiation the entire set of resources it will process. This means that resources, at least at the higher levels of the hierarchy, may be both allocated and locked during allocation for the transaction. If the transaction locks the resource in non-intent mode, no other locks need be acquired (but concurrency on such data may be reduced). Similarly, batch transactions may be able to specify all of the resources they need at allocation. On the other hand, interactive transactions (e.g., generalized query transactions) may be unable to specify the resources required until the transaction is running. While running, they may need to lock resources down to the record level to maximize potential concurrency.

While the data base manager allocation process is acquiring the locks on behalf of the transaction, the lock manager could make use of the knowledge that allocation is in process. The lock manager could realize that all locks acquired during allocation will be held until the corresponding deallocation phase of transaction termination. This means that the resource locks acquired at allocation could be freed by the lock manager as a group and would not need to be individually unlocked by the data base manager deallocation process. This "block unlock" would allow certain optimizations in the unlock process.

The second transaction processing point of interest to the lock manager is the commit point (Ref. 5). The commit point (sometimes referred to as the synchronization point or quiet point) is a declaration by the transaction that it has reached a point in its processing where the data on which it has operated are consistent. In particular, reaching this point implies that the previous "dirty" data of this transaction may now be considered valid and may be exposed to other transactions. This point occurs at successful completion of the transaction, but it may also be declared while the transaction is running. When the commit point is declared, the lock manager unlocks all non-allocation locks gathered on behalf of the transaction during processing (as stated above, allocation locks are released at deallocation). This simplifies the processing which the rest of the data base manager must perform at a commit point by implicitly handling the transaction's data locks.

The final transaction processing point of interest to the lock manager is the transaction backout. This point occurs when the transaction has failed and the changes that it made have been removed from the data it processed. As above, the resources processed by the transaction are no longer "dirty" (since the changes have been removed) and the data may again be made available to other transactions. At a transaction backout the lock manager releases all nonallocation locks held by a transaction (allocation locks may also be freed if deallocation takes place at transaction backout).

DEADLOCK

Deadlock occurs when a set of transactions can never be granted the resources they requested because of a cycle of lock holders and waiters among the transactions. The simplest deadlock would be T(1) holding resource lock R(a) and requesting resource lock R(b) while T(2) holds R(b) and requests R(a). The deadlock would occur if both transactions indicated they wished to wait for the resource lock to be granted:

```
         R(a)                        R(b)
          |                           |
        held by                     held by
         T(1)                        T(2)
          |                           |
    waited for by               waited for by
         T(2)                        T(1)
```

Figure 5. Deadlock Situation

In Figure 5, T(1) is waiting for T(2) to release R(b), and T(2) is waiting for T(1) to release R(a). Obviously, neither action will occur in the normal course of events.

The deadlock problem can be approached in several ways. The interested reader is referred to any or all of References 2, 3, 5, 6, 7, and 9. In general, the approaches fall into three categories: avoidance, prevention, and detection/resolution. Avoidance schemes require that resource locks be identified as a part of transaction scheduling, and the data base manager allows scheduling of only those transaction combinations which it can determine are "safe" (i.e., will not deadlock). The shortcomings of this approach are that the data base manager is very pessimistic in its scheduling, and that the transaction must specify all resources which it may process. With this approach, the data base manager's scheduler would not allow T(1) and T(2) in Figure 5 to run concurrently against the data base, since the potential for deadlock exists. Scheduling only "safe" combinations of transactions insures that deadlocks will not occur, but if the likelihood of deadlock is low, the adverse effect on concurrency may not be justified. In addition, the mere potential for use of a resource is sufficient to prevent scheduling, whether the resource would actually have been used or not. Reduced schedulability makes this approach undesirable in most data base systems. This technique was attempted by early releases of IBM's Information Management System (IMS2) but was abandoned in favor of a detection approach.

Prevention schemes insure against deadlocks by requiring that resource locks be acquired in a certain system-defined order. With such a scheme, a deadlock like that in Figure 5 would not occur, since either R(a) or R(b) would be first in the acquisition order, making the request sequence of either T(1) or T(2) impossible. This technique is useful when only a small set of resources must be allocated and an ordering can logically be imposed. Many operating systems use this approach. The problem with this approach is that when a transaction is processing within a data base, it is usually impossible to predetermine which records will be requested, and hence it is impossible to acquire the resource locks initially in the correct order. Any time an out-of-order request is made, all resource locks lower in the order must be freed, then reacquired. This overhead and the potential interference from other transactions makes the approach undesirable for most data base systems.

The last approach to deadlock reflects most of the recent work on the subject. In this scheme, the deadlock is allowed (or nearly allowed) to occur, is detected, and is then resolved. The first problem is to determine when to attempt to detect the deadlock. Detection can be attempted:

1. Any time a request waits,

2. Periodically during normal system processing, or

3. At transaction timeout or data base system wait.

There are advantages and disadvantages to each of these approaches. If detection is attempted each time a request must wait, then the deadlock will be discovered before it is allowed to occur. Opponents of this approach note that in most cases a deadlock will not be found, so the processing is "wasted". Proponents point out that transactions are seldom forced to wait for a resource and that this is already handled as an exception case.

If deadlock detection is done periodically, then the deadlock will be allowed to occur and will be discovered by the detector during one of its passes. Opponents of this approach note that the deadlock will tie up transactions until it is detected. Proponents claim that since deadlocks are so infrequent, there is no effect on the normal throughput of the system, that the period may be adjusted such that the deadlock does not go undetected for very long, and that much less time is wasted searching for deadlocks.

The transaction timeout or data base system wait techniques are generally less popular than the other two methods. In transaction timeout, the transaction is allowed to wait a certain amount of time for a resource, after which some action is taken to handle the possiblity of deadlock. This action consists of either beginning a deadlock detection process or failing the timed out transaction. The first alternative is very similar to periodic detection; the second has the shortcoming that an inappropriate transaction may be chosen as the victim. If deadlock detection is put off until a data base system wait occurs, then the deadlock will be detected only after the entire system has come to a stop. According to Macri (Ref. 9) this technique was originally used in the DMS 1100 system but was later abandoned in favor of a search-at-transaction-wait approach. The overriding drawback of the system wait approach is that the entire data base system must grind to a halt before the deadlock can be detected. This leads to unacceptable variations in system performance.

Once a deadlock has been detected, by whatever means, the problem becomes how to resolve it. Again, there are several approaches, each with its merits and drawbacks. The obvious solution to a deadlock detected at request wait is to fail the transaction that issued the request. While this may be the obvious and probably easiest solution, it is far from the best. In resolving a deadlock this way, the lock manager must be concerned with the cost to the system of selecting a transaction as a victim, rather than the ease with which the victim is selected. The victim should be the transaction which involves the least total work to backout. This total includes both the processing that the transaction has accomplished as well as the work necessary to backout the transaction. Typical criteria for victim selection include:

- Number of log records written (and hence, the number of distinct backout actions which must be performed)
- Number of data base records or buffers modified (another indication of potential backout activity)
- Processing time used by the transaction (which may not be reflected in either of the above two numbers)
- Some transaction priority scheme.

The lock manager must choose some of these or other criteria to assess the "worth" of the transactions which are involved in the deadlock. Once the worth of each of the participants is determined, resolution amounts to selecting the least "worthy" transaction as the victim. This involves resuming the data base manager process representing the victim with an indication that the transaction which was being processed has been selected as a victim and has not been granted the lock. The data base manager process would then fail the transaction, causing backout. As noted above, this backout process would cause the lock manager to release all resource locks gathered on behalf of the transaction, thus resolving the deadlock.

A few other characteristics of the deadlock problem are also worth mentioning. First, the lock manager must be careful not to select a transaction that is already a victim and is backing out. This problem could arise if, during backout, the data base manager found it necessary to acquire resource locks (e.g., buffer locks which had been released when the initial request processing was complete). Selection of a backing out transaction as a victim would leave the data base manager with no way to resolve the deadlock, since attempting to backout a transaction in this state would have no meaning. This problem can be avoided in one of two ways. First, the data base manager can permit only one transaction at a time to be in the actual process of backing out. Thus, if a transaction which was backing out became involved in a deadlock, the data base manager could select a victim other than the backing out transaction, mark the victim for later backout, and preempt the resource from the victim. This procedure requires the data base manager to exercise a significant amount of care during backout, and to backout only one transaction at a time. An alternative is for the data base manager to disallow lock acquisition during backout. If no locks may be requested, no deadlock can occur. The disadvantage of this approach is that it requires all locks which might be needed during backout to be retained until either a backout occurs or the transaction reaches a commit point.

Finally, the deadlock may contain more than one cycle, as illustrated in Figure 6.

```
      R(i)                R(j)                R(k)
       |                   |                   |
     held by             held by             held by
      T(1)                T(2)                T(4)
       |                  T(3)                 |
  waited for by            |              waited for by
      T(2)                 |                  T(3)
                      waited for by
                          T(1)
                          T(4)
```

Figure 6. Multicycle Deadlock

This figure shows four transactions which have deadlocked on three data locks. Again, the lock manager has to decide whether to take the simple or the "optimal" approach. The simple approach would be to detect each cycle independently and resolve each independently. This, however, may be the wrong approach from the data base system perspective. The lock manager must select the victims not only on the basis of whether T(1) and T(4) are, individually, of less "worth" than the sum of T(2) and T(3) but also whether the sum of T(1) and T(4) is of less "worth". This determination will indicate whether the deadlock should be resolved by failing T(1) and T(4) or T(2) and T(3).

SUMMARY

The lock manager performs both basic and extended services related to serialization of the data resources managed by the data base manager. Options are available to the lock manager in several areas of its processing. The specific lock manager implementation should be a set of these options selected to best support the data base system as a whole.

SHARING WITHIN A SINGLE DATA BASE MANAGER

The three main users of the lock manager will be the transaction processing manager, the data base record manager, and the data base buffer manager. (The data communication component, while probably a user of the lock manager, is not discussed in this paper.)

TRANSACTION PROCESSING MANAGER

The transaction processing manager is responsible for controlling transactions within the data base system. Once it is decided, through some mechanism not described here to run a certain transaction, the transaction manager must insure that the transaction is brought to a point where it can be scheduled (allocation). It then initiates the transaction, handles processing point requests, and finally, controls the termination of the transaction (deallocation).

The locking considerations of the transaction processing manager involve allocation and deallocation of data bases to the transaction. As part of the process of making the transaction ready to run, data bases which are to be used are locked in the mode required to support the transaction. It may be unreasonable to require that all the data bases which the transaction may process be locked, particularly in general interactive query transaction. However, the advantage of allocating as many resources as possible before transaction initiation is that the likelihood of deadlock is reduced if allocation completes successfully. If allocation cannot complete, due to deadlock, the backout which must be done is trivial (simply release all locks and retry allocation).

The reader may notice a similarity between this approach and the deadlock avoidance approach discussed in the previous section. The difference is that this scenario does not require all resources to be allocated. This means that deadlock may occur and must be handled.

Dynamic allocation refers to the ability to allocate data bases while the transaction is running. Dynamic allocation, if allowed by the data base manager, is another point at which the transaction processing manager must use the lock manager to lock data bases. The locks will be the same whether the allocation is done before transaction initiation or dynamically. In both cases, the data base(s) will be acquired by the transaction processing manager on behalf of the transaction in the mode dictated by the type of processing to be performed by the transaction. The query transaction would acquire the resource locks in share or intent share mode (depending on the consistency needed and the concurrency to be allowed). The update transaction would acquire the resource locks in exclusive, intent exclusive, or shared and intent exclusive (SIX) mode (again depending on the consistency and concurrency desired).

Release of the data locks acquired during allocation may occur at three points during the transaction:

1. When the transaction ceases to process the data protected by the locks.

2. At a commit point, or

3. At transaction deallocation as part of transaction termination.

If the data base has been allocated for read access, release of the resource locks may be at any of these points. However, if the data base has been allocated for update and updates have been made, it is undesirable to release the resource locks before a commit point. The rationale for this is that until a commit point is reached, the transaction may be forced to backout. If locks are released and a backout is necessary, then the "dirty" data that the locks protected will be exposed to other transactions.

It may also be undesirable to release data base locks at a transaction commit point unless the transaction has completed processing of the data base. The reason for this is that once the locks on the data base have been released by the transaction, they become available to other transactions, which may acquire them in an incompatible mode. If the transaction is a background or batch type, this may be the result desired, but it should be remembered that the transaction may take longer than expected to complete its processing. Additionally, if locks are released it is impossible to retain positioning across a commit point. This may or may not be a desirable attribute.

The release of resource locks acquired during initial or dynamic allocation is always safe (and necessary) at transaction deallocation. The release of these locks at a commit point prior to deallocation, while possible, may lead to unnecessarily long processing times. These times would be particularly noticeable with interactive transactions.

RECORD MANAGER

The record manager implements the support for the operators identified at the transaction interface. In fulfilling this function, the record manager hides most of the data base manager internal structure and processing. The record manager is responsible for presenting a record or set of records to requesting transactions. The types of locking required by the record manager depend on the data manipulation interface supported and the capability of the data base system to support transaction views of data other than the stored format. This includes materialization of the record which the transaction views from underlying stored forms, format changes, field reorderings, etc. In producing the record requested by the transaction, the record manager must lock all constituent parts of the record to insure consistency. This process may be as simple as locking a single data base record or as complicated as locking a set of physical records which make up the desired logical record. This processing is performed by the data base manager on behalf of a transaction request. The manner and extent of the locking necessary should be invisible to the transaction.

Several data base manager commands have direct locking implications for the record manager. The most obvious of these is the update type operation. Transaction T(1) may update a data base by inserting a new record, deleting an existing record, or modifying an existing record. In each of these cases, the record manager should insure that the data changes introduced by T(1) are not compromised by changes of other transactions until T(1) has completed or reached a commit point. Since problems only arise when concurrent processing and update are both allowed, the record manager need not be concerned if high-level non-intent locking is done. For low-level (e.g., record) locking, the considerations are described below.

The record manager protocol of locking a modified record will, block subsequent transactions from processing the "dirty" data. This block will last until the modifying transaction either commits or fails.

The problem associated with insertion and deletion of records by a transaction is more subtle. If T(1) inserts a record into the data base, the record should not be visible to other transactions processing the file. The initial concern is that other transactions not see the "dirty" data of T(1). In addition, however, it may be desirable that other transactions needing to process the file must be blocked by the inserted record until the fate of T(1) is determined, if their processing would include the inserted record. If T(1) is successful, any transactions which were blocked in their processing are now permitted to proceed and see the newly inserted record. If T(1) fails, the record is "removed" and any transactions that were blocked by the insert are allowed to proceed with processing. Such a protocol is necessary to insure the protection of other transactions from "phantom" records.

A "phantom" record (Ref. 1, 12) is: 1) one which is not necessarily part of a consistent version of the data base or 2) one which appears between a transaction's processing and reprocessing of the same data base before commit. In the first case, if the locking protocol is not observed, transaction T(2) may process the entire data base with record locking and yet not see a consistent copy, even though locks are held until commit. For example, T(1) inserts record R(a), and then inserts record R(b). If T(2) is not blocked by the first insert, it is possible for T(1) to successfully complete and for both R(a) and R(b) to appear in the data base before T(2) arrives at R(b) in its processing. In this case, T(2) sees a state of the data base which never really existed. In the second case, T(1) may see a "phantom" record inserted by T(2) between T(1)'s first and second processing of the data. For example, suppose T(1) has processed the data base once and now T(2) is scheduled, inserts a record visable to T(1) and completes successfully. If T(1) now makes a second pass over the data base, it will see the record inserted by T(2). Engles (Ref. 1) calls this the problem of inconsistent analysis and indicates that its only solution lies in the prevention of "phantoms" by the record manager.

The problem of deletion has the same characteristic. In deleting a record for a transaction which is still in process, the record manager must not permit other transactions to process past the deleted record. In this case, if the transaction fails, the deleted record(s) will suddenly reappear in the data base. A final complication to this problem is that the record manager must permit the transaction responsible for the modification, insertion, or deletion to see the results of its action if it attempts to re-reference a modified record. Blocking the original transaction leads to a certain deadlock if re-reference ever occurs.

The read operators supported at the record manager interface present a simpler set of requirements. Locking a high-level resource in shared mode frees the record manager from any locking requirements, since the records are certain not to change. Such an approach reduces concurrency by disallowing update transactions against the locked data. Record locking increases concurrency by allowing both readers and updaters to reference the data, but it necessitates locking each time a record is materialized for a transaction. The locks acquired would be the same as those previously described in the update discussion. This is necessary to avoid the consistency problems discussed above. Reading transactions would be blocked by updating transactions which had not completed.

Gray (Ref. 4) notes that there are two ways in which a data base manager may allow a transaction to dispose of read locks. Logically, since no update has been made and no"dirty" data created, the lock may be released when the transaction has ceased to be interested in a record it has read (e.g., it has moved the cursor to a new record). A potential problem is that it is possible for a transaction to process the data base twice and see two different sets of data. Suppose T(1) is only reading data and wishes to enhance concurrency by locking at the record level. As T(1) processes the data base, the record manager locks each record for T(1) as long as T(1) is interested in the record, but it releases the lock(s) when T(1) moves on to the next record. It is now possible for T(2) to update some of the records which T(1) has processed and then commit. If, upon completing processing of the data base, T(1) reprocesses the data base, a different set of results may be obtained, due to the changes made by T(2). This problem may be solved by holding all locks (both for read and update until a transaction commits or completes.

While most transactions will require protection from "dirty" data, some will be insensitive to the problem. Those transactions which need only an approximation of the exact state of the data base may not desire protection from "dirty" data at the cost of longer execution times. The record manager supports these transactions with an unlocked read interface. In processing for such a transaction, the record manager needs to be aware of the possibility of situations which would not normally occur. A record which has been selected, or in fact an entire data base, could disappear while the unprotected transaction was processing. The record manager must detect and communicate such situations back to the transaction. The record manager does not, however, insure consistency beyond this point. The potential problems make these types of transactions the exceptions.

Another area of concern for the record manager is the paths by which data is accessed. If only linear (flat) views of the data base are supported by the data base manager and there is no support for access to records except sequentially, the record manager need concern itself only with protection of the sequential paths to the data. If the data base may be accessed in hierarchical fashion, directly, or in a network or relational fashion, the record manager must be able to lock paths to the record as well as the record itself. Again, if only one path to the data is supported, the problem can be solved by locking elements in the path in the same mode in which the record is to locked, but if more than one path is available, this approach is insufficient. In general, any update made by a transaction must cause the record manager to lock the data and make the change. In addition, the record manager must lock any paths affected by the update and update the paths to reflect the change. This may include updating indices over the date, and/or modifying chains to reflect the status of the update, depending on the way in which the data base manager supports data paths.

BUFFER MANAGER

The buffer manager is the function of the data base manager which manages the permanent copy of the data bases. In addition to managing the external media, the buffer manager manages the buffers which make up the data base while they are in processor memory. This is the first area in which the buffer manager must employ the lock manager. If a transaction makes an update to a record, the record manager must insure that the record is logically locked. The buffer manager, on the other hand, must insure that the buffer space in which the record exists is not subject to change or reuse before the transaction completes. If the update made by the transaction is a modification to a field of an existing record (which does not change the record length), there is no need to lock the buffer, since the locked record within the buffer will block concurrency. If the update is an insert or delete, or a change in length occurs, the associated modification of buffer space must be processed by the buffer manager. This includes locking the modified portion of the buffer. The lock may be acquired on the affected space, but a simpler approach is to lock the entire buffer on behalf of the updating transaction. The rationale behind locking the buffer is to prevent another transaction from attempting to update a record in some fashion while the fate of the updates made by the first transaction remain undecided.

An example of the potential danger is the following: Suppose transaction T(1) deleted a record from a data base. The record manager would insure that any concurrent transactions which tried to follow paths through the deleted record were blocked by the delete until the fate of T(1) was decided. However, if T(2) inserted a record which was to be placed in the same buffer as the record deleted by T(1), the record might be placed in the same spot as the record deleted by T(1). If T(1) failed later in its processing, there would then be no way for it to reinsert the record which it had (temporarily) deleted.

Buffer managers may choose to handle this problem in one of several ways. One approach is to mark the space as deleted but, by internal protocol, not reuse the space until T(1) has either successfully completed or failed. The buffer manager may choose not to reuse the space at all, in which case the space in the buffer is not reusable until a reorganization (garbage collection) is done. Another approach is to lock the buffer until the fate of T(1) has been decided and then expose the resultant state. The lock would only block other transactions attempting to update the same buffer, and then only until T(1) completed.

SUMMARY

In this section, the author has shown how several data base manager processes can use locking facilities when operating on behalf of the transactions. The uses made of the locks reflect a transaction's method of processing data under the control of the data base manager. This section dealt only with the most obvious problems encountered when sharing is carried out within a single data base system.

CONCLUSIONS

By now, the reader will have realized that this paper does not contain any radical innovations in the area of data sharing. However, it should give a better understanding of the various data base manager functions which are involved when data sharing is allowed. The divisions of data base manager functions described here are rather arbitrary and reflect the author's bias. However, the problems outlined and the solutions proposed are applicable to any data base system which supports data sharing. The problems, not addressed here, of sharing among multiple data base managers offer excellent opportunities for both research and extension of current data base systems.

REFERENCES

1) R. W. Engles, "Currency and Concurrency in the COBOL Data Base Facility", Modelling in Data Base Management Systems (ed. G. M. Nijssen), North Holland 1976

2) G. Gardarin and P. Lebeux, "Scheduling Algorithms for Avoiding Inconsistency in Large Databases", Third International Conference on Very Large Data Bases, ACM 1977

3) G. Gardarin and S. Spaccapeitra, "Integrity of Data Bases: A General Lockout Algorithm with Deadlock Avoidance", Modelling in Data Base Management Systems (ed. G. M. Nijssen), North Holland, 1976

4) J. N. Gray, R. A. Lorie, G. R. Putzolu and I.L. Traiger, "Granularity of Locks and Degrees of Consistency in a Shared Data Base", Modelling in Data Base Management Systems (ed. G. M. Nijssen), North Holland, 1976

5) J. N. Gray, "Notes on Data Base Operating Systems", Advanced Course on Operating Systems, Technical University of Munich, Germany, July 28-August 5, 1977

6) "Information Management System/Virtual Storage (IMS/VS)", System Programming Reference Manual, IBM Form No. SH20-9027-2

7) P. F. King and A. J. Collmeyer, "Database Sharing - An Efficient Mechanism for Supporting Concurrent Processing", Database Management Systems, Vol 1, (ed. Ben Shneiderman) AFIPS Press, 1976

8) L. J. LaPadula, "Harmonious Cooperation of Processes Operating on a Common Set of Data, Part 1", The MITRE Corporation, MTR-2254 Vol 1, Contract F19628-71-C-0002 (671A), Bedford, Massachusetts, December 1972

9) P. Macri, "Deadlock Detection and Resolution in a CODASYL Based Data Management System", Proceedings, International Conference on the Management of Data, ACM, 1976

10) D. Ries and M. Stonebraker, "Effects of Locking Granularity in a Database Management System", ACM Transactions on Database Systems (TODS), ACM, September 1977

11) D. Ries and M. Stonebraker, "Locking Granularity Revisited", Memorandum No. UCB/ERL M78/71, Electronics Research Lab, U. C. Berkeley, October 1978

12) K. P. Eswaran, J. N. Gray, R. A. Lorie and I. L. Traiger, "The Notions of Consistency and Predicate Locks in a Data Base System", CACM 19, November 1976

Data Base Architecture, Bracchi/Nijssen, eds.
North-Holland Publishing Company

COPING WITH DEADLOCK IN DISTRIBUTED SYSTEMS

David B. Lomet

IBM Thomas J. Watson Research Center
Yorktown Heights, New York 10598

While methods have been developed that cope well with deadlock in centralized systems, it is only recently that this issue has been treated in distributed systems. This paper presents an algorithm that prevents deadlock in distributed systems without the need to centralize resource contention information. The algorithm is based on previous deadlock avoidance methods for centralized systems. The paper presents a model for distributed systems. Then, based on a discussion of distributed graphs, conditions are given that permit distributed detection of potential cycles. These conditions lead us to make assumptions concerning non-local activity in the distributed system. Using this framework, the application of the centralized deadlock avoidance algorithm to distributed systems follows naturally.

I. Introduction

With the emergence of very low cost computer systems, there has been an increasing desire to effectively distribute this computational power to the geographic locations where it will actually be used. A restraint on this tendency has been the need, in many applications, to access a shared data base. Problems having to do with data base consistency and recovery are fairly well understood in a centralized system. Distributing the data base geographically has, however, magnified these problems and compounded the complexity of their solutions. Nonetheless, there has been recent progress on distributed data bases. A fairly extensive bibliography on this and related work appears in [6].

In this paper, we describe a method of preventing deadlocks in a distributed data base system. Our approach is an adaptation of our methods of deadlock prevention in a centralized system[3,4]. In this paper, and, as is commonly done, we treat deadlock issues in terms of the management of locks requested and released by multiple processes. While consistency is what concerns data base users, consistency requirements are translated into locking requirements by the data base system.

II. Distributed Systems

In our model of a distributed system, such a system is composed of a number of dispersed geographical locations which possess both computational power and resources, i.e. some part or parts of the data base. Such locations are called sites. A request by an individual for manipulation of the data base results in the creation of a job, sometimes called a transaction. Such a job may require data base resources from several sites. In order to access this data, the job must spawn one or more processes that provide the computational power of the job. A process of a job must exist at each site containing data required by the job, and only processes at a site may access data at that site. Thus. our model of distributed systems consists of four components, geographical locations or *sites*, transactions or *jobs*, *processes*, and data base *resources*.

Some additional attributes of our model of distributed systems that need to be emphasized are the following.

1. A job may have several proceses, distributed over several sites, and more than one of them may be active simultaneously. This is similar to the model suggested in [1,5], and is more general than the model of [6].
2. Processes of a job may communicate freely with each other, but the only interaction between jobs is via competition for resources.
3. If all the processes of a job can acquire the data base resources they require, then the processes of a job will all terminate, as will the job. More specifically, the processes of a job will not deadlock or be subject to indefinite delay under such conditions.
4. If some process of a job is denied resources because of competing use of the resources by a process of another job, it is possible for all the processes of the job to become dependent on the progress of the blocked process, and hence for them all to become blocked(inactive).

A distributed data base system is illustrated schematically in Figure 1.

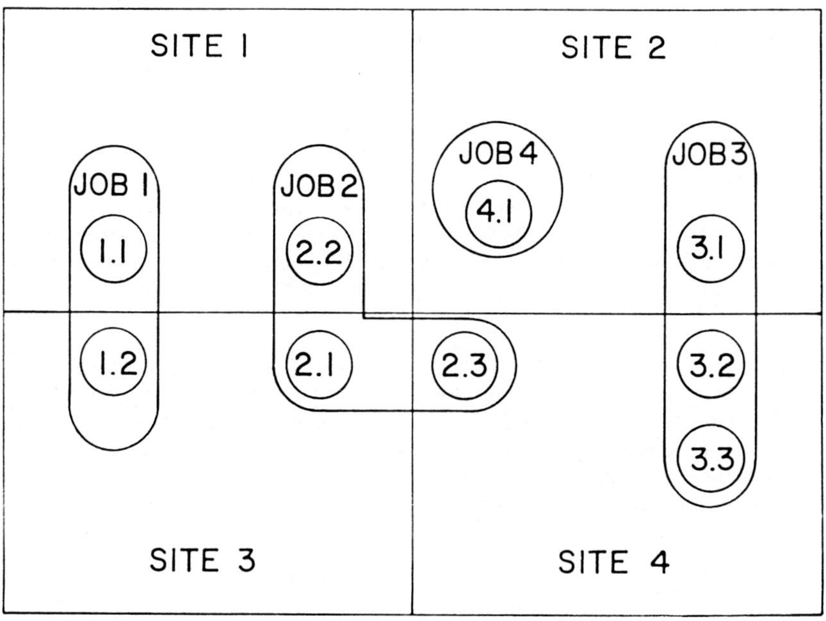

Figure 1: A schematic view of a distributed data base system.

III. Deadlocks

This section will review, and in some cases, modify, the terms in which we have previously defined deadlock and its avoidance. The modifications arise because of the change in our underlying system model. Thus

Notation 1: The set of resources held by a process p_j of a job J_i at time t, for its exclusive[shared] use is denote by $H_E(J_i.p_j,t)[H_S(J_i.p_j,t)]$.

In order to capture the meaning intended for the locking(holding) of resources in either the exclusive or the shared mode, the following constraint must be satisfied.

Constraint 2: $H_E(J_i.p_j,t) \cap [H_E(J_k.p_l,t) \cup H_S(J_k.p_l,t)] = \phi$ for $i \neq k$.

The above constraint implies that if a process of one job is holding resources in the exclusive mode, no other process of any other job can simultaneously hold those resources. It permits, however, multiple processes of multiple jobs to hold resources shared.

Since we are concerned with what happens when a job needs to hold a resource that, if permitted to do so, would lead to a violation of Constraint 2, we introduce notation for the requests of processes that have yet to be satisfied. Thus

Notation 3: The set of resources requested by a process p_j of a job J_i at time t for its exclusive[shared] use is denoted by $R_E(J_i.p_j,t)[R_S(J_i.p_j,t)]$.

Then a process is resource delayed whenever constraint 2 would be violated as follows.

Definition 4: A process p_j of job J_i resource delays a process p_l of job J_k at time t if

$$(H_E(J_i.p_j,t) \cap [R_E(J_k.p_l,t) \cup R_S(J_k.p_l,t)]) \cup [H_S(J_i.p_j,t) \cap R_E(J_k.p_l,t)] \neq \phi.$$

There are, in our model, other circumstances in which one process might delay another. These occur within a job as a form of communication or synchronization wait. Thus

Definition 5: A process p_j of job J_i wait delays process p_k of the same job J_i at time t if p_k is waiting in some way, unspecified but permitted in our model, for p_j.

The relation 'resource delays' we denote by $RD(J_i.p_j,J_k.p_l)$, while the relation 'wait delay' we denote by $WD(J_i.p_j,J_i.p_k)$.

Deadlock can now be defined in terms of circular delay or waiting. In order to do this, we define the delay graph as follows.

Definition 6: The delay graph $G_D(t)$ is a time varying directed graph $<N_D(t),E_D(t)>$ such that

a. the set of nodes $N_D(t) = \{J_i.p_j \mid J_i$ is a job and p_j is a process of $J_i\}$.

b. the set of edges $E_D(t) = \{(J_i.p_j,J_k.p_l) \mid RD(J_i.p_j,J_k.p_l) \vee WD(J_i.p_j,J_k.p_l)\}$.

Then we finally have a definition of deadlock as follows.

Definition 7: A system is deadlocked whenever its delay graph $G_D(t)$ possesses a cycle.

IV. Deadlock Avoidance

In order to avoid deadlock, we must take care to fully appreciate the role played by jobs in our model. In particular, the edges of the delay graph $G_D(t)$ that are between processes of a job are not under the control of the lock manager system. Because of this, if deadlock is to be avoided, it must be done by controlling the existence of edges between processes in different jobs. The crucial observation thus is that cycles can be avoided in the delay graph if and only if cycles involving only jobs in this graph are also avoided. This observation depends on the assumption that processes within a job do not deadlock among themselves, i.e. no cycles will exist that are totally within a job.

Deadlock avoidance requires a declaration, called a claim, prior to any locking, of resources, that informs the system of all resources that might be locked(held) by a process. Thus we have

Notation 9: The set of resources claimed by a process p_j of job J_i at time t for its exclusive[shared] use is denoted by $C_E(J_i.p_j,t)[C_S(J_i.p_j,t)]$.

As with holds, there are constraints that must be satisfied by claims, and by the holds and claims of any given process as well. These constraints are

Constraints 10: For $X \varepsilon \{E,S\}$,

a. $C_X(J_i.p_j,t_2) \subseteq C_X(J_i.p_j,t_1)$, where $t_1 \leq t_2$, i.e. claims cannot be increased.

b. $H_X(J_i.p_j) \subseteq C_X(J_i.p_j)$

The reasoning above concerning jobs leads us to define claims and holds for jobs.

Definition 11 The set of resources claimed by a job J_i at time t for its exclusive[shared] use is denoted by $C_E(J_i,t)[C_S(J_i,t)]$ and is defined as follows.

$$C_X(J_i,t) = \cup\{C_X(J_i.p_j,t) \mid \text{all } p_j \text{ in } J_i\}, \text{ where } X \varepsilon \{E,S\}.$$

Similarly we have

Definition 12: The set of resources held by job J_i at time t for its exclusive[shared] use is denoted by $H_E(J_i,t)[H_S(J_i,t)]$ and is defined as follows.

$$H_X(J_i,t) = \cup\{H_X(J_i.p_j,t) \mid \text{for all } p_j \text{ in } J_i\}, \text{ where } X \varepsilon \{E,S\}.$$

Analogously to the notion of 'delay', we now define the notion of one job potentially delaying another.

Definition 13: A job J_i potentially delays a job J_j at time t if

$$(H_E(J_i,t) \cap [C_E(J_j,t) \cup C_S(J_j,t)]) \cup [H_S(J_j,t) \cap C_E(J_j,t)] \neq \phi.$$

We denote this relation by $PD(J_i,J_j)$.

The notion of potential delay captures the fact that if a process in job J_i holds any resources claimed by a process in J_j, then that process will be delayed if it tries to lock those resources. Further, in our model, all the other processes of J_j might, because of this, also be blocked or delayed. It is this potential delay among jobs that deadlock avoidance methods must monitor. Therefore, the holds-claims graph, renamed here the potential delay graph, is presented.

Definition 14: The potential delay graph $G_{PD}(t)$ is a time varying directed graph $<N_{PD}(t),E_{PD}(t)>$ such that

a. the set of nodes $N_{PD}(t) = \{J_i \mid J_i \text{ a job and } C_X(J_i,t) \neq \phi\}$.

b. the set of edges $E_{PD}(t) = \{(J_i,J_j) \mid PD(J_i,J_j)\}$

Then, repeating the central result for deadlock avoidance, we have the following theorem.

Theorem 14: A system state is safe, i.e. deadlock can always be avoided regardless of the subsequent resource requests of the processes of the jobs, if and only if the potential delay graph $G_{PD}(t)$ is cycle free.

To prove this theorem for the potential delay graph above requires but minor modifications to the proof presented for the holds-claims graph in [4]. There is no way to prevent delay edges among processes within a job. Hence, there is no way to prevent completion of a delay cycle among processes unless a delay cycle is prevented among jobs. Such edges can be prevented if and only if cycles in the potential delay graph are prevented. Note that if a deadlock detection and recovery strategey is pursued, that the delay graph G_D is used in which processes are nodes, while deadlock avoidance requires the potential delay graph where jobs are nodes.

V. Distributed Graphs

In this section some general results are established concerning graphs, and what can be guaranteed concerning them when only partial knowledge is available. In particular, we start with a graph which we call the global graph G_G. This graph is an abstraction of the delay or potential delay graphs of the preceding section. It is the graph about which we wish we had complete information. There are a number of local graphs, which we denote by G_i, that represent that part of the graph that exists at a particular site. This local graph is, however more than merely a fragment of G_G, as we shall see. A distributed graph is then defined as

Definition 15: A distributed graph is a set of local graphs $\{G_i\}$ in which $N_i \cap N_j$ ($E_i \cap Ej$) may be non-null for $i \neq j$.

We can then define what we mean by a combined graph.

Definition 16: A combined graph of a distributed graph $\{G_i\}$ is denoted by $G_C = \langle N_C, E_C \rangle$ where

a. $N_C = \cup\{N_i \mid G_i$ in the distributed graph$\}$ and

b. $E_C = \cup\{Ei \mid G_i$ in the distributed graph$\}$.

Our purpose in introducing distributed graphs is to enable us to discuss distributed decision making in resource contention systems. Thus, based only on separate knowledge concerning each of the local graphs, we wish to either detect or prevent cycles from forming in G_G and G_C. What we are looking for is a situation in which there are cycles in G_G and G_C only if there are cycles in at least one of the local graphs. Notice that we are willing to be conservative. That is, cycles may appear, or threaten to appear in the local graphs without such a situation existing in G_G and G_C.

There are two situations about which we need to be on our guard. Obviously, we wish to be aware of cycles or impending cycles in G_G. However, problems arise caused by cycles in G_C, even when no cycles exist in G_G. These cycles can result in what has been called scheduling deadlocks, i.e. situations in which the system state is safe (or not deadlocked) but in which, nonetheless, no progress is made. These problems are illustrated in Figure 2.

What is needed in order to make a local determination as to whether cycles exist globally is to have local information concerning global connectivity. For this reason, we introduce the notion of local connectivity.

Definition 17: A distributed graph $\{G_i\}$ satisfies the local connectivity condition if, whenever (n_i,n_j) is in E_C^*, then (n_i,n_j) is in E_k^* for some local graph G_k in the distributed graph.

Then, Claim 18 below follows immediately.

Claim 18: If the distributed graph $\{G_i\}$ satisfies the local connectivity condition, then the combined graph G_C will contain a cycle only if one or more of the local graphs G_k of the distributed graph contain a cycle.

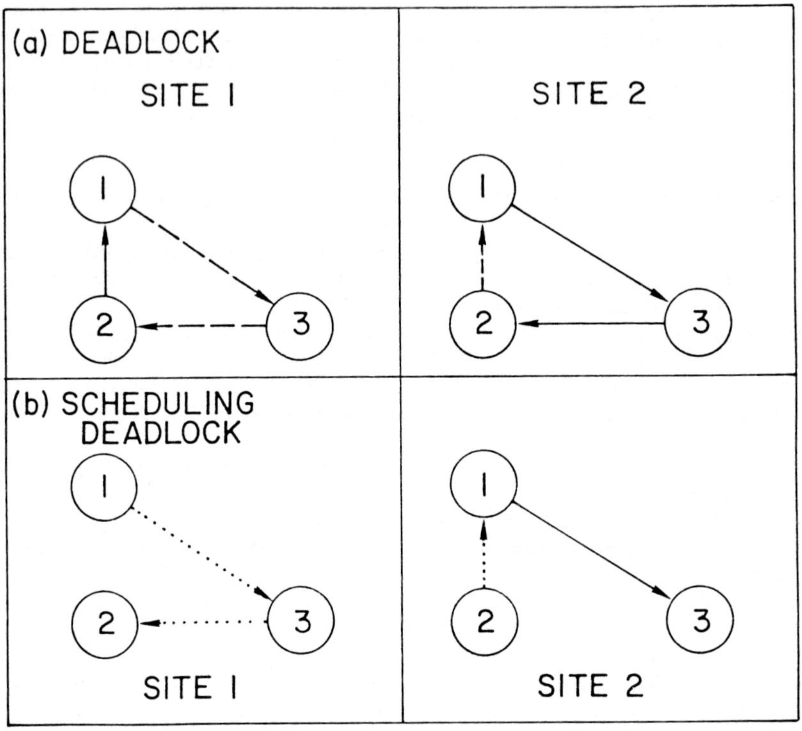

Figure 2: Distributed systems in which (a) deadlock and (b) scheduling deadlock occur. A real edge is indicated by ______, an edge assumed by the site by ......, and a real edge not known at the site by ------.

Finally, we are able to determine the presence of cycles in the global graph G_G under the following condition.

Claim 19: If $G_G \subseteq G_C$, i.e. if $N_G = N_C$ and $E_G \subseteq E_C$, then G_G will contain a cycle only if one or more of the local graphs G_k contain a cycle and the distributed graph $\{G_i\}$ satisfies the local connectivity condition.

VI. Hybrid Methods

Rosenkrantz et al, in [6], recognized the utility of distinguishing purely local processes from the global processes when they introduced the notion of hybrid methods for distributed systems. With hybrid methods, complete information is known with regard to local nodes and local connectivity while assumptions are implicity made concerning global nodes. Their formulation was appropriate only for their model of distributed systems. However, the same basic idea can be applied here. Thus, we first define local and global nodes as follows.

Definition 20: A node n_i of a distributed graph $\{G_k\}$ is
a. global if there are local graphs G_j and G_k in the distributed graph and n_i is in $N_j \cap N_k$ and $j \neq k$.
b. local if it is not global, i.e. if n_i is a member of the nodes N_j of only one graph G_j of the distributed graph.

Having distinguished local from global nodes, we observe that connectivity between nodes in G_C, at least one of which is local, is present in a local graph or does not exist. This leaves only connectivity between globals to consider and leads us to the following condition.
Definition 21: A distributed graph $\{G_i\}$ satisfies the local connectivity of globals condition if, whenever (n_i,n_j) is in E_C*, then (n_i,n_j) in E_k* for n_i, n_j global nodes and G_k a local graph.
Thus, the following claim permits us to substitute the local connectivity of globals condition for the local connectivity condition.
Claim 22: If the local connectivity of globals condition is satisfied by a distributed graph $\{G_i\}$, then the local connectivity condition is also satisfied.

The advantage of the above distinctions and claims is that it focuses our attention on where the difficulty in treating distributed graphs, and hence distributed systems, lies. The source of the difficulty is exactly in acquiring information concerning the global connectivity of nodes that span sites of the distributed system. There are many approaches to acquiring this information or of making assumptions concerning it. The problem that must be overcome in all the approaches is to assure the consistency of the information or the assumptions at any given time. Note that we emphasize both the consistency and the time factor. Approaches that attempt to broadcast complete information on global connectedness must be concerned that the information presented is valid across all sites at the time it is to be used. Approaches in which assumptions replace the need for exact information, like the approach described in the next section, can ease the problem of timeliness but consistency remains critical.

VII. Connectivity Based on Node Ordering

If communication of information concerning connectivity of nodes in a distributed system is to be kept low, assumptions must be made concerning that connectivity. In particular, as indicated in the preceding section, these assumptions must be made with respect to the connectivity of global nodes. The idea is to associate a number with each global node which depends on some fixed property of the node. Then, we can use the ordering among integers to derive the assumed connectivity. Since all local sites have access to this static property of the global nodes, the assumptions concerning node connectivity are the same at all sites.

One important property of the node ordering suggested above is that so long as the node ordering connectivity assumptions are not violated, i.e. so long as actual connectivity of the global nodes is a subset of the connectivity assumed by the ordering, then the local connectivity of globals condition is satisfied. Thus, cycles in the global graph are all detected as cycles in the local graphs by claims 22 and 19. A second important property of node ordering is that cycles arise in G_C, aside from purely local cycles, exactly when the node ordering based connectivity is violated. The result is expressed in the following claim.

Claim 23: If cycles are prevented in local graphs of a distributed graph $\{G_k\}$ where each local graph includes edges between global nodes whenever the node ordering assumption requires that the nodes be connected, then cycles will be prevented in G_C, and hence in G_G.

Rosenkrantz [6] has made use of node ordering among globals to detect the potential for deadlock. Thus, if all assumed connectivity represented actual connectivity in G_G, then the method successfully detects deadlock. Actually the method in [6] imposes an ordering on all nodes, global and local. This does not aid in detecting deadlock, but makes it possible to assure that indefinite delay is avoided.

One convenient method by which to order nodes is by the time that they enter the graph. Such a method involves what is called timestamping. To timestamp events in a distributed system, however, presents a more difficult chore than in a centralized system. Fortunately, Lamport[2] has solved this problem and we shall assume that a mechanism based on his work is available.

For deadlock detection, any number may be associated with a node when it is entered into the graph so long as it differs from the numbers of the existing nodes. This is so because the new node never has any other real edges in the delay graph since real edges form only when requests are delayed or the process issues an explicit wait. For deadlock avoidance however, if complications are to be avoided, strict time sequencing must be enforced in the node ordering. The graph of Figure 3 illustrates such a situation. The problem arises because real edges to the new node may exist at the moment that the node is entered and these may conflict with the connectivity assumed by the node ordering. Strict time sequencing of the nodes, i.e. if g_i is older than g_j, then (g_i,g_j) is in E_k, for all G_k in which the nodes occur, assures that this problem is avoided. Why? Because, any real edges in the graph between a new node, g_{new} and an existing node, g_i are such that it is (g_i,g_{new}) that is an edge, not (g_{new},g_i). An edge exists in the potential delay graph from g_{new} to some other node only if g_{new} is holding some resources, and an entering node does not hold resources. But, since g_{new} enters G_{PD} with a claim, the holdings of some other node g_i may be such that $PD(g_i,g_{new})$ is true.

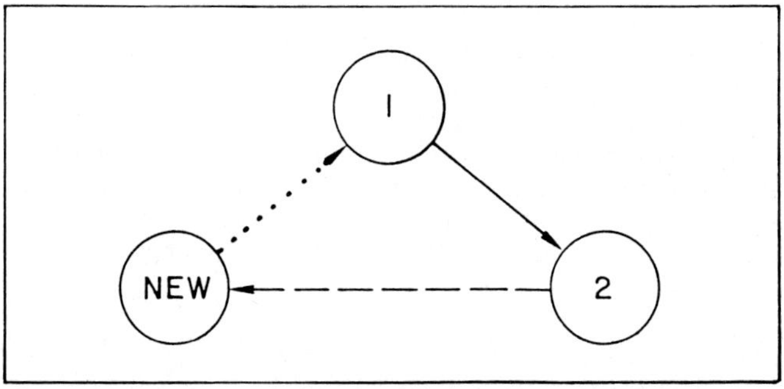

Figure 3: A potential delay graph in which g_{new}, if it enters with assumed out edges, produces a cycle. Real edges are indicated by ______, assumed out edges of the new node by ......, and real edges of the new node ------.

VIII. A Distributed Deadlock Avoidance Method

In this section, a deadlock avoidance method is described that, drawing on the analysis of the preceding three sections, works for distributed systems. Specifically, the method makes use of the potential delay graph in which jobs are nodes. The responsibility for keeping the potential delay graph cycle free is distributed to the local graphs or sites of the distributed system. This is done by assuring that the local connectivity of globals condition is satisfied via an ordering of nodes. The ordering of nodes is in strict time sequence, as required for the potential delay graph. The actions required in order to perform the operations of entering jobs into the system, requesting, and releasing resources and the exiting of jobs from the system are each described.

Job Entry: A job is presumed to enter the distributed system at a particular site as a result of a user initiated request for some service. Before the job or any of its processes can hold the resources needed to satisfy this user request, the following activities must be performed.

a. The set of resources that may be needed must be determined. This is the requirement that a claim, distinguishing exclusive use from shared use, is needed for deadlock avoidance methods. A separate claim must be determined for each site in which resources are needed.
b. A timestamp for the job must be obtained. This will require communication with all sites[2].
c. The site specific claim information, along with the timestamp of the job, must be communicated to each site that contains resources claimed by the job. This step may be combined with step b. to reduce somewhat the required communication.
d. At each site, the assumed connectivity of the global nodes must be updated by creating edges from all older global nodes to the newly entered job.

Request for Resources: When a process running at some site requests additional resources, the effect of the request on the local potential delay graph must be computed with the request attributed to the job containing the process. If the holding of the resources does not change the local graph, or if a change occurs but the graph remains acyclic, the request is granted. If a cycle would result were the requested resources to be held, then the requesting process must be delayed. We have previously discussed two ways that this delay can be handled. These are basically the following.

1. The requesting process is placed on a queue of delayed processes[3].
2. The granting subsystem for the job is formed together with an indication of the delayed process[4]. This method assures that indefinite delay is avoided and if consistently performed in this manner, will approximate a FIFO scheduling policy. The proof that this method works requires a modification of the proof in [4] but is a straightforward induction. The key observation is that any granting subsystem for a global will never contain younger globals.

Release of Resources: While a process is never delayed by releasing resources, previously delayed processes may be resumed. The two methods above require the two different actions described below whenever the releasing resources changes the potential delay graph.

1. The queue of delayed processes must be accessed and for each delayed process, a safety test must be made to determine if its delayed request can now be satisfied. If so, then the delayed process is removed from the queue and resumed.

2. If the change occurred within a granting subsystem, the granting subsystem must be recomputed. If the result is a granting subsystem containing only the delayed job, then the requesting process of this job can be resumed. Further, if the granting subsystem changes(shrinks) and the subsystem itself is contained within another granting subsystem, these steps are repeated until either a granting subsystem doesn't change or until there is no containing granting subsystem. The nesting of granting subsystems then plays the role of the delayed process queue but a number of such 'queues' may exist and a method of terminating the examination of the 'queue' exists.

Job Exit: In order for a job to complete, and hence exit from the system, processes of the job must all be informed. This involves intra-job communication which is not exposed to the resource contention system. However, it is not critical that all processes of the job terminate simultaneously, only that they all eventually terminate and leave the system. Thus, whenever a job finishes at a particular site, it can be removed from that site without further ado, and without any additional communication between sites by the resource contention system.

IX. Discussion

With distributed systems, we run into two conflicting desires when trying to optimize system performance. On the one hand, we wish to maximize the number of processes that can execute concurrently. This leads to a desire for precise information on which to make decisions in response to requests for resources. On the other hand, communication in such systems can be expensive, both in money and in time. Processes can be delayed not just due to resource requests, but also because they are waiting for a communication response related to an attempt to acquire precise information.

The approach taken here minimizes inter-site communication at the expense of lost concurrency. We do not know the circumstances under which this leads to the best performance. However, we present an informal argument which suggests that the approach taken is a reasonable one. It consists of the following points.

1. Communication of precise information so as to maximize concurrency results in the loss of some real concurrency while processes wait for the information to arrive. The magnitiude of this loss, and how it compares to accepting explicit loses in concurrency is not known.
2. The number of processes that must run concurrently in order to maximize system thruput need not be greater than that required to yield the optimal level of multiprogramming at each site. Given a system with a large number of simultaneous users, losses in concurrency produced by the global assumptions may be completely unimportant.
3. Where losses in concurrency may be more important is in attempting to provide uniform response times for similar jobs. A large number of active jobs permits the system to more effectively average the response times by timesharing among this larger set of jobs. If most jobs are short, however, even this may not be a serious problem.

One other performance consideration relates to the pros and cons of deadlock detection with recovery versus deadlock avoidance. The results of this comparison are likewise uncertain, but the same argument concerning possible lost concurrency suggests that avoidance should be competitive. Its competitive position is enhanced in distributed systems by the increased cost and complexity of recovery in such systems. Such recovery requires considerable extra communication, resulting in extensive delay of the process being recovered, and degrades general system performance by increasing the number of communication interrupts that each site must service.

X. Bibliography

1. Gray, J., Notes on data base operating systems. in *Operating Systems, an Advanced Course,* Chapter 3.F, Springer-Verlag, Berlin (1978), 394-481.
2. Lamport, L., Time, clocks, and the ordering of events in a distributed system. Comm. ACM 21,7(July, 1978), 558-565.
3. Lomet, D., A practical deadlock avoidance algorithm for data base systems. 1977 Proceedings of ACM SIGMOD Conf. on Management of Data (Aug. 1977) Toronto, Canada, 122-127.
4. Lomet, D., Subsystems of processes for the prevention of indefinite delay with deadlock avoidance. IBM Research Report RC6897 (Dec. 1977) Yorktown, N. Y. (to appear in IEEE Trans. on Software Eng.)
5. Menasce, D. and Muntz, R. Locking and deadlock detection in distributed databases. Proc. Third Berkeley Workshop on Distributed Data Management and Computer Networks (Aug. 1978) Berkeley, Calif., 215-232.
6. Rosenkrantz, D., Stearns, R., and Lewis, P., System level concurrency control for distributed database systems. ACM Trans. on Database Systems 3,2(June, 1978) 178-198.

Data Base Architecture, Bracchi/Nijssen, eds.
North-Holland Publishing Company

COMMITMENT IN A DISTRIBUTED DATABASE

George Colliat
Honeywell Information System
Phoenix,Arizona 85005 USA

Charles Bachman
Honeywell Information System
Billerica, Massachussetts, 02154, USA

abstract: This paper reviews the concept of commitment applied to an information processor, the implications when the information processing is distributed over several nodes of a network and the protocols necessary to handle such a distributed commitment. The implications over the mutual roles of the various cooperating programs is discussed along with the programmer's view of the distributed commitment.

Introduction

In order to maintain the integrity of a database, techniques are necessary to control the access of the database by many concurrent users and to recover the database to a consistent point in the event of failure. In order to synchronize the concurrency control and the recovery , points of consistency of the database are usually introduced by most existing commercial systems; these points are alternatively named FREE [4], CHECKPOINT [12] or COMMITMENT [9]. The last issue of the COBOL Journal of development [1] introduces the COMMIT verb to declare such a consistency point and defines its relationship to concurrency control and recovery (ROLLBACK verb).

All these techniques are well known when the database is localized on a single computer system. However these techniques must be extended when the database is distributed over several nodes of a computer network. In particular protocols must be defined to control concurrency declare commitments and recover from failures. This paper reviews the definition of commitment and some of its implications in case of a single process accessing the local database. Then the problem of commitment in accessing a distributed database is analyzed. The concept of a commitment hierarchy is introduced in order to permit the commitment of the work of any number of cooperating processes. The message exchange protocols necessary to support the commitment functions are then introduced . Finally the impact on the programmer's interface is considered.

The word "process" will be used to indicate a well defined sequence of elementary actions . Consequently a process will represent a conventional computer process as well as the association of a human operator and a terminal device. The communication between cooperating processes is performed through the exchange of messages. It is assumed in this paper that a reliable message delivery system is available; this means that the sequence of delivery of the messages exchanged between two processes is quaranteed and that in the event of a connection failure the sender is always notified before any subsequent message is successfully transmitted. In other words a message cannot be lost without the sender being notified of the failure.

I. SINGLE PROCESS COMMITMENT

Definition:

> A commitment is a guarantee by the computer system that all actions performed between two commitment points are final. They can be altered only by an explicit request from outside the computer system.

The committed actions of the computer system are meaningful only in the sense that they are visible outside the computer system. They are essentially of two kinds:

- database updates, which can be made visible outside the computer system through various query and report facilities.
- messages, which report outside the computer system the actions of the computer in the form of CRT display, printer listings, punched cards, etc.

Central to the need for a commitment concept is the fact that with the increasing sophistication of the computer system, it becomes very difficult to know whether a message from the computer system reports an action which has taken place, will take place or, although it has taken place, may be backed out. Many batch systems display the report listing only when the batch job is terminated, thus giving the reader an accurate account of what actually happened. With on-line transaction processing systems, however, the response time and the recovery requirements are such that a message display on a CRT is not always indicative of what happened; if the system were to crash immediately after the display, it is sometimes doubtful that the reported actions actually took place as described or were not wiped out by some recovery action.

Impact Of Recovery On Commitment

Most commercial systems provide recovery capabilities -termed "roll back" in this paper- such that in case of failure, the process actions can be backed out to a known point. This roll back usually takes place automatically upon occurrence of any serious hardware or software failure without any human intervention. The following corollary results from the definition of a commitment:

Corollary 1. A process cannot be rolled back to a point prior to a commitment point.

Impact Of Concurrency Control

In the absence of a practical technique to prevent deadlocks when a database is concurrently accessed by many transactions and locking is used to avoid interference, most systems utilize a deadlock detection technique. They allow deadlocks to occur and then detect them and break them by rolling back one of the transactions involved in the deadlock loop. Since roll backs cannot extend prior to a commitment point, all deadlocks must be breakable by rolling back a process to its most recent commitment point. This implies that all database records must be released from concurrency protection at commitment point; otherwise a situation like the one in Figure 1 could develop.

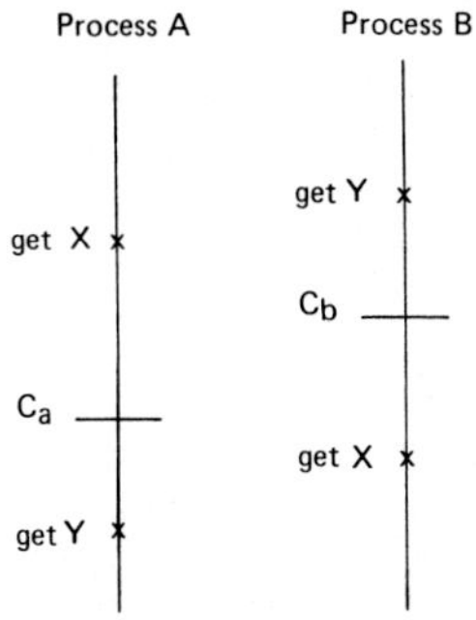

Figure 1

Each vertical line represents a portion of the life of a process with time flowing top-down.

Process A can only release X by rolling back prior to commitment point Ca.

Process B can only release Y by rolling back prior to commitment point Cb. Both are impossible, the deadlock cannot be broken.

Theorem 1. All database objects subject to concurrency control and liable to cause deadlocks must be released at commitment time.

Impact On Database Currencies

Most database systems maintain a set of implicit or explicit pointers which locate the user program within the database. CODASYL type of DBMS refer to these pointers as currencies: current of realm, current of set, current of record-name, current of program. Many verbs rely on the value of these currencies which have been established by previously executed verbs. If the records corresponding to these currencies are released from concurrency control, other processes may modify these records or even delete them; it is consequently essential to nullify all currencies corresponding to these released records at commitment time.

Theorem 2. All database currencies must be nullified at commitment time.

Impact On Database Usage

Because concurrency locks are released at commitment time, the database user must be aware of commitment points and must program accordingly. In particular all the interrelated read and updates of a database must be executed in the same commitment unit. For instance, if the following relation must hold between records A, B and C:

$$A + B = C$$

and if an update is made to A, then C must also be updated in the same commitment unit in order for the relation to hold true. This type of constraint is typically true for an accounting entry, where both debit and credit entries must be made in the same commitment unit. Another way to look at this is to say that commitment units are "independent" and could be executed in any sequence. In other words, the "invariant" of the database must be maintained at the end of a commitment unit in the same way as the invariant of a monitor must be kept [8,10].

Theorem 3. The invariant of the database must be maintained at the end of a commitment unit.

II. COMMITMENT IN A NETWORK OF DISTRIBUTED DATABASES

The constraint that interdependent database operations must be executed in the same commitment unit is particularly challenging when the database is distributed over several nodes of a computer network. We will first analyze the case of two and then three nodes in order to see some of the synchronization problems and the possible solutions. Then we will define a general commitment protocol to handle any number of nodes.

1. Commitment With 2 Nodes

Lets assume that the two processes P1 and P2 (Figure 2.a) must update their local database in a coordinated manner, that is either both updates are executed or neither is done. They notify each other of what updates are to be done by exchanging one or several messages. Then each one of them executes the following operations:

- Perform the database update.

- Notify the partner that the update was done properly.

- Wait for notification from the partner that the partner's update was done properly.

- Commit the local updates.

If there is no failure, the above scheme works very well since each process makes sure that both its functions and the partner's functions are properly executed before the commitment is declared. However, if P1 fails just after notifying P2 (Figure 2.b), then it performs a roll back to the beginning of the commitment unit thus undoing its function. P2 which was notified of P1 success commits its updates. By the time P2 is notified of P1 failure, it is too late for P2 to roll back and the rules for commitment have been violated:

P1 did not perform its function.
P2 committed its function.

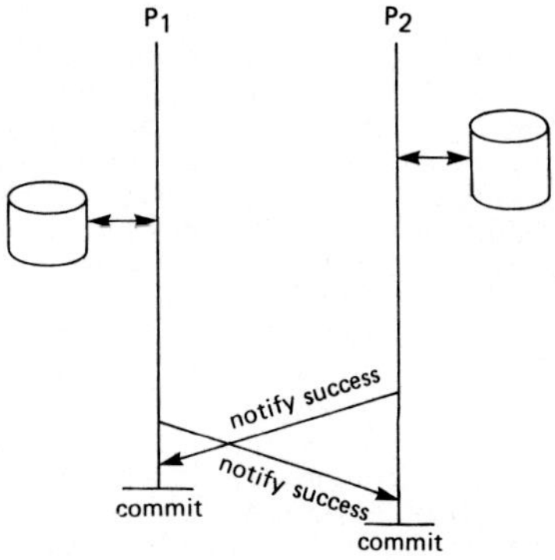

Figure 2.a

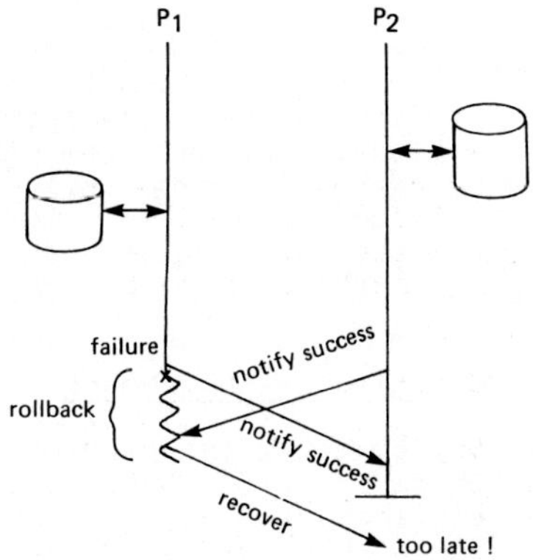

Figure 2.b

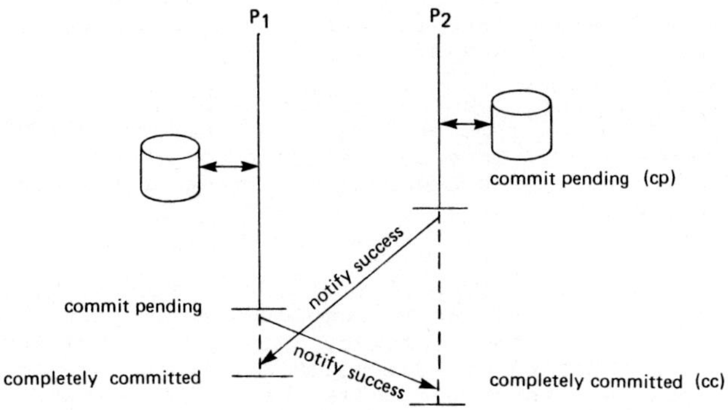

Figure 2.c

This is a typical race condition which is easily prevented. (Figure 2.c) P1 should not roll back after notifying P2 because its job is finished; it should roll back only if P2 fails in which case all updates must be undone. This can be done by recording a "commit-pending" mark on a local journal. In case of failure, this mark will remind the process not to roll back although the job has not been committed. Only a failure from P2 could cause such a roll back after the recording of the "commit-pending" mark.

In order to satisfy Corollary 1., the complete commitment of the local work is accompanied by the recording of a "completely-committed" mark on the local journal, so that in case of subsequent failure, the system knows not to roll back.

Rule 1. After the local part of the commitment is properly done, record a "commit-pending" mark and notify the partner of the success. After receiving successful commitment notification from the partner, commit the local work and record a "completely-committed" mark. After recording the "commit-pending" mark, roll back only if so requested by the partner. After recording the "completely-committed" mark never roll back.

2. Commitment With 3 Nodes

Let's try to apply the previous rule when the database is distributed over three nodes. Lets assume moreover that Process P1, requests some help from Process P2 which in turn requests help from Process P3. In other words, P1 and P3 do not know the existence of each other.

If we apply Rule 1, the situation of Figure 3.a should develop. After successfully executing its local functions, each process records a "commit-pending" mark, notifies his partners, waits for a successful notification from them, commits the local commitment unit and records a "completely-committed" mark.

However, if P1 fails the situation of Figure 3.b may develop. P2 is notified of failure too late It cannot roll back according to Rule 1 because it has already successfully notified P3.

One way this problem can be avoided is by having P2 wait for the successful notification from both P1 and P3 before notifying each one of them. (Figure 3.c). This determines a precedence order: P2 must be notified first of P1's success before it can notify P1 of its own successful completion.

After having completed its part of the work successfully and having been notified that both P1 and P3 completed their part successfully, P2 commits its work and notifies P1 and P3 of the successful commitment. If either P1 or P3 reports a failure or if P2 itself detects a failure, then P2 rolls back its work and broadcasts a recovery message to P1 and P3. In this sense P1 and P3 can be viewed as subordinate to P2 which has the ultimate authority to decide their mutual commitment. This is noted:

$$P2 > P1$$
$$P2 > P3$$

We say that P2 is superior to P1 and P3.

Since P2 has received successful notification from P1 and P3, when P2 notifies them it can be seen that the "commit-pending" mark and "completely-committed" mark collapse into a single mark. This is due to the fact that P2 does not have a superior.

In this example, each process has zero or one superior and zero or two subordinates. It can easily be shown that the commitment protocol can be enforced properly for processes having any number of subordinates.

Figure 3.d illustrates the case where P1 is subordinate to P2 and P2 is subordinate to P3. In this case failure by either P1 or P2 after it has entered the commitment pending state will have no effect and the commitment process may continue. Failure by P3 at any time up until it commits will cause P1 and P2 to be recovered. After that time it will have no effect.

However, the question remains, can a process have more than one superior? It can easily be seen in Figure 3.e that this is not possible in general. If P2 is subordinate to both P1 and P3 then a failure of P1 might be reported to P2 after P3 has already been notified thus preventing P2 roll back according to Rule 1. and violating the commitment requirements. This shows that in general a process cannot have more than one superior. However if a process had two superiors which were themselves subordinate directly or indirectly of the same process, then it can be easily shown that the commitment process would work correctly. Unfortunately there is to the authors' knowledge no general algorithm to validate in the presence of two or more superior processes that they are dependent directly or indirectly on the same process without undue overhead. Until such an algorithm is determined, the rule will be used that a process may have only one superior, ignoring the more relaxed rule.

From this second example, we can draw a second rule of behavior which is a refinement of Rule 1 in order to be applicable to any number of processes which cooperate in a commitment unit of work. Figure 3.f illustrates a process behavior according to Rule 2.

<u>Rule 2</u>. Any two correspondent processes which are connected by a message flow to produce a unit of committed work must be tied by a hierarchical relationship: one process is the subordinate, the other one the superior. A process may have any number of subordinates but at most one superior.

When a process has successfully completed its part of the work and after it has received a successful commitment request from all its subordinates it records a "commit-pending" mark, and requests commitment from its superior if there is one.

After recording the "commit-pending" mark, the process rolls back only if so requested by the superior process.

After receiving a commitment acknowledgement from its superior if there is one, the process completes the commitment of its local work, records a "completely-committed" mark and broadcasts a commitment acknowledgement to all its subordinates.

After recording the "completely-committed" mark, the process may never roll back.

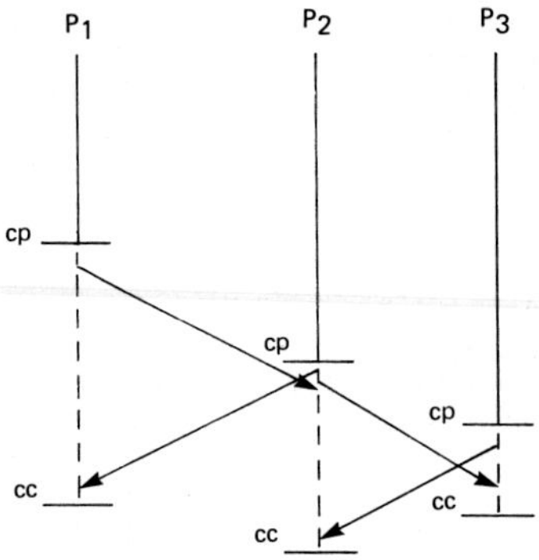

Figure 3.a

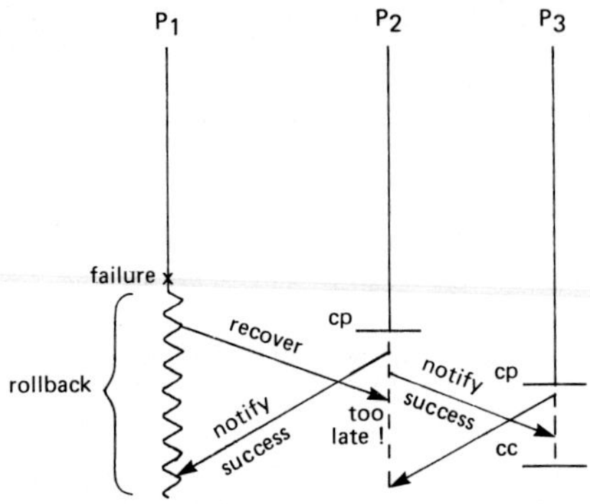

Figure 3.b

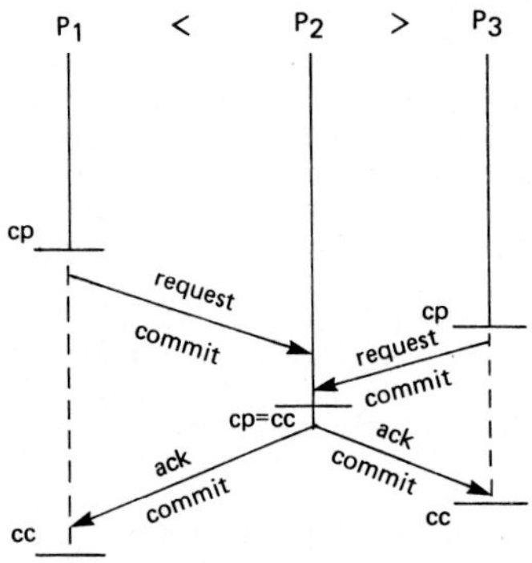

Figure 3.c

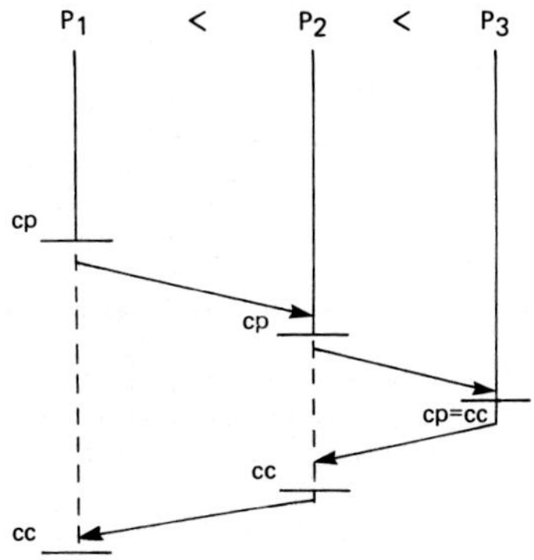

Figure 3.d

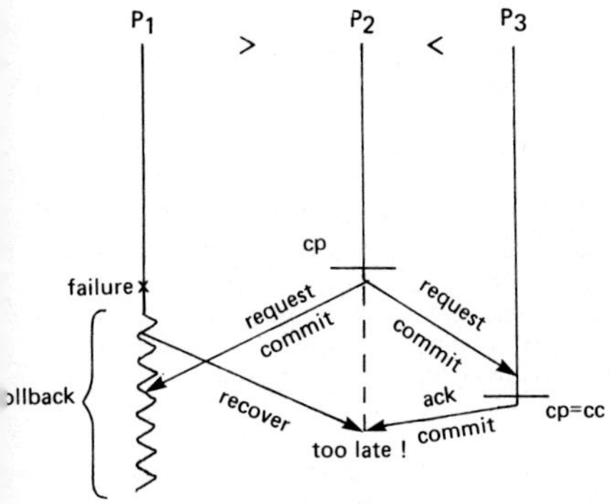

Figure 3.e

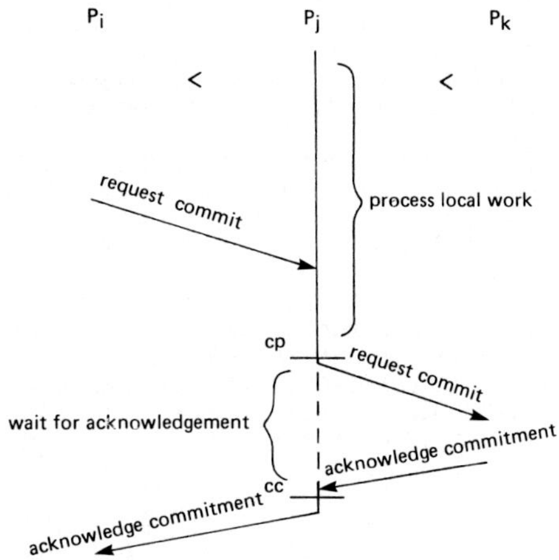

Figure 3.f

3. General Commitment Hierarchy

We have shown in the previous examples that the processes which cooperate in a commitment must follow a certain ordering relation in their commitment protocol such that each process has at most one superior and any number of subordinates. As long as there is always one node which does not have a superior, this ordering is characteristic of a tree (Figure 4.a).

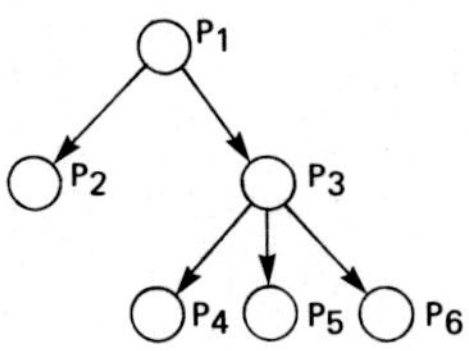

Figure 4.a

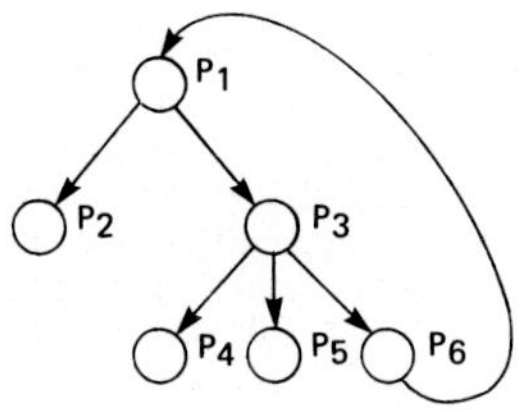

Figure 4.b

Each branch of the tree is represented as an arrow. The arrow P1 --► P2 means that there is a message path between P1 and P2 and that P1 is superior to P2 in the commitment hierarchy. The commitment protocol can be seen as a flow of commitment requests originating from the leaves of the tree. Every node, except the top of the tree (the master of the commitment), has a unique superior path which leads toward the master; when it has finished its local functions and after it has received a commitment request from all its subordinates, it records a local "commit-pending" mark and then requests commitment from its superior. After it has received a commitment acknowledgement from its superior, it records its local "completely-committed" mark and then broadcasts the commitment acknowledgement to all its subordinates.

Thus the commitment requests flow up the tree from the leaves to the master and then the commitment acknowledgements flow down the tree from the master to the leaves. If any node in the tree fails before issuing a commitment request to the superior, it broadcasts a roll back message to all its correspondents and recovers its processing .

It can be seen that once the master is committed, then every node in the hierarchy is committed, since no roll back message may be issued any longer. It is only a matter of time for the commitment acknowledgement to flow down the tree to the leaves.

Note that it was assumed that one node did not have a superior, this was called the master of the commitment. If we lift this restriction a loop might be created like in Figure 4.b. It can easily be seen that the flow of commitment request could never get started since there is no leaf in the loop and consequently each member of the loop could wait forever to get a commitment request from its subordinate.

Rule 3.

> Rule 2. must be restricted such that there may be no circularity of the processes connected by their subordinate/superior relationship.

4. Impact On Message Exchange Protocols

The following message exchange protocols are necessary in order to support the commitment of a distributed unit of work:

- Establish the commitment hierarchy.
- Commit a unit of work.
- Recover a unit of work.

The message paths which connect the cooperating processes which process a transaction may be preestablished through some administrative utility. However, in the most general case these paths will be established as the need arises. It then becomes necessary to check dynamically that the tree is properly structured. Whenever a connection is negotiated between two processes, each process must make sure that the following conditions hold:

- Each process must have at most one superior.
- There must be no "commitment loop".

It is an easy matter to check the first condition. Whenever a process initiates a message path connection it declares its intention to take the role of superior or subordinate on the message path. It cannot take the subordinate role if it would have more than one superior. The process which is to accept the message path connection checks the new commitment role it must assume against those it is already assuming. If this would result in its being connected to two superiors, then it rejects the connection, otherwise it accepts it.

The second condition is unfortunately much more difficult to check. There is not, in the authors' knowledge, any general algorithm to accomplish this verification without undue overhead. Until such an algorithm is discovered, the following mechanism can be used. It detects any loop but also rejects some valid commitment trees depending on the order in which the connections are established.

When Process Pi seeks to establish a message path with process Pj, it indicates whether it would be an "end-point" in the commitment hierarchy; i.e., it would be either a leaf or the top of the tree, after the message path is established. If Pi would be an end-point, there is no loop possible and the message path is established. If Pi would not be an end-point and Pj would be an end-point after the message path is established, then the connection is accepted since again no loop is possible. However, if Pi would not be an end-point and Pj would not be an end-point after the message path is established, then the connection is rejected although no loop necessarily exists.

The protocol to commit a unit of work is described by Rule 3. The "commitment request" and "commitment acknowledgement" messages can be transmitted in the normal data flow as special protocol messages. It must be noted that on many systems the message exchange protocol between two processes is "two-way alternate" meaning that the processes take turns sending messages. When a process is finished sending messages for one interaction, it passes the "turn" to the other process which may then send messages as soon as it has received the turn. The implications on the commitment protocol for a "two way alternate" message exchange system are the following:

- The subordinate must have the turn before sending a "commitment request" message and must pass the turn along with the request to the correspondent.

- The superior and the subordinate both reestablish the "initial turn" with the "commitment acknowledgement". The initial turn for the message path may be with either the superior or subordinate process.

The first implication follows from the definition of two way alternate. The second implication is based on the independence of commitment units. At the beginning of the commitment unit the state of the database is always defined by its invariant, independently of the previous commitment unit. Likewise for messages, the turn should be independent of the prior commitment unit, thus making commitment units truly independent of one another.

The protocol to recover a unit of work is implied by Rule 2. Three states of the commitment unit as seen by the process must be considered:

- The "active" state, from the time the first database access is performed or the first message is sent or received until the "commit-pending" mark is recorded.

- The "commit-pending" state, from the recording of the "commit-pending" mark until the recording of the "completely-committed" mark.

- The "completely-committed" state, after the recording of the "completely-committed" mark.

There are three major cases for recovery depending on the state of the commitment unit which exists when the failure is detected.

a) When the commitment unit is in the "active" state:

The process may broadcast at any time a "recovery request" message stating that it wants to recover to the time of the beginning of the commitment unit, to all the correspondents with which it is cooperating. It then rolls back its own work to the beginning of its commitment unit, waits for a recovery acknowledgement from each correspondent then restarts processing. If the node fails the same actions are taken.

If a process receives a "recovery request" message, stating go back to the beginning of the commitment unit, it will acknowledge the request, broadcast "recovery request" messages to all its other correspondent processes, rollback its own work to the beginning of its commitment unit, wait for recovery acknowledgements, then restart processing.

b) When the commitment unit is in the "commit-pending" state:

The process is blocked pending termination of the commitment pending state so that it cannot request recovery on its own behalf. However if it receives a recovery request from its superior stating to go back to the beginning of the commitment unit, then it will acknowledge the recovery request, broadcast "recovery request" messages ,stating that it wants to recover to the time of the beginning of the commitment unit , to all its subordinate processes, rollback its own work to the beginning of its commitment unit, wait for the "recovery acknowledgement" message, then restart processing.

If the node fails, the process will broadcast recovery messages to each of its correspondents, stating that it wants to recover to the time when it entered the commitment pending state.

If a process receives a recovery request stating that the correspondent wants to go back to the time when it entered the commitment pending state, then it will acknowledge the requests but take no other action.

If a subordinate process receives a recovery request message stating go back to the time when the superior entered the "completely committed" state, it will notify the superior requestor that it is still in the commit pending state.

c) when the commitment unit is in the "completely-committed" state:

If the node fails the process will send out recovery requests stating that it wants to rollback to the time when it entered the "completely committed" state.

If the process receives a recovery request message from its correspondent stating that the correspondent wants to recover to the time it entered the "completely committed" state, the request is acknowledged and no other action is taken.

If the process receives a recovery request message from a subordinate process stating that it wants to recover to the time it entered the "commitment pending" state, then the request is acknowledged, a commitment acknowledgement message is subsequently sent.

These algorithms can be easily implemented by associating a "phase number" with each process. This phase number is incremented whenever the process sees a state change of the commitment unit. The recovery request may then carry the phase number and depending on its value:

-request a recovery of the commitment unit, or
-request the repositioning of the message path, or
-acknowledge the receipt of a "commitment request".

Figure 5 gives some examples using this technique. Note that in Figure 5.d, because P2 is at the top of the commitment hierarchy, the "commit-pending and "completely-committed" marks are collapsed into one and consequently the phase number is incremented by two; upon reception of the recovery request P2 can only reposition its message path to the beginning of n+2 and thus resend the commitment acknowledgement.

5.0 IMPACT ON PROGRAMMER INTERFACE

CODASYL has recently defined [1] a COMMIT verb and ROLLBACK verb. As they stand these verbs address only the local database management area. If the concept of "two-way " message paths is introduced, which in the authors' opinion is an absolute requirement for distributed database management, then care must be taken that the program has the turn on all message paths before the COMMIT verb can be accepted. In other words, the programmer must realize that the effects of COMMIT are not local, they are broadcast to all cooperating programs.

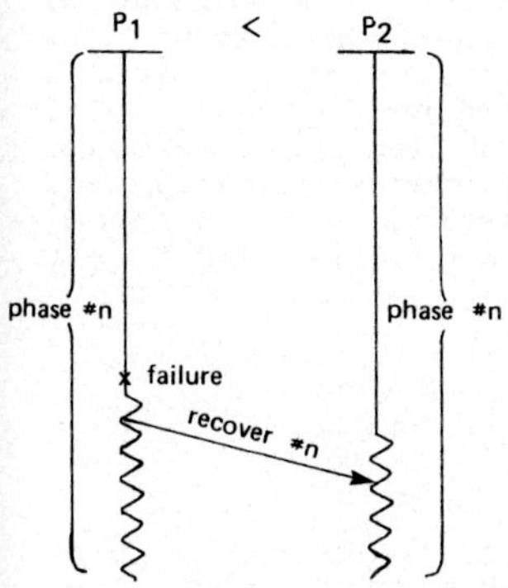

P_1 and P_2 rollback to beginning of commitment unit

Figure 5.a

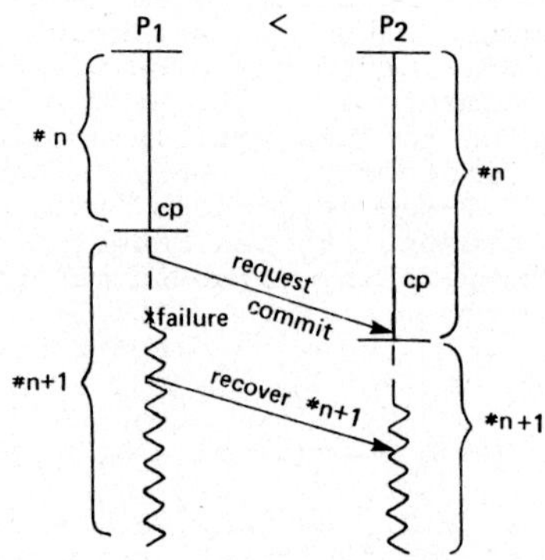

P_1 rollback to beginning of phase n+1

P_2 rollback to beginning of phase n+1

Figure 5.b

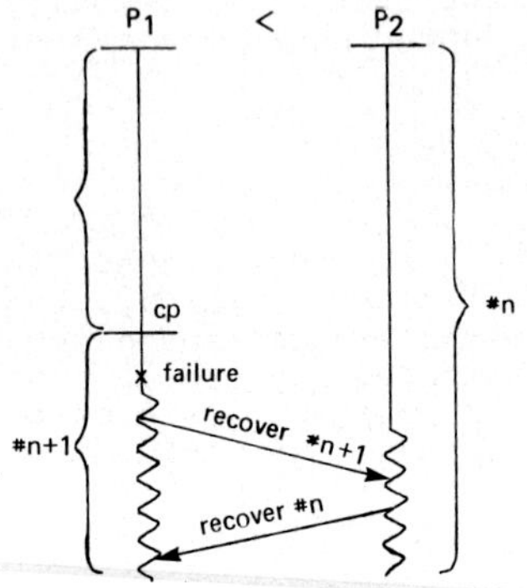

P_1 and P_2 rollback to beginning of commitment unit

Figure 5.c

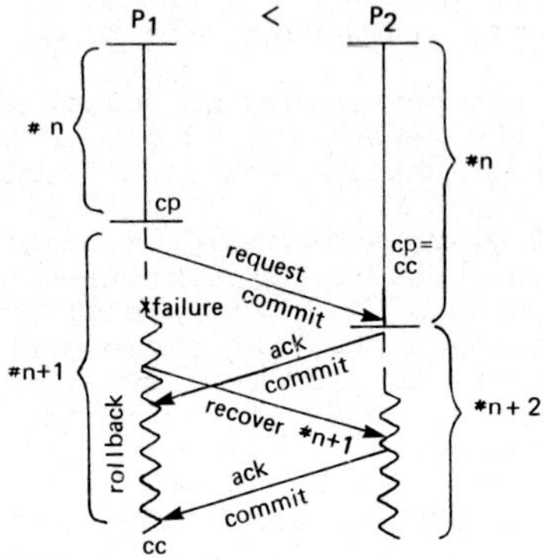

P_2 acknowledges commitment again

Figure 5.d

CONCLUSION

The concept of commitment which is fairly well known in local database management, can be extended to distributed database management, as long as the proper protocols are respected. It was shown that if the distributed database extends over 3 or more nodes of the network then a structure of commitment hierarchy is necessary. Some protocols were presented to establish the commitment hierarchy, commit a unit of work and recover a unit of work. The space allocated to this article does not permit a detailed exposure of these protocols. Only their general functionnality was introduced. These protocols used in conjunction with deadlock detection protocols [6] can make the distribution of databases over a network of cooperating database managers a reality.

References

1 CODASYL COBOL Journal of development 1978,

2 Courtois, P.J., Heymans, F., and Parnas, D.L. Concurrent control with "readers" and "writers". Comm. ACM 14, 10 (Oct 1971), 667 -668.

3 Everest, G.C., Concurrent Update Control and database integrity. Data base management north-holland/american elsevier, 241-268.

4 Fossum, B.M., Data base integrity as provided for by a particular data base management system. Data base management north-holland/american elsevier, 271-288

5 Fisher R.S and Maryarski F.J., Rollback and Recovery in distributed database management systems. Proceedings of the ACM 77 annual conference, 33-38

6 Goldman, B, deadlock detection in computer network. MIT thesis June 1977.

7 Gray, j.N., Notes on Database Operating Systems, Operating Systems: an advanced course, Springer-Verlag Berlin Heidelberg 1978 , 465-471

8 Hoare. C.A.R. Monitors: an operating system structuring concept. Comm. ACM 17, 10 (Oct. 1974), 549-557.

8 Honeywell Data Management IV, Transation processor reference manual DF 44.

10 Howard, J.H. Proving monitors. Comm. ACM 110, 5 (May 11076), 273-2710

11 Lampson B. and H.Sturgis, Crash Recovery in Distributed Data Storage Systems, Xerox Palo Alto Research Center Technical Report ,1976

12 IBM, Information Management System reference manual.

13 Stonebraker,M., Concurrency Control and Consistency of multiple copies of data in distributed INGRES. Electronics Research Laboratory, College of Engineering, Berkeley 1978.

RECOVERY

Data Base Architecture, Bracchi/Nijssen, eds.
North-Holland Publishing Company

RECOVERY BASED ON TYPES

Joost S. M. VERHOFSTAD

Digital Equipment Corporation
1925 Andover Street
Tewksbury, MA Ø1876
U S A

Abstract

Data base systems can often be regarded as systems consisting of several levels. Each level may have certain recovery mechanisms incorporated. This paper discusses a model that can be used to link recovery with types and to discuss such recoverable multi-level systems. An example system is discussed to illustrate the principles. The relation of the mechanisms described to high level languages and other areas is also briefly discussed.

Key words and phrases: data base, file, multi-level system, recovery.

1. Introduction

Data base management systems can often be regarded as consisting of several levels, which could, for example, be: a hardware level (possibly with an intelligent controller), a driver level, a file system level, a record management level and a DBMS level. The levels may provide various recovery techniques, possibly for different purposes. With the advent of distributed systems such layered approaches with associated recovery techniques have become of more interest, since lower levels are often represented differently on different components in the network.

The multi-level systems discussed in this paper consist of a hierarchy of levels in which all, except for the "bottom" level, are procedural levels. The "bottom" level is an interpreter level, which is either the hardware or micro-code. A procedural level consists of a set of procedures that can be invoked by higher levels. A procedural level provides one or more new data types to higher levels, while an interpreter level completely redefines an interface with the system. More formal definitions of procedural and interpreter levels have been given elsewhere [1]; however, the informal definitions given above are sufficient for the purposes of this paper.

A way in which levels can be built as so-called recoverable type managers, which provide recovery for the new data types they implement, has has been described elsewhere [16] [18]. The basic principles for building recoverable multi-level systems are described in this paper. An example of a multi-level data base system is then considered to show how different recovery techniques used in different levels interact. The term data type, or type for short, is used to mean a definition of a named class of operands. The distinction between data structures and data types depends upon the current level of abstraction [7]. The representation of a data type includes: (1) a storage structure, (2) a set of operations for creating, destroying, modifying, and examining the structure, and (3) an interpretation of the storage structure (i.e. a mapping from its values to values of the abstract type). It is the function of a level in a multi-level system as discussed in this paper, to represent one or more new data types. A level is responsible for the data integrity of the types it represents and may therefore provide or use various recovery techniques.

Levels of abstraction are used as in important tool or concept for construction (e.g. [12]) or discussing (e.g. [8]) data base systems. Levels represent new types. The recovery techniques employed in different levels are used to restore objects of different types. Recovery is based on types in this paper because it is argued here that the data recovery operations should be part of the type representation and therefore of levels in a multi-level system.

The example of a recoverable multi-level data base system is discussed in Section 2. Section 3 briefly explains the major mechanisms for building recoverable multi-level systems. Section 4 then uses the model described in Section 3 to explain how the various recovery techniques in the example system of Section 2 are used, what their functions are, and how they interact. Section 5 discusses how the model could be used to embed the recovery mechanisms in high level languages. Finally, Section 6 discusses the relation of this work with other areas and draws some conclusions.

2. An Example of Recovery Techniques used in Different Levels of a Data Base Management System

An example of a multi-level system in which different levels incorporate different recovery techniques is described in this section and illustrated in Fig. 1.

Level 5	user processes
Level 4	DBMS
Level 3	record management
Level 2	file system
Level 1	I/O modules
Level Ø	hardware

Fig. 1. A Multi-Level Data Base Management System

Level Ø, the hardware level, incorporates techniques to deal with particular failures in the hardware. One example of this is the use of secondary memory devices that have spare sectors which are automatically used to replace damaged sectors in memory. This is done at the drive and/or controller level and is completely masked from the software.

Level 1 contains the I/O modules (drivers) in the system; it provides block I/O to secondary memory devices. This level deals with certain errors by doing a read after write and retry after failure. These recovery techniques are masked from higher levels.

Level 2 consists of the file system; it maintains files which are containers for user data. The file system maintains duplicates of files, called shadows, on different devices. The user only specifies that he wants shadows to be maintained, when he creates the file. After the file has been created the user "sees" only one file on which he operates; the file system updates all copies of a file when an operation on the file is done. All of the copies of the file always have the same value, before and after an operation on the file is performed. This shadow mechanisms makes files highly available: if one copy is destroyed or disconnected, the system continues to use the remaining copies. This technique is especially useful in distributed systems and therefore used in many such systems [11].

The record management system, which provides different access methods to files, is contained in level 3. This level regularly produces a complete backup copy of all of the files that have been updated since the last time backups were taken. It also maintains a journal with entries containing before and after images of records (i.e. old and new values) for each record that is updated. Each time a record is updated an entry is written to the journal. These recovery data are used for the following purposes:

a. Rebuilding of secondary storage devices.

   If all of the information on, say, a disk is lost, then the information is reconstructed, possibly on another physical disk, using both the backup copies of the files that were on the original disk and the journal. The backup copies of the files lost are restored on the disk and the after images of records are used to roll the files forward to the most recent consistent state. The after images are the new values of records updated since the creation of the backup copies.

b. Backing out of one or more processes.

   A process may have to be backed out for many reasons, some of which are: deadlock resolution, a system crash and process abort. Backing out is done by using before images of records on the journal to roll backward. This will undo the updates performed by the process being backed out.

Level 4 is the data base management level, which implements user data bases. This level uses the differential file technique [13] [17] to keep the new values of the records that a process updates in a separate list. All these updates are applied to the data base when the process finishes. The TRAX system [5] uses this technique, which is called "staging of files" in TRAX, to be able to do very efficient transaction recovery when necessary: recovery simply involves discarding the differential file for that transaction. Before the data base is updated, the list of updated records is written out to secondary storage. If a crash occurs during the processing of this list, this processing can simply be restarted.

Level 5 is the user level. The user specifies scopes of recovery which are the units of processing that must appear as atomic actions: if an error occurs in such a unit of processing, then the whole unit is backed out (its effects are undone). A scope of recovery is equivalent to a sphere of control as defined by Davies [4]. A scope of recovery could, for example, be implemented as a transaction [6], a recovery block [9], a terminal session or a batch program. The way in which such a scope is syntactically specified is not important for the discussion of recovery techniques in multi-level data base systems in this paper.

Many of the techniques such as staging, journaling or shadowing may be optional. It is not clear whether each user or a database administrator should choose the options required. It is also not clear how to decide which options to use, since the interactions between the techniques are not obvious. The following sections discuss a model and the example of this section with this model, to demonstrate those interactions.

3. The Principles of Recoverable Multi-level Systems

A model for recoverable multi-level systems has been described and discussed elswehere and a prototype system based on that model has been implemented [16] [18]. This section will briefly explain the model without explaining in detail why and how the mechanisms work the way they work. The model is simply used to discuss multi-level systems like the one described in the previous section, and makes it possible to understand the functions of the various recovery techniques used in different levels. An alternative model exists [14] and has been compared with the model presented here [1].

First it is necesssary to define the notion of "recoverable". A <u>recoverable object</u> is an object for which recovery is done automatically by the underlying machine (i.e. the complete set of levels below the given level) when an error occurs inside a scope of recovery in the level using the object. The recovery performed must be backward recovery, because the error recovery mechanisms are below the level in which the error occurs. Backward error recovery involves roll back and state restoration. Forward recovery, which involves the use of redundancy to make the system robust in the face of failures (e.g. TMR), can only be used to deal with an error if it is done within the level in which the error occurs. In fact this is what distinguishes forward and backward error recovery. Both kinds of recovery have been fully discussed elswhere [10] and their formal definitions are not of importance for the purpose of this paper. A recoverable type is a type the objects of which are recoverable, while objects of an unrecoverable type are not recoverable.

The model for recoverable multi-level systems is described below:

1. A level L, which provides a new type T, can provide implicit recovery for this type (i.e. make this type implicitly a recoverable type), by mapping it exclusively on other recoverable types provided by lower levels.

   Fig. 2 illustrates how this works in our model: level L maps objects of type T on objects of types $t_1, \ldots, t_n$. When an error occurs in the user level, the error recovery mechanism in the underlying machine of level L will be invoked to restore objects of types $t_1, \ldots, t_n$. This implicitly restores objects of type T.

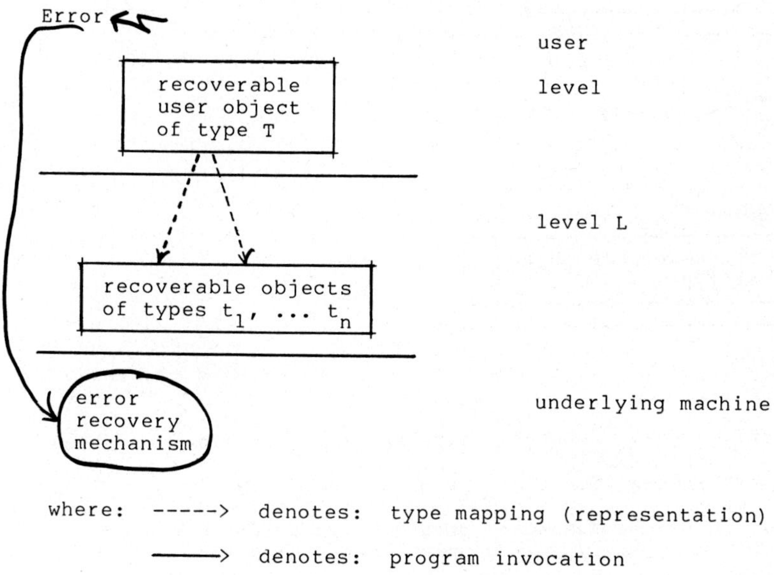

Fig. 2

2. A level L can provide explicit recovery for a new type T by mapping it on unrecoverable types provided by lower levels and also implementing a recovery mechanism for the new type. This recovery mechanism is invoked when an error occurs in a higher level so that this level's recovery mechanism will restore objects of the newly provided type, used by higher levels.

Fig. 3 illustrates this: level L maps objects of type T on objects of types t_1, ..., tn. When an error occurs in the user level then the error recovery mechanism in level L is invoked to restore objects of type T, used in higher levels.

Restoration of objects of type t is done in level L by operating on objects of types t_1, ..., t_n, which are used to represent it. Level L <u>provides</u> type T, it cannot <u>use</u> T.

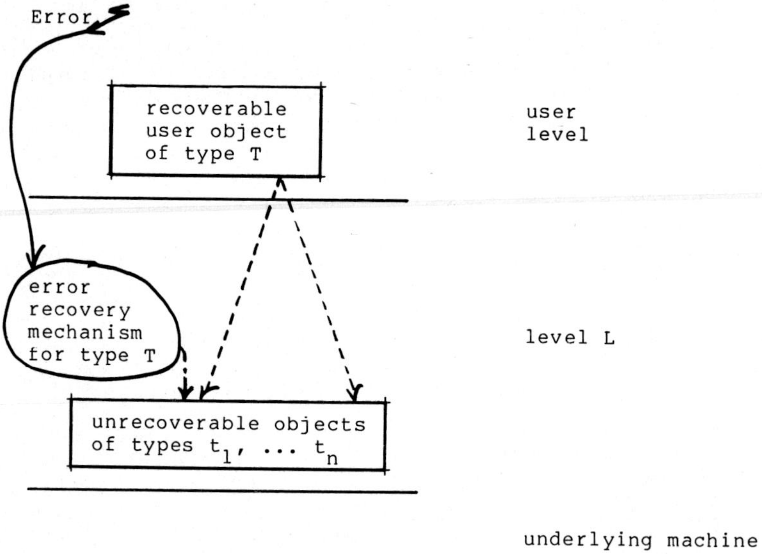

where: -----> denotes: type mapping (representation)

——> denotes: program invocation

— · —> denotes: program (mechanism) operates upon data pointed to

Fig. 3

3. The recovery mechanism, for example in a level L (See Fig. 3), works as follows:

   a. Levels above level L invoke operations in level L to operate on objects of type T. These operations may be invoked from within a scope of recovery. In that case the objects of type T operated upon, may have to be restored. When required, these objects are restored to the states they were in at the beginning of the recovery scope. This is done to restore the state as seen by the user. Level L will store sufficient information to be able to restore the objects of type T. This information is called recovery data and is stored in a so-called recovery cache (from now on simply called cache).

b. When an error occurs in a higher level, inside a scope of recovery, then the recovery mechanism in level L is invoked to process the cache, that is it restores the values of objects of type T using the information stored in the cache.

This recovery mechanism is illustrated in Fig. 4. The cache processing operation, invoked on error, restores those objects of type T. It uses the information put in the cache by the implementation of the operations on objects of type T.

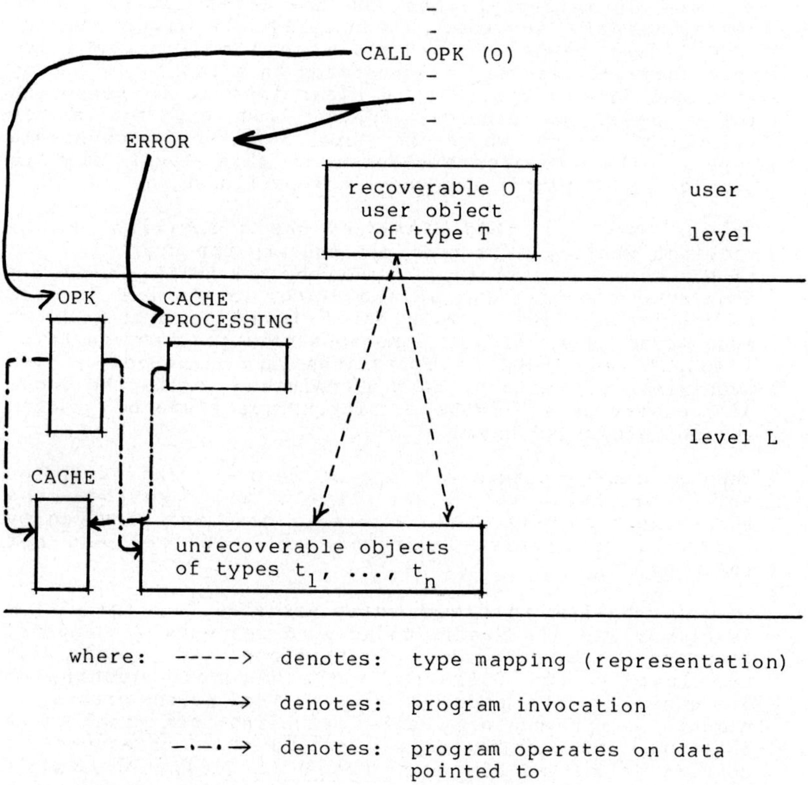

Fig. 4

4. A level providing explicit recovery for a new type provides also the following three operations that are part of the recovery mechanism:

   a. ENTER; this operation is invoked by any higher level when it enters a new scope of recovery.

   b. ACCEPT; this operation is invoked by any higher level when it exits a scope of recovery successfully.

   c. UNDO; this operation is invoked by any higher level when an error occurs in it: the UNDO operation is the cache processing operation shown in Fig. 4.

   These three operations respectively prepare to collect recovery data, clean up the cache and thereby commit the scope of recovery and process the cache.

   This also implies that when a program in a level i enters a scope of recovery, then all the lower levels' ENTER operations are invoked,. Similarly all lower levels' ACCEPTs and UNDOs are invoked when that program exits that scope of recovery or generates an error in it. From this and from 2 above it is clear that it is senseless for a level to provide explicit recovery for a new recoverable type which it maps on other recoverable types: the recovery mechanism in this level used to provide the explicit recovery is superfluous.

   It has been described elsewhere how a facility can be provided whereby a program can specify the start and end of his scope of recovery and whereby all ENTER - ACCEPT - and UNDO - operations of the lower levels are invoked automatically [16]. This paper is not concerned with such mechanisms; what is important here is that the ENTER - ACCEPT and UNDO - operations are invoked. Also mechanisms to restart the program piece inside the scope of recovery or to invoke an alternative piece of program are not discussed here.

5. When a program enters a scope of recovery and generates an error then all lower levels will restore the recoverable objects used by that program and provided by those lower levels. Unrecoverable objects are not restored.

   In order to deal with such unrecoverables, a program or a level may use its own redundancy an recovery mechanisms. These built-in mechanisms are therefore used to deal with the level's own failures. The recovery mechanisms discussed in (1) and (4) are to deal with errors in higher levels and are called <u>cacheing mechanisms</u>. An internal recovery mechanism dealing with unrecoverable objects is called a <u>logging mechanism</u> [16]. An example to illustrate the difference between logging and cacheing is the following:

A data base system level can provide transaction recovery for the higher level (the user of the data base) by using a journaling mechanism. This journaling is to provide recovery for higher levels and is therefore cacheing as described above. In order to deal with internal failures for which no underlying recovery mechanisms are provided the data base system may, for example, use two journal tapes to be able to deal with a failure of a tape unit. Such a recovery mechanism is logging as described above since it is not to provide recovery for higher levels, but to provide internal error recovery: higher levels are not even aware of the presence of a logging mechanism.

Cacheing makes backing out of higher level programs possible, whereas logging simply provides more reliability in the underlying machine to higher levels. For example, if a level L provides a new unrecoverable type file and uses an (internal) logging mechanism to deal with failures in the file system level L, then the file system will be more reliable. If the level provides recoverable files explicitly, then the cacheing mechanisms provide the ability to back out higher level (i.e. user) programs. Failures in the file system level cannot be dealt with internally, in that case. If they were dealt with internally then they would not be visible to the user in a higher level. Now that they are not, they must be passed on as a user error, thus causing the user to be backed out, which is possible as long as the cacheing mechanism itself still functions properly.

4. The Example Explained as a Recoverable Multi-level System

The example of Section 2 is discussed below in terms of the model for recoverable multi-level systems described in the previous section.

Level Ø in the example is the hardware. It does not provide any recoverable types to higher levels. This level is the "bottom" level and the only interpreter level in the system. Since it does not provide recoverable types it does not do any cacheing. However, it can deal with certain failures transparently to the software. The built-in recovery mechanism provides more reliable hardware and is a logging mechanism as described above. The self-provided scope of recovery is a disk operation: if it fails, it is restarted after repair. The scope of recovery is provided by level Ø for level Ø.

Similarly level 1 uses a logging mechanism and does not do any cacheing to provide recoverable types. Level 1 maps unrecoverable type page on unrecoverable type disk block. Type disk block is provided by level Ø, while type page is provided by level 1 and used by level 2. Although the disk hardware is quite reliable, an operation implemented in level 1 could fail for many reasons (such as a transient failure on the channel). In order to deal with such internal failures, it uses an internal recovery mechanism which is therefore a logging mechanism. Operations on disk pages are thus made very reliable; situations in which they fail are almost always those in which the whole disk is lost or unavailable.

Level 2 maps unrecoverable files on unrecoverable pages. So this level does not provide user recovery: when a higher level program fails, this level will not restore files. However, this level uses a logging mechanism to cope with failures in performing the required (by higher levels) file operations. Even though it is up to the user to specify whether or not he wishes this mechanism to be used for his file, it is not a cacheing mechanism, because it provides reliable file operations, not user recovery.

Level 3 maps recoverable file records on unrecoverable files. In other words, this level provides user recovery: users of objects of this new recoverable type "record", will have their records restored if they fail. This level therefore implements a cacheing mechanism. The cacheing mechanism consists of the creation of backups and journaling, which are used to restore user objects to the states they were in before the user of those objects entered his scope of recovery. However, no recovery is possible if level 3 itself fails (for example because of a system crash). Level 3 can backout a user: when the user of recoverable records invokes the level 3 UNDO operation, then this will cause restoration of those records. However, a failure in level 3 cannot always be passed on to the user, since the representation of the user objects, or worse the cache, may have been corrupted in an unrecoverable manner.

If level 3 wants to be able to recover from its own failures it needs to use a logging mechanism. Such a logging mechanism could save old values of unrecoverable objects operated upon before the operation is done. This level operates on file words, the old values of which could be saved before being updated. It has been shown [16] [18], that the cacheing and logging mechanisms can be combined to serve both purposes, if a level operates only on unrecoverable objects that are used to represent the recoverable objects provided. Indeed all that is involved in this case is a so-called write-ahead log protocol [6] which assures that a record is journaled before it is updated in the file. A failure in the file system can now be recovered from or be passed on to the user as a user error.

This combined cacheing/logging mechanism makes it possible to recover from any failure as long as the cacheing/logging mechanism functions properly. Since journals are often written to magnetic tapes and tapes are notoriously unreliable, many systems use a duplicate journal implemented on two separate tapes. This duplication of the journal makes journals highly reliable. Similarly two backups of the set of files can be kept: the most recent backups and the ones created before those. The journal will have to go back to the oldest backups in this case. The whole cacheing/journaling mechanism is highly reliable with these duplications.

Level 4 maps a recoverable data base on the tuple (set of differential files, set of recoverable file records). The set of differential files are unrecoverable data structures which could be tables in the virtual address space on (unrecoverable) files on disk. The differential files contain the new values of records as described in Section 2. Since recoverable objects are partially mapped on unrecoverable objects, a cacheing mechanism is required. The cacheing mechanism is very simple because of the way the mapping function works: state restoration here simply involves discarding the differential file entries for the user. The mapping function will, after this recovery action, map the user's data base records on the original file records as explained in Section 2. No separate data structure is required to keep old values of file records, for the following two reasons:

a. The recoverable file records are not updated while the user is in his scope of recovery.

b. The file records are already recoverable and could be restored implicitly if they were updated while the user is in his scope of recovery. In fact, as described in Section 3, it would be impossible to provide explicit recovery if data base records were directly mapped on recoverable file records.

When the user is at the need of his scope of recovery he will call the ACCEPT provided by level 4 (see Section 3). This ACCEPT operation writes the values of the records in the differential file to the recoverable file records. In order to do so reliably the ACCEPT operation could do this writing from insie a scope of recovery by calling the ENTER operation provided by level 3 at the beginning, and the ACCEPT operation provided by level 3 after successful completion. After a failure the journal will then be used to back out this level 4 ACCEPT operation. Alternatively, the operator or system could invoke the level 4 operation that processes the differential files during restart after a crash, or in general when the whole system is started, before doing anything else. Those differential files must therefore be on non-volatile memory from the moment the user of the data base exits his scope of recovery. The system must in that case be able to recognize that the differential files are ready for processing (i.e. the user has exited his scope of recovery). This alternative technique does not normally make sense, because it is a logging mechanism used for objects that are unrecoverable since no scope of recovery is used. It would be much simpler to use a scope of recovery and let the lower level perform the recovery automatically. the only case in which this alternative technique makes sense is when the recovery mechanisms provided do not allow the user to specify what to do after recovery: in this case a retry is required. This self-constructed logging mechanism includes such a retry after failure. The difference between the retry and no retry after failure is the point at which commitment takes place: with retry it is when the user in level 5 calls level 4's ACCEPT; without retry it is when level 4's ACCEPT finishes.

No extra mechanisms are required for using level 4's cacheing mechanism as a logging mechanism. A failure in level 4, such as a deadlock or a malfunction in the data base management system of level 4, could very simply be passed on to the user for the same reason.

The technique used by level 4 is usually referred to as the two-phase commit [6]. The special mapping function makes recovery for higher levels very simple; most complications arise with the final commit, which in our example is the level 4 ACCEPT operation.

The discussions above show how logging is always local to a level and totally unrelated to other levels and their recovery mechanisms. Logging simply makes the level more reliable. If two subsequent levels perform cacheing for objects that are mapped onto each other then there is a strong relationship in the sense that the one usually makes the other cacheing mechanism superfluous. If the recovery technique used by a level has to be made more reliable, then this should be done in a different way, for example by duplicating the journal as suggested for level 3 of our example. The differential file technique as a recovery technique in level 4 does not interfere with journaling in level 3, because this particular cacheing mechanism of level 4 is only used to undo the operations on the unrecoverable objects on which the data base is partially mapped. The new recoverable type data base is only partially mapped on recoverble types. The operations on objects of this recoverable type file record, which are only performed in level 4's ACCEPT, can be undone automatically (i.e. by lower levels). This explains the relationships between the recovery techniques used by different levels.

Models like the one described in this paper become especially of interest when systems are complex. For example, many distributed data base systems have a top level providing one logical data base to the user while mapping this data base on data bases or files on different independent systems. These systems may use different recovery techniques for different purposes. In these situations it is important to understand how the recovery techniques used by the top level providing the user interface, interact with recovery techniques used on local systems for files or data bases. The model described here can, as shown in the example of this section, be used to understand, describe or construct such systems.

5. The Provisions of Recovery Mechanisms with High-level Languages

A level that explicitly provides a new recoverable type, could be specified in a SIMULA-like language [2] by a so-called recovery class as shown in Fig. 5. Such a recovery class would be used as a prefix by user programs wanting to use the new type. The compiler would envelop the user's scope of recovery with the ENTER and ACCEPT procedures and make sure that the UNDO is invoked when an error occurs. The way in which the latter is done patially depends on the facilities provided by the lower levels. The compiler can, for example, generate all kinds of checks in user programs, such as range checks, and invoke the undo when such a check indicates an error.

Similarly a compiler could provide a level (class) with the facility to specify the ENTER, ACCEPT, and UNDO operations that are part of a logging, rather than cacheing mechanism. The operations can then be used to envelop recovery scopes in the programs in the level itself, rather than to envelop recovery scopes in programs that use the level. These facilities for classes can be extended to monitors. The problems involved with this are much more complicated and discussed elsewhere [14].

If a programmer could also specify invariants or assertions, as for example in ALPHARD [19] or some data base query languages [15], then the ENTER, ACCEPT and UNDO procedures could be specified by the programmer as part of the type checking mechanisms. In ALPHARD they could be specified as a part of a "form" and be invoked before an object of that form was updated, after it was updated successfully (i.e. the assertions and invariants were still valid) or unsuccessfully respectively. In a data base management system these operations are to be invoked before a scope of recovery is entered, when it is exited successfully or unsuccessfully respectively.

	new type recovery class level k;
level k's cache	begin integer array cache (1: length);
increased when user enters a scope of recovery, decreased when he exits	integer recovery-scope-level;
the ENTER procedure provided by level k	enter procedure begin ...... end;
the ACCEPT procedure provided by level k	accept procedure begin ...... end;
the UNDO procedure provided by level k	undo procedure begin ...... end;
operation 1 on the new type	procedure operation 1 (.....) begin ...... end;
operation p on the new type	procedure operation p (.....) begin ...... end;
	end;

Fig. 5. A Recovery Class

6. Relation to Other Areas and Conclusions

The mechanisms discussed in this paper could be used to provide protection or consistency checks. It is often very difficult to find out in advance whether a given operation or set of operations on the data base breaches any of the protection or consistency rules, without performing the operation first. Using a scope of recovery the operation, or set of operations, can be performed first. Subseqently, a test can be done and recovery be performed if any rule is breached. If the recovery facilities are available using high level languages, then such tests could easily be invoked automatically at the right places. The advantages of this method are that the tests are likely to be easier to specify and evaluate. In that case non-breachers will pay for less overhead required to enforce the rules.

This paper has shown how the model for recoverable multi-level systems presented, serves as an extremely useful framework for evaluating the use of different recovery techniques in one system.

REFERENCES

[1] Anderson, T., Lee, P.A., Shrivastava, S.K.: A Model of Recoverability in Multi-Level Systems, Technical Report 115, Computing Laboratory, the University of Newcastle upon Tyne, England. To appear in IEEE Trans. on Software Engineering (1977).

[2] Birtwistle, G.M., Dahl, O-J., Myhrhaug, B., Nygaard, K.: SIMULA BEGIN, (Auerbach Publishers Inc., Philadelphia, Pa., 1973).

[3] Chamberlin, D.D., et al: SEQUEL 2: A Unified Approach to Data Definition, Manipulation and Control, IBM J. R&D 2Ø, 6, (November 1976).

[4] Davies, C.T.: A recovery/integrity architecture for a data system, Report TR Ø2-528, IBM, San Jose, Calif., (19 May 1972).

[5] Introduction to TRAX, Order No. AA-D327A-TC, (Software Distribution Center, Digital Equipment Corporation, Maynard, MA. Ø1754, August 1978).

[6] Gray, J.N.: Notes on Data Base Operating Systems, Technical Univ. Munich, 1977, (Elsevier North-Holland, Inc., New York, 1977).

[7] Guttag, J.V.: The specification and application to programming of abstract data types, PhD. thesis, Dept. of Computer Science, University of Toronto, Canada, (1975).

[8] Madnick, S.E., Alsop, J.W.: A modular approach to file system design, SJCC (1969) 1-13.

[9] Randell, B.: System structure for software fault tolerance, IEEE Trans. Software Eng., SE-1, 2, (June 1975) 22Ø-232.

[1Ø] Randell, B., Lee, P.A., Treleaven, P.C.: Reliability issues in computing system design, ACM Computing Surveys 1Ø, 2, (June 1978) 123-165.

[11] Rothnie, J.B., Goodman, N.: A survey of research and development in distributed database management, in: Proceedings of the Third International Conference on Very Large Data Bases. (IEEE and ACM, October 1977) 48-62.

[12] Senko, M.E., Altman, E.B.: DIAM II and levels of abstraction. The physical device level: a general model for access methods, in: Systems for large data bases, P.C. Lockman and E.J. Neuhold (eds.),(North-Holland Publishing Company, 1976) 79-94.

[13] Severance, D.G., Lohman, G.M.: Differential Files: Their Application to the Maintenance of Large Databases, AMC Trans. Database Syst. 1, 3 (September 1976) 256-267.

[14] Shrivastava, S.K., Banatre, J-P.: Reliable resource allocation between unreliable processes, IEEE Trans. Software Eng., SE-4, 3, (May 1978) 23Ø-241.

[15] Stonebraker, M.: High level integrity assurance in relational data base management systems, Memorandum No. ERL-M473, Univ. of California, Berkeley, (August 1974).

[16] Verhofstad, J.S.M.: The construction of recoverable multi-level systems, Ph.D. Thesis, Univ. Newcastle upon Tyne, UK, (August 1977).
[17] Verhofstad, J.S.M.: Recovery techniques for database systems, ACM Computing Surveys 10, 2, (June 1978) 167-195.
[18] Verhofstad, J.S.M.: Recovery in multi-level systems, submitted for publication.
[19] Wulf, W.A., London, R.L., Shaw, M.: An introduction to the construction and verification of Alphard programs, IEEE Trans. Software Eng., SE-2, 4, (December 1976) 253-265.

Data Base Architecture, Bracchi/Nijssen, eds.
North-Holland Publishing Company

ENHANCEMENT OF CONCURRENCY IN DATABASE SYSTEMS BY THE USE OF SPECIAL ROLLBACK METHODS

G. Schlageter

Universität Dortmund, Informatik III
Postfach 500 500, D-4600 Dortmund 50
W.-Germany

In this paper a possibility to enhance parallelism in database systems is discussed which avoids the riks of rollback propagation. The approach relies on the use of some information about the operations to be performed on the database objects, such that the concurrency control can decide whether a requested lock can be granted without risk of rollback propagation or not. In case of transaction rollback, propagation is avoided by exploiting commutativity of operations. The approach may considerably improve system performance because it allows to selectively enhance parallelism, for instance in frequently used regions of the database. Where the required information about operations is not available to the concurrency control, the conventional restrictive "keep to the end of transaction" locking protocol is automatically applied.

1. Introduction

One of the main problems in the design of a database system is the selection of an appropriate concurrency control. Though the basic problems and principal solutions are well understood now /Bay, EGL, Gra, Sch/, many practical issues are still open, especially issues of implementation and economy. An important point which has hardly been discussed so far in the literature, is that the synchronization mechanisms required in practice should be flexible, i.e. first of all adaptable to the actual application.

The selection of a concurrency control is greatly influenced by the recovery problem, and there seems to be a tradeoff between the degree of parallelism in the system and the recovery cost in case of transaction rollback: the more we exploit "free" locking protocols, for instance, the more we have to pay in the case of transaction rollback. In practice, this results in the application of very restrictive synchronization mechanisms, which do not allow high parallelism in the database for many commercial applications.

The aim of these restrictive synchronization mechanisms is to guarantee that a running transaction can always be rolled back without affecting other transactions in the system (sphere of control /Dav/). The obvious way to achieve this goal is to lock all objects required by a transaction to the end of the transaction. If less restrictive locking protocols are applied, this unilateral transaction rollback is no longer guaranteed: other transactions may have accessed objects released by a transaction T before the end of T; so, if T fails, these transactions must be rolled back too, and this process may propagate to further transactions. Thus, the central issue in a discussion about the degree of parallelism in a database, given the granularity of locking, is this problem of "rollback propagation".

The "keep locks to the end" strategy is sufficient in many applications. However, there are applications where protocols of this type may produce bottlenecks in the system. Consider, for example, the situation where many persons simultaneously do order processing or execute invoicing transactions, all accessing in parallel the part file, the customer file, etc. Each transaction updates the quantity-at-hand information in the part records it accesses. If the records stay locked to the end of a transaction, all other transactions which also require some of these part records must wait - and thus depend on the speed of the corresponding clerk. The situation may get even worse, if all transactions of a certain type update statistical information, such as total value of the invoices prepared. Note that in these cases the bottleneck cannot be removed by choosing a finer granularity of lockable units, but only by special synchronization measures.

Now, virtually all investigations on concurrency control stay on the elementary level of read and write actions on objects in the database, they do not consider the operations actually performed on the objects. In this paper we want to show that more flexible synchronization mechanisms can be developed, if the concurrency control makes use of only little information about the operations to be performed on the objects.

To get a rough impression, consider an example: assume that transactions "invoicing" add the amount of invoice to a sum record R. All transactions of this type perform commutative operations on R, i.e. the final value of R does not depend on the sequence in which the operations are performed. Assume that the following happens: transaction T adds s to R and then releases R before its end; transaction T_1 locks, updates and releases R; T fails, and is rolled back. Applying conventional methods, T_1 would also have to be rolled back. However, since we know that the operations of T and T_1 on R are commutative, we only need to subtract s from the current value of R in order to rollback T, T_1 needs not to be considered. Rollback propagation cannot happen in this case, though T releases an object before its end. This fact could be exploited when designing a concurrency control: if the concurrency control has the knowledge about the operations performed on R, and about the operation to be performed on R by a new transaction T, it should be able to decide whether R can be accessed by T without risking rollback propagation, or not. So, in many cases parallelism can be enhanced without paying for it in the case of transaction rollback.

It is not required to have such information for all operations or for all transactions. But where the information is available we can loosen the restrictive synchronization rules to a large extent without again introducing the problem of rollback propagation. In fact, synchronization mechanisms relying on this basic idea allow to selectively enhance parallelism in a database, e.g. for frequently used portions of it.

2. The use of information about operations

In this chapter we briefly want to outline how current investigations on concurrency might be extended if operations are to be considered instead of read and write actions only. A more formal and complete treatment of the subject will be given elsewhere.

The synchronization of the transactions running simultaneously on the database must be done such that serializability of the transactions is guaranteed, that is there must exist a serial execution of all transactions which has the same overall effect as the actual parallel execution. We must consider this general requirement more in detail:

Let $E = \{e_1,...,e_m\}$ be the set of operations a transaction can perform on an object of the database; E may contain, for instance, a read operation, an add operation, a multiplication operation, an assignment operation, etc. The (parallel) execution of a set $\mathcal{T} = \{T_1,...,T_n\}$ of transactions produces, for each object v of the database, a sequence S(v) of operations on v. $e_i < e_j$ means that e_i is executed before e_j in the corresponding sequence; e(T) means that e was executed by transaction T. Assume that all operations are indivisible. The set of operation sequences S(v) produced by the given execution of $\mathcal{T}$ is called the schedule of this execution.

Now consider the dependency graph $G = (\mathcal{T},U)$, the nodes of which are the transactions, and the arcs of which are defined as follows:

$$U = \{(T_i,T_j) \mid \exists\ v, e(T_i), e(T_j): e(T_i) < e(T_j) \text{ in } S(v)\},$$

that is, an arc (T_i,T_j) exists, if, in some sequence S(v), T_i executed an operation before T_j.

Theorem 1:

A sufficient condition for the execution of $\mathcal{T}$ to be serializable is that G does not contain a cycle.

(For a detailed discussion see /Sch/, for instance. Note, however, that the notion of a schedule is different there from the one used here: there the set E = {read action, write action} of operations is considered, and only conflicting operations are ordered in the schedule, that is, the observed order of two succeeding read operations is considered immaterial from the very beginning.)

Obviously, therorem 1 is unnecessarily restrictive, if E contains commutative operations: whenever two succeeding operations e_i and e_j, $e_i < e_j$, are commutative, they might as well have been executed in the reverse order, $e_j < e_i$, without changing the final value of object v. Let us call two succeeding commutative operations interchangeable. Obviously, two schedules which can be transformed one into the other by interchanging interchangeable operations are equivalent in the sense that they both produce the same final state of the database, and the same output of the transactions to the user. (To see the latter, note that only the operations in E are executable by a transaction, thus only that information can be output by a transaction to the user which has been accessed by an explicit read operation.)

So a more useful serializability criterion is the following:

Theorem 2:

The execution of τ is serializable, if either its dependency graph is acyclic, or if there exists a schedule equivalent to the one of this execution the dependency graph of which is acyclic.

In other words: an execution is serializable if there exists a series of interchanges of interchangeable operations such that the schedule of the execution becomes acyclic.

As usual we assume that serializability is to be enforced by locking the objects according to some protocol. (We cannot discuss here the possibility of simply observing the running execution, and of intervening if we recognize some nonserializable situation.) Protocols which guarantee serializability or various degrees of consistency are well known now, however on the basis of read and write actions only. The fundamental protocol is the so-called two-phase lock protocol which requires that all locks are acquired before the first lock is released /ESW/. This protocol guarantees that there is one moment of time where all objects required by a transaction are actually locked.

According to the two-phase lock protocol objects can be released at different points of time. This improves the possibility of parallelism, but at the same time rollback propagation may occur. So, in practice only a very restricted two-phase protocol seems to be applicable, namely to keep all objects of a transaction locked to the end of the transaction.

In general, the basic two-phase protocol must be satisfied also if we consider operations instead of read and write actions (this is so because we have no detailed information about the logical interconnection of objects, etc.). We do not need to discuss here in detail, how locking is done in this case. For instance, a lock-command might be used in which the operations from E which are to be performed by the transaction, are indicated:

lock (object designation, list of operations to be performed).

As usual, the object then is released by a command unlock (object designation).

Our concern is to loosen the strong restriction imposed because of the rollback propagation problem, by using the information about the operations at run time. In terms of the schedule: the concurrency control must observe the developing schedule of the execution, and must exploit situations where operations are interchangeable on some objects. As has already been demonstrated by an example in chapter 1, in this case an access to an object released before the end of transaction is allowable, since rollback propagation may be avoided in a simple way by the recovery system.

Before we can develop a synchronization mechanism which makes use of information about operations in the above sense, we must briefly discuss the rollback problem in the outlined environment.

The rollback problem

Consider a sequence $S(v,t) = e_1,\dots,e_i,\dots,e_n$ of operations performed on object v up to time t.

Operation e_i is called locally erasable (in S), if all operations e_k, $i<k\leq n$, are commutative to e_i.

A locally erasable operation e_i can be undone in S by making e_{n+1} the inverse operation to e_i, without considering in detail the operations e_k, $i<k\leq n$. Now, consider a transaction T which performed operation e on v and then released v before its end. If T must be rolled back, the recovery system has to check whether e is locally erasable in S(v,t). If it is, operation e is undone by performing the inverse operation of e, i.e. by producing the sequence $S' = e_1,\dots,e,\dots,e_n,\bar{e}$, where $\bar{e}$ is the inverse operation to e. So, rollback propagation does not happen due to the undoing of e. Of course, rollback propagation may happen due to other operations of T which were not locally erasable at the point of failure of T.

Obviously, a transaction T can be rolled back at time t without rollback propagation, if all its operations on released objects v are locally erasable in S(v,t). Such a transaction is also called a locally erasable transaction (at time t).

Compare this approach to the classical rollback scheme using before-images: there the object value before the operation e_i is restored into the database, and all transactions which have performed operations e_k, $k>i$, are rolled back.

In the above scheme rollback propagation only happens if some operation e_j following e_i is not commutative to e_i. In this case, however, either only the transaction which performed e_j, or this transaction and the ones that performed the subsequent operations must be rolled back (see below); the operations e_m, $i<m<j$, stay unaffected by the rollback. That is, to undo e_i in the sequence $e_1,\dots,e_i,\dots,e_j,\dots,e_n$, e_j the first operation not commutative to e_i, one either need not apply corrective operations at all (e_j a read operation) or one produces the sequence $e_1,\dots,e_i,\dots,e_j,\dots,e_n$, $\bar{e}_n,\dots,\bar{e}_j,\bar{e}_i$.

The fact that in this approach only not locally erasable operations may give rise to rollback propagation could be essential, for instance in commercial databases: there we often have frequently used regions in the database (accumulative data, statistical data) which are permanently modified by a large set of transactions, all the modifications being commutative (additions to current value, for instance). Provided that the outlined rollback scheme is used, it is permissible to release these special objects before the end of transaction without risking rollback propagation.

3. High Parallelism without Rollback Propagation

In this chapter a synchronization mechanism is developed which prevents all possibility of rollback propagation but nevertheless allows to achieve a much higher degree of parallelism than by the use of conventional "rollback propagation proof" lock protocols. As will be seen, the advantages of the mechanism described in the following may be considerable in commercial applications.

We assume that we explicitly distinguish between different operation types, and that the concurrency control knows the type of each operation performed on an object (perhaps a type "unknown" might be necessary). The basic idea is then as follows:

1. the transactions apply any protocol they like provided that is satisfies the two-phase restriction;
2. we introduce a mechanism which guarantees that a transaction can only perform safe operations; an operation of a transaction T is said to be safe at time t, if it must never be undone due to the rollback of any non-terminated transaction T' ≠ T.

A mechanism of the above type would obviously guarantee that rollback propagation can never happen in the case that a non-terminated transaction must be rolled back: since a transaction can only perform safe operations it will never be affected by the rollback of any other non-terminated transaction. The problem is to decide when a given operation is safe.

To develop a mechanism of the required type we assume that the concurrency control distinghuishes between two states of an object:

- temporarily released: released by some transaction (unlock), but the transaction not yet terminated;
- safely released: not locked, and not temporarily released by any transaction.

Thus, at the moment a transaction T requests a lock to perform an operation e on object v, v is either temporarily released or safely released; we apply the following rules:

(1) object v temporarily released (by transaction T'):
the lock is only granted if the operations of T' in S(v,t) are commutative to e. If not, the lock is only granted after T' has terminated. (Note that there may be several transactions which released v temporarily.)

(2) object v safely released: access can be granted immediately.

Consider the example of figure 1. At time t_1 transaction T_1 releases v_1; T_1 performed an addition operation on v_1, so T_2 which also wants to perform an addition operation can access v_1 immediately. At t_2 transaction T_2 releases v_1 and terminates; nevertheless v_1 remains in the state "temporarily released" because T_1 is still active; so T_3 which wants to perform a multiplication operation on v_1 has to wait until t_3 (non-commutativity of operations).

The following two assertions are rather obvious now:

Lemma 1:

If the rules (1) and (2) are applied, each operation is only executed when it is safe.

(In the case of commutativity of rule (1), the undoing of an operation is avoided by the mechanisms discussed in chapter 2.)

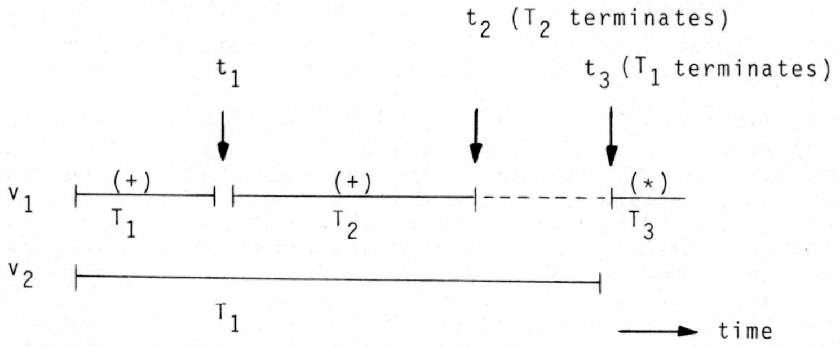

Figure 1: Example for the different states of objects (see text)

Lemma 2:

If the rules (1) and (2) are applied, rollback propagation due to the rollback of a non-terminated transaction cannot occur.

The implementation of the synchronization mechanism is almost straightforward: essentially some feature must be introduced which enforces that rule (1) is satisfied. Consider the following principal solution:

For each object v two queues, q_v and q_v' are maintained. q_v indicates the transactions actually locking the object, and those waiting for the object to be released. q_v' indicates the transactions which have released v, but are not yet terminated, i.e. if q_v' contains an element, v is in the state "temporarily released". So, transaction T moves from q_v to q_v' when it releases v, provided that it does not terminate at the same time, and it leaves q_v' when it terminates (see figure 2). The entries in the queues must also contain an indication of the operation types to be performed resp. performed by the transactions (the actual operations need not to be described here); a bit vector would be sufficient here, for instance.

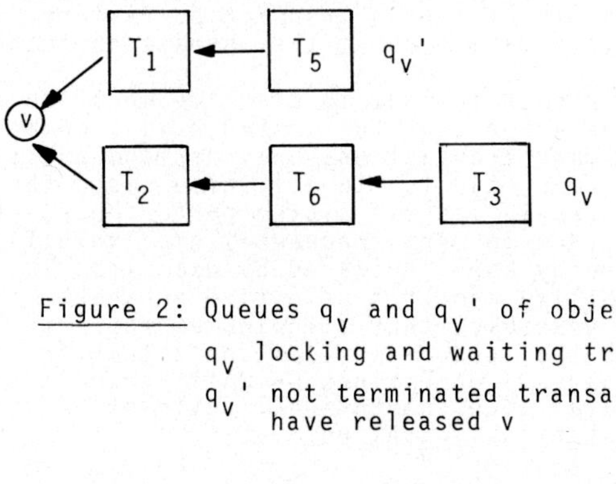

Figure 2: Queues q_v and q_v' of object v:
q_v locking and waiting transactions
q_v' not terminated transactions which have released v

q_v' retains the part of S(v,t) which is of interest in rule (1). If transaction T wishes to lock v and v is not locked, the concurrency control can perform the commutativity check of rule (1) using q_v'.

In many applications it is not necessary to distinguish between many classes of commutative update operations. So, in a commercial environment, it may be sufficient to have only "commutative" and "non-commutative" operations, where the class of commutative operations is formed by the additive operations. Note that read operations of transactions which read and write objects must be considered not commutative to any update operation, since the read operations may provide input parameters for write operations; however, in contrast to an update operation, the elimination of a read operation does not require any measures by the recovery system, so read operations should form a special class of operations for the system. If we have only commutative and non-commutative operations the decision process expressed in rule (1) is extremely simple.

Finally, we want to stress that this mechanism does not require that all transactions and their operations are well known; if no information is available to the database management system, it has to assume that an operation is not commutative. Thus, the mechanism offers great flexibility, it gives the possibility to enhance parallelism where it is necessary, where this is not required it applies the conventional restrictive locking strategy.

4. Conclusion

A possibility to enhance parallelism in database systems has been discussed which loosens the restrictive "keep locks to the end" protocol, but avoids the risk of rollback propagation. The approach relies on the use of some information about the operations to be performed on the database objects, such that the concurrency control can decide whether a requested lock can be granted without risk of rollback propagation or not. In case of transaction rollback, propagation is avoided by exploiting commutativity of operations.

According to the proposed synchronization mechanism each transaction can lock the required objects according to its real needs, i.e. it can lock objects at the moment it needs them and it can release each object when it is no longer needed, with the only restriction that the two-phase lock protocol is satisfied. So, a high degree of parallelism is possible; it is the job of the concurrency control to prevent parallelism only in those cases where it might result in rollback propagation in case of a transaction failure. This is done by the use of the information about the operations to be performed.

It is important to recognize that in practice we often have commutativity of operations, as for instance in a commercial environment, where many transactions only perform additions and subtractions on certain objects. In all these cases the outlined approach may considerably improve system performance, especially also because bottlenecks due to very frequently used objects can be avoided, as has already been indicated by examples. The approach offers great flexibility, so that selective enhancement of parallelism in the database is possible, thus allowing appropriate tuning of the system according to the special application situation. The approach does not require that all operations be well known in advance; where no information is available conventional restrictive locking strategies are automatically applied.

References

/Bay/ Bayer, R.: Integrity, Concurrency, and Recovery in Databases. Proc. ECI Conference 1976, Lecture Notes in Computer Science 44, 1976

/Dav/ Davies, C.T.: Data Processing Spheres of Control. IBM Syst. J. 17 (1978)

/EGL/ Eswaran, K.P., et.al.: The Notions of Consistency and Predicate Locks in Database Systems. Comm. ACM 19 (1976)

/Gra/ Gray, J.: Notes on Data Base Operating Systems. In: Operating Systems, Lecture Notes in Computer Science 60, 1978

/Sch/ Schlageter, G.: Process Synchronization in Database Systems, Transactions on Database Systems, 3 (1978)

Data Base Architecture, Bracchi/Nijssen, eds.
North-Holland Publishing Company

OPTIMIZATION OF LOGGING AND RECOVERY IN A DATABASE SYSTEM

Theo Härder   Andreas Reuter

Technical University Darmstadt
West Germany

A special log strategy based on an indirect mapping scheme from logical pages to slots on disk is introduced. The basic idea is to use the old copy of a modified page on disk as its before image saving a considerable portion of the log activity normally required. The proposed concept allows very fast in-progress-transaction backout in case of a transaction failure. In case of a system failure the UNDO-processing of incomplete transactions can be performed efficiently while REDO-operations of completed transactions are avoided. The evaluation of a cost model indicates a substantial gain w. r. t. log I/O compared to conventional log strategies.

1. Introduction

In a database system, a number of entities representing objects, facts, relations etc. of the miniworld, an application oriented section of the real world, are stored as data. As an important goal, the database system has to preserve the consistency of the stored information, that is, the database should reflect the state of the miniworld at any time (system enforced integrity). In order to control the consistency of the stored data a set of assertions often called consistency constraints has to be defined in the system. It is assumed that the state of the database is consistent if the stored entities of the state satisfy all the consistency constraints.

The consistency of the system is endangered whenever an update operation is performed. In order to modify the database one may need to temporarily violate the consistency of the system state (see /3/). Therefore, consecutive actions of a user have to be grouped into sequences called transactions which transform the database from a consistent state into a new consistent state. Transactions serve as units of consistency, that is, at the end of a transaction the consistency constraints must be satisfied. In order to guarantee consistency the system will only accept complete transactions. A transaction which does not reach its logical end (EOT = end of the transaction) has to leave the system in a state as if this transaction had never happened.

In a multi-user system allowing the access to shared data each transaction has to achieve certain locking protocols isolating its access to the temporarily inconsistent data. Here we are not concerned with the problem of locking strategy and granularity. We are assuming two-phase lock protocols according to (/3/) keeping exclusive locks on the updated data until EOT of the updating transaction, that is, the shrinking phase of the lock protocol (unlock) is concentrated to EOT.

This special two-phase lock protocol implies a stronger assumption than the general two-phase lock protocol postulates. In general, updates in a shared database should be visible to other users as soon as possible. The appearence of failures of various kinds at any time enforces the above restrictions in practical cases.

In order to allow an isolated recovery from failures during a transaction all changes must be hidden from all other users until EOT. By processing EOT a transaction commits its updates and looses the right to undo the changes performed. The related data are unlocked and the changes become visible to the community of the users. To undo or correct changes in case of a detected error after EOT another kind of mechanism has to be performed. Because other users may have seen the committed updates some kind of compensation has to be achieved (e. g. broadcast the detected error and the consequences to all users); see /2/.

System enforced integrity necessarily requires the control and preservation of the logical and physical integrity of the database. For this reason, a database system has to cope with various types of failures (hardware and software). A special subsystem called log (and recovery)component is catering for an appropriate set of preventive measures allowing the successful recovery in case of failure and the minimization of the amount of work that is lost. Usually the following types of failures and their expected frequency of occurrence can be classified as follows (/4/,/5/).

Transaction failure: Such a failure is locally recoverable w. r. t. the database system and affects only a particular transaction or number of transactions. The database system is assumed to continue without interruption and to perform some corrective actions in this situation. Typical examples of errors causing such failures are timeout, user detected error, resource limits, deadlock, protection or integrity violation. This type of failure is expected to appear very frequently, e. g. one or several times an hour during database operation.

System failure: This kind of failure affects the entire system behavior and every action has to be stopped immediately. It is assumed that the current contents of system buffers in main memory are lost; but the data on nonvolatile storage (disk, tape) is kept unaffected. Sources of such system failures are errors in critical tables, operating system crashes or hardware downs. This type of failure is supposed to be less frequent, e. g. one or several times a day/week.

Media failure: This type of failure is caused by a nonrecoverable error detected on nonvolatile storage device containing (recoverable) data of the database. It is assumed that the system cannot cope with this kind of error in normal operation. Usually it is irrelevant whether or not the system can close the session in a controlled manner and avoid an additional system failure. Examples of such errors are disk head crash, parity errors or loss of the storage device. This type of failure is expected to be very infrequent, e. g. one or several times a year.

In order to cope with failures in an appropriate way some principles of error recovery should be considered.

General principle: The amount of work that is lost in case of an error should be minimized. In particular, locally recoverable errors should be treated locally avoiding recursive backout, that is, only the transaction concerned should be backed out ("undone"). Appropriate isolation by locking the referenced data objects until EOT has to be provided. In case of a deadlock detected the transaction or set of transactions causing minimum costs should be undone.

Principle for complete transactions: If a transaction completes successfully the system definitively accepts its updates at EOT and guarantees their physical integrity to the user. Therefore, all changes of complete transactions have to survive each possible failure, that is, they have to be repeated in their original sequence, eventually.

Principle for imcomplete transactions: The changes of incomplete transactions which cannot proceed due to transaction failure or are aborted due to system failure have to be undone completely in reverse order. The UNDO-sequence of all different transactions in case of a system failure can be chosen arbitrarily, because the concerned transactions were isolated w. r. t. each other and had not committed their updates.

According to these principles appropriate recovery mechanisms of the log component have to be designed for the various failure types.

In case of a transaction failure an in-progress-transaction backout has to be performed. The recovery action consists of aborting the transaction and undoing its changes in reverse order. *(R1 = selective UNDO-operation of a transaction).*

In case of a system failure, after reloading the system the following recovery actions have to be performed:

If some updates of completed transcations are lost (e. g. the updated pages in the system buffer are not forced to disk at EOT), the updates of these transactions have to be repeated in their original sequence within the particular transaction and in EOT-sequence of the related transactions *(R2 = partial REDO-operation in case of a system failure).*

The effects of all incomplete transactions have to be undone as if these transactions had never happened. *(R3 = global UNDO-operation in case of system failure).*

After detecting a media failure a reconstruction of the recent possible consistent database state has to take place. The recovery mechanism is usually based on a consistent backup version of the database which is gained by copying the database periodically to tape. Using the latest available copy the recovery proceeds by performing REDO-operations of all transactions completed since the generation of the copy. *(R4 = complete REDO-operations in case of media failure).*

In order to be able to perform the four different recovery mechanisms (R1 - R4) the log component has to collect appropriate information for all update operations allowing the UNDO- or REDO-recovery. Roughly speaking two different kinds of logging are possible. Using logical logging only the update operation code with all its parameters is written to the log file allowing the system the complete UNDO- and REDO-operation in case of a failure. In particular, consecutive updates of access path data derivable from the original update operation are not logged at all. On the other hand, physical logging saves the states of the related data before and after performing the update operation and writes the so-called before-images and after-images to the log file. All changes as a result of an update operation - user data and access path data - are recorded in the log file.

Logical logging will be considerably shorter than physical logging and favour the normal mode of operation (w. r. t. gathering log information). In principal the logical log information of an operation can always be written to the log file in one physical I/O-operation. Physical logging is often obtained by keeping a transaction log at the physical disk page level rather than at the logical record level (IMS,DMS 1100, UDS). Every page altered by an update operation is written twice (old + new value) to the log file, resulting in a number of physical I/O operations for the log file per single update.

In case of recovery physical logging is very fast allowing a pure exchange of data while logical logging may be very slow due to the complete repetition of the update operations including user data and access paths.

Given the expected error frequencies, transaction and system failure recovery (R1 - R3) have to be optimized for performance reasons, while media recovery (R4) may be treated with less efficiency. Our goal in this paper is to design a storage mechanism and an output policy for altered database pages which allow very fast UNDO-operations in case of recovery R1 and R3 and avoids REDO-recovery in case of system failure (R2). While it is also possible to speed up the media recovery (R4) by applying physical page logging for the REDO-information we are adopting logical logging for REDO-purposes because of the expected failure rates.

It is assumed that the minimum locking granularity of a transaction is a database page and that all exclusive locks are kept until EOT allowing isolated backout.

This concept of page locking is supported in many database systems and does not seem to introduce too many restrictions; see /7/.

2. Storage organization of the database

Database systems using update-in-place operations on disk (e. g. each page is always written back from the system buffer to the same slot) have to perform physical page logging for UNDO-purposes applying the WAL-principle (Write Ahead Log) in order to survive a system failure during a write operation and to avoid media recovery in this case. (Media recovery is always extremely expensive no matter which kind of REDO-logging is performed). Hence, for each altered page at least two physical I/O operations have to be performed. The goal of our concept is to write an altered page only once for the update operation and the related UNDO-log. As a consequence, we cannot use update-in-place operations on disk. Applying an indirect mapping-scheme every write operation of a page causes the allocation of a new slot. The basic idea is that we use the newly written page P_i' and its original copy P_i for a twofold purpose:

As long as the transaction T is in progress P_i' and P_i are locked exclusively by T. P_i serves as the UNDO-log information until EOT of T. After EOT of T P_i is released (given back to the pool of free slots) while P_i' is committed. This method of relating slots containing the old and the new image of a page, respectively, is very similar to the storage organization proposed by Lorie /6/. But while Lorie's scheme does not allow for in-progress-transaction backout (R1-recovery) our approach does due to the special method of UNDO-logging.

In order to explain the details of this mechanism we have to introduce an appropriate storage organization of the database.

The storage organization could be based on one potentially infinite linear address space. To increase flexibility and to improve control it is preferable to partition a large database into segments (areas). At the physical level the database can be seen as a collection of segments S_k $(1 \leq k \leq m)$. Each segment S_k constitutes a linear address space which is decomposed into logical pages P_i $(1 \leq i \leq s_k)$ of uniform size L. The pages contain the stored entities (user data) called logical records and access path data (system data). Logical records and access path structures are connected by references in various ways. An appropriate addressing machanism has to be introduced to implement these references in an efficient manner. Addressing an entity in a particular location of a segment by using the relative byte address from the beginning of the segment is a disastrous concept because all address references have to be changed as soon as the entity is moved. The addressing mechanism should allow some degree of freedom w. r. t. the movement of the referenced entity.

In our storage organization we propose the so-called TID concept described in /1/ or some variation of this addressing mechanism. An approved implementation technique for TID's being a concatenation of a page number along with a byte offset from the bottom of the page combines the speed of a byte address pointer with the flexibility of indirection. The page number allocated in a logical address space allows an indirect reference to the actual physical storage slot. The offset denotes a special entry which contains the byte location of the referenced entity in the page. Hence, the TID concept offers two different kinds of indirection - at the page level and within the page.

The chosen addressing mechanism allows the explizit and dynamically changing mapping of logical pages to physical slots of identical size on disk.

Let us assume for simplicity reasons that a separate disk space D_k consisting of d_k slots $(d_k > s_k)$ is provided for each segment S_k. (It is also possible to provide only one disk space D for all segments S_k). The entire number of slots of D_k has not to be allocated in physical contiguity on a disk. Different sets of contiguous slots controlled by an extent table are conceivable. Because contiguity between different extents is not necessary, D_k as well as S_k can be increased dynamically.

In order to facilitate the search for a free slot when a page is allocated a bit map of d_k bits called MAP_k is maintained such that

$$MAP_k(j) = 1 \text{ if slot } j \text{ is occupied,}$$

$$MAP_k(j) = 0 \text{ if slot } j \text{ is available.}$$

The mapping of segment S_k to disk space D_k is represented by using a vector V_k - often called a page table (/6/). $V_k(i)$ contains the number of the slot used to store page P_i. A null value indicates an undefined page.

Some other information concerning the available space in a page serving for the free placement administration has to be maintained in a database system. It is advantageous to pack related information which is often used and changed jointly, physically close together. Hence, $V_k(i)$ should contain additionally the free space information of page P_i.

The following figure describes our storage organization for a segment S_k.

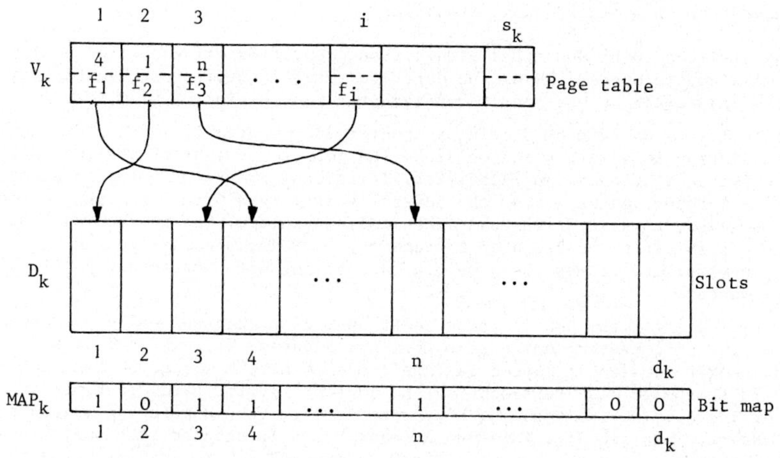

Fig.1: Mapping between pages and slots

An actual implementation of V_k could be chosen as follows: Each entry of V_k consists of

- *a 4 byte subentry containing the slot number w. r. t. D_k, which is considered to be the physical address of the logical page P_i, ($V_k(i,1)$).*
- *a 2 byte subentry containing the actual number of free bytes (f_i) in the logical page P_i serving for free placement administration. Assuming a page size of 2K or 4K some of these bits can be usded optionally for other purposes ($V_k(i,2)$).*

In general, MAP_k and V_k are larger than the maximum practicable size of a physical record (unit of data transfer). Therefore, they must be split into blocks of uniform size B.

3. Description of the UNDO-log algorithm

As already mentioned in section 2, the main disadvantage of the update-in-place concept is the necessity of additional write accesses concerning the UNDO-information (before image).

Depending on the organization of the log file an overhead of 100% up to 300% of physical I/O can be produced. The question of logging pages or entries is of minor importance w. r. t. this point. The second problem of such a log strategy is the triggering of all update operations by the WAL-discipline.

In our log concept we are using the fact that we get the before image of a page for free when an altered page is written to a different slot.

In the following we shall explain how the basic idea of writing changed pages into new slots can be refined in such a manner that transaction-oriented logical consistency points (see /5/) can be achieved without an additional UNDO-log. The detailled analysis in section 6 will show that only a small portion of the saved write accesses for the before images has to be spent on other I/O due to the algorithm. Hence, the result will be a considerable reduction of log overhead.

3.1 Generation of a transaction identifier

The log strategy to be described requires an identifier for each transaction performing update operations on the database. This identifier should be easy to generate and remain unique over a sufficiently long period of time.

One could try to do this by storing a counter incremented by 1 for every updating transaction in a safe place on disk. The actual contents of that counter could serve as a transaction identifier. It is easy to see that the first overflow of a 4-byte-counter would take several years, even with high transaction rates. However, this algorithm has a great disadvantage. The counter must be stored to disk after the begin of a transaction (BOT), because even in case of a system failure it must be possible to continue with the actual contents of the counter.

The following algorithm avoids these additional disk accesses while preserving the property of long-term uniqueness. When the database is generated or a consistent backup version is copied to tape (checkpoint), a so-called "initial value" is stored to disk representing the contents of the hardware timer in units of 1/8sec. (We are assuming here that no more than 8 updating transactions can be started per second). Whenever a transaction is started, the same kind of value is obtained from the hardware timer, decreased by the initial value and taken as the transaction identifier. With a 4-byte identifier the value generated by this algorithm remains unique over a period of 17 years.

3.2 Data structures for UNDO-information management

The implementation of our log strategy requires a number of fields in the header of every page of the database. They are to maintain the connection between the slot containing the updated page and the slot containing its before image, the connection between all slots containing pages updated by the same transaction etc. These fields might be declared as follows:

```
DCL 1 PAGE_HEADER,
      2 LOGICAL_PAGE_ #           FIXED(32), /* DATA SUPPORTING THE */
      2 . . .                                /* DATA MANAGEMENT     */
      .
      .
      2 LOG INFORMATION,
        3 LAST_CHANGE_BY_TA        FIXED(32), /* LOG DATA SERVING    */
        3 COPY_OF_SLOT             FIXED(32), /* FOR UNDO-PURPOSES   */
```

```
      3 BACK_PTR_IN_TA              FIXED(32),
      3 FORW_PTR_IN_TA              FIXED(32),
    2 . . .
    .
    .
    .
```

The logical page number of a page should be stored in the page itself in any implementation. Hence, it does not count as a special log information. The 4 words of log information occupy only 0,78% of a 2K page, a tolerable expense compared to the amount of data necessary for the maintenance of a separate log file. The fields of the structure LOG_INFORMATION declared above are to contain the following data:

- LAST_CHANGE_BY_TA — Identifier of the transaction which caused the last update of the page
- COPY_OF_SLOT — Number of the slot, in which the page was stored before it was updated by the transaction, whose identifier is saved in LAST_CHANGE_BY_TA (before image pointer)
- BACK_PTR_IN_TA — Number of the slot, which contains the previous page changed by the same transaction
- FORW_PTR_IN_TA — Number of the slot, which contains the next page changed by the same transaction

Additionally, we need a (rudimentary) logfile, which contains as many records (in direct access) as concurrent transactions are allowed. The record structure might be declared as follows:

```
DCL  1 BOT_FILE_ENTRY,
       2 ID_OF_ACTIVE_TA          FIXED(32),
       2 UNDO_ANCHOR(*)           FIXED(32),
       2 USER_INFORMATION,
         3 START_TIME             FIXED(32),
         3 . . .
         .
         .
         .
```

The fields of this structure contain the following data:

- ID_OF_ACTIVE_TA — Identifier of the transaction, whose BOT-handling caused this record to be written. As will be explained in the following, the "log-file" contains only records about incomplete transactions, and therefore it will be called BOT-file in the following.
- UNDO_ANCHOR(*) — Number of the slot, which contains the first page changed by this transaction. There will be one anchor for each segment in the database.

Though the total size of the BOT-file will be very small, it cannot be kept in main storage only. Because of recoverability in case of a system failure it must be stored in a safe place. But of course, there will be a table for the active transactions in main storage as well.

3.3 Maintenance of transaction-dependent UNDO-information

In this section we want to explain the details of our log strategy from a logical point of view, i. e. it is shown, how the different types of pages and slots are chained, how the vectors V_k and MAP_k are updated and so on - irrespective of questions of buffer management etc. These issues will be treated in a separate section. To simplify the discussion we shall always consider one segment denoted by index k.

At the beginning of a new transaction (BOT) which is going to update the database (and we are only talking about this type of transaction), first of all the transaction identifier (IT) is generated. The IT is then stored in the table of active

TA's and in the BOT_FILE_ENTRY-structure. An empty record in the BOT-file is found, which is to receive the BOT_FILE_ENTRY of the new transaction. But before this record is actually stored in the BOT-file, the UNDO_ANCHOR-field is set for all segments to be updated by the transaction, although the transaction has not yet changed any page at all. This action saves an additional write access to BOT-file during the update of the first page. We obtain the number of a free slot from the MAP_k-vector, store it into UNDO_ANCHOR(k), mark the slot in MAP_k as being occupied and write the BOT_FILE_ENTRY to the log file. Now, the successful BOT of the transaction is acknowledged to the user's program.

When the first page (P_i) changed by the transaction with identifier IT has to be written onto disk, the following steps have to be performed:

a) Get the slot number stored in UNDO_ANCHOR(k) (its number be s_i')
b) Store IT into LAST_CHANGE_BY_TA
c) Store the number of the old slot of P_i (the number be s_i) into COPY_OF_SLOT
d) Move 0 into BACK_PTR_OF_TA to denote this page as the first one to be changed by transaction IT
e) Find a free slot via the MAP_k-vector (its slot number be s_{i+1}') and store it into FORW_PTR_IN_TA
f) Write page P_i into slot s_i'.

For all the following pages, which are changed by transaction IT essentially the same steps have to be performed. Only in step a the number of the new slot s_i' has to be obtained from FORW_PTR_IN_TA of the previous page, and in step d BACK_PTR_OF_TA must point to the slot with that very page.

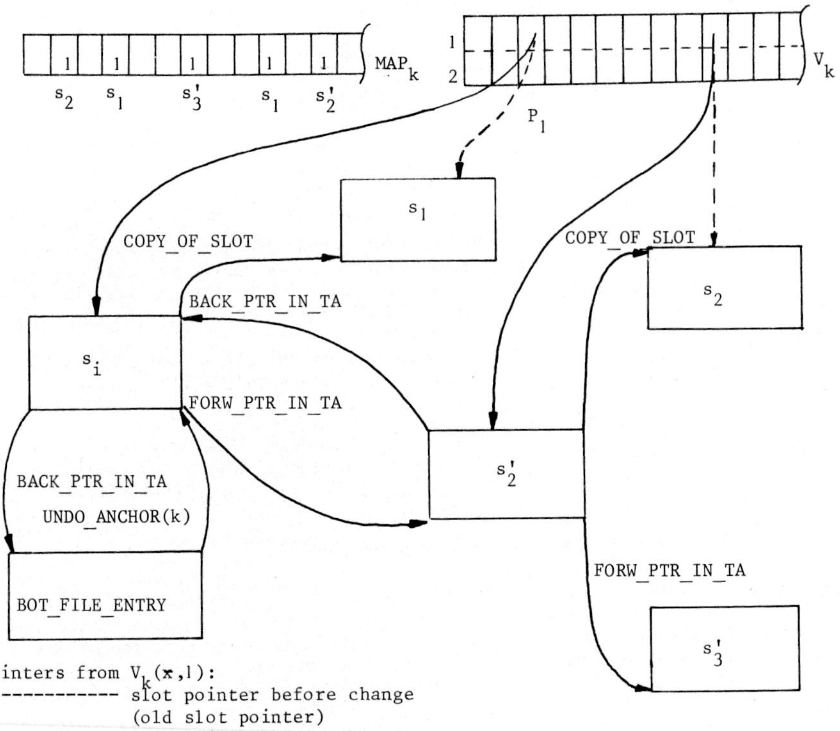

Pointers from $V_k(x,1)$:
------------- slot pointer before change (old slot pointer)
_____________ slot pointer after change (actual slot pointer)

Fig. 2: Chains of UNDO-information

Thus we have spent only one write access per page and nevertheless we have succeeded in storing the contents of the new page to disk connected with its before-image and with its predecessor and follower in the chain of pages changed by the same transaction.

For every page changed by the transaction IT for the first time, the following table entries have to be updated (the logical page be P_i):

- *$V_k(i, 1)$ must point to the new slot s_i'*
- *MAP_k (s_{i+1}') has to be set to 1*
- *$V_k(i, 2)$ has to be changed according to the update performed by transaction IT*.

Note that FORW_PTR_IN_TA of P_i points to an empty slot reserved for the next update of IT.

Note that the old page s_i must not yet be released in MAP_k.

A page updated and forced to disk several times within a transaction is always assigned to the same slot.

Figure 2 shows the concatenation of old and new slots in the way described after two pages have been changed.

3.4 Write disciplines implied by the log algorithm

Let us now consider, which write discipline must be observed for the different kinds of data involved in the log algorithm to guarantee recoverability under all possible failure conditions. We do not write any separate log information for a changed page, so the "write ahead log"-principle does not apply here, but in fact there are some equivalent rules, which we shall specify now. The necessity of these rules will become obvious in section 5.

- Let P_i and P_j be two pages changed by the same transaction IT. If FORW_PTR_IN_TA of page P_j points to the new slot of P_i or equivalently, BACK_PTR_IN_TA of P_i points to the new slot of P_j, then P_i has to be written to its new slot before P_j is written. Otherwise the situation might occur, that the FORW_PTR_IN_TA chain is broken and some updated pages of IT are inaccessible for the recovery routine. If both, P_i and P_j have been written already to their new slots due to previous changes of transaction IT, then this rule does not apply.
- Let P_i be a page changed by transaction IT. After the first change of this page, it has to be written to its new slot before the corresponding entries V_k (i,x) are written to disk. Otherwise the situation might occur, that in case of a failure $V_k(i, x)$ is written and P_i is not. Then the old contents of $V_k(i, x)$ would be unrecoverable, because they can only be obtained from the old slot referred to by COPY_OF_SLOT of P_i, which was assumed not to be written.
- All entries of MAP_k affected by transaction IT have to be written at EOT of IT.

The first rule is not very restrictive; in fact, in many cases it is not contradictory to a normal LRU-buffer-management-algorithm. The third rule is rather simple, too. Some problems, however, do arise from the second rule. It says, that the necessity of writing data pages can be triggered by the need to replace a block of the vector V_k, which contains changed entries. This may cause conflicts due to the first rule and has an additional impact on the buffer management. Therefore, we state that even the changed blocks of vector V are not written until EOT. This is a great advantage in the most common cases of recovery (R1, R3), as will be shown in section 5.

But, of course, if we want to keep all V_k-entries of all transactions in main memory until EOT, we cannot expect to do this in the normal database-buffer. This problem will be discussed in detail in section 4.

4. Access and update of pages

In the previous section we have explained the essential steps of the log-algorithm from a logical point of view. We described which pages and table entries have to be updated in which way, but we did not mention the impact of these actions on the storage structure of our database system. Here we want to consider, what has actually to be done, if we want to read, change and write a page, a vector etc.

It is assumed that the database system has three kinds of buffer pools:

- *A page buffer PB for pages* P_i
- *A block buffer BB for blocks of vector* V_k *and* MAP_k
- *An entry buffer EB for those entries of* V_k *that have been changed by an active transaction. The entries changed by the same transaction are linked together in an appropriate way. Together with the actual copy of the* V_k*-entry the old slot number of page* P_i *is stored in EB. Note that EB can serve as a global lock table, which has to be maintained in a database system regardless of the chosen log strategy.*

All the steps described below do only apply to the case of normal processing. For recovery actions after any kind of failure see section 5.

4. 1 Read access to a page

Although the different steps should actually be specified in a flow-diagram, it will be sufficient for our purpose to list them as follows:

a) *If* P_i *is already in PB, immediate access is possible, otherwise*

b) *If* $V_k(i, x)$ *is already in EB, set* $j = V_k(i, 1)$*, go to step d otherwise*

c) *If the block of* V_k *containing* $V_k(i, x)$ *is not in BB, fetch it and set* $j = V_k(i, 1)$

d) *Read page* P_i *stored in slot j into PB (possibly after the selection of a page to be replaced).*

4.2 Modification of a page

A modification of page P_i causes the actions of the log-algorithm described in section 3 to be performed. The predecessor in the log chain delivers the number of slot s_i' for page P_i being forced to disk. Entry $V_k(i, 1)$ has to be changed to point to s_i'. According to the write discipline explained in section 3.4 we do not change this entry in the block buffer BB, but we save its new value in the entry buffer EB. Hence, the steps necessary can be summarized as follows:

a) *If* P_i *has been changed previously, only* $V_k(i,2)$*, found in EB has to be changed depending on the update performed(*P_i *will be written to the same slot as before)*
otherwise

b) *Find a free slot* s_{i+1}' *via* MAP_k *according to the nearest neighbor-principle and store it into* FORW_PTR_IN_TA *of* P_i

c) *Store the number of* P_i*'s old slot in the respective EB-entry*

d) *Store the entry* $V_k(i,x)$ *into EB and connect it with the previous entry changed by the same transaction*

e) *Modify* $V_k(i,x)$ *according to the rules given in section 3.*

f) *When* P_i *is forced to disk: get the new slot number* s_i' *from* FORW_PTR_IN_TA *of the previous page in the log chain and write* P_i *to slot* s_i'*. The contents of*

FORW_PTR_IN_TA of the actual head of the log chain pointing to the next s_i' *to be used can be kept in main storage; hence, no read of the previous page is necessary to obtain this information.*

4.3 Modification of a block of vector V_k

Because of the write discipline implied by our log algorithm we have decided in section 3.4 not to write any modified blocks of vector V_k until EOT. Therefore, we have to keep the old and the new values of the changed entries in different places. The entrv buffer EB introduced at the beginning of this section serves as an intermediate storage for those entries of V_k, which have been changed by an active transaction. Whenever a page is changed for the first time, the respective entry of V_k is stored in EB, as described in section 4.2. The entries of the vector blocks in BB remain unchanged until EOT. When transaction IT terminates normally, V_k is updated performing the following steps:

a) If the entries in EB changed by IT are exhausted, write all flagged blocks of BB to disk
otherwise

b) Find the next entry $V_k(i,x)$ *in EB changed by IT*

c) If the block containing $V_k(i,x)$ *is not in BB: fetch it*

d) Replace the old contents of $V_k(i,x)$ *in BB by the new ones*

e) Flag the respective block in BB .

We have not yet considered, whether the usual LRU replacement algorithm can be applied to BB, because of the strong dependencies between BB and EB. Probably a CLOCK-algorithm modified by a counter for the number of transactions that actually refer to the same block in BB would achieve better results (see /9/). Due to the limited space we must leave this problem open.

4.4 Modification of a block MAP_k

We stated in section 3.4 that changed blocks of MAP_k must not be written until EOT. Therefore, we have to keep the old and new values of the changed MAP_k-bits in different places. To simplify the discussion the complete MAP_k-vector and a current copy of MAP_k are supposed to be kept in main memory. Fig. 3 shows the two copies of MAP_k required for a transaction-oriented modification at EOT.

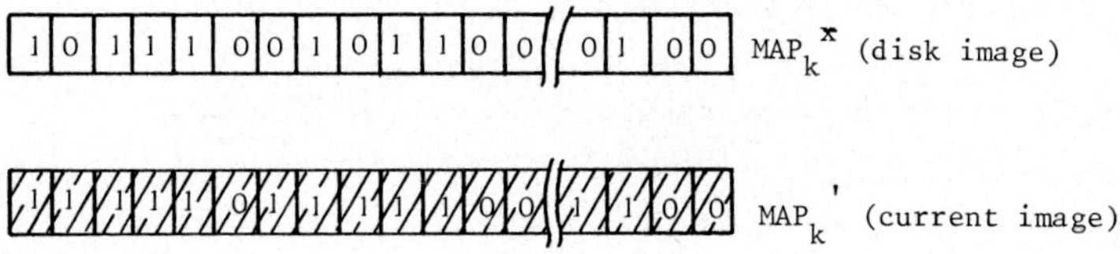

Fig. 3: Representation of MAP_k in main memory.

The so called "disk image" contains the image of MAP_k actually stored on disk. Due to the EOT write discipline applied, it reflects only changes of complete transactions. The "current image" is the "working storage" for MAP_k serving for the bookkeeping of all changes due to active transactions. Hence, all modifications of MAP_k mentioned in section 3 apply only to the "current image", while the "disk image" contains the last consistent state.

When transaction IT terminates normally, the change of MAP_k caused by IT must be added to MAP_k^* (disk image) and the affected blocks must be written back onto disk. The following steps have to be performed:

a) If the list of entries changed by IT in EB is exhausted, write the flagged blocks of MAP_k^* to disk
otherwise
b) Find the next entry changed by IT in EB
c) Find the new slot number s_i' of the resp. entry and set $MAP_k^*(s_i') = 1$
d) Find the old slot number s_i of the resp. entry and set $MAP_k^*(s_i) = 0$ and $MAP_k'(s_i) = 0$
e) Flag the resp. block of MAP_k^*.

5. Normal termination and recovery actions

5.1 EOT-handling

Almost all steps to be performed have already been discussed in detail. The EOT-procedure consists of the following actions in the given sequence:

a) Write all pages in PB changed by the terminating transaction IT back onto disk (if not already)
b) Write the blocks of vector V_k changed by IT (see section 4.3)
c) Write the blocks of vector MAP_k changed by IT (see section 4.4)
d) Destroy all entries belonging to IT in EB
e) Delete the record in BOT-file corresponding to transaction IT
f) Write an EOT-record to the REDO-log file
g) Send an acknowledgement of the successful termination to the user's program.

5.2 Recovery action R1

R1 is defined as an in-progress-transaction backout, i. e. the respective transaction cannot proceed to its normal EOT and must be aborted. Note that all changes of the vector V_k and MAP_k caused by this transaction are not reflected by the images of these vectors on disk. Some pages updated by this transaction will, of course, have been written to disk. But none of these pages is referred to by the corresponding table entries of V_k and MAP_k on disk, so we can simply treat them as free pages. Thus we actually have to perform the following simple steps:

a) Delete the record in BOT-file corresponding to transaction IT
b) Reset $MAP_k'(s_i') = 0$ for all entries s_i' changed by IT (using the list in EB)
c) Destroy all entries belonging to IT in EB.

5.3 Recovery action R2

The failure situation requiring recovery action R2 can never occur in our environment. A transaction is treated as incomplete until all pages and blocks changed have been written to disk (see section 5.1). Hence, in case of a failure either recovery action R3 or R4 has to be applied.

5.4 Recovery action R3

Only incomplete transactions to be rolled back after a system failure are recorded in the BOT-file. The field UNDO ANCHOR(k) in each record is the beginning of the transaction's log chain. Before we explain the processing of this chain, we have to distinguish two possible cases: either the transaction to be rolled back had already initiated its EOT-handling when the failure occurred, or it had not. This decision is done by reading the slot which the field UNDO_ ANCHOR(k) points to and the V_k-entry corresponding to the page stored in that slot. (It is assumed that the V_k-block belonging to the first page in the log chain is written first during EOT). If the V_k-entry does not point to the new slot, the EOT-handling for this transaction had not yet affected the vector blocks. A simplified R1 recovery can take place, that is, the deletion of the corresponding BOT-entry. Otherwise, the updates caused by the transaction to be rolled back have already affected the stored data; therefore they have to be undone explicitly by performing the following steps:

a) *Traverse the entire log chain beginning with UNDO_ANCHOR(k) by proceeding via FORW_PTR_IN_TA*

b) *If LAST_CHANGE_BY_TA of the current page is not equal to the transaction identifier actually processed, the end of the log chain is found otherwise*

c) *Read the V_k-entry corresponding to the page found (P_i)*

d) *Set $V_k(i,1)$ = COPY_OF_SLOT*

e) *Recover $V_k(i,2)$ by using the actual value f_i*

f) *Read the MAP_k-entries corresponding to the slot actually processed (its number be s_i') and to the slot pointed to by COPY_OF_SLOT (s_i)*

g) *Set $MAP_k(s_i') = 0$, $MAP_k(s_i) = 1$*

h) *When the end of the log chain has been found: rewrite all changed blocks of V_k and MAP_k, delete the record in BOT-file corresponding to the rolled back transaction.*

This recovery action has to be applied to all transactions recorded in the BOT-file irrespective of their sequence. Finally, we have to consider one special error that might occur due to our write policy. Since a page may be written to the same slot repeatedly, a system failure during the write operation may leave such a slot in an unreadable state. This does not cause any problem, however, because a transaction, which was just writing a page cannot have modified any vector blocks. Hence, the contents of the unreadable slot are of no interest. A simplified R1 recovery can be accomplished. Note that it does not make any difference, whether or not we process the log chain in reverse order. Every page has only one before image, so the sequence of restoring V_k and MAP_k is not important. The recovery algorithm depends on the uniqueness of the transaction identifiers. Therefore, whenever the "initial value" is reset (see section 3.1) a backup copy of the database has to be written to tape and the fields LAST_CHANGE_BY_TA in all slots must be set to 0.

5.5 Recovery action R4

Media recovery is of minor interest for our discussion. In section 1 we preferred logical REDO-logging to be performed. But a physical log strategy may be chosen as well. Note that REDO-log information concerning the vectors V_k and MAP_k has not to be collected because their contents can always be reconstructed by using the data pages in case of a media failure recovery. For further discussion of this issue see /10/.

6. Evaluation of a cost model

It is desirable to estimate the performance ot the proposed log strategy in order to show potential gains compared to conventional log concepts, e. g. with page logging for UNDO- and REDO purposes. This is typically done by an analytic model tailored to a database organization. The chosen model has to be evaluated by applying a workload consisting of a number of "typical" transactions to it. Analyzing a log strategy we are focussing on the total number of output operations required for normal processing and logging. As a measure of quality, we are particularly interested in the relationship between normal output and additional output for logging. We have to consider output operations from system buffers concerning the propagation of the updates to the database and the storing of the various log information to a safe place (UNDO-log files on disk/ REDO-log files on tape). Our model consists of a two-level storage hierarchy: buffers for pages (PB) and blocks (BB) in main memory and slots on disks or similar devices. The unit of data transfer between main memory and disk is a page or a block of fixed size. Write operations to tape for REDO-purposes may be done in variable length physical records.

Records in a database are often connected to a number of access paths (sets, search keys). In order to model update operations on records in sufficient detail precise assumptions on the storage structures for records and access paths, their related frequency distributions on values of inverted attributes and the replacement algorithm controlling the system buffers have to be introduced resulting in a wide range of parameters. Since many of these parameters are unknown to the analyst it is hopeless to gain an accurate model for all conceivable cases. Therefore, our goal is to reduce the complexities of operation by introducing appropriate simplifications. Nevertheless, our model should allow an indication of the principal behavior of the proposed concept w. r. t. the log activity.

Two different kinds of transactions performing u (sequential/random) update operations are considered. Every update operation is supposed to change a single page. An altered page has to be written back to disk (before or at least at EOT) causing update operations in the related page table V and bit map MAP. Additionally, an appropriate log action is required for REDO-purposes. A complex update operation on a record connected with several access paths can be described in our model by a number of single page updates.

In order to express the range of an update transaction a page interval (Δs) is introduced. A clustering behavior of a transaction's updates can be characterized by a special cluster factor (c). Uniform probabilities are assumed for the selection of a page to be updated and to be replaced in the system buffers.

Let us restrict our analysis to one segment S and one disk space D. Then, the storage system related parameters are:

- s = number of logical pages in S
- d = number of physical slots in D ($d>s$)
- l = $d-s$ = number of slots for UNDO-logging
- B = size of a block for page table V and bit map MAP
- t = length of an entry in V
- e_B = B/t = number of entries per block
- v = s/e_B = number of blocks for V
- m = $d/(8 \cdot B)$ = number of blocks for MAP
- r = average number of REDO-entries per physical record
- p_P = number of buffers in PB (available for a transaction)
- c_P = cost to write a page to disk
- c_B = cost to write a block to disk
- c_T = cost to write a physical record to tape
- c_L = cost to write an entry to the log file (UNDO)

In order to describe the output costs, the following transaction oriented parameters have to be introduced:

- u = number of updates per transaction
- Δs = update interval of a transaction in number of pages

c = average number of updates per page in case of clustering (c>1)
N_P = number of pages written
N_V = number of page table blocks written
N_M = number of bit map blocks written
N_R = number of REDO-records written

6.1 Cost estimates for a sequential transaction

It is assumed that the transaction performs u updates in an interval of Δs pages where the pages are accessed sequentially in one direction. Hence, the number of pages touched is

$$n_S = \begin{cases} s & \text{for } u \geqslant \Delta s \\ u & \text{for } u < \Delta s \quad \text{(unclustered case)} \\ u/C & \text{for } u < \Delta s \quad \text{(clustered case)} \end{cases}$$

Sequential processing in our model implies that the transaction traverses the interval of pages in one direction. Therefore, an altered page has to be written only once, irrespective of buffer replacement strategy. Hence,

$$N_{PS} = n_S .$$

The n_S pages are allocated to new slots causing updates of some blocks of the page table. Note that the page interval Δs is not aligned with the block boundaries. The expected number of modified blocks to be written back can be calculated by

$$N_{VS} = \left\lfloor \frac{\Delta s}{e_B} \right\rfloor + \frac{2e_B}{2e_B - (\Delta s \bmod e_B)+1} .$$

The estimation of the modified blocks of the bit map assuming a nearest neighbour strategy for the slot allocation can be done using the same arguments. Δb is supposed to be the interval of bits in MAP touched by the slot allocation. Hence,

$$N_{MS} = \left\lfloor \frac{\Delta b}{8B} \right\rfloor + \frac{2 \cdot 8 \cdot B}{2 \cdot 8 \cdot B - (\Delta b \bmod 8B)+1} \quad \text{with } \Delta b = \begin{cases} \frac{\Delta s}{s} \cdot d & \text{for } \frac{n_S}{\Delta s} \leqslant \frac{1}{s} \\ n_S \cdot (\frac{s}{1}+1) & \text{for } \frac{n_S}{\Delta s} > \frac{1}{s} \end{cases}$$

The expense of REDO-logging considering separate indication of BOT and EOT can be expressed by

$$N_{RS} = \begin{cases} \left\lceil \frac{u+2}{r} \right\rceil & \text{for physical/logical entry logging} \\ n_S + 2 & \text{for physical page logging} \end{cases}$$

The resulting cost function for a sequential transaction taking into consideration two explicit write operations for the UNDO-log (BOT+EOT) is

$$C_{OS} = N_{PS} \cdot c_P + N_{SV} \cdot c_B + N_{MS} \cdot c_B + 2 \cdot c_L + N_{RS} \cdot c_T . \qquad (1)$$

6.2 Cost estimates for a random transaction

A transaction performs u updates in an interval of Δs pages choosing every page with equal probability $\frac{1}{\Delta s}$ for every subsequent update operation. Hence, the number of pages touched by the transaction is

$$n_R = \Delta s(1-\frac{1}{\Delta s})^u \approx \Delta s(1-e^{-u/\Delta s}).$$

n_R is the lower bound of write operations because multiple outputs of a referenced page are possible due to the limited number of page buffers. Assuming that a transaction can use p_p page buffers the number of actual write operations can be calculated as follows:

$$N_{PR}=\begin{cases}\Delta s\cdot(1-e^{-u/\Delta s}) & \text{for } u\leqslant u_o\\ \Delta s\cdot(1-e^{-u/\Delta s})+(u-u_o)\cdot(1-\frac{p_p}{\Delta s})\cdot(1-\frac{\Delta s}{u}(1-e^{-u/\Delta s})) & \text{for } u> u_o\end{cases}$$

u_o is the expected number of updates which can be performed without replacing a modified page from the p_p page buffers. Hence, u_o is implicitly given by

$$p_p = \Delta s\cdot(1-e^{-u_o/\Delta s}).$$

The number of modified blocks of V and MAP to be written back onto disk can be calculated using the assumptions of the sequential case. Hence,

$$N_{VR} = N_{VS},$$
$$N_{MR} = N_{MS}.$$

REDO-logging yields the following number of I/O operations:

$$N_{RR}=\begin{cases}\left\lceil\frac{u+2}{r}\right\rceil & \text{for physical/logical entry logging}\\ N_{PR} + 2 & \text{for physical page logging}\end{cases}$$

The resulting cost function for a random transaction is

$$C_{OR}=N_{PR}\cdot c_P+N_{VR}\cdot c_B+N_{MR}\cdot c_B+2\cdot c_L+N_{RR}\cdot c_T. \qquad (2)$$

6.3 Comparison with a conventional log strategy

We are assuming that a hypothetical system is performing physical UNDO-logging driven by the WAL discipline. No matter which kind of storage organization is chosen some sort of administrative data has to be maintained, e. g. the free placement information. The write overhead for this kind of data during normal processing is supposed to be equal to N_V output operations being an extremely conservative estimate w. r. t. some existing systems. Taking into consideration the WAL principle for pages and administrative data, two additional write accesses indicating BOT and EOT for the UNDO-log and the expense of the REDO-log, our cost function for the expected number of output operations for a transaction in the hypothetical system is

$$C_H=2\cdot N_p\cdot c_p+2\cdot N_V\cdot c_B+2\cdot c_L+N_R\cdot c_T. \qquad (3)$$

In order to compare the qualitiy of the log concepts, we compute the fraction of log overhead w. r. t. the entire output costs. By using equation (1) or (2) the following relationship is gained:

$$L_O=(N_M\cdot c_B+2\cdot c_L+N_R\cdot c_T)/C_O. \qquad (4)$$

Here, N_V is considered to be normal output required for administrative data. Equation (3) leads to the following relationship:

$$L_H=(N_P\cdot c_P+N_V\cdot c_B+2\cdot c_L+N_R\cdot c_T)/C_H. \qquad (5)$$

Another kind of measure relating the total output costs of the different log strategies to each other is given by the following qualitiy measure

$$Q=C_O/C_H. \qquad (6)$$

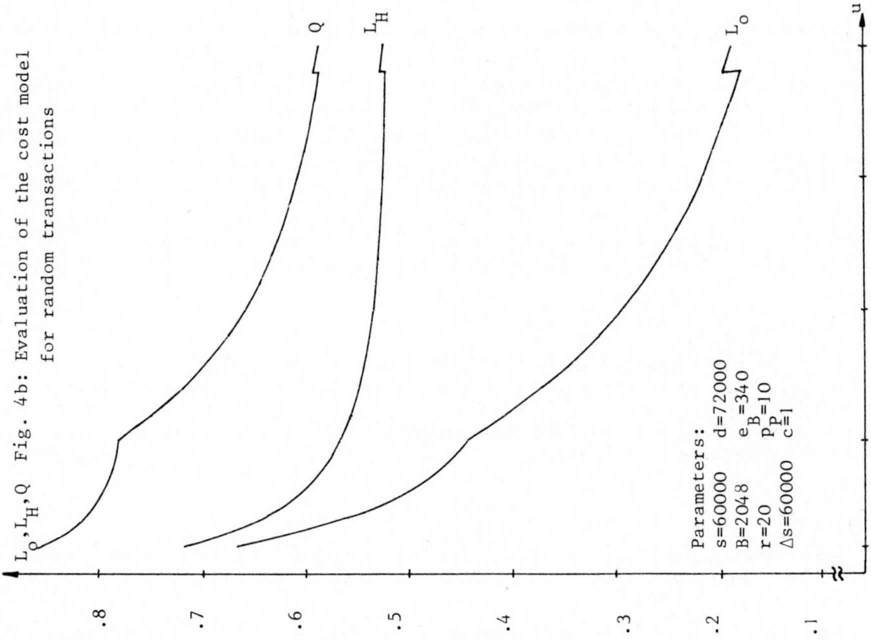

Fig. 4b: Evaluation of the cost model for random transactions

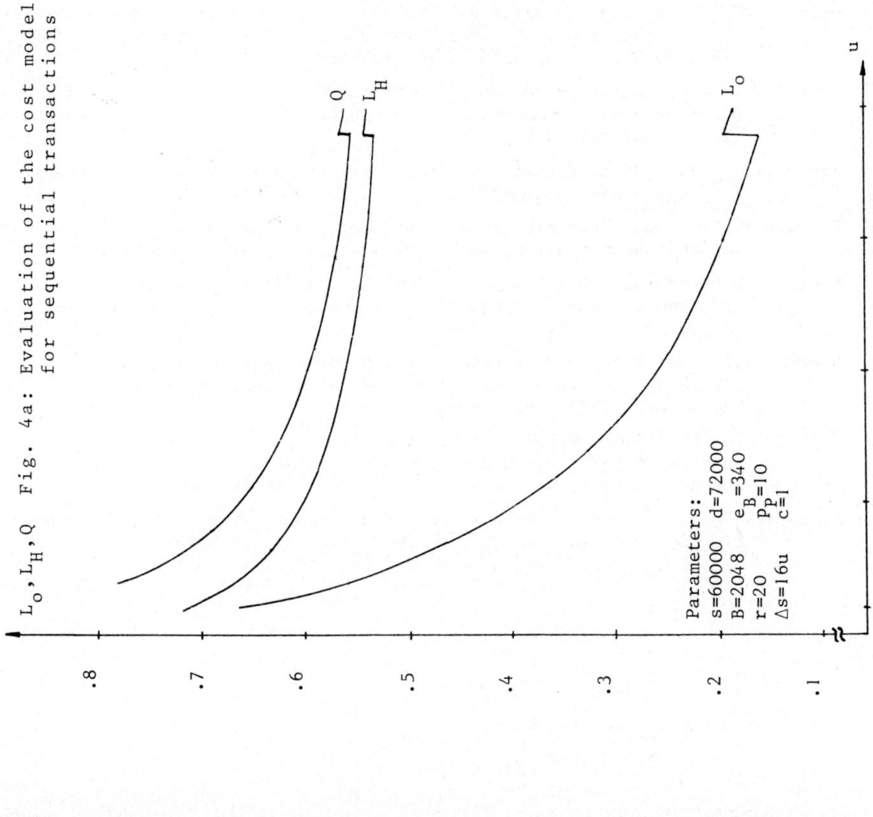

Fig. 4a: Evaluation of the cost model for sequential transactions

The evaluation of our cost model as shown in Fig. 4a and 4b reveals the following facts:

- *The total number of output operations of our concept is substantially smaller than those required by the conventional one. The evaluation of Q indicates that the ratio of* C_O/C_H *is about 1/2 for common update transactions.*
- *The log overhead w.r.t. the total output is decreasing much faster with growing numbers of updates in our concept than in the conventional one (*L_O *versus* L_H*).*
- *There is no significant difference in both concepts between sequential and random transactions in the case of unclustered updates (c=1).*

Acknowledgement

This research was supported in part by the Federal Ministry of Research and Technology (Grant o81 5186) and by the Siemens AG, Division of Data and Information Systems.
We wish to thank the referees for their valuable hints clarifying some issues of our first version of the paper.

References

/1/ Astrahan,M.M. et al.: System R: Relational Approach to Data Base Management, in: ACM Transactions on Database Systems, Vol. 1, No. 2, June 1976, pp. 97-137.

/2/ Davies,C.T.: Data Processing Spheres of Control, in: IBM Systems Journal, Vol. 17, No. 2, 1978, pp. 179-198.

/3/ Eswaran,K.P., Gray,J.N., Lorie,R.A., Traiger,I.L.: The Notions of Consistency and Predicate Locks in a Database System, in: Comm. of the ACM, Vol. 19, No. 11, Nov. 1976, pp. 624-633.

/4/ Gray,J.N.: Notes on Data Base Operating Systems, in: Lecture Notes in Computer Science 6o, Advanced Course on Operating Systems, Springer-Verlag, Berlin, 1978.

/5/ Härder,T.: Entwurfsüberlegungen zur Protokollfunktion eines Datenbanksystems, in: Angewandte Informatik, Vol. 2o, No. 1o, Oct. 1978, pp. 423-431.

/6/ Lorie,R.A.: Physical Integrity in a Large Segmented Database, in: ACM Transactions on Database Systems, Vol. 2, No. 1, March 1977, pp. 91-1o4.

/7/ Ries,D.R., Stonebraker,M.: Effects of Locking Granularity in a Database Management System, in: ACM Transactions on Database Systems, Vol. 2, No. 3, Sept. 1977, pp. 233-246.

/8/ Sherman,S.W., Brice,R.S.: Performance of a Database Manager in a Virtual Memory System, in: ACM Transactions on Database Systems, Vol. 1, No. 4, Dec. 1976, pp. 317-343.

/9/ Severance,D.G., Lohmann,G.M.: Differential Files: Their Application to Maintenance of Large Databases, in: ACM Transactions on Database Systems, Vol. 1, No. 3, Sept. 1976, pp. 256-267.

/1o/ Verhofstad,J.S.M.: Recovery Techniques for Database Systems, in: ACM Computing Surveys, Vol. 1o, No. 2, June 1978, pp. 167-195.

MULTILEVEL ARCHITECTURES OF DATA BASE SYSTEMS

Data Base Architecture, Bracchi/Nijssen, eds.
North-Holland Publishing Company

MULTIMODEL EXTERNAL SCHEMAS FOR CODASYL DATA BASE MANAGEMENT SYSTEMS

Carlo Zaniolo
Sperry Research Center, Sudbury, MA 01776
U.S.A.

ABSTRACT

The problem of designing and supporting relational and hierarchical views over CODASYL network schemas is considered. These include specialized views which only support specific applications and general purpose views which must support general query and updates and preserve the information content of the underlying data base. A solution is proposed based on the integrity constraints on logical data resulting from certain declarations in the CODASYL Data Definition Language. Then a discipline is given to design schemas for better logical data definition, higher data independence and easier mapping to multimodel external schemas. The implication for data independence and efficiency of execution of these views and associated DML are explored.

1. INTRODUCTION

Relational capabilities in a CODASYL Data Base Management System [CODA 73, CODA 78] will bring significant benefits; these include ease of use, data independence and high level Data Manipulation Languages (DML's). The last two features in particular become even more important as data base machines and distributed databases are coming to age.

Also multiple hierarchical views would be highly desirable. Hierarchies have the quality of fitting very naturally the requirements of specific applications. Historically a great number of applications have been developed using hierarchical data organizations. Thus a hierarchical view capability in a CODASYL system could make application development easier, would facilitate user's migration to an integrated data base environment, and promote data independence and compatibility across different data base systems.

Unfortunately CODASYL 78 [CODA 78] despite numerous improvements introduced with respect to CODASYL 73 [CODA 73] is still oblivious to the need for multiple views of data and for high level DML's. A number of critics [FESA 78],[CLER 78] have suggested that the inadequacy of external schema facilities represent the most prominent area in which CODASYL 78 specifications fall short of the guidelines set by the ANSI/X3/SPARC study group on Database Management Systems [ANSI]. In this paper we show that multimodel external schemas are attainable within the framework of CODASYL 78 DDL once a well structured schema design methodology is adopted. We will use the term "view" as a synonym of external schema.

2. RELATIONAL VIEWS OVER EXISTING CODASYL DBMS's

Previous research has proven that it is possible to define relational views over existing CODASYL DBMS's to support general purpose relational DML (both query and update) [JOHN 78a, LARS 78, ZANI 79]. In this section we review the work discussed in [ZANI 79] were we adopted a bottom-up approach by assuming that schema and data base are given and that the relational views are simply added on to the old system thus preserving the exsisting data base and application programs. Further work [GOLD 79] has produced an automatic schema translator which has been applied to a number of exsisting CODASYL 73 schemas with encouraging results.

2.1 The Basic Approach

The term logical data will be used here to denote information of interest to the enterprise world outside the data processing department. Thus logical data will describe "real world" entities, attributes and relationships such as employees, their salaries, their employment history. A relational view of the data base consists of a set of time varying relations representing only logical data [CODD 72, DATE 77]. One or more candidate keys are defined for each relation. These keys specify integrity constraints which the user must respect when modifying the content of the relations by insert delete or update commands. Thus while a relational schema describes only logical data and it is actually designed after the integrity constraints characterizing this data, a CODASYL 73 schema describes four different aspects of data. These concern:

1. logical data and its structure,
2. physical organization of data,
3. data manipulation,
4. privacy of data.

Therefore our basic strategy for designing relational views over network schemas first identifies those declarations of a CODASYL schema which are source of logical data definition, then derives a set of view relations which make logical data on its structure visible while concealing information relating to physical structure and data manipulation (information on privacy may also be part of the view but this topic is outside the scope of this report.) Three objectives are of paramount concern in our view design. These are:

a. Information Preservation: The logical content of the underlying data base must be entirely accessible through the relational view which can therefore support general query and retrieval capabilities.

b. Updatability: This is the property of a view to conform to real data behavior. Updates (i.e. insert, delete and modify requests) supply the critical test for this behavior. Every request which respects the constraints expressed by the view must produce the expected result. Only udates which violate these constraints must be rejected as erroneous.

c. Data Independence. This is a very important and pervasive objective in a DBMS architecture. As we shall see later there are many facets to this objective and different degrees of data independence are practically obtainable with different types of views and DML's. For our relational views we pursue what can be regarded as the ultimate level of data independence: complete visibility of logical data and their structure combined with invisibility of implementation dependent details. Applications written against these views may still depend on the persistence of the logical relationships used but not on the invariance of the underlying implementation.

2.2 Z-Diagrams

A first source of logical data definition in a CODASYL schema is the description of record types and of the data items making up these records. A second source is the association between owner and member records established by the various set types in the schema. The nature of this association depends on whether this set was declared as (insertion is) MANUAL or AUTOMATIC and (retention is) MANDATORY or OPTIONAL. A third source is the declaration of certain data item combinations to be DUPLICATES NOT ALLOWED (DNA) in the location mode of a record. This establishes that no two record occurrences can have the same value for a DNA combination at any

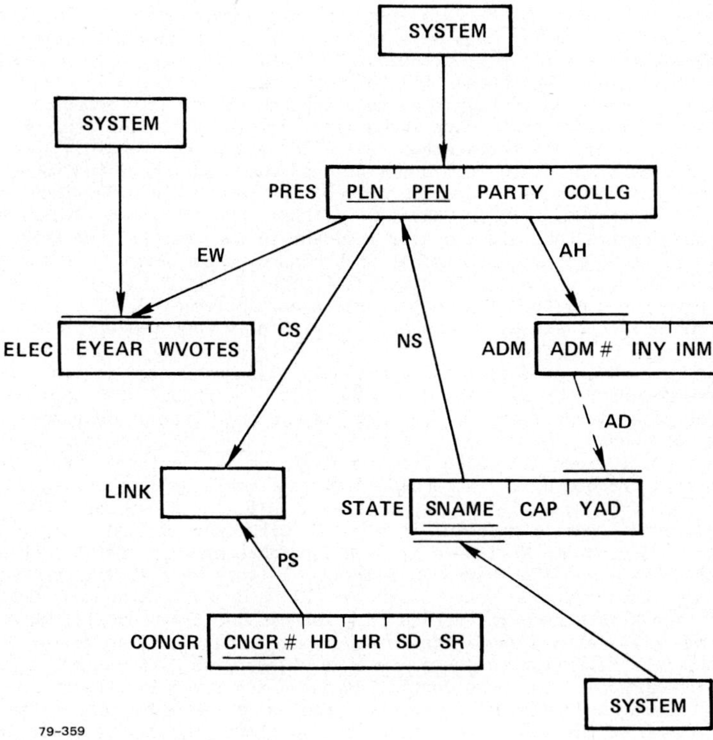

79-359

LEGEND

PRES: president's record

- PLN: president's last name
- PFN: president's first name
- PARTY: president's party
- COLLG: president's college

ADM: administration record

- ADM#: administration number (relative to a given president)
- INY: administration inauguration year
- INM: administration inauguration month
- IND: administration inauguration day

STATE: state record

- SNAME: state name
- CAP: state capital
- YAD: year admitted (into the U.S.A.)

ELEC: election record

- EYEAR: election year
- WVOTES: election winner's votes

CONGR: congress record

- CNGR: congress number
- HD: house democrats
- HR: house republicans
- SD: senate democrats
- SR: senate republicans

LINK: link record

- EW: election won set
- CS: congress served set
- PS: president served set
- NS: native son set
- AH: administration headed set
- AD: admitted during set

FIG. 1 Presidential Data Base.

given time. A fourth source are the DNA declaration for sets. These establish that no two member records in the same occurrence of a DNA set have identical value for the specified combinations of data items in the member record. In order to visualize these four sources of data definition we have enriched the current data structure diagrams to a form called Z-diagrams [ZANI 79]. Figure 1 uses this representation to define the schema for the data base discussed in [TAYL 76]. Rectangular contours are used to represent records; the record name appears next to the contour. The (elementary) data items are displayed inside the contour. AUTOMATIC MANDATORY sets are represented by solid arcs, the remaining sets are represented by dashed arcs. Data item combinations which are specified DUPLICATES NOT ALLOWED (DNA) in the location location mode of the record are underlined inside the contour. For instance, this is the case of PLN, PFN of record PRES. A bar outside a contour denotes that all the sets incident to the bar are specified with the option DNA for the data item combination spanned by the bar. For instance, ADM# was declared DNA for set AH. For simplicity some of the data items appearing in [TAYL 76] have been omitted and names have been abbreviated. The structural complexity of the original example, however, is faithfully captured by Figure 1.

The effect of the DNA declarations previously discussed is to establish a one-to-one correspondence between the data base key of a record type and certain combinations of data items, taken from this record and its predecessors (i.e. owners, owners of owners, and so on), which we call synonyms. Formally synonyms can be defined as follows. A data item combination X, declared DNA for the location mode of a record R, is a candidate synonym for the database key of R, denoted @R. Also X is a candidate synonym for @R if X is declared DNA on a singular (SYSTEM-owned) set. Moreover if a set S with owner R1 and member R2 is declared DNA on a combination X2, where X1 is a candidate synonym for R1, then the union of X1 and X2 is a candidate synonym for @R2. In this case X1 will be said to be a predecessor synonym for the union of X1 and X2. Synonyms must be non-redundant thus X is a synonym for @R if X is candidate synonym for @R and no proper subset of X is also a candidate synonym. If the set S above is MANUAL and/or OPTIONAL the X is called a pseudo-synonym. Otherwise X is called a proper synonym. The synonyms for our presidential database are given in figure 2. Each node of this hierarchy (except the root) denotes a synonym: the data item combination is given at the left of the node, the corresponding database key at the right of the node. Solid edges lead to proper synonyms and dashed edges to pseudo-synonyms. A database key may have more than one synonym (proper or otherwise). E.g. for @STATE there is the proper synonym SNAME and then there is (PLN, PFN, ADM#, YAD). This record is a pseudo-synonym since set AD is not an AUTOMATIC MANDATORY set; thus in correspondence to a given value of @STATE the values of ADM# and PLN, PFN may be missing. Moreover many ownerless occurrences of STATE can exist and share the same value for YAD.

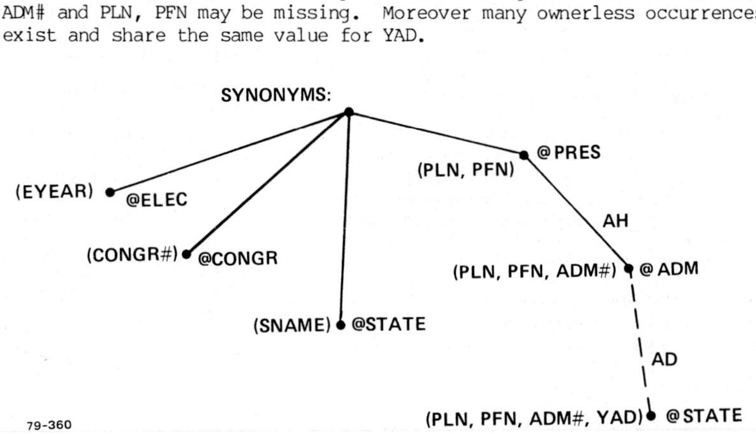

FIG. 2 The synonym structure of the Presidential Data Base Schema.

2.3 View Design

The view design algorithm is driven by the synonym structure of the original schema. A relation is generated for each record type of the schema. The relation corresponding to a record type R has as attributes:

1. the data items of R, plus
2. for each non-singular set owning R a proper synonym for the database key of the owner record (when more than one such synonym exists a choice can be made subject to conditions to be discussed later).

Figure 3 shows the set of relations corresponding to the schema of figure 1. For simplicity each relation is named after the corresponding record type in the schema. As shown in [ZANI 79] this set of relations preserves the logical information of the underlying database and schema both with respect to content and structure. In a CODASYL system both sets and records contain logical information. Each relation captures the information corresponding to a schema record by including all its data items; moreover by including a synonym for each of its owner records it captures the information associated with its owner sets. Thus the view relations cut across record boundaries to capture logically related data items. For instance in the STATE relation of figure 3 we find the data items from the STATE record (SNAME, CAP, YAD), respectively denoting the name, the capital and the admission year for a state, plus the data items PLN, PFN, and ADM# from its predecessor records denoting the president name and the administration under which the state was admitted.

The constraints on logical data resulting from the underlying schema declarations are captured and visualized by the relational view using two simple constructs. One is the allowable null patterns the other the (candidate) keys of each relation. The allowable null patterns specify which attribute combinations are allowed to have a null (undefined) value. A combination Y of attributes of R is is an (allowable) null pattern for R, when R can contain tuples where every Y-attribute is null and every other attribute is not null. Moreover, if no proper subset of Y is a null pattern then Y is said to be minimal. Now, Y is a minimal null pattern for a view relation R if it is a synonym for the data base key of a record owning R in a set which is MANUAL and/or OPTIONAL. Thus every combination migrated along a dashed arc in the Z-diagram becomes a minimal null pattern. Thus (PLN, PFN, ADM#) is a minimal null pattern for STATE in figure 3. In our figures minimal null

PRES (PLN, PFN, PARTY COLLG, SNAME)

ADM (PLN, PFN, ADM#, INY, INM, IND)

STATE (SNAME, CAP, YAD, PLN, PFN, ADM#)
x x x - - -

ELEC (EYEAR, WVOTES, PLN, PFN)

LINK (PLN, PFN, CNGR#)

CONGR (CNGR#, HD, HR, SD, SR)

FIG. 3 The relational view for the Presidential Data Base of Fig. 1.

patterns are described by rows where "x" stands for any non-null value and "-" for the null value. Also every set DNA combination with the NULL ALLOWED phrase attached becomes a minimal null pattern. The allowable null patterns of our view relations are either minimal or a union of minimal patterns. A tuple will be called fully defined if it contains no null value.

One or more keys are defined for each relation in the view. In our figures they are denoted by suitably underlining the attributes comprising the key. Different styles of underlining are used to denote distinct keys within the same relation. Formally a combination X of attributes of R is a candidate key for R if the following two conditions are satisfied:

(1) Uniqueness Constraint: At any instant in time there is at most one tuple of R having a given fully defined value for X,

(2) Minimality: property (1) does not hold for any proper subset of X.

Thus a key uniquely and irredundantly identifies the tuples of a relation; however, two or more tuples of a relation can share the same key value if this is not fully defined. Keys whose value is always fully defined (i.e. they do not intersect any allowable null pattern) will be called proper keys; the other will be called pseudo-keys. All keys in figure 3 are proper, except for (PLN, PFN, ADM#, YEAR). Thus while a given president and administration could at most have admitted one state per year, any number of states could have been admitted on the same year under a missing (null) president and administration; these could for instance be the original thirteen states that started the Union.

In addition to the uniqueness constraint candidate keys establish the foreign key constraint. This was first introduced by researchers in the area of Database Abstraction and Aggregation [SMIT 77]. These workers suggest that a candidate key X should be regarded as a unique identifier of a conceptual object, which is defined and described by the relation, say R1, where X appears as key. Instances of values of X in any other relation, say R2, should be interpreted as references to the conceptual object described and defined in R1. Thus making a reference from R2 to an object not defined in R1 must be regarded as conceptually incorrect. If one wants to refer in R2 to a undefined R1-object he must do so by using a null X-value. Formally therefore:

Foreign Key Constraint: If a key X of relation R1 is also an attribute combination of relation R2 then every X-value appearing in R2 must also appear in R1 (i.e. the X-projection for R2 must be a subset of the X-projection of R1).

Since our relations obey the foreign key constraint they are analogous to the "well defined relations" introduced in [SMIT 77] in order to make the relational data model more suitable for data base abstraction and aggregation. This analogy was previously noted in [JOHN 78a]. Thus in figure 3 a president name (PLN, PFN) cannot appear in LINK, ELEC, ADM or STATE unless it also appears in PRES.

If X is an attribute combination for the view relation R, and X is a proper synonym or a pseudo-synonym for @R, then X is respectively a proper key or a pseudo-key for R. Indeed for each fully defined value of X there exists at most one occurrence of record R, thus a unique value for the data items in this record and its predecessors. In the schema of figure 1 no synonym exists for @LINK. The semantics of the application at hand suggests that multiple LINK records connecting the same pair of PRES and CONGR records are not meaningful and should not occur. Therefore in constructing relational views over the given schema of figure 1 one can treat (PLN, PFN, CNGR#) as a de facto synonym and use it as the key for the LINK relation of figure 3. However, a better solution is to enforce this integrity constraint through schema declarations. This is only achievable by using the DNA declarations in conjunction with SOURCE data items. Thus e.g. one can include in LINK a SOURCE data item CNGR# from CONGR and then declare set CS DNA on CNGR#.

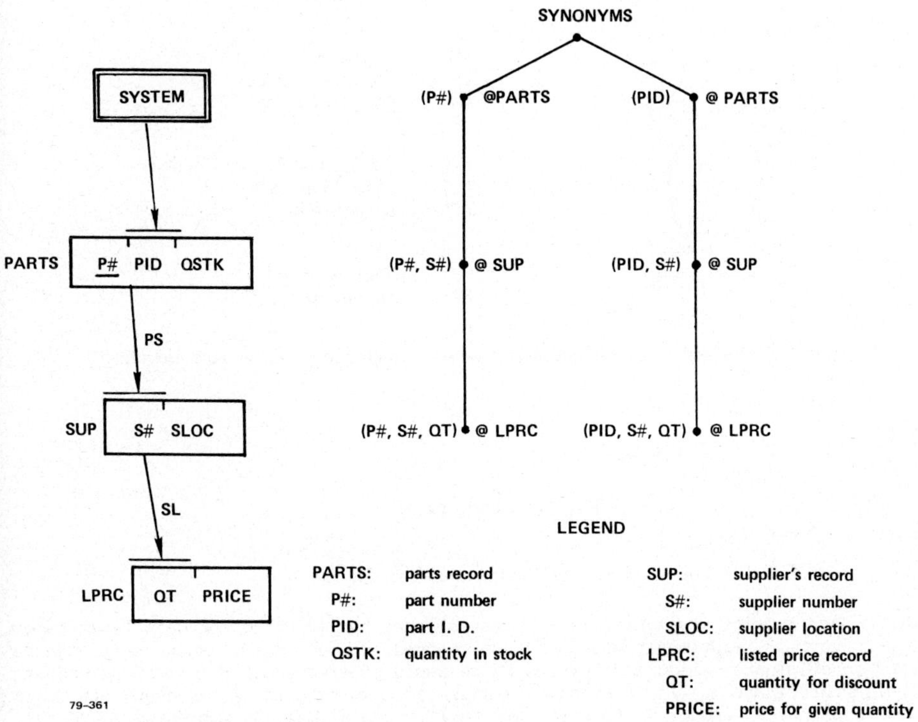

FIG. 4 Parts, their suppliers and listed price under a quantity-discount policy.

A: PARTS (P#, PID, QSTK)
B1: SUP (P#, S#, SLOC)
C1: LPRC (P#, S#, QT, PRICE)

A: PARTS (P#, PID, QSTK)
B2: SUP (PID, S#, SLOC)
C2: LPRC (PID, S#, QT, PRICE)

FIG. 5 Two updatable views for the schema of Fig. 4.

Therefore the availability of SOURCE items, not offered by many existing implementations, will greatly enhance the logical definition capabilities of CODASYL DDL. Section 3 of this paper will further expand on this topic.

Let us discuss now view design for schemas, such as the one in figure 4, where the data base key of some record has more than one proper synonym. As previously discussed the attribute set of a relation Rl, for each set S owning Rl, includes a proper synonym for @R2, where R2 denotes the owner of S. If @R2 has more than one proper synonym the one used must be contained in (thus a key of) relation R2. The two relational views of figure 5 satisfy this condition. Instead a view consisting of relations A, Bl and C2 would not satisfy it since (PID, S#) is a synonym of @SUP which is not a key for Bl. Thus it can not be used in relation LPRC. Indeed such a view would not be updatable since the fact that (PID, S#) is a foreign key in LPRC and the associated integrity constraint would be hidden from the user.

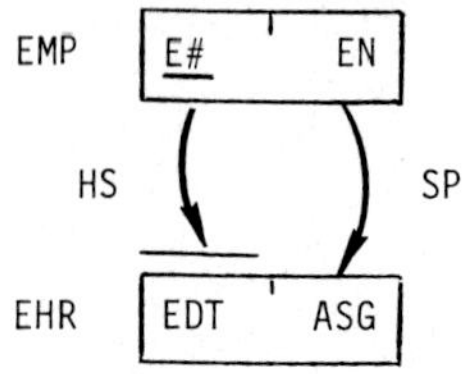

Legend

EMP: employee record
E#: employee number
EN: employee name

EHR: employee history record
EDT: effective date
ASG: assignment

HS: history set
SP: supervisor set

FIG. 6 Employees, their previous assignments and their supervisors at each assignment.

EMP (E#, EN)

EHR (E#.HS, EDT, ASG, E#.SP)

FIG. 7 The relational view for the schema of Fig. 6.

Since the foreign key constraint is established by matching the data item names across various relations these cannot be changed independently. Role names can be used to eliminate naming ambiguities which would otherwise occur in schemas such as the one of figure 6. If a synonym is migrated down to a record R along its owner set S then the use of S as role name always avoids naming ambiguity [GOLD 79]. Moreover there exists a natural correspondence between the CODASYL set construct and the relational role construct [JOHN 76, LARS 78]. As shown in figure 7 the role name is attached to the data item name following a dot.

2.4 Discussion

The two main problems in supporting relational DML on our view relations are (1) correctness and (2) efficiency. Update requests (i.e. insert, delete and modify operations) supply the critical test for correctness. The translation of these requests must be correct in the sense that they affect the view content exactly as the user requested (of course excluding concurrent updates by other users). For certain views however correct translation is impossible [PAOL 77],[DAYA 78]. For instance say that the view of figure 5 is changed by moving the attribute QSTK from A to B1. The relation,

SUP'(P#, S#, QSTK, SLOC) (2.1)

so obtained presents update anomalies since the functional dependency of QSTK on S# is now hidden to the user [CODD 72, DATE 77]. Thus a request such as "change the QSTK value in the tuple of SUP' identified by its key value (p1, s1)" cannot be translated correctly. Indeed if part p1 appears in many tuples of SUP' (i.e. p1 is supplied by many suppliers) and a change is made in the QSTK value of the unique occurrence of the PARTS record identified by a P# value of p1 then all these tuples will be affected. Then the resulting effect upon the view content is different from what the user requested. Alternatively the policy could be chosen of disallowing execution of this update request by returning an error message to the user. This also would come as a surprise to the user since his request is seemingly correct in terms of the view. In either case the user cannot understand and/or predict the result of his DML execution without understanding the schema and, possibly, the behavior of the view support subsystem. In brief, the view would fail to insulate the user from the complexity of the underlying system.

At the contrary the views produced by our design algorithm are updatable since every integrity constraint enforced by the schema (thus expressed in the Z-diagram) is now captured by keys and null patterns of the view [ZANI 79]. Thus for every update request, which is correct in terms of the view, there exsists a sequence of low level DML commands (executable say against a COBOL or a PL/I subschema) which produces exactly the expected results. Updatability is the main quality which distinguishes these views from other relational views over network schemas which have been proposed in the past [ADIB 78, ZANI 77].

A number of implicit assumptions were made in applying the view design algorithm (e.g. we have assumed that repeating groups and multi-member sets do not occur and that every owner record has a proper synonym). The approach previously discussed is robust since it can be extended to overcome these restrictions [ZANI 79]. In some cases, however, a price must be paid for these extensions since they produce relations which are more complex, and contain some implementation dependent constructs. Thus they supply a reasonable solution only in a situation where a CODASYL 73 schema and data base are given and one wants to add relational capabilities without modifying them. While this is certainly a meaningful framework in the short term perspective, since it saves the cost of data base conversion and program translation, it is reasonable to assume that new installations and the evolution of present ones will bring about a scenario where CODASYL database schemas are designed for better data independence and support for multiple views. In the next section we present a discipline for schema design to obtain these objectives. In consonance with such a forward-looking perspective we use the framework of '78 DDL [CODA 78] which, most likely, will guide future developments of CODASYL implementations. The problem of efficient execution of high level DML will be discussed in that context.

3. WELL STRUCTURED SCHEMAS

The CODASYL 78 DDL contains a number of features which provide for better and more uniform definition of structure of logical data. Most useful in this regard are:

1. The capability of specifying that the value of a data item in a record is to be the same as the value of a data item in some owner record of it, if one exists otherwise this value is null, by using the SOURCE clause in this member record declaration. When a data item A of record R is specified SOURCE IS A' OF OWNER OF S (where A' is a data item in the S-owner R') then we will say that <u>A is A' migrated along S from R' to R</u>.

2. The capability of specifying any number of combinations of a record to be keys for this record. Only keys declared with the option DUPLICATES NOT ALLOWED (DNA) are of logical significance. A <u>DNA</u> key for record R wil be called <u>minimal</u> if no smaller subset of it is also a DNA key for R. A DNA key will be called a <u>pseudo-key</u> if it contains data items migrated along a set declared INSERTION IS MANUAL and/or RETENTION IS OPTIONAL, otherwise it is called a <u>proper key</u>.

The combined use of migrated data items and DNA keys provides a simple and powerful vehicle for logical data definition. For each record R in the schema the designer will migrate down data items from its predecessors as required to construct a proper synonym combination for @R, then he declares this combination to be a DNA key for R. Figure 8, for instance, shows how this technique can be applied to our Presidential Data Base. In our diagrams we underline the DNA keys, as usual. Moreover if the data items of a DNA key X are migrated along a set S, then the initial end point of the arc representing S will be positioned in correspondence to the X-underlining. For simplicity we assume here that no renaming of migrated data items occurs except for the addition of role names required to avoid ambiguities.

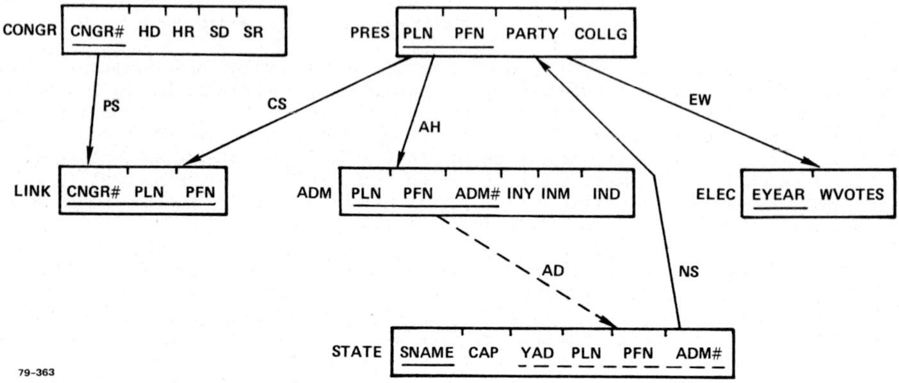

FIG. 8 A well-structured, minimally migrated schema for the Presidential Data Base.

For instance in figure 8 the proper keys of PRES and CONGR were migrated down to their common member LINK to form a proper key for this record. This specifies that at the most one LINK occurrence exists for any given congress-president pair. The symmetry of this solution makes it preferable over the alternative approach, discussed in the previous section, of migrating down the data base key of one owner along one set and declare a DNA on the other set. Again we must remember that the PLN, PFN and CNGR# fields need not be physically stored in the actual LINK records; thus it is possible to have a transition from a schema such as the one in figure 1 to the one of figure 8 without data base conversion. [JOHN 78a, JOHN 78b, LARS 78] applied transformations based on this strategy to CODASYL 78 schemas and subschemas to obtain informationally equivalent schemas and/or subschemas which exhibit the salient properties of both network and relational model. Three degrees of key migration where there discussed: 1) none at all, 2) value-based --- migration sufficient to result in identification of all tenants of a set occurrence by common value of corresponding items, and non-membership in any set occurence by the null value 3) (possibly additional) migration so that each record contains a DNA record key which is the concatenation of DNA record keys and DNA set keys corresponding to each record-set path via which occurrences of the record may uniquely be identified by value. Previous authors also discuss concepts related to value-based sets [WHIT 74, KALI 76]. However the logical structures obtainable using source data items and DNA keys exceed the ones obtainable without them (even if set DNA declarations are used). A first example of this is supplied by plex (multiply owned) records such as LINK in figure 8. A second example is supplied by figure 9. This schema

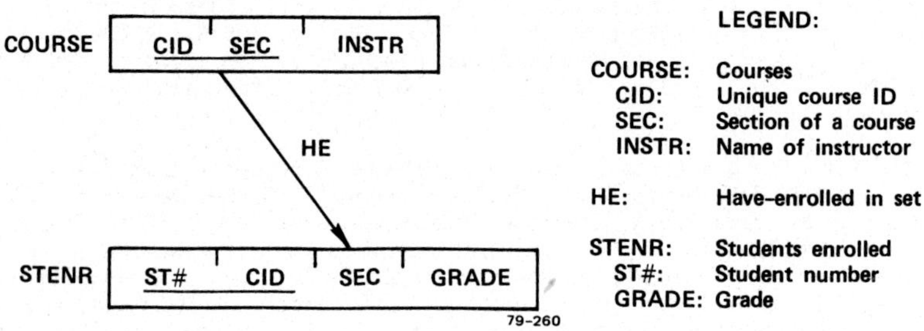

FIG. 9 Course enrollment and grades for a school term.

specifies that for each class (i.e. a course and a section) there is at the most one instructor (INSTR). It also specifies that a student cannot enroll in two different sections of the same course. Thus there is at most one section (SEC) and grade (GRADE) for each pair (ST#, CID). The integrity constraints specified by this schema cannot be expressed without the use of migrated data items (even when DNA on sets are used). Thus there is a need for a new discipline for schema design which exploits these more powerful data definition capabilities. A solution to this problem is proposed in the next section.

3.1 Schema Design

CODASYL 78 supplies a powerful framework for logical data definition. Unfortunately there is a great risk in power for, if not used with discipline, it leads to complexity, redundancy, inconsistency and inefficiency. A clear example of such problems can be found in our presidential data base taken from [TAYL 76] where EYEAR is declared DNA both in a singular set and in set EW. The second DNA is redundant and source of inefficiency. Its only effect is to slow down DML execution since it causes the system to check the second condition along with the first stronger one when executing an update operation. Similar considerations can be made for the record STATE where SNAME is declared DNA on a singular set after being specified DNA in the location clause. Our experience with a number of schemas has shown that this sort of problems become even more serious and frequent as we move from this textbook examples to real life schemas. Thus there is a strong need for better logical schema design in the framework of CODASYL DDL. The use of migrated data items can also be a source of potential problems. As we discussed in section 2.4 an undisciplined migration of data items from owners to members may result in an anomalous update behavior marked by spurious side effects. A a designer must to avoid these problems by supplying the user with a schema which is well behaved and simple to comprehend. Finally we want the schema to be well suited for supporting multiple external views in general and relational views in particular. For the purpose of avoiding the problems discussed above and supplying a better framework for multiple view support we propose the notion of well structured schemas. A CODASYL 78 schema is well structured when the following conditions are satisfied:

(1) One or more DNA keys are declared for each record type in the schema and,
  a. every such key is minimal,
  b. one at least of these keys is proper.
(2) for each set S the data item combination migrated along S must be a subset, proper or otherwise, of a proper key of the owner record of S.
(3) for every set S neither the combination migrated along S nor a subset of it is a DNA key for the member record of S.

For simplicity we assume that no DNA option is used in set declarations: their function in defining constraints on logical data is now performed by DNA keys combined with migrated data items.

Condition (1)a. forbids redundant DNA declarations. Condition (1)b. ensures that the occurrence of every record in the data base is content-addressable on the basis of the values of its data items and the ones migrated from its predecessors. Condition (2) allows the designer to choose for each set S a proper DNA key of the owner record and then to migrate down to the member record either all or some or none of the data items of this key (role names may be appended to the migrated data items as needed to avoid name ambiguities). There are two solutions of interest. In one a whole proper key of the owner is migrated down to the member for each (non-singular) set in the schema; schemas so designed will be called fully migrated. In the other only those items which participate in some DNA key for the member record are migrated (i.e. as needed to obtain complete definition of logical constraints); schemas so designed will be called minimally migrated. The well structured schema of figure 8 is minimally migrated. The one of figure 9 is fully migrated. A minimally migrated schema can be obtained by removing SEC from STENR.

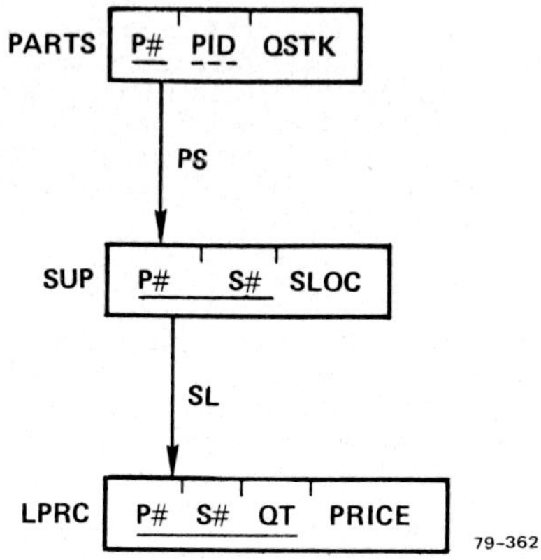

FIG. 10 A well-structured version of the schema of Fig. 4.

The transformations which lead from a fully migrated into a minimally migrated schema and vice-versa are obvious. Figure 10 shows a well structured schema for the example of figure 4. This schema is both fully and minimally migrated.

Condition (3), combined with (2), ensures that the corresponding relational views have important normal form properties that we discuss later. Moreover without this condition two records in the schema could have the same DNA key (either a record could have the same key as its predecessor or two successors of the same record could have the same key). Also if (3) is removed one could, for instance, declare SEC alone to be a DNA key for STENR, thus contradicting the assumption that (CID, SEC) is a minimal key for COURSE.

When more than one proper key exists for a given record, the designer can migrate down to the member records any of them; (different keys can be migrated down to different members). For the schema of figure 10, for instance, one could have chosen to migrate PID instead of P#. Thus this schema can be changed into an equivalent one by simply replacing P# in SUP and LPRC by PID. The two schemas are equivalent in the sense that they define the same semantic constraints. In general, given a well-structured schema W1 where some owner records have multiple proper keys the following transformation can be used to transform W1 into an equivalent schema W2 (a related transormation called "key switch" was proposed in [LARS 78] using the set selection construct):

Equivalence Transformation Step: If the following conditions are satisfied,

a. W1 contains a record R with two proper keys X1 and X2,
b. R owns a set S1 along which X1 was migrated to the member record R1,
c. every DNA key in R1 and its successors either contains or does not intersect X1,

then consider every set S such that (1) S is either S1 or a successor of S1 and (2) a combination $Y \supseteq X1$ has been migrated along S. For each such S replace the combination Y in the member record of S, say R2, by $(Y - X1) \cup X2$ (the symbols "$\cup$" and "$-$" respectively denote set union and set difference.) Moreover if Z is a key for R2 the $(Z - X1) \cup X2$ becomes a key for R2.

Every schema W2 obtained from W1 by the equivalence transformation step just described is still well formed and equivalent to W1 as it defines the same integrity constraints on data. In general two minimally migrated or fully migrated

schemas will be said to be equivalent if there is a sequence of equivalence transformation steps leading from one to the other. Two schemas are equivalent when their fully migrated or minimally migrated versions are equivalent.
Note the importance of condition c. for the equivalence transformation. For instance if the COURSE record in figure 9 has a second proper key, say CLASS#, this cannot replace the (CID,SEC) pair in STENR since the resulting schema would not be equivalent (indeed the functional dependency (ST#,CID) → SEC would be lost).

3.2 Relational Views

The set of relations corresponding to a fully migrated well structured schema W contain a relation R for each record type R in W, where:

1. the attribute set of relation R consists of the data items of record R,

2. the keys of relation R are the DNA keys of record R,

3. for each MANUAL and /or OTIONAL set S owning record R there is a minimal null pattern X for relation R, where X denotes the attributes migrated along S.

Given a well structured schema W each set of relations corresponding to a fully migrated schema equivalent to W supplies an information-preserving updatable view over W. The relational view for our schema of figure 9 is given in figure 11. The relational views for schemas of figures 8 and 10 are the ones of figures 3 and 5. It is also interesting to note that these relational views over well structured schemas are Fourth Normal Form [FAGI 77] (assuming that all tuples are fully defined since a definition of this normal form in the presence of null values is not available). Thus they avoid the various anomalies and problems which are connected with the presence of multidependencies [ZANI 76], [FAGI 77]. Fully migrated schemas are a subclass of the valued-based schemas discussed in [JOHN 78b, LARS 78]. Clearly each view corresponding to a value-based schema is information preserving. However a migration of data items beyond those comprising a proper key (thus in violation of well-structure condition (2)) may result in the loss of the normal form and updatability properties previously discussed.

The relational views thus derived can supply the user with a congenial interface to support high-level relational DML's such as SEQUEL or Query by Example [DATE 77]. Using such languages the user may then define other relational views over these basic ones (e.g. relation 2.1 could have been derived in this way.) In general, however, these views will not preserve the information content of the underlying data base nor support update requests correctly [DAYA 78]. Thus they must be classified as specialized views.

Regarding the problem of supporting high level DML on these views, we note that since access paths and physical organization of data are invisible in the view, responsibility for efficient execution would be taken over by the view support subsystem. This must take into account the characteristics of the requested transactions and the organization of the underlying data base to dynamically select access paths and perform aggregate operations to optimize DML execution. An important question yet unresolved is how efficient this execution can be and in particular how the execution cost for a query on the view compares against the execution cost of (a) the same query on a truly relational data base system and (b) an equivalent application program written against, say, a COBOL subschema.

{ COURSE (<u>CID</u>, SEC, INSTR)
  STENR (<u>ST#, CID</u>, SEC, GRADE)

FIG. 11 The relational view corresponding to schema of Fig. 9.

(a) CODASYL 73 and even more CODASYL 78 include provision for a powerful range of storage structures and access methods. They are comparable with the ones used by various relational data base implementations, including some of the more sophisticated ones. For instance the CODASYL framework provides for clustering, indexing and linking of records; as described in [ASTR 76] these are the basic storage organizations provided by system R. This similiarity of strorage structures suggests that high level DML on view relations may execute as efficiently in a CODASYL system as in a truly relational system.

(b) An answer to this second question clearly depends on how sophisticated the query-optimization subsystem is. First of all this system must be capable of recognizing which joins of the given query are supported by the underlying sets in the schema. For instance say that a query formulated against the view of figure 3 requires the join of PRES, LINK and CONGR (possibly along with some restrictions and projections). Then the optimization subsystem must be able to recognize, as any COBOL programmer would, that this join can simply be implemented as a navigation through the sets CS and PS. The COBOL programmer would also decide from which record to start his navigation (this record will be called the root record). He may start from the PRES record then, for each such record occurrence, find all its LINK members, then for each such a member find its CONGR owner. Or he can start from CONGR and then visit LINK and PRES. Or he could choose LINK as the root and then visit the PRES and CONGR records. A choice between the different navigation strategies is dictated by their relative cost which is usually measured by the number of page faults generated. This in turn depends on the physical clustering between owners and members, on the availability of indexes and owner pointers, in brief on data base characteristics defined by schema declarations which we abstracted from in building our relational views. One may conjecture that a sophisticated optimization subsystem having access to all this information can perform in this area as well as the COBOL programmer. Moreover, there are cases in which the DML support subsystem can actually outperform the application programmer by using techniques which are too complex for the every day programmer.

The programmer however may hold an edge over the view support subsystem because of his knowledge of the real world. For instance a programmer will probably know that a condition on STATE such as "YAD = 1951" is much more selective than a condition on PRES such as "PARTY=democratic". It is hard for the view support subsystem to factor in this sort of information despite its importance in selecting efficient access paths and execution strategies. When dictionaries containing information about sets and record population and other data base statistics will be maintained, information previously available only to the programmer can then be used by the view support subsystem as well. Eventually the execution cost for applications using high level DML on relational views may become comparable with the cost of applications using procedural languages on network subschemas.

These views with their high level DML offer significant advantages with respect to data independence. An application program written against a network subschema cristalizes a particular choice of access path. When the underlying storage schema is changed this access path may become very inefficient to use. Thus the performance of this application program may be dramatically compromized although, if the schema is unchanged, it still runs correctly. For instance in the previous example, involving a navigation through sets CS and PS, a change in owner pointers or indexes for these sets may invalidate the programmer's previous choice. However applications using high level DML on relational views do not embody any choice of access path. As a given execution strategy becomes inefficient the view support subsystem will choose another one. Thus the performance of the application may still suffers but not as severely as in the previous case. Likewise when the storage schema is changed to provide a better access path navigational DML programs must be rewritten to take advantage of it. Not so for programs written in high level DML against the relational views. Thus while the three schema level architecture of CODASYL 78 has the potential for better data independence much of this potential is realized only when high level DML against relational views is used.

4. HIERARCHICAL VIEWS

In this section we discuss the problem of designing hierarchical views over network schemas both as specialized and general purpose views. In the next section we present an approach which ensures simple DML mapping and efficient execution.

4.1 Access Structures

The style of data retrieval and manipulation most naturally supported by hierarchical data base systems is the one where access begins at the top (the root of the hierarchy) and proceeds downward from a parent to its children. Hierarchical views based on the concept of access structure support very effectively this simple style of data processing. Access structures can be viewed as a generalization of the well known concept of access paths. Formally an access structure over a network schema is a rooted unordered tree whose nodes and directed arcs respectively denote records and sets of the schema. In an access structure an arc S with initial endpoint A and final end point B denotes the set S with owner A and member B. Figure 12 shows an access structure over the presidential data base schema (the top node denotes the root of the tree.) Note that a record name, e.g. STATE in figure 12, may appear more than once in a access structure. Set names may also appear more than once. There is a unique path leading from the root node to every other node. An arc will be called a member arc if its initial end point is in the path leading from the root to its terminal end point. It is called an owner arc otherwise. In figure 12 the arcs labeled CS, AH and AD are member arcs while the ones labeled NS and PS are owner arcs.

An access structure can be transformed into a hierarchical view by eliminating the owner arcs. Each owner arc S, with initial end point R1 and terminal end point R0, is simply replaced by a node (R0, R1.S). Every arc connected to either node R0 or node R1 is then connected to the new node (R0, R1.S). Elimination of the owner arcs takes place in a top-down fashion, i.e. arcs which are closer to the root are eliminated first. After the elimination of the various owner arcs the structure reduces to a rooted tree where all the arcs are member arcs and the nodes have the form (R0, R1.S1,...,Rn.Sn) where R0 and R1 are respectively the member and the owner of S1, R1 and R2 denote the member and the owner of S2,...and so on. Since all the sets are member sets the arrowheads on arcs become redundant and are eliminated. We refer to the graphs so obtained as reduced access structures.

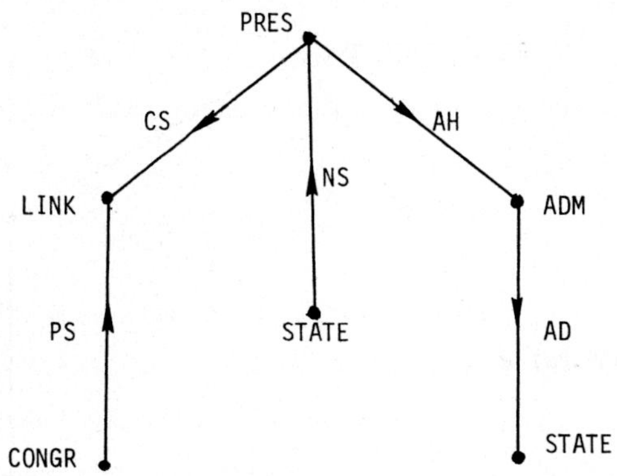

FIG. 12 An access structure on the Presidential Data Base Schema of Fig. 9.

Figure 13 shows the reduced access structure for figure 12. Finally the reduced access structure is transformed into a hierarchical view by replacing each node (R0, R1.S1,...,Rn.Sn) by a record R constructed as follows:

(1) eliminate from each record Rj, $0 \leq j \leq n-1$, the data items migrated along Si, i=j+1.

(2) if this node is connected to its parent by an arc labeled S eliminate from R0 the data items migrated along S.

(3) every remaining data items in R0, R1,...,Rn becomes a distinct field of R (roles names will be added as needed to ensure that field names are unique within R).

Thus R contains all the data items of R0, R1,...,Rn except for possible duplicates among these records or between R and its parent record. The hierarchy defined by the access structure of figure 12, over the schema of figure 8, has as root a record with fields the data items form PRES and STATE i.e. (PLN, PFN, PARTY, COLLG, SNAME, CAP, YAD, PLN.NS, PFN.NS, ADM#.NS). Note that PLN and PFN occur twice since for each president we also find the president who admitted to the Union the home state of that president. The record corresponding to the node (LINK, CONGR.PS) has as fields the data items of record CONGR in figure 8. The records corresponding to ADM and STATE have as fields the data items of the corresponding records in figure 8 with the respective exception of (PLN, PFN) and (PLN, PFN, ADM#). Not all these attributes need to appear in the final view since the user will be given the option of dropping those fields which are not of interest for his application.

There is a simple correspondence between the content of our hierarchical view and the content of the underlying data base. To an occurrence of a record (R0, R1.S1,...,Rn.Sn) in the view there corresponds a unique occurrence of a record R0 in the underlying data base; this R0 occurrence uniquely identifies its S1-owner R1, and the S2-owner of this, ... and so on. Thus it is simple to map, DML requests on the view into DML commands executable against the underlying network schema. For the hierarchy defined by figure 13, for instance, a GET NEXT request for record (LINK, CONGR.PS), within its current (PRES,STATE.NS) parent, is simply translated into a GET NEXT command for set CS followed by a GET OWNER for set PS. The data items from these records are finally merged and presented to the user as if they were all part of the same record. Thus it is easy to see how a top-down

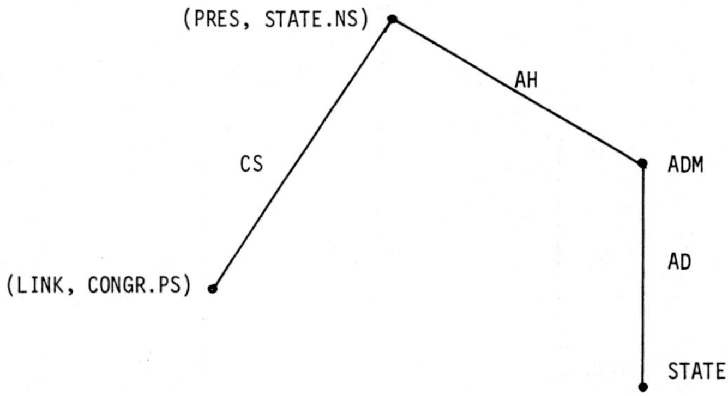

FIG. 13 The selection structure of Fig. 12 after the elimination of owner arcs.

access on the view hierarchy, starting from its root, it is in fact translated into a navigation on the underlying schema as described by the access structure defining the view. Thus to obtain a suitable hierarchical view the user will select an access structure which ensures efficient support for his intended application, much in the same way as if he was working against a network subschema. Thus applications written against these views will have the same pros and cons in terms of execution efficiency and data independence as the ones of applications written against network subschemas (see section 3.2 for a further discussion).

In summary the access structure approach supplies a simple and efficient way to define and support hierarchical views over network schemas. However, these views are not general purpose for the following reasons:

i) under the simple DML translation strategy outlined above, these views support efficiently only certain applications and not others. For instance, the view defined by figure 12 is not suited for queries seeking information on a congress identified by its CNGR# . Clearly richer and more complex DML's could be provided to allow accessing lower level records directly without going through the root record. Even then two problems would remain:

ii) a loss of content information results from the presence in the access structure of owner arcs, or member arcs corresponding to MANUAL and/or OPTIONAL sets. Thus although STATE appears twice in figure 12 every state of the original Union which gave birth to no president cannot be accessed using the corresponding view.

iii) some updatability problems follow from the lack of information preservation (e.g. how is the user going to know that his request to insert a new record conflicts with the key value of another record if he cannot see all the records ?) Moreover as the records in these views merge two or more schema records the update anomalies discussed for relational views will also occur here.

4.2 General Purpose Hierarchical Views

The concept of ID of a record supplies a simple construct for defining uniqueness constraints in a hierarchy:

Record ID: A combination X of fields of a record R in a hierarchy is an ID for R if the following conditions hold: (1) no two occurrences of R can have the same parent and the same fully defined value of X (where root records are assumed to share the same owner), and (2) no subset of X has this property.

One or more ID's will be defined for each record in the hierarchy. The union of an ID of R with an ID from each of its ancestors will be called a key for R.
In our figures we show ID's for records in a hierarchy by simply underlying them. Different styles of underlying will be used to distinguish distinct ID's. Thus e.g., in the hierarchy of figure 14, QT is the only ID for LPRC; (P#, S#, QT) and (PID, S#, QT) are the two keys for this record. Null values may also be allowed for some records in the view. When so we represent only the minimal null patterns in analogy with what was done for relational views.

An access structure T over a well formed schema will be called conformal when every arc of T has the following properties (say that S is the set corresponding to this arc),

(a) it is a member arc,

(b) S is not MANUAL and/or OPTIONAL,

(c) the set of data items migrated along S is a key for the owner of S and a subset of each key of the member of S.

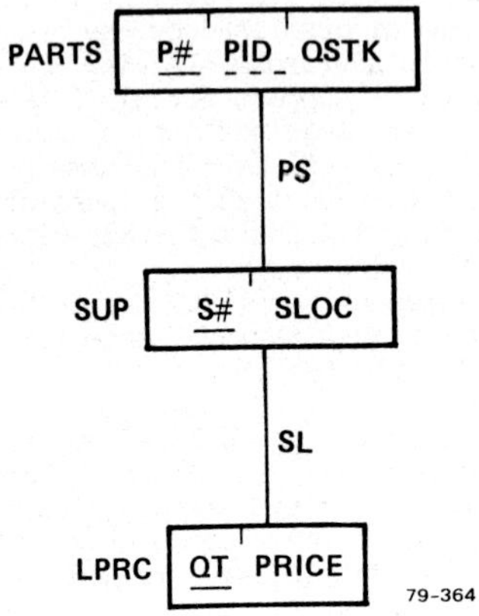

FIG. 14 A conformal hierarchy over the schema of Fig. 10.

For conformal access structures no elimination of owner records occurs and we name the records in the view after the records in the schema. The hierarchical view so derived will also be called conformal. Now the keys for a record R in a conformal hierarchy are simply the DNA keys for record R in the schema. Moreover X is a minimal null pattern for R if X in the schema is migrated to R along a set which is either MANUAL and/or OPTIONAL.

Now we have that a family of conformal hierarchies over a well formed, fully migrated schemas is information preserving and updatable if each record of the schema appears exactly once in the view. Figure 15 gives such a view for the schema of figure 8. Conditions (a) and (b) and the presence in the view of every schema record ensure preservation of information content. Condition (c) ensures that the DNA keys of the schema are defined by the ID's of the various records in the hierarchies. Given a well structured fully migrated schema W the following algorithm produces an updatable information-preserving view with a minimum number of hierarchies:

1. remove from W all sets which do not satisfy conditions (a) and (b) above,

2. for each record with n > 1 owner sets remove n-1 of these sets,

3. let the remaining connected components of the schema define the conformal access structures for the view.

This algorithm applied to the schema of figure 8 produces two different views. One is the one shown in figure 15, the other can be derived from this by letting LINK (with fields PLN, PFN) be the child of CONGR.

Note that the relational views described in the previous subsection are just a special case of conformal hierarchies (i.e. the hierarchy reduced to its root). Conversely conformal hierarchies can be viewed as an interesting generalization of our relational views. As the view contains many hierarchies a query may also encompass many of them. In figure 15, for instance, to retrieve information about congresses associated with a certain president the query language must allow the user to specify that a join on CNGR# must take place between the hierarchies rooted in PRES and CONGR. A DML which provides joins and other high level operations on hierarchically structured relations has been proposed in [BRAC 72]. These

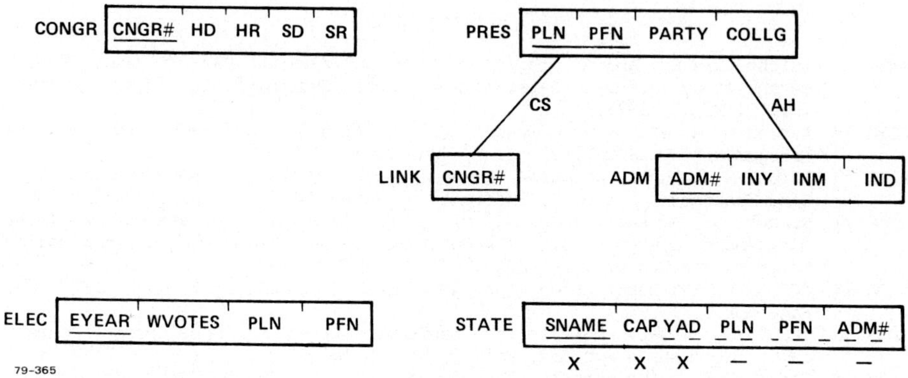

FIG. 15 An information-preserving, updatable hierarchial view for the Presidential Data Base Schema.

hierarchical views in conjuction with such a DML will provide a general purpose, high level, data independent interface to the underlying database. The various considerations made in section 3.2 about data independence and DML optimization for applications written in high level DML on relational views can be extended to applications using high level DML on these conformal hierarchies.

As we compare these conformal hierarchies vis a vis with our previous relational views, the former appear to be somewhat simpler only for schemas as the one of figure 10 which themselves are hierarchical in flavor. For more complex schemas one ends up with a large family of shallow hierarchies as the one of figure 15. The foreign key constraint which also holds for hierarchies is somewhat harder to visualize for these than for relations. E. g. the user must be aware that since (PLN, PFN, ADM#) is a key for record ADM in figure 15 every new value of this key used in STATE must first appear in ADM and its parent PRES. Thus a set of relations is somewhat simpler to understand than a family of shallow hierarchies. Therefore it appears that hierarchies are more suited for the role of specialized views, such as the ones previously discussed, than for the one of general purpose views.

5. CONCLUSION

In this paper we have presented an effective approach to the design of relational and hierarchical views over network schemas. The approach is based on the identification and use of certain CODASYL schema declarations which define the structure of logical data. The concept of well structured schemas was introduced to provide better logical data definition and easier mapping to multimodel external schemas. Algorithms were given to design relational and hierarchical views which are general purpose since they preserve the information content of the underlying data base and provide support for both queries and update operations. Also we considered specialized views, i.e. those can only serve the needs of certain applications, and we indicated that the strength of hierarchies lies in this area. Finally the implications of the various views and associated DML in terms of data independence and efficiency of execution were examined.

AKNOWLEDMENTS. I am grateful to Murray Edelberg and Jay Goldman for the contribution they offered in the course of many discussions and consultations.

References

ANSI Tsichritzis D. and A. Klug (Eds) "The ANSI/X3/SPARC DBMS Framework Report on the study group on Database management Systems,", Information Systems Vol. 3, No. 3, 1978.

ASTR 76 Astran M. M. et als "System R: Relational Approach to Database Management", TODS Vol. 1, No. 2, June 1976.

ADIB 78 Adiba, M. and C. Delobel "A Cooperation System for Heterogeneous Data Base Management Systems", Information Systems, Vol. 3, No. 3, 1978.

BRAC 72 Bracchi G., A. Fedeli, P. Paolini "A Language for a Relational Data Base Management System", Sixth Annual Princeton Conference on Information Sciences and Systems, Princeton, N. J. 1972.

CODA 73 "CODASYL Data Description Language Journal of Development, June 1973" NBS Handbook 113.

CODA 78 "CODASYL 78 Data Description Language Journal of Development, January 1978" Information Systems, Vol. 3, No. 4, 1978.

CLEM 77 Clemons, E. "The external Schema and CODASYL" VLDB 78, Sept. 13-15, 1978, West Berlin, Germany.

CODD 72 Codd, E. F. "Further Normalization of the Data Base Relational Model" Data Base Systems, Courant Computer Science Series, Vol. 6, Prentice Hall, New York, 1972.

DATE 77 Date, C. J. "An Introduction to Data Base Systems" Addison-Wesley, 2nd Ed., New York 1977.

DAYA 78 Dayal, U. and P. A. Bernstein, "On the Updatability of Relational Views" VLDB 78, Sept. 13-15, 1978, West Berlin, Germany.

FAGI 77 Fagin, R. "Multivalued Dependencies and New Normal Form for Relational Data Bases" TODS, vol. 2,no. 3, Sept. 77.

FESA 78 Proceedings of the Second DBMS Feasibility Workshop, National Bureau of Standards August 22-23, 1978 Gaithersburg U.S.A. (to appear).

GOLD 79 Goldman, J. "Automated Generation of Relational Schemas for CODASYL Databases," Sperry Research Center Research Paper SCRC-RP-79-13, March 79 (submitted to VLDB 79).

JOHN 76 Johnson J.R. "Subschema Declared Data Names/ Virtual Source Items/ QLP Subschemas," June 1976, Sperry Univac Research Rpt. 00728.

JOHN 78a Johnson H.R., Larson, J.A. and Lawrence, J.D. "Transformations between Network and Relational Data Models", March 1978, Sperry Univac Research Rpt. 00729.

JOHN 78b Johnson, H. R., Larson, J. A. and Lawrence, J. D., "A Common Data Base Architecture", IEEE Workshop on Data Management and Storage Hierarchies, Sept. 6-8, 1978, Lake Arrowhead, California (Sperry Univac Research Rpt. TMA 00730.)

KALI 76 Kalinichenko, L.A. "Relational-Network Data Structure Mapping," Modelling in Data Base Managment Systems, G.M. Nijissen Ed., North Holland 1976.

LARS 78 Larson J.A., H.R. Johnson and J.D. Lawrence "Multimodel Data Base Management," Sperry Univac Research Rpt. TMA 00731.

PAOL 77 Paolini P. and G. Pelagatti "Formal Definition of Mappings in a Data base" ACM SIGMOD 77, Aug. 3-5 1977, Toronto, Canada

SMIT 77 Smith, J. M. and Smith, C. P. "Data Base Abstractions: Aggregation" CACM Vol. 20, No. 6, June 1977.

WHIT 74 Whitney,V.K.M. "Relational Data Managment Implementation Techniques," Proc. ACM SIGFIDET Workshop 1974.

ZANI 76 Zaniolo, C. "Analysis and Design of Relational Schemata for Data Base Systems", (Ph.D. thesis), Comp. Sc. Dpt. UCLA, UCLA-ENG-7769, July 1976.

ZANI 77 Zaniolo, C. "Relational Views in Data Base Systems: Support for Queries", COMPSAC77, November 8-11, 1977, chicago, Illinois.

ZANI 79 Zaniolo, C. "Design of Relational Views over Network Schemas," Proc. ACM SIGMOD Int. Conf., Boston, May 29-June 1, 1979.

Data Base Architecture, Bracchi/Nijssen, eds.
North-Holland Publishing Company

ISSUES IN BUILDING A RELATIONAL INTERFACE ON A CODASYL DBMS

Laszlo I. Mercz

Control Data France
01210 Ferney-Voltaire, France

The ultimate role of any database management system is to support information systems. The information system is formally defined with a conceptual schema, which is the most comprehensive in meaning. External schemas are derived from the conceptual schema. The CODASYL'78 database proposals are evaluated and found to be insufficient for providing a semantically complete, formal description for the conceptual schema. Therefore, it is not possible to derive a complete relational view from a CODASYL schema. In contrast with the CODASYL'78 proposals, a procedural external schema and related data manipulation operators are outlined, which can coexist with normalized relational views on the same information base.

1 - INTRODUCTION

Since the three level architecture for future database management systems is widely accepted (Nijssen (2)), each time a new data model is proposed, its place of the new model in the overall architecture must be defined.

Its position must be precisely determined, because the requirements at each level are quite different :

conceptual schema - correctness of the information system,

external schema - convenience for user and programmer efficiency,

internal schema - optimization of computer efficiency.

The reasoning behind the choice of one data model or another is not simple, each has a certain set of properties and its user has to decide which properties he wants. So it is generally admitted, that multiple models should coexist at the external schema level to offer that choice. Similarily, multiple internal schemas are needed - perhaps for distributed databases.

On the other hand, as concerns the conceptual model for an information system, only one model, the most appropriate, has to be selected.

Recently, it again was suggested, that the CODASYL specifications are appropriate to describe the information at the conceptual level (O'Connell (22), Manola (23)). Moreover, it is asserted that a correct n-ary normalized relational view can be derived from a CODASYL'71, CODASYL'73 or CODASYL'75 schema description and the existing database need not be converted : "Previous research has proven that it is possible to define relational views over existing CODASYL DBMS's to support general purpose relational DML (both query and update). That research followed a bottom-up approach by assuming that the schema and the data base are given and the relational views are simply added on to the old system. Such approach is totally evolutionary as it preserves existing data base and application programs." (Zaniolo (1) published in this volume). This point of view might sound like music to the ears of some users, but it merits a little bit more detailed investigation.

Prior to actually evaluating the validity of deriving and operating semantically consistent external views on a CODASYL schema, I will first summarize the important properties of the conceptual schema, of being a faithful description of an enterprise (Senko (3)), i.e. as the description of the information system which reflects the most comprehensive meaning (Nijssen (2)).

I will then discuss briefly the coexistence architecture, where different kinds of external schemas coexist on the common conceptual schema and use the same information base. The external schema can be a classical n-ary normalized relational, a procedural with canonical data manipulation operators or a binary relational and possibly many other kinds of views.

It is important to recognize that the semantics of each external schema are derived from the semantics of the conceptual schema. The conceptual/external transformation rules govern the mapping of the constructs and the operators of the two schemas. Therefore in the discussion of models it is necessary to regard both the operands and the operators, since without them any assessment would be incomplete.

Then I will shortly review of the possibility of incorporating the CODASYL'78 specifications into the overall architecture and what could be its place. It turns out, that the CODASYL'78 schema DDL has too much functional redundancy which makes it complex, and yet it is incomplete to fully capture meaning, as major parts of the semantics of the information system are scattered over the application programs. Since the CODASYL'78 schema has several semantic leaks, one cannot derive an n-ary normalized relational view from it for retrieval or update purposes.

Nevertheless, an external schema and related data manipulation operators are needed for problem solutions with procedural programming languages like PASCAL (or COBOL, FORTRAN), so in the next section I will outline such a procedural facility which, can be contrasted with the CODASYL'78 DDLs and DML.

Lastly, we compare on two diagrams the assertion to use CODASYL schemas as a central schema and what I see as a desirable and possible coexistence of relational and procedural veiws on a common conceptual schema.

2 - THE CONCEPTUAL SCHEMA IN THE COEXISTENCE ARCHITECTURE

2.1 - Correctness by the conceptual schema

The final role of any database management system is to support information systems.

As a useful engineering approximation, an information system can be regarded as a black-box between people who communicate with each other. This communication generally could be regarded as speech, a set of sentences of a language. To continue this analogy with linguistics, just as the principles of grammar define the rules for meaningful sentences in any human language, similarily, a grammar may be defined for sentences which make sense for an information system. The conceptual schema is such a prescriptive grammar (Nijssen (2)).

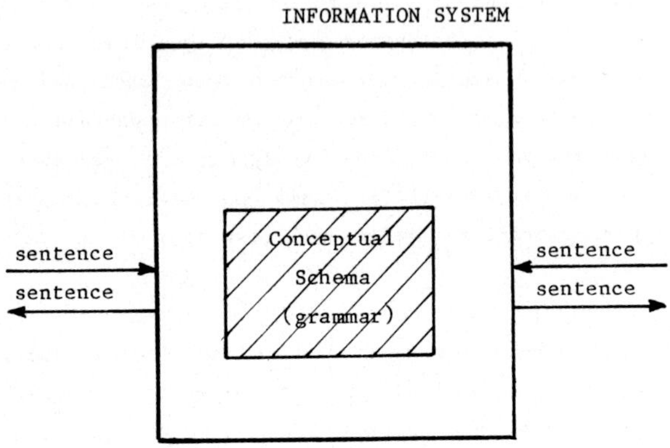

Figure 1 : The conceptual schema captures the meaning for an information system

The properties of the conceptual schema have been gradually defined over the past five years, by individual researchers, and by organizations such as the IFIP Database Working Group 2.6. Among the properties found desirable were (Nijssen (2)) :

(i) the conceptual schema should be general and powerful to describe any discrete structure, without imposing any restriction on the mental model of the users ;

(ii) the conceptual schema should be simple, easy to read and easy to formulate by the users after a short training (without any computing or database education) ;

(iii) the conceptual schema should be formal, it must be a system in the sense of logic ;

(iv) the conceptual schema should be easy to change to accomodate the evolution of the enterprise ;

(v) the conceptual schema should be easily transformable to the various user's models all the while preserving semantic consistency.

An important corollary of the characteristics (iii) and (v), is that any model proposed for the conceptual schema has to comprise both the structures and the operators on them.
As stated earlier, a conceptual schema is a prescriptive grammar of the information system. In the ENALIM approach (Evolving NAtural Language Information Model of G.M. Nijssen (2)), any input and output to the system is regarded as a sequence of elementary or compound sentences, which satisfy this grammar. Thus, the conceptual schema is composed of object name types connected with elementary sentence types, and many semantic constraints on these elementary sentences. For instance, an information system dealing with US Presidents, would contain a sentence type for the following sentence : "J.F. Kennedy was born in Massachussetts". For most people, who are familiar with the subject a sentence" J.F.K. was born in Mass" would mean the same thing as the previous one. This is illustrated on the lower part of Figure 2 with a Nijssen-diagram. Thus using names or nicknames of presidents and full or abbreviated names for states does not matter for humans, just a question of naming conventions. This part of the conceptual schema is the significational level. For a more thorough treatment see (27).

The upper part of Figure 2 shows a higher level of abstraction, where things are independent of assigned names. This is the ontological level, usually much more stable. Here we can talk about "president" not "president name" "president-number" or "president-nickname". In practice, many difficult problems can be resolved easily with this level of abstraction. For instance, merging databases with different naming conventions can be handled with ease. Also, the so called irreducible n-ary relations can be reduced at the ontological level, since one can always define an object type without finding a good name for it.

Clearly, using two levels and the naming bridge between them for the conceptual schema permits capturing more meaning of the modeled enterprise. For the manipulation of the elementary sentences of the conceptual schema two update operators are needed : STORE and DELETE elementary sentences. With these operators, conceptual transactions are defined so that at the end of the execution of each transaction all semantic contraints are satisfied.

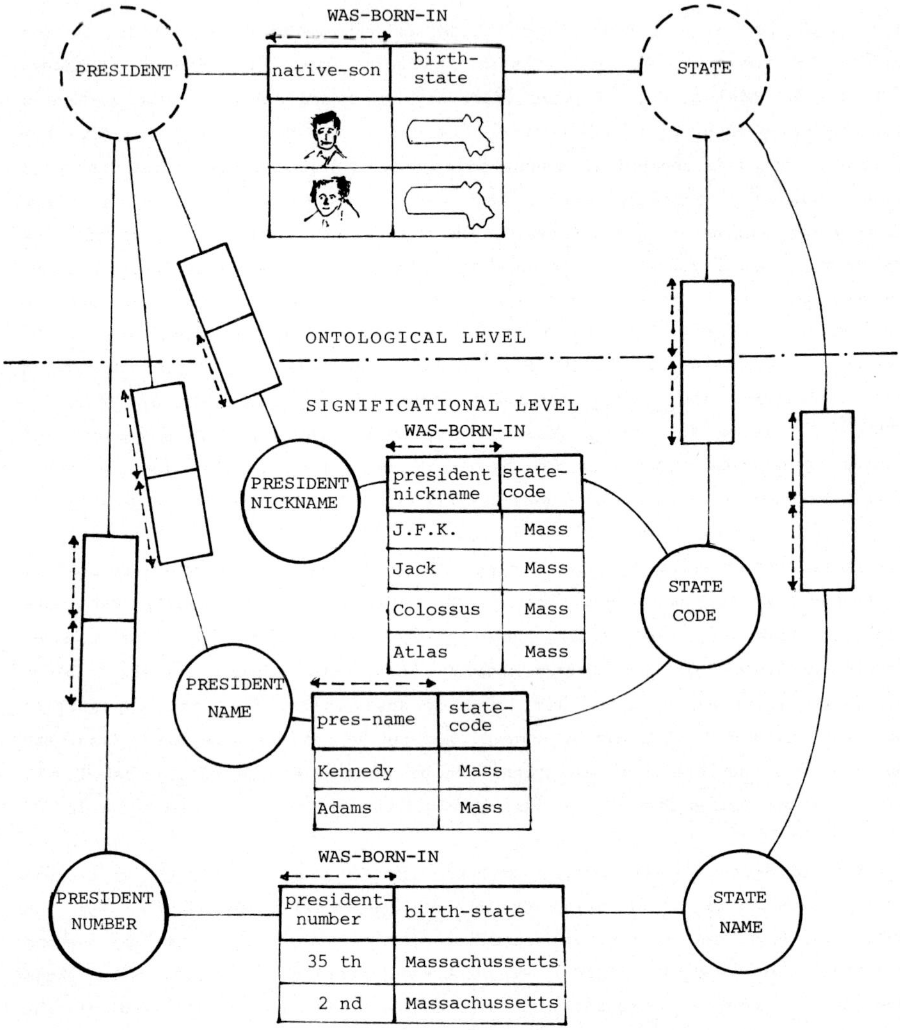

Figure 2 : Nijssen-diagram to show the name assignment in the conceptual schema.

2.2 - Coexistence at the external schema level

The need for external schemas is manifold. Perhaps the most important is to isolate the existing applications from the evolution of the conceptual schema. But also to simplify the task of the users by allowing them to ignore parts of the information base which are of no interest to them and provide a familiar, convenient view to work with.

Since the external schemas and related data manipulation operators of an information system are used by many people, their single, most important, property is convenience. Freedom of choice is one of the ingredients of convenience. Therefore many different kinds of external schemas must be able to coexist on the same information base via a common conceptual schema. For practical, industrial-scale applications at least the following types are desirable :

- An elementary sentences (or binary associations) external schema for the information analysts, together with an accessing language such as FORAL Light Pen (Senko (26) ;

- An n-ary normalized relational external schema mainly for queries and occasional updates ; the normalized relations are derived from the conceptual schema, so they will be undoubtedly well normalized ; with a domain and a tuple oriented relational language (Pirotte (6)) ;

- A procedural external schema with canonical data manipulation operators for the bulk of daily operations in transaction processing mode ; such a facility is briefly outlined in Section 4.

Recently most academic research has been concentrated on n-ary relational models, the problems of normalization and non-procedural languages. Non-procedural languages often provide improvements over procedural languages, but not always. Many practical, industrial problems with recursive nature (e.g. bill of material, network planning etc.) can be better handled in procedural languages (Mercz (24)). Procedural languages also have been critized for their one-record-at-a-time logic. The program logic may be set oriented even if records are delivered serially. Also, many business transactions are inherently one-thing-at-a-time sort of processes.

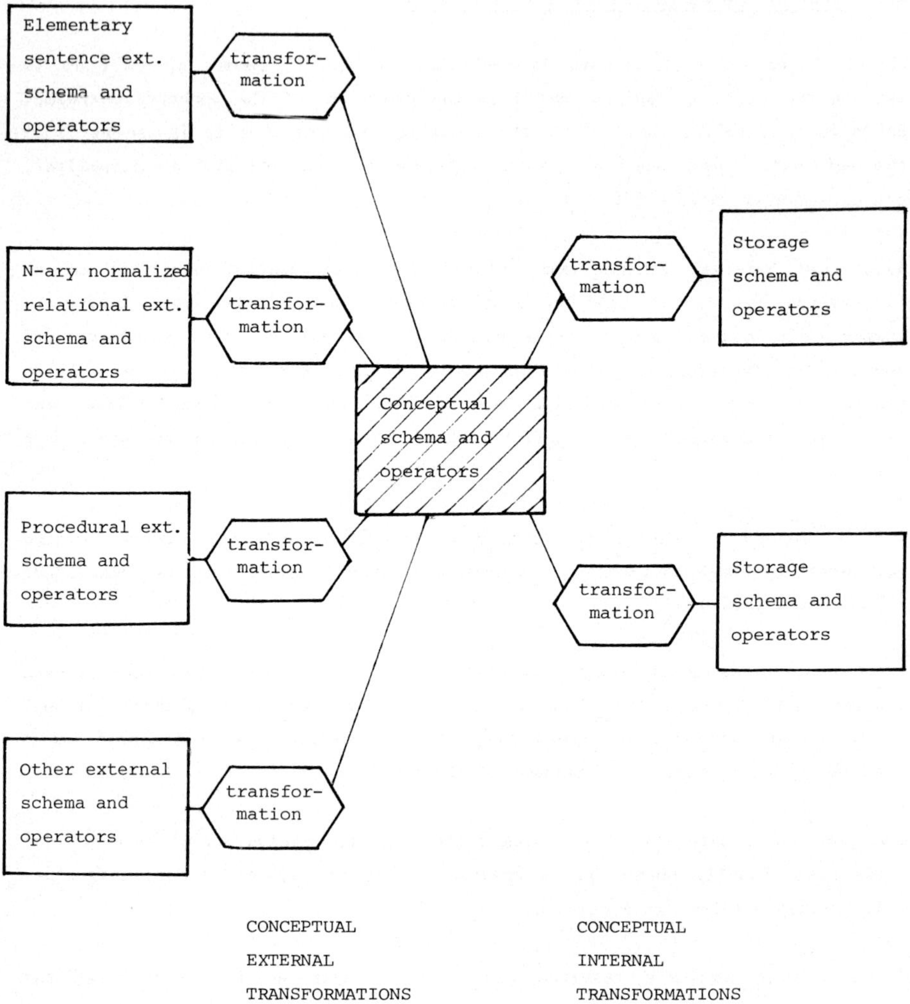

Figure 3 : The place of the conceptual schema in the coexistence architecture. Stripes indicate where semantics are defined.

As illustrated in Figure 3, the place of the conceptual schema is central in the architecture. It must be the most comprehensive in meaning, since all external schemas are derived from the conceptual schema. The external view of the information base does not have an independent existence, it is completely defined by applying the transformation function to the conceptual schema. The transformation (mapping) between the conceptual and external schemas preserves semantic consistency, and permits accurate transformation of both the structures and the operators in both directions.

With the early database management systems only a minor part of the meaning is defined at the central schema level, with most of the semantic scattered over one or many application programs, or simply not captured at all. This is why database application programming was a perennial task, and changes in requirements of the enterprise caused massive re-programming.

For a formally defined information system the conceptual schema should be the most comprehensive in meaning. Then from such a conceptual schema which is rich in semantics, many external schemas may be derived (formally) on which application programs can be written and indeed very often generated. These kinds of information systems should be supported by future database management systems. Today, it is possible for a large business application to generate about 60 percent of the source code of the update programs (Mercz and Nijmeijer (4)).

3 - A BRIEF ASSESSMENT OF THE CODASYL'78 PROPOSALS

Several versions of the CODASYL database proposals were evaluated over the last ten years and some of its major flaws clearly identified. In fact, a previous IFIP Conference in this series was dedicated to an "In-depth Technical Evaluation of CODASYL DDL" (held in Wepion in 1975, Proceedings : Data Base Description edited by B.C.M. Douque and G.M. Nijssen by North-Holland, 1975). During this conference "implementers, users and language designers including some members of the CODASYL committees, jointly tried to analyze the DDL, in order to preserve the strong points, and, if needed, to propose improvements for weak points... About 40 percent of the time was spent on discussions... A major result of all discussions was a list of recommendations to be presented to the CODASYL DDLC". The long list of recommended changes were fairly fundamental in nature, and should constitute required reading for those intending to build on

CODASYL systems. Some of the most relevant papers are : Nijssen (11, 12), Taylor (13), Huits (14), Robinson (15), Kay (16), Tsichritzis (17), Waghorn (18 and Biller (19).

In 1978 CODASYL published a new version of DDL (7), evaluated by Hutton in (20) and a COBOL sub-schema and DML (8) which incorporates several of the Wepion recommendations, but neglects the solution of other problems.

3.1 - CODASYL'78 schema DDL for conceptual schema ?

With the new version of the CODASYL proposals some proponents suggested, that the CODASYL schema DDL is appropriate for the conceptual schema, the sub-schema DDL and DML is appropriate for an external schema facility and the storage schema DSDL is appropriate for the internal schema, (O'Connell (22), Manola (23) and others.)

The first difficulty in discussing the two proposals is that the descriptions are not formal enough, even the terminology used by the two committees is different and sometimes contradictory (e.g. ORDER clause). The division into schema DDL on one part and sub-schema DDL plus DML on the other is perplexing.

The following are the main constructs and operands in CODASYL'78 :

. Record type : an information bearing structure, a juxtaposition of data items, optionally identified by a record key. The record manipulation operators are : STORE, DELETE, MODIFY, FIND, GET, each with several formats.

  Another information bearing structure can be embedded in the record type : the data aggregate (vector or repeating group). For data aggregates no data manipulation operators are provided so they are always handled with the functions of a host language.

. Set type : a combination of four different things :

  First, an information-bearing structure to relate one occurrence of an owner record type with many occurrences of one or more member record types.

  Second, a semantic constraint. Set membership can be AUTOMATIC/MANUAL for insertion, FIXED/MANDATORY/OPTIONAL for retention ; plus the STRUCTURAL CONSTRAINT clause.

Third, an access path for retrieval and for updates, defined by the set selection expression.

Fourth, still another information bearing structure with the ordered set ; this manipulated with ORDER.

CODASYL sets are manipulated with INSERT, REMOVE and STORE, DELETE, MODIFY, each operator with several formats.

. Area type : a container for record occurrences of one or more record types, sometimes another information bearing structure. The operators are OPEN, CLOSE, and the placement of a given record occurrence (WITHIN) is either predefined in the schema, sub-schema or dependent or the application program.

To illustrate the complexity of the single function to modify the information base, the following syntax is proposed in CODASYL'78.

```
MODIFY [record-name] [ { INCLUDING } { ALL             } MEMBERSHIP ]
                       { ONLY      } { {set-name-1} ... }

MODIFY {identifier-1}... [ INCLUDING { ALL             } MEMBERSHIP ]
                                     { {set-name-1} ... }

CONNECT [record-name] TO { {set-name-1} ... }
                         { ALL              }

DISCONNECT [record-name] FROM { {set-name-1} ... }
                              { ALL              }
```

What is most striking with the CODASYL'78 specifications is, that in spite of functional redundancies and unnecessary complexity, they are not complete to capture all meaning in the schema but in many cases it is up to the application programmer to define the semantics. The major semantic leaks of the CODASYL'78 are :

(1) No place in the schema to define domains (object type names) and semantics of domains (e.g. value space). How, then, the system can know that "budget" and "salary" are comparable but "budget" and "age" are not ? At best, the meaning can be found in the application programs.

(2) The smallest manipulable structures for the DML are the record types. Such undefined relationships between data items may imply spurious relationships between real life entities. Therefore - as was proven by binary proponents - smaller structures are needed for an accurate description.

(3) Data aggregates are always manipulated within the host language programs and generally it is not possible to capture and transform their meaning (for instance, if in a personal record, children's name is a repeating group, the application can arrange them in order of birth, or order of girls then boys, etc. only known by the application programmer).

(4) Since set types are information bearing, when set membership is MANUAL the application programmer must use INSERT, when the set membership is OPTIONAL he must use REMOVE. Whatever the set membership is, the set selection expression can be by APPLICATION, at the end, defined by the programmer.

(5) The set order is information bearing, so when set ORDER is TEMPORARY, an application program can reorder (not LOCALLY) the set occurrences.

(6) The areas - which are mapped to one or more realms in the sub- schema - are sometimes information bearing constructs : the WITHIN clause of the record type may state that an occurrence is to be stored in an area (AREA-ID is parameter), where the parameter is defined in the program at execution-time, and later some record selection expression operates on realms (WITHIN realm-name), again the semantics is up to the user.

Because the CODASYL'78 schema is incomplete in meaning, one can not derive semantically complete n-ary relational views from it.

When evaluating the possibility of using the CODASYL'78 schema DDL for the conceptual schema, we can make the following remarks :

(i) CODASYL'78 is not general enough, for example, to derive binary association views ;

(ii) CODASYL'78 is not sufficiently simple to formulate enterprise descriptions ;

(iii) CODASYL'78 is not formal enough, therefore cannot be used for formal system descriptions "even CODASYL specialist sometimes cannot agree upon the semantics... We have taken as an example the CODASYL DML and illustrated, that by means of formal description techniques ambiguities in the language can be revealed" says Biller in (19) ;

(vi) CODASYL'78 schemas are not easily changeable. "Automatic database program conversion of CODASYL systems seems to be extremely difficult" states the conclusion of (21) by Schneiderman ;

(v) CODASYL'78 schemas, because of incompleteness in meaning, are not transformable to other views as the binary or n-ary normalized relational views.

Perhaps, it would be useful to improve the CODASYL'78 specifications to make a good external schema facility. Provided with a formal description of a CODASYL'78 like model, references to a vague "network model" could be avoided.

4 - A PROCEDURAL EXTERNAL SCHEMA WITH CANONICAL OPERATORS

Having a conceptual schema described - where all semantic constraints are explicitely defined by predicates or procedures - an external schema can be rather simple and the data manipulation operators can be reduced to a canonical form. Procedural programming languages, like PASCAL and COBOL, FORTRAN etc. can use such an external schema so that the original file handling facility is replaced or complemented with an access to the database "in situ". In this section, an informal outline of such a procedural facility is proposed.

This external schema uses three primary concepts :

. record type : the only information bearing construct,

. logical access path : for out-of-the-blue and intra-record population retrieval,

. coset (acronym for COdasyl SET) link : for inter-record population retrieval.

The record type (the term is familiar in programming languages) is a template for a structure consisting of a fixed number of data items. The conceptual/external schema transformation makes this record type conform to an n-ary normalized relation of a relational external schema, both corresponding to a compound sentence formed from elementary sentences of the conceptual schema. No aggregates are needed : neither vectors nor repeating groups.

The user or the programmer visualizes the information base as a collection of record occurrences of each record type known in the external schema. From the programming language standpoint, record types are abstract data types, on which a uniform set of canonical update operators are defined :

STORE record-type-name RECORD,
DELETE record-type-name RECORD,
MODIFY record-type-name RECORD.

When one of these operators is executed, all relevant semantic constraints of the conceptual schema are reinforced.

In contrast with the very concise update operators, a procedural language needs a diversified set of retrieval functions.

For intra record type processing, on each record type an arbitrary number of logical access paths can be defined. (An access path of the external schema is independent, whether supported by a b-tree or a database machine or nothing at all in the internal schema). An access path on any concatenation of data items partitions into subsets the population of the record type. In each subset, there is one or more synonym record occurrences. An access path can be ordered for retrieval convenience. Also, synonyms can be ordered by any data item(s) of the record type.

The retrieval operator via an access path can :

```
        / record-type-name RECORD VIA access-path-name                              \
        |                                                                           |
        | {FIRST}                                                                   |
OBTAIN <  {NEXT }  record-type-name RECORD VIA access-path-name                      >
        |                                                                           |
        | {NEXT }  [{DUPLICATE}]                                                    |
        \ {PRIOR}  [{DIFFERENT}]  record-type-name RECORD VIA access-path-name      /
```

This OBTAIN function should be considered complete, in the sense that any task requiring procedural retrieval can be efficiently performed by means of a sequence of calls on this operator.

However, for convenience of inter record type processing, an alternate retrieval construct can be introduced, called coset. A coset type is a link between two record types called owner and member, such that one occurrence of the owner record type is linked to many occurrences of the member record type. The coset is based on the equality of values of data item(s) of the owner and member occurrences (derived from a common object type name of the conceptual schema). A coset can be ordered by any data item(s) of the member record type.

The syntax for retrieve by coset is fairly simple :

```
        {FIRST}
OBTAIN  {LAST }  record-type-name RECORD WITHIN coset-name COSET,
        {NEXT }
        {PRIOR}
```

```
OBTAIN OWNER record-type-name RECORD WITHIN coset-name COSET.
```

Using cosets, any general structure can be described at the external schema level (hierarchies, networks, recursive structures in any superposition), with a very neat semantic definition. But a coset is just a retrieval link in the external schema, so it is independent of the underlying structural constraints (if any) defined in the conceptual schema.

A more detailed description of this procedural external schema and its canonical data manipulation operators, and some recent experiences by using it on large scale projects can be found in (4).

5 - DISCUSSION

As reviewed in section 3, the CODASYL'78 schema DDL allows that major part of the semantics of the information system are scattered over on the sub-schemas and a number of application programs, as illustrated on Figure 4. Since any n-ary relational view needs a complete description of meaning, it is incorrect to assume that one can derive a usable relational view from an incomplete CODASYL'71, CODASYL'73, CODASYL'75 or CODASYL'78 view.

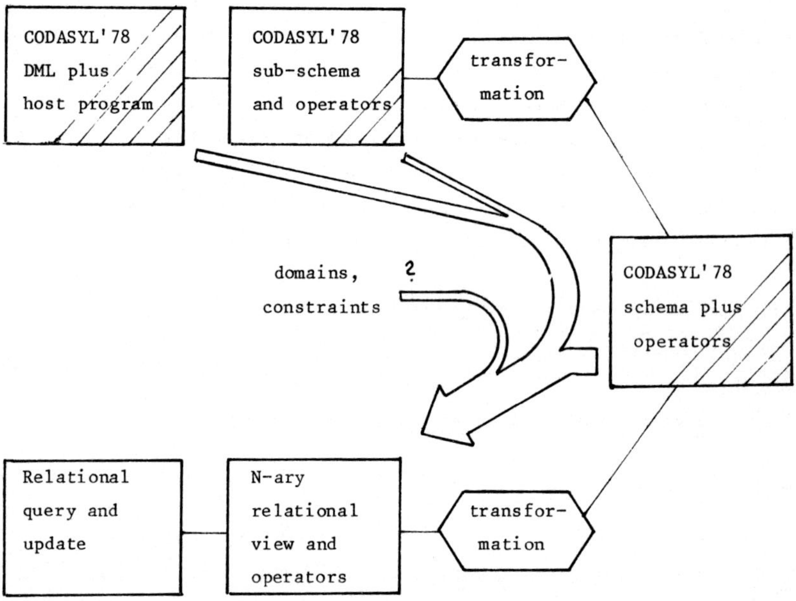

Figure 4 : Assumption to define relational views on a CODASYL DBMS. Stripes indicate where semantics are defined.

As it is desirable to have both n-ary normalized relational views and procedural external views on the same information base, Figure 5 shows the coexistence architecture, as it was implemented in 1975 (Nijssen (2)).

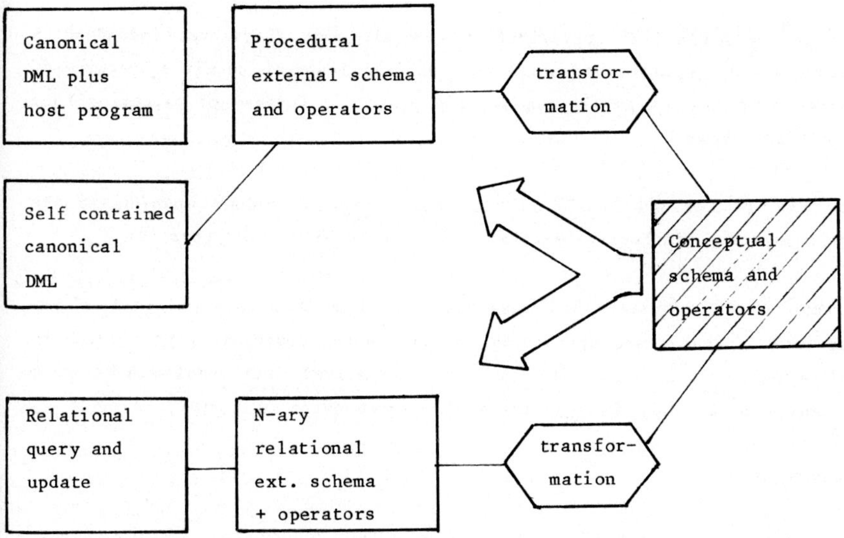

Figure 5 : Coexistence of procedural and relational external schemas on the same conceptual schema. Stripes indicate that semantics are defined in the conceptual schema.

The concentration of all semantics in the conceptual schema is desirable objective. After that, remains the real challenge of constructing a bridge between the real world and the conceptual schema.

6 - CONCLUSIONS

Briefly, what has been argued in this paper ? Essentially three things :

First, that the CODASYL'78 specifications contain many functional redundancies in constructs and operators and still have several leaks to permit dispersion of major parts of semantics in the application programs, instead of capturing them in the central schema.

Second, that as the CODASYL'78 schema cannot capture enough meaning of the information system, complete relational views cannot be derived from it.

Third, that it is desirable and possible to define a simple external schema facility (both operands and operators) for procedural programming ; and such an external schema can coexist with an n-ary normalized relational schema on a common conceptual schema, which is the most comprehensive in meaning.

ACKNOWLEDGEMENT

I am grateful to G.M. Nijssen for the stimulating discussions on information systems. Many thanks to my colleagues at Control Data Europe within the CYBER-EDMS development team, who have implemented a coexistence database management system including several versions of the procedural facility outlined in this paper.

REFERENCES

(1) C. Zaniolo : Multimodel External Schemas for CODASYL Data Base Management Systems. In Data Base Architecture, North-Holland, 1979.

(2) G.M. Nijssen : On the Gross Architecture of the Next Generation Database Management Systems. Information Processing 77, p.327-335. North-Holland, 1977.

(3) M.E. Senko : Conceptual schema, abstract data structures, enterprise descriptions. International Computing Symposium 1977, p.85-102. North-Holland, 1977.

(4) L.I. Mercz, E.A. Nijmeijer : A Procedural External Schema and Canonical Data Manipulation Operators for Application Programming. Control Data Europe, 1978, to appear.

(5) G. Pelagatti, P. Paolini, G. Bracchi : Mappings in Database Systems. Information Processing 77, p.447-452. North-Holland, 1977.

(6) A. Pirotte : Linguistic Aspects of High-level Relational Languages. Infotech State of the Art Report : Data Base Technology. Vol.2. P.272-300.

(7) CODASYL DDLC. Journal of Development 1978.

(8) CODASYL COBOL Committee. Journal of Development 1978.

(9) S. Todd : Automatic Constraint Maintenance and Updating Defined Relations. Information Processing 77, p.145-148. North-Holland, 1977.

(10) Y. Dayal, P.A. Bernstein : On the Updatability of Relational Views. Transactions 1978 IEEE.

(11) G.M. Nijssen : Two Major Flaxs in the CODASYL DDL 1973 and Proposed Corrections. Inform. Systems Vol.1. p.115-132. Pergamon Press, 1975.

(12) G.M. Nijssen : Set and CODASYL Set or Coset. Data Base Description, p.1-70. North-Holland, 1975.

(13) R.W. Taylor : Observation on the attributes of database sets. Data Base Description, p.73-84. North-Holland, 1975.

(14) M.H.H. Huits : Requirements for languages in data base systems. Data Base Description, p.85-108. North-Holland, 1975.

(15) K.A. Robinson : An analysis of the uses of the CODASYL set concept. Data Base Description, p.169-181. North-Holland, 1975.

(16) M.H. Kay : An assessment of the CODASYL DDL for use with a relational subschema. Data Base Description, p.199-214. North-Holland, 1975.

(17) D. Tsichritzis : A network framework for relational implementation. Data Base Description, p.269-282. North-Holland, 1975.

(18) W.J. Waghorn : The DDL as an industry standard ? Data Base Description, p.121-167. North-Holland, 1975.

(19) H. Biller, W. Glatthaar, E.J. Neuhold : On the Semantics of Data Bases : The Semantics of Data Manipulation Languages. Modelling in Data Base Management Systems, p.239-267. North-Holland, 1976.

(20) D. Hutton : DDL'78, a Critical Assessement of the CODASYL Data Description Language 1978. Infotech State of the Art Report : Data Base Technology. Vol.2, p.115-129.

(21) B. Schneiderman : A framework for automatic conversion of network database programs under schema transformations. Information Technology, p.279-288. North-Holland, 1978.

(22) M.L. O'Connell : The 1978 CODASYL Data Base Specifications. Infotech State of the Art Report : Data Base Technology. Vol.2, p.257-270.

(23) F. Manola : An Evolution of the New CODASYL and ANSI/SPARC Data Base Proposals. INFOTECH State of the Art Report : Data Base Technology. Vol.2, p.131-150.

(24) L.I. Mercz : How to increase database programming productivity. Infotech State of the Art Report : Data Base Technology. Vol.2, p.151-183.

(25) R.L. Stamper : Physical Objects, Human Discourse and Formal Systems. Architecture and Models in Data Base Management Systems, p.293-311.

(26) M.E. Senko : FORAL LP - Making Pointed Queries with a Light Pen. Information Prcessing 77. p.635-640. North-Holland, 1977.

(27) G.M. Nijssen : Modelling in data base management systems. Invited paper to be presented at EURO-IFIP 1979, London, Sept. 1979. Proceedings by North-Holland.

Data Base Architecture, Bracchi/Nijssen, eds.
North-Holland Publishing Company

SUPPORTING VIEW UPDATES IN RELATIONAL DATA BASES

François BANCILHON
IRIA-LABORIA
BP 105, 78150 Le Chesnay
FRANCE

A data base view is a portion of the data base structured in a way which is relevant to the user's application. However, such views are not actually implemented; they are simply "defined" by the user. Therefore, update requests issued by the user within the context of his view must be translated into updates on the underlying data base. It is the purpose of this paper to formalize the notion of view and view update and study the translation process. This is done in the context of the relational model for data bases.
We first define formally the notion of a view and that of a view update and its translation into a data base update. We then propose a method for translating view updates : together with the user defined view, we define a "complementary" view such that the data base can be computed from the view and its complement; a view update is then translated in such a way that only the view is changed while its complement remains unchanged ("translation under constant complement"); conditions are given for this translation to be semantically consistent. Next, we show that a view can have many different complements and that the choice of a complement determines an update policy. Finally, we establish the generality of our method by showing that any translation of a view update is a translation under some constant complement.

I - INTRODUCTION

A data base is generally used by a community of users. Most of these users are actually interested in only a small part of this data base and they do not necessarily want to see this part of data named and structured as the data base administrator has decided. To meet these two user requirements most data base management systems provide a facility known as the "user view". That user view defines the specific subset the user is interested in together with the structuring he desires.

As long as the user interaction with the data base consists only of queries, it is fairly easy to support this facility : the view definition function is used to translate the user's queries from view queries into queries on the actual data base. However things get more complex when the user is allowed to update his view. The goal of this paper is to study the tranlation process for updates : given a view update how can we translate it into a data base update ? Several authors have already adressed this problem [Dayal and Berstein 78, Furtado and Sevcik 78, Paolini and Pelagatti 77] and the difficulty is now well known : there seems to be many possible translations for a given update in the general case and most authors restrict their attention to the case where one single translation exists.
The main contributions of our study are :

1 - there is <u>never</u> a single translation of a view update (unless of course the view

is empty or equivalent to the data base or the update leaves the view unchanged)

2 - This is because the information given by the view description is not sufficient to translate the update and we identify the complementary information that must be given together with the view to uniquely specify an update translation.

3 - Finally we define a translation scheme, that is a method to generate all possible translations of a given update, and show that it is universal.

This study is done in the framework of the relational model. After briefly reminding the basic definitions from that model, we define formally the notion of a view and an update. This allows us to formulate the view update problem. Then we introduce a mathematical model that permits the specification of a method to handle view updates. Finally we show that there can be different manners of handling updates and that more information is needed about the view definition to choose among these different alternatives. The extra information needed is characterised as another view, "complementary" to the user's view.
Finally the generality of the view update handling method is demonstrated. However, the actual implementation of the method and the study of the necessary algorithms are not presented here and are under current study.

II - THE RELATIONAL MODEL

In this section, we review the basic definitions from the relational model and we introduce our notation. Central to the relational model is the notion of a relation. A relation is specified by a relational descriptor of the form :

$$R(A_1:D_1,\dots,A_i:D_i,\dots,A_n:D_n)$$

R is the relation name, the A_i's are the attribute names and the D_i's are the associated domains. We shall not be too concerned with domains and they will be left implicit, thus denoting the descriptor by $R(A_1,A_2,\dots,A_n)$. The attribute set $\{A_1,\dots,A_n\}$ is usually denoted by U.

With the relation descriptor $R(A_1:D_1,\dots,A_n:D_n)$, we can associate specific values, that are finite subsets of the cartesian product $D_1 \times D_2 \times \dots \times D_n$. Values of the descriptor will in general be denoted by subscripting the relation name R, i.e ;

$$R_\tau \subseteq D_1 \times D_2 \times \dots \times D_n$$

Relation values are represented in the usual tabular form, where rows represent tuples and columns attributes.

A data base consists of one or several relations taking at each instant specific values. Thus a data base is defined by a set $R = (R_1,R_2,\dots,R_p)$ of relational descriptors that we call the data base descriptor.
With that descriptor, at each instant t, we can associate a data base value $R_t = (R_{1t},R_{2t},\dots,R_{pt})$ by assigning a value R_{it} to each relation R_i of the data base. The set of values that the data base can take is the data base schema, denoted S. That schema is in general specified by a set of integrity constraints that the values must satisfy. In the absence of integrity constraints, the schema is called the free schema, denoted by $S_F(R)$. It consists of all the possible values that the data base descriptor can take. Examples of integrity constraints are functional dependencies as defined in [Codd 72]. The reader will be assumed familiar with the notions of projection and join of relations : the projection of the relation value R_τ on the attribute subset X is denoted $R_\tau(X)$ and the join of the two relation values $R_{1\tau}$ and $R'_{1\tau}$ is denoted $R_{1\tau} * R'_{1\tau}$.

III - THE VIEW UPDATE PROBLEM

A data base usually consists of a number of relations shared by different users. It has been structured by the data base administrator, and this structuring can be done in many different ways (even third or fourth normal forms are not unique). It is therefore very conceivable that a given user, on one side is not interested in the entire data base and on the other side would like to see his data structured in a different manner. The notion of the user's view was specifically introduced to meet these two requirements : It allows the user to define exactly what part of the data he is interested in and to name and structure his data as he desires, thus creating his own virtual data base.

Consider for instance the data base descriptor :

R_1(EMPLOYEE,DEPARTMENT)

R_2(DEPARTMENT,MANAGER)

and an associated schema specified by the two functional dependencies :

$$\text{EMPLOYEE} \xrightarrow{R_1} \text{DEPARTMENT}$$

$$\text{DEPARTMENT} \xrightarrow{R_2} \text{MANAGER}$$

A user of this data base might be concerned only with the relationship between employees and managers. Consequently he would like to view the data as a single base relation

R_3(EMPLOYEE,MANAGER)

defined from the original ones by joins and projections. How are we going to give the user the ability to operate on R_3? It is of course not practical to build the actual R_3 relation : for each new user's view we would have to implement a new relation. Therefore, we simply want to give the user the feeling that the R_3 relation is available to him. When the user wants to query his relation, we <u>translate</u> his query on R_3 into a query on R_1 and R_2. For instance :

"List all employees working under manager Jones"

Will be translated into :

"List all employees working in a department whose manager is Jones"

As one can see, queries can be handled in a fairly straightforward manner; this paper is concerned with the problem of handling updates which happens to be much more complex.

Let us summarize the study of the previous example by saying that there are three concepts involved :

(i) the view descriptor R_3

(ii) the view value, i.e. the actual value taken to be the user's view at a given instant and,

(iii) the view definition function, i.e. the process by which we can compute the view value from the data base value.

Let us now state this formally.

Definition III-1.

Let $R = (R_1,R_2,\ldots,R_n)$ be a data base descriptor and let S be a schema defined on R. Let $r = (r_1,r_2,\ldots,r_p)$ be another data base descriptor called the view descriptor. A view is a mapping $f : S \rightarrow S_F(r)$. □

That is, the view f associates with each data base value R_τ of S a view value $r_\tau = f(R_\tau)$ of $S_F(r)$. In general we shall use uppercase letters for variables concerning the data base and lower case letters for variables concerning the user's view. Usually not all values of $S_F(r)$ are view values. The set f(S) which consists of all the values that the view descriptor can take is the view schema. It can also be specified by a set of integrity constraints (in ANSI/SPARC terminology it is the user's subschema).

We shall denote by M(S) the set of view mappings that can be defined on S. These mappings are usually specified through a set of computation rules. We shall not specify here what set of computation rules is adopted, since the theory we present is independent of the type of rules chosen. Only when we want to implement actual algorithms should we worry about that problem. Throughout the paper, all examples will involve well known rules from relational algebra and arithmetic. For instance, the projection mapping is defined as follows :

Let $R = (R_1,R_2,\ldots,R_n)$ be the data base descriptor. The projection mapping $\Pi R_i(X)$ is the function that associates with the data base value $R_\tau = (R_{1\tau},\ldots,R_{i\tau},\ldots,R_{n\tau})$ the view value $R_{i\tau}(X)$, i.e. $\Pi R_i(X)(R_\tau) = R_{i\tau}(X)$, $\forall$ $R_\tau \in S$.

From now on, we shall make the following abuse of notation : we shall write $R_i(X)$ for the mapping $\Pi R_i(X)$. It should however be kept in mind that by $R_i(X)$ we do not mean the descriptor nor the actual view value but the mapping.

Let us now review the example presented at the beginning of this section to clarify these definitions :

The data base descriptor is :

$$R = (R_1(EMP,DEPT)\ ,\ R_2(DEPT,MGR))$$

And the associated schema is specified by the functional dependencies :

$$R_1 : EMP \rightarrow DEPT \quad ; \quad R_2 : DEPT \rightarrow MGR$$

The view descriptor is :

$$r(emp,mgr)$$

The view definition function is the mapping f defined by :

$$r_\tau(emp,mgr) = (R_{1\tau}(EMP,DEPT) * R_{2\tau}(DEPT,MGR))(EMP,MGR)$$

This defines a view schema specified by :

$$r : emp \rightarrow mgr$$

We now turn to the definition of updates. An update U on a schema S is a function from S into S, that associates with each data base value $R_\tau \in S$, its updated version $U(R_\tau)$. Actually updates can be defined as sequences of tuple-insertions, tuple-deletions and tuple-modifications and whenever we consider examples they will appear under that form. However, to discuss the problem of update semantics it is sufficient to stay at the level of generality where an update is just any mapping $U : S \rightarrow S$.

This definition implies that all updates are well defined, i.e. that $U(S) \subseteq S$. In other words, by taking any data base value $R_\tau \in S$ and applying update U we get a new value $U(R_\tau)$ that satisfies the integrity constraints of the schema, i.e. $U(R_\tau) \in S$.

As an example consider the data base described by

R(PART,PRICE)

and the associated schema specified by the integrity constraints :

$$\text{PART} \rightarrow \text{PRICE} \quad \text{and } \forall\, x \in R_\tau,\ x.\text{PRICE} \geq 0.$$

The function U defined by "Decrease the price of part Bolt by $5" is not an update since it might lead to a semantic inconsistency (a negative price if the price of a bolt is less than $5). While the function U' defined by "decrease the price of part Bolt by $5 if that price is greater than $6" is an update.

We have now described in formal terms a view as a mapping $f : S \rightarrow f(S)$ and a view update as a mapping $u : f(S) \rightarrow f(S)$. Let us look into the view update problem.

At a given time τ, the data base is in the state R_τ; the user's view is in the state $r_\tau = f(R_\tau)$. The user wants to update his view by u, i.e. change from state r_τ to state $r'_\tau = u(r_\tau)$. The problem is that r_τ does not physically exist (at least in the general case). Therefore, if we want to update something it must be R_τ. Hence we must change from state R_τ to a new state $R'_\tau = U(R_\tau)$. That new state must of course be such that the view that stems from it is what the user expects i.e. r'_τ . Therefore we can write

$$f(U(R_\tau)) = u(f(R_\tau))$$

This is represented by fig. III-1.

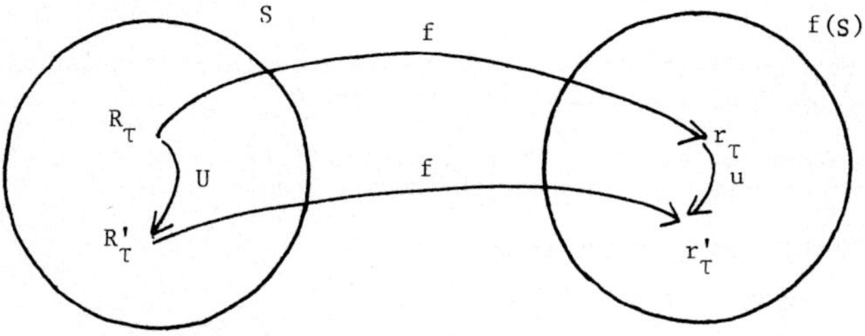

Fig. III-1 : Updating a view

Since this property must be true for all $R_\tau \in S$ we have $f \circ U = u \circ f$. We can also say that the following diagram commutes :

$$\begin{array}{ccc} S & \longrightarrow & f(S) \\ U \downarrow & & \downarrow u \\ S & \underset{f}{\longrightarrow} & f(S) \end{array}$$

This leads us to the following definition :

Definition III-2.

Let S be a schema, let f be a view on S and let u be an update of f(S). We say that update $U : S \rightarrow S$ is a translation of u iff $f \circ U = u \circ f$. □

As anybody familiar with the problem knows, there might be several possible translations of a given update u. For instance we can think about changing in the data base things which are totally unrelated to the view. It is also clear that some of these translations are meaningless. In order to restrict our attention to meaningfull ones we introduce the notion of admissibility :

Definition III-3.

Let S be a schema, let f be a view on S, let u be an update on that view and let $U : S \rightarrow S$ be a translation of u. We say that U is admissible iff $u^n(f(R_\tau)) = f(R_\tau)$ $\Rightarrow U^n(R_\tau) = R_\tau, \ \forall R_\tau \in S, \forall n \geq 0$. □

The admissibility condition simply states that if the user does a sequence of updates on his view that leaves this view invariant ($u^n(f(R_\tau)) = f(R_\tau)$) then the original data base should remain unchanged. For instance if the user asks for the insertion of some tuple in his view and this tuple is already present the view is going to remain unchanged. It is only natural to require that the original data base won't be modified either. Or if the user inserts a tuple then deletes it, it should be expected that nothing has changed.

It should be noted that our condition of admissibility is a weak one (other studies of the problem demand much stronger properties). Nevertheless, our set of admissible translations obviously contains all bona fide ones and we show in section VII that every admissible translation has a meaning. Therefore we consider that the condition of definition III-3 adequately describes the set of meaningful translations.

From now on we shall restrict our attention to admissible translation and by "translation" we shall mean "admissible translation".

Now, given a schema S, a view f and an update u of this view there are four basic questions that one must ask to solve the update problem :

(i) Does there exist a translation U of u ?

(ii) Is it unique ?

(iii) If it is not, how can we choose among the candidates ?

(iv) How can we effectively compute the translation U.

This paper essentially deals with the three first questions. We do recognize that the fourth one is very important but it has seemed to us that a good understanding of the first three was necessary to answer the fourth.

In the litterature the first ones to tackle this problem were the designers of relational systems. In INGRES [Stonebraker 75] and in System R [Chamberlin et al 75] views are implemented by query modification and in the case of system R they are also used for protection. For view updates the approach generally taken is to simply forbid them.

The first formalisation of the problem is in [Paolini and Pelagati 77] where it is studied in the context of mapping several user views into one single conceptual schema. In [Furtado and Sevcik 78] the effect of specific update operations (insert, delete and modify) on views obtained by operations from a relational algebra is studied together with the problem of preserving semantic consistency. Finally, in [Dayal and Berstein 78] a formal criterion for translation is given and algorithms, to do the actual translation in the case where schemas are specified by functional dependancies are presented. This last paper is more oriented toward the computational aspect of the problem and we shall discuss it in more detail later.

IV - THE MATHEMATICAL MODEL

In this section we develop the mathematical framework needed to solve the update problem. Our first task is to study the set M(S) of views that can be defined on schema S. As mentioned in the previous section we do not worry about the content of M(S) but rather about its structure.

Definition IV.

Let S be a schema. Let f and g be two mappings of M(S). We say that f is greater than g or that f determines g (denoted $f \geq g$), iff

$$f(R_1) = f(R_2) \Rightarrow g(R_1) = g(R_2) \qquad \forall \; R_1, R_2 \in S \qquad \square$$

Example : Let the data base be described by a single descriptor R(U) and let X and Y be two subsets of the set of attributes U, then :

$$Y \subseteq X \Rightarrow R(Y) \leq R(X)$$

For instance in R(EMPLOYEE,DEPARTMENT,MANAGER) :

R(EMPLOYEE) ≤ R(EMPLOYEE,MANAGER)

Example : Let the data base be described by :

R_1(EMPLOYEE,DEPARTMENT), R_2(DEPARTMENT,MANAGER,NUMBER-OF-EMPS)

Let the associated schema be specified by :

R_1(DEPARTMENT) = R_2(DEPARTMENT)

R_1 : EMPLOYEE → DEPARTMENT

R_2 : DEPARTMENT → MANAGER, NUMBER-OF-EMPS

and the "NUMBER-OF-EMPS" attribute represent the actual number of employees per department.

Then we have :

R_1(EMPLOYEE, DEPARTMENT) ≥ R_2(DEPARTMENT,NUMBER-OF-EMPS)

Example : Let the data base be described by :

R(PART #, COST, SALEPRICE,PROFIT)

Let the associated schema be specified by :

PART # → COST,SALEPRICE,PROFIT

and ∀ x, x ∈ R_T, x.PROFIT = x.SALEPRICE - x.COST.

Then we have :

$$R(PART \#, COST, SALEPRICE) \geq R(PART \#, PROFIT)$$

As these examples indicate, $f \geq g$ means that whenever we know the value $f(R\ )$ we also know (i.e., we can compute from $f(R_\tau)$) the value $g(R_\tau)$. Note however, that this is a relation between mappings and not between relation values.

This relation can be interpreted as follows : Let S/f and S/g be the quotient sets of S by f and g, respectively. Recall that S/f is the partition induced by f on S (where two relation values R_1 and R_2 belong to the same bloc of the partition iff $f(R_1) = f(R_2)$). Also recall that the partition S/f is said to be a refinement of the partition S/f iff each block of S/f is contained in a block of S/g. The following theorem is a consequence of definition IV-2.

Theorem IV-1.

$f \geq g$ iff S/f is a refinement of S/g. □

And an immediate consequence is that :

Theorem IV-2.

The relation $\geq$ is reflexive, transitive but not antisymmetric. □

Theorem IV-1 implies that the only information we need for ordering f and g is the partitions S/f and S/g. As the relation $\geq$ is not antisymmetric, we introduce the equivalence relation associated with it.

Definition IV-3.

Let f and g be two mappings of M(S). We say that f and g are equivalent (denoted $f \equiv g$) iff $f \geq g$ and $g \geq f$. □

It follows from Theorem 2 that $f \equiv g$ iff $S/f = S/g$ i.e., iff f and g induce the same partition on S.

We denote by 1_S the identity mapping on S and by 0_S the "always true" mapping on S that associates with any value $R_\tau \in S$ the value "true". The partition induced by 1_S is the one where each block consists of a single element (i.e., 1_S is equivalent to any injective mapping of M(S)). The partition induced by 0_S consists of only one block equal to S (i.e. 0_S is equivalent to any constant mapping). The following theorem is an immediate consequence of definition IV-2.

Theorem IV-3.

$\forall\ f \in M(S),\ 0_S \leq f \leq 1_S$ □

We now give an example of equivalence :

Let us consider again the data base described by :

$R_1(EMP,DEPT)$

$R_2(DEPT,MGR,NUMB\text{-}OF\text{-}EMP)$

with the integrity constraints given above.

We define the mapping f by :

$$f(R_{1\tau},R_{2\tau}) = R_{1\tau}(EMP,DEPT) * R_{2\tau}(DEPT,MGR)$$

and we have $f \equiv 1_S$. This simply means that the new view is equivalent to the original schema in the sense that we can recompute the original relations from the view.

In summary, two mappings f and g are equivalent if knowing the value $f(R_\tau)$ we can compute the value $g(R_\tau)$ and conversely, for every R_τ in the schema . Note again that this notion of equivalence applies only to mappings and not to relation values.

We now define a binary law on M(S) :

Definition IV-4.

Let f and g be mappings from M(S). Their product $f \times g$ is a mapping of M(S) defined by $f \times g(R_\tau) = (f(R_\tau), g(R_\tau)),\ \forall\ R_\tau \in S$. □

Example : Let the data base be described by R(EMP,DEPT,MGR) and the schema be specified by the functional dependencies : EMP → DEPT and DEPT → MGR.

Then $1_S \equiv$ R(EMP,DEPT) × R(DEPT,MGR). This is a classical result from decomposition theory. Note, however, that it has nothing to do with joins : the mapping $f \times g$ simply represents the juxtaposition of view f and view g. When this juxtaposition of views produces a schema equivalent to S then the views are "complementary".

Definition IV-5.

Let f be a mapping of M(S). A complement of f is a mapping g of M(S) such that $f \times g \equiv 1_S$. □

Of course, if g is a complement of f then f is a complement of g. Note that 1_S is a complement of 0_S.

Example : Let the data base be described by R(NAME,ADDRESS,TEL), let the schema be specified by the functional dependancy : NAME → ADDRESS,TEL and let f = R(NAME,ADDRESS). Then g = R(NAME,TEL) is a complement of f.

Intuitively the complement $g(R_\tau)$ of $f(R_\tau)$ is the "extra information" that we must give together with $f(R_\tau)$ to be able to recompute R_τ. It should be noted that 1_S is the complement of any f in M(S). This shows that any mapping has at least one complement.

V - TRANSLATING UNDER A CONSTANT COMPLEMENT

Let us now discuss the view update problem in intuitive terms. At a given time the data base has some value R_τ. The user is interested only in his own data $r_\tau = f(R_\tau)$ and he wants to update it by changing it to some $r'_\tau = u(r_\tau)$. Our problem is to translate that change u in f(S) into a change U from R_τ to some R'_τ in S. One simple way to do such a translation is to consider the user's view r_τ as a "subset" of the data base and to update that subset while leaving the rest of the database unchanged. Such a method is fairly natural at first view. Consider for instance a data base described by :

$$R_1(\mathrm{EMP,AGE,SAL,DEPT}),\quad R_2(\mathrm{DEPT,MGR})$$

and consider the view defined by

$$R_1(\mathrm{EMP,AGE,SAL,DEPT})$$

i.e. by restricting our attention to one single relation.

If we want to update an employee record, this can be done easily while leaving the value of R_2 unchanged. In this case the notion of the "rest" of the data base is fairly straightforward since it can be partitionned into two "independent" parts. However, in the general case it might be more difficult to define the "rest" and it might also be more difficult to update one part while leaving the other constant.

Consider again the data base described by :

R_1(EMP,DEPT), R_2(DEPT,MGR,NUM-OF-EMP)

together with the integrity constraints given above.
And the view defined by R_3(EMP,MGR).

What is the "rest" of the data base ? (i.e., what is left out of R_3 ?) It could be R_1(EMP,DEPT) or R_2(DEPT,MGR) or R_2(DEPT,MGR,NUMB-OF-EMP).

At this point it is appropriate to make use of the notion of complement as defined in the previous section. For instance the view

R_1(EMP,DEPT)

is a complement of R_3 and it indeed represents what we intuitively understand as the "rest" of the data base.

Now that we have a view f and its complement g, the translation problem can be restated as follows : in the state R_τ of the data base, the user's view has value $r_\tau = f(R_\tau)$. The user wants to move from value r_τ to r'_τ. Since g is a complement of f, we can replace the data base value R_τ by the equivalent couple $(f(R_\tau),g(R_\tau))$. Under this equivalent representation, if we want to change r_τ to r'_τ while leaving g constant, all we have to do is move to the new representation $(r'_\tau,g(R_\tau))$. Then, since $f \times g \equiv 1_S$, we can recompute $U(R_\tau)$ from $(r'_\tau,g(R_\tau))$ by applying $(f \times g)^{-1}$. This process is illustrated by Figure V-1.

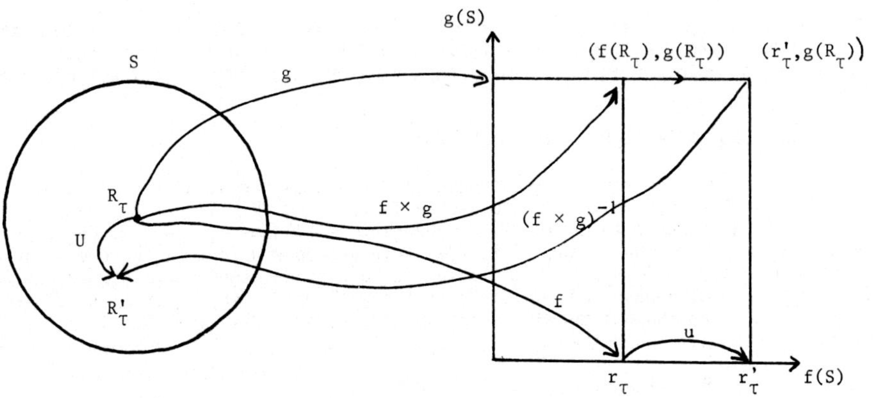

Figure V-1

On the left hand side of the figure, we have the data base schema S and a data base value R_τ. On the right hand side, we have an equivalent representation obtained by replacing R_τ by $(f(R_\tau),g(R_\tau))$. To modify the view value $f(R_\tau)$ while leaving $g(R_\tau)$ constant, we simply move along a line parallel to the f-axis. Then we come back to the original schema, through $(f \times g)^{-1}$ (which exists because $f \times g \equiv 1_S$).

Definition V-1.

Let S be a schema, let $f \in M(S)$ be a view and let u be an update of that view. Let g be a complement of f. The translation of u under constant g (or the g-translation of u) is the mapping U defined on S by :

$$U(R_\tau) = (f \times g)^{-1} (u(f(R_\tau)), g(R_\tau)), \quad \forall R_\tau \in S \qquad \square$$

The following Theorem is an immediate consequence of this definition :

Theorem V-1.

Let S be a schema, let $f \in M(S)$ be a view, let u be an update of f(S), let g be a complement of f and let U be the translation of u under constant g then :

(i) $$f(U(R_\tau)) = u(f(R_\tau)), \qquad \forall R_\tau \in S$$

(ii) $$g(U(R_\tau)) = g(R_\tau), \qquad \forall R_\tau \in S$$

Part (i) of the theorem states that U is indeed a translation of u and part (ii) states that this translation is done under constant g.

U has been defined as a mapping on S. However we should worry about the fact that U must be an update of S. When we defined updates, we insisted on the fact that an update should always lead to a semantically consistent new state i.e. :

$$\forall \; R_\tau \in S, \; U(R_\tau) \in S \quad \text{or} \quad U(S) \subseteq S.$$

Let us now see if the translation of U under constant g satisfies this condition : For $U(R_\tau)$ to belong to S we must have

$$(u(f(R_\tau)), g(R_\tau)) \in f \times g(S)$$

or $\exists R_1 \in S$ such that :

$$(u(f(R_\tau)), g(R_\tau)) = f \times g(R_1)$$

or $u(f(R_\tau)) = f(R_1)$ and $g(R_\tau) = g(R_1)$.

Since this must be true for any $R_\tau \in f^{-1}(r)$ it must be the case that :

$$g(f^{-1}(r)) \subseteq g(f^{-1}(u(r))) \quad \forall \; r, \; r \in f(S).$$

This condition is illustrated in Figure V-2.
Figure V-2-a, shows the case where $U(R) \in S$ and Figure V-2-b, shows the case where $U(R) \notin S$.

These remarks can be summarized by the following definition :

Definition V-2.

Let S be a schema, $f \in M(S)$ be a view, u be an update of that view, and g be a complement of f. u is consistently translatable under constant g iff :

$$g(f^{-1}(r)) \subseteq g(f^{-1}(u(r))), \qquad \forall \; r, \; r \in f(S) \qquad \square$$

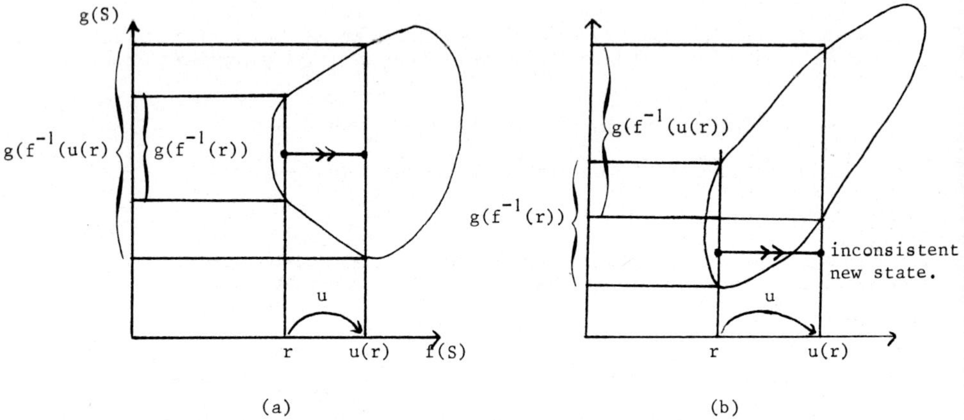

Figure V-2

And as an immediate consequence we can state the following theorem :

Theorem V-2.

Let S, f, u and g be as above. If u is consistently translatable under constant g, then the g-translation U of u is an update on S. In that case we say that U is the consistent g-translation of u. □

In general, when taking any S, f, u, and g, u is not consistently g-translatable. Let us investigate some examples to see what different cases we can encounter :

Example : Let the data base be described by :

R_1(EMP,DEPT); R_2(PART #,PRICE)

Let the view f be defined by f=R_1 and its complement g be R_2. Then in this case any update u on R_1 is consistently R_2-translatable. This is generally the case when the view and its complement are fully independent.

Example : Consider the data base described by

R_1(STUDENT,EXAM,HOUR) ; R_2(EXAM,HOUR)

And an associated schema specified by :

STUDENT,HOUR → EXAM and EXAM → HOUR.

R_1(EXAM,HOUR) ⊆ R_2(EXAM,HOUR)

Let the view f be R_1(STUDENT,EXAM). Then g = R_2(EXAM,HOUR) is a complement of R.

Consider the update u on f defined by :

"Student Smith drops Math exam"

This update is consitently g-translable (i.e. we can in all cases update R_{1t}(STUDENT,EXAM) while keeping R_{2t}(EXAM,HOUR) unchanged and stay in a semantically consistent state).

On the contrary consider update u' defined by :

"Student Smith registers to Latin exam"

u' is not consistently g-translatable since in some cases this update would lead us to a semantically inconsistent state (a violation of STUDENT,HOUR → EXAM, i.e. a timetable conflict).

Finally, we are unable to exhibit any practical example of a couple (f,g) where no update but the identity (which is of course always consistently g-translatable for any g) is consistently g-translatable. However the case cannot be theoretically excluded. We end this section by presenting a complete example of an update translation.

Consider a data base described by :

R_1(EMP,SAL,DEPT)

R_2(DEPT,MGR,# EMP)

Because we do not want to burden this presentation with lengthy notation, we shall assume that we have defined a count mapping that computes the number of attribute values related to another attribute value. Then the associated schema can be specified by the following integrity constraints :

(1) R_1 : EMP → SAL,DEPT

(2) R_2 : DEPT → MGR,# EMP

(3) R_2 (DEPT,# EMP) = count ($R_{1\tau}$(DEPT, EMP))

(4) R_{1t}(DEPT) = R_{2t}(DEPT)

Now, we define the following view descriptor :

r(EMP,DEPT,MGR)

And the view mapping f :

r_τ(EMP,DEPT,MGR) = $R_{1\tau}$(EMP,DEPT) * $R_{2\tau}$(DEPT,MGR)

The view g = R_1(EMP,SAL) is a complement of f. Consider now, the data base value R_τ = ($R_{1\tau}$,$R_{2\tau}$) given by :

$R_{1\tau}$	EMP	SAL	DEPT
	Smith	10000	Car
	Martin	12000	Car
	Jones	11000	Sales
	Doe	10000	Sales
	Adams	12000	Sales

$R_{2\tau}$	DEPT	MGR	#EMP
	Car	Martin	2
	Sales	Adams	3

It yields the view value represented by :

r_τ	EMP	DEPT	MGR
	Smith	Car	Martin
	Martin	Car	Martin
	Jones	Sales	Adams
	Doe	Sales	Adams
	Adams	Sales	Adams

Consider the update on that view defined by

"Move Jones to the car department"

This would yield (in the user's mind) the new view value :

r'_τ	EMP	DEPT	MGR
	Smith	Car	Martin
	Martin	Car	Martin
	Jones	Car	Martin
	Doc	Sales	Adams
	Adams	Sales	Adams

The complement g, in the original data base value, takes the following value :

$g(R_\tau)$	EMP	SAL
	Smith	10000
	Martin	12000
	Jones	11000
	Doc	10000
	Adams	12000

Now we must recompute U(R) by applying the mapping $(f \times g)^{-1}$ to the new data base value $(r'_\tau, g(R_\tau))$. The inverse mapping $(f \times g)^{-1}$ is defined by :

$$R_{1_\tau}(EMP,SAL,DEPT) = (r_\tau(EMP,DEPT) * R_\tau(EMP,SAL))$$

$$R_{2_\tau}(DEPT,MGR,\#EMP) = r_\tau(EMP,MGR) * R_4(DEPT,\#EMP)$$

where $R_4(DEPT,\#EMP)$ = <u>count</u> $(r_\tau(EMP,DEPT))$.

The application of this inverse mapping yields the following new data base value :

R_1	EMP	SAL	DEPT
	Smith	10000	Car
	Martin	12000	Car
	Jones	11000	Car
	Doc	10000	Sales
	Adams	12000	Sales

R_2	DEPT	MGR	#EMP
	Car	Martin	3
	Sales	Adams	2

We do not suggest by this example to use this method for computing the new data base value ! We are only interested here in the semantics of the update process.

VI - THE MULTIPLICITY OF COMPLEMENTS

In the preceeding section, we proposed a translation scheme for view updating. This scheme is based on the separation of the data base into the user's view $f(R_T)$ and its complement $g(R_T)$. The question immediately arises whether this complement is unique. The answer is no, as the following theorem shows.

Theorem VI-1.

Let $f \in M(S)$. Let g be a complement of f. If $g' \geq g$ then g' is a complement of f, $\forall g' \in M(S)$.

□

Proof : As $g' \geq g$, $g'(R_1) = g'(R_2) \Rightarrow g(R_1) = g(R_2)$, $\forall R_1,R_2 \in S$. Therefore, $(f(R_1),g'(R_1)) = (f(R_2),g'(R_2)) \Rightarrow (f(R_1),g(R_1)) = (f(R_2),g(R_2))$, $\forall R_1,R_2 \in S$. That is, $f \times g'(R_1) = f \times g'(R_2) \Rightarrow f \times g(R_1) = f \times g(R_2)$, $\forall R_1,R_2$. It follows from definition 2 that $f \times g' \geq f \times g$. As g is a complement of f we have $f \times g \equiv 1_S$, hence $f \times g' \geq 1_S$. It follows from Theorem IV-3 that $f \times g' \leq 1_S$. Therefore, $f \times g' \equiv 1_S$, and g' is a complement of f. Q.E.D.

This result is intuitively satisfactory : It means that if we can reconstruct the original data base by adding g to f then we can certainly do so by adding to f anything "bigger" than g.

Now that we know that there can be different choices for the complement, let us see how these choices might affect the translation process.

Theorem VI-2.

Let $f \in M(S)$. Let g and g' be two complements of f such that $g' \geq g$. Let u be an update of f(S). If u is consistently g'-translatable then (1) u is consistently g-translatable and (2) the g'-translation of u is equal to the g-translation of u.

□

Proof : (1) We have to show that : $g(f^{-1}(r)) \subset g(f^{-1}(u(r)))$, $\forall r \in f(S)$. As u is g'-translatable, we have : $g'(f^{-1}(r)) \subset g'(f^{-1}(u(r)))$, $\forall r \in f(S)$.

This implies that $\forall R_1 \in f^{-1}(r)$ there exists $R_2 \in f^{-1}(u(r))$ such that $g'(R_1) = g'(R_2)$. Since $g' \geq g$, it follows that $g(R_1) = g(R_2)$. That is, $\forall R_1 \in f^{-1}(r)$ there exists $R_2 \in f^{-1}(u(r))$ such that $g(R_1) = g(R_2)$. Therefore, $g(f^{-1}(r)) \subset g(f^{-1}(u(r)))$, $\forall r \in f(S)$. Q.E.D.

(2) Let U be the g'-translation of u.

Then $U(R) = (f \times g')^{-1}(u(f(R)),g'(R))$, $\forall R \in S$, and $g'(U(R)) = g'(R)$. Since $g' \geq g$, it follows from (1) that $g(U(R)) = g(R)$ i.e., $U(R) = (f \times g)^{-1}(u(f(R)),g(R))$.
Q.E.D.

Example : Let the data base be described by :

R_1(EMP,SAL,DEPT) and R_2(DEPT,MGR,#EMP)

with the usual meaning attached to these relations.

Let the view be $f = R_1$(EMP,SAL,DEPT). A complement of f is $g_1 = R_2$(DEPT,MGR,#EMP). But another one is $g_2 = R_2$(DEPT,MGR).

Consider for instance the problem of translating the update u = "raise all employees salaries by 5%". u is consistently translatable under g_1 and g_2 constant and clearly both translations have the same result. However if we think of the update :

u' = "hire employee Jones with salary 10000 in the car department"

u' is consistently g_2 translatable, but it is not consistently g_1 translatable.

Theorem VI-2 implies that as the complement g (of a view f) becomes smaller the set of g-translatable updates becomes larger. Thus, given a view f, we have interest in choosing the smallest possible complement of f for the translation process. This fact leads to the notion of a minimal complement.

Definition VI-1.

Let $f \in M(S)$. A minimal complement of f is a mapping $g \in M(S)$ such that (i) g is a complement of f and (ii) if g' is a complement of f and $g' \leq g$ then $g' \equiv g$. □

We saw earlier that the complement of a view f is not unique. We now ask the question : is the minimal complement unique ? The answer is again no, as the following theorem shows.

Theorem VI-3.

A mapping $f \in M(S)$ has a unique minimal complement iff $f \equiv 1_S$ or $f \equiv 0_S$. □

Before proving this theorem let us emphasize that we consider uniqueness up to an equivalence.

Proof : If a mapping f has a unique minimal complement g, then

$\forall g'$ comp of f $\quad g' \geq g$.

The proof is as follows : we take a mapping f non equivalent to 1_S and non equivalent to 0_S and we exhibit a g' complement of f and not greater than g.

Proposition 1 : $f \not\equiv 0_S$ and $f \not\equiv 1_S \Rightarrow \exists B_1 \in S/f \ \exists B_2 \in S/f$ such that

(i) $\quad B_1 \neq B_2$

(ii) $\quad |B_1| \geq 1$ and $|B_2| \geq 2$

Proof 1 : $f \not\equiv 0_S \Rightarrow S/f \neq \{S\}$

$\Rightarrow$ There are at least two distinct non empty blocks in S/f

$f \neq 1_S \Rightarrow S/f \neq S$

$\Rightarrow$ One block in S/f has at least a two elements.

Q.E.D.

Proposition 2 : g omplement of f $\Rightarrow \exists a \in B_1, \exists b \in B_2$ such that $g(a) \neq g(b)$.

Proof 2 : Recall that for g to be a complement of f, we must have $S/(f \times g) = S$ that is the partition induced by g on the blocks of S/f must consist of single element blocks.

Assume now that $\forall a \in B_1, \forall b \in B_2$

$$g(a) = g(b)$$

Then by transitivity $\forall b_1 \in B_2, \forall b_2 \in B_2$

$$g(b_1) = g(b_2)$$

And the partition induced by g on B_2 is not single element. Q.E.D.

Proposition 3 : Let g' be defined by :

$g'(x) = g(x)$, $\forall x \in S, x \neq a, x \neq b$

$g'(a) = g'(b) = K$ where K is some new value such that $K \notin g(S)$ then we have :

(i) g' complement of f

(ii) g' not $\geq$ g

Proof 3 :

(i) Each block B_i of S/f is partitioned in single element blocks by g', and therefore g' is a complement of f

(ii) $g'(a) = g'(b)$
and $g(a) \neq g(b) \Rightarrow g'$ not $\geq g$ Q.E.D.

This concludes the proof of Theorem VI-3.

It follows from this theorem that there can be an infinity of even minimal complements of a given view. Then, according to our translation scheme there is an infinity of ways to translate an update. Do all these different ways have a practical meaning ? In other words, can we find examples of "realistic" f, g_1 and g_2 such that (i) g_1 and g_2 are distinct complements and (ii) the g_1-translation and the g_2-translation of a "realistic" update of f are meaningful ? The answer is yes and we shall present such examples later. First, let us discuss further the multiplicity of complements and its practical consequences.

In [Dayal and Berstein 78] it is argued that "... an update u on a view f(S) is translatable if there is a unique update U on S producing the desired update on f(S) such that ...". Then, later, the authors argue that the uniqueness criterion is controversial : "... We do not feel comfortable with this choice but could not find more attractive alternatives [...] admittedly, our correctness criteria have weaknesses. However, these weaknesses are due to gaps in our understanding of update semantics in the relational model..."

Indeed, it appears that the uniqueness criterion is the best choice in case, when the only information available is the description of the view. However, as the authors observe, "... the view definition function [...] is often not sufficient to express the semantics of the relationship between update operations on the view and on the [original] schema...". Our conclusion here is that the extra information we need is exactly the description of a complement of the view.

We present now some examples of views and multiple complements.

Example : Let the data base be described by :

R(PRODUCT,COST,SALE-PRICE,PROFIT,PROFIT-RATE)

and an associated schema specified by :

(i) PRODUCT $\rightarrow$ COST,SALEPRICE,PROFIT,PROFIT-RATE

(ii) $\forall x \in R_\tau$, x.COST ≥ 0 and x.PROFIT ≥ 0

x.PROFIT = x.SALEPRICE - x.COST

x.PROFIT-RATE = x.PROFIT/x.COST.

Now define a view r(PRODUCT,COST) by the f mapping

r_τ(PRODUCT,COST) = R_τ(PRODUCT,COST)

and consider the update u described by

"Decrease the cost of all products by 5%"

The three mappings

g_1 = R(PRODUCT,SALEPRICE)

g_2 = R(PRODUCT,PROFIT)

g_3 = R(PRODUCT,PROFIT-RATE)

are all complements of f, and u is g_i-translatable for i=1,2,3. These three translations correspond to three different update policies : in the g_1-translation the saleprice will remain constant while profit and profit rate will increase, in the g_2-translation the profit will remain constant, the sale price will decrease and the profit rate will increase and in the g_3-translation the profit rate will remain constant while the saleprice and the profit will decrease. These three translations are all acceptable policies and neither practical nor theoretical arguments can allow us to disregard one or another. This is simply because the view definition function is not sufficient information to decide on the update policy, while for instance (f,g_1) is a full description of the view f. It is up to the user to decide which update policy is appropriate for his application.

Example : Let the data base be described by

R_1(EMP,DEPT)

R_2(DEPT,MGR,MGR-SAL,SECRETARY)

and the associated schema be specified by

R_1 : EMP $\rightarrow$ DEPT

R_2 : DEPT $\leftrightarrow$ MGR

R_2 : MGR $\rightarrow$ MGR-SAL,SECRETARY

Consider the view :

$$f = R_2(\text{DEPT},\text{MGR})$$

and the update

u : "permute the managers of departments A and B".

The following mappings are three different complements of f

$$g_1 = R_1(\text{EMP},\text{DEPT}) \times R_2(\text{DEPT},\text{MGR-SAL},\text{SECRETARY})$$
$$g_2 = R_1(\text{EMP},\text{DEPT}) \times R_2(\text{MGR},\text{MGR-SAL},\text{SECRETARY})$$
$$g_3 = R_1(\text{EMP},\text{DEPT}) \times R_2(\text{MGR},\text{MGR-SAL}) \times R_2(\text{DEPT},\text{SECRETARY})$$

In all three cases the translation U of u permutes the managers of departments A and B. But this is done under a different "policy" each time. For instance, in the first case the managerial salary of the department remains unchanged. Also, the secretary stays with the department. In the second case, neither the salary nor the secretary of the manager change. In the third case the salary of the manager remains unchanged and the secretary stays in the department. Thus, the three complements of f correspond to three different "realistic policies" under which a permutation of managers can be done in a company.

VII - UNIVERSALITY OF TRANSLATION UNDER CONSTANT COMPLEMENT

To summarize the previous sections, we have first defined the translation of an update u on view f as an update U on schema S such that :

(i) $$f \circ U = u \circ f$$

(ii) $$u^n(f(R_\tau)) = f(R_\tau) \Rightarrow U^n(R_\tau) = R_\tau, \qquad \forall\, R_\tau \in S.$$

This defined a set $T_f(u)$ of translations of u. Then we studied a specific translation scheme : the translation U under a constant complement g defined by :

$$U(R_\tau) = (f \times g)^{-1}\,(u(f(R_\tau)),g(R_\tau))$$

It was then shown that for a given f there was no unique g but a multiplicity, which defined a set $T_f^c(u)$ of translations of u under all constant complements i.e. :

$$T_f^c(u) = \{U \mid \exists \text{ complement } g \text{ of } f \text{ such that } U \text{ is the consistent } g\text{-translation of } u\}$$

The first question to ask is whether the g-translation of u is indeed an admissible one as defined in section III., i.e., whether $T_f^c(u) \subseteq T_f(u)$.

Theorem VII-1.

Let S be a schema, let f be a view and u an update of that view, let g be a complement of f. The consistent g-translation of u is an admissible translation of u. □

Proof : It was shown in theorem V-1, that the g-translation of u is indeed a translation. So all we have to show is that it is admissible. Assume

$$u^n(f(R_\tau)) = f(R_\tau).$$

Then
$$U^n(R_\tau) = (f \times g)^{-1}(u^n(f(R_\tau)),g(R_\tau))$$
$$= (f \times g)^{-1}(f(R_\tau),g(R_\tau))$$

$$= (f \times g)^{-1}(f \times g(R_\tau))$$
$$= R_\tau$$
Q.E.D

The next question concerns the generality of the translation scheme that we presented : Does there exist other ways of translating updates ? Fortunately the answer is no, i.e. any translation of u is its translation under some constant complement g of f as we now state :

Theorem VII-3.

Let S be a schema, let f be a view, let u be an update of that view and let U be an admissible translation of u. Then there exists a complement g of f such that U is the g-translation of u. In other words

$$T_f(u) \subseteq T_f^c(u).$$ □

Proof : We define on S a binary relation by :

$$R_\tau \equiv R'_\tau \quad \text{iff } \exists n \geq 0 \text{ such that } U^n(R_\tau) = R'_\tau$$
$$\underline{\text{or}} \quad \exists n \geq 0 \text{ such that } U^n(R'_\tau) = R_\tau$$

It is clear that $\equiv$ is an equivalence relation. We can therefore define the quotient set $S/\equiv$ and the induced mapping $g : S \rightarrow S/\equiv$, that associates with each R_τ its equivalence class $[R_\tau]$, i.e.

$$g(R_\tau) = [R_\tau] , \quad \forall R_\tau.$$

Claim : g is a complement of f.

To show this, we must prove that $f \times g \equiv 1_S$, i.e. that $f \times g$ is injective or in other words :

$$f \times g(R_1) = f \times g(R_2) \Rightarrow R_1 = R_2 , \quad \forall R_1 \text{ et } R_2 \text{ in S.}$$

Let R_1 and R_2 be two values such that $f \times g(R_1) = f \times g(R_2)$
Then by definition of $f \times g$ we have

$$f(R_1) = f(R_2) \qquad (1)$$

and

$$g(R_1) = g(R_2) \qquad (2)$$

(2) $\Rightarrow \exists n \geq 0$ such that $R_2 = U^n(R_1)$ (3)

The fact that U is a translation of u implies that :

$$u^n(f(R_1)) = f(U^n(R_1)) \qquad (4)$$

(3) and (4) $\Rightarrow u^n(f(R_1)) = R_2$ (5)

(5) and (1) $\Rightarrow u^n(f(R_1)) = f(R_1)$ (6)

(6) and the fact that U is an admissible translation of u implies that :

$$U^n(R_1) = R_1 \qquad (7)$$

(7) and (3) $\Rightarrow R_1 = R_2$ Q.E.D.

We have shown that g is a complement of f. By the definition of g we have :

$$g(U(R)) = g(R), \quad \forall R \in S$$

which shows that U is a g-translation. Q.E.D.

This theorem shows that every translation is a translation under some constant complement g of f. Therefore the translation under constant complement is a totally general method of translation.

VIII - CONCLUSION

In this paper we have studied the problem of updating relational views. We have defined a view as a mapping $f : S \to f(S)$ and an update as a mapping $u : f(S) \to f(S)$.

The view update problem consists in translating u into an update $U : S \to S$. The usual definition of the update translation, i.e. $f \circ U = u \circ f$ was adopted and we introduced an admissibility condition, stating that if a sequence of updates leaves the view unchanged then their translation should leave the data base unchanged too.

Then we presented a specific "method" for update translation : together with a view f, we defined a complementary view g, such that from the couple $(f(R_\tau), g(R_\tau))$ the original data base value R_τ can be recomputed. The translation under constant g consists of modifying the $f(R_\tau)$ component, while the $g(R_\tau)$ component remains unchanged. Conditions for this translation to be well defined were exhibited. It was then argued that different complementary views could be chosen and that their choice would correspond to the choice of an update policy of the data base.

Finally this translation method was proved universal, by showing that every admissible translation can be done by this method.

The main contributions of this paper consist of showing :

(i) that all update translations are translations under some complement

(ii) there is no unique better way of translating an update but just different update policies

(iii) the choice of a policy is the choice of a complementary view g.

These three points suggest the following approach for handling updates

1 - choose a complement g

2 - check that it is a minimal complement of f

3 - whenever update u is attempted, check whether u is g-translatable

4 - translate u by the formula $(f \times g)^{-1}(u(f(R), g(R))$

In this paper we have not dealt at all with the problem of the practical implementation of these four steps. Steps (1)(2) and (3) are very much dependent on the schema S, i.e. on the type of integrity constraints that we want to consider. This seems to imply that many decisions will be taken by humans (the DBA) at these steps. Obviously step 4 must be realized by a program and the brute force application of the formula is unacceptable. So efforts for further research should go in that direction.

REFERENCES

[Chamberlain et Al 75] Chamberlain, D.D., J.N. Gray, and D.D. Traiger, "Views, authorization and locking in a relational data base system", Proceedings of AFIPS NCC, Vol 44, 1975.

[Codd 72] Codd, E.F., "Further Normalization of the database relational model", in Data Base Systems, Courant Computer Science Symposium 6, R. Rustin, Ed. Prentice Hall, Englewood Cliffs, 1972, pp. 33-64.

[Codd 74] Codd, E.F., "Recent investigation in a Relational data base systems", information Processing 74, North Holland Pub. Co, Amsterdam 74, pp 1017-1021.

[Dayal and Berstein 78] Dayal, U. and P.A. Berstein, "On the updatability of Relational views", Proceedings of the 4th International Conference on very large data bases, West Berlin 78.

[Furtado and Sevcik 78] Furtado, A.L. and K.C. Sevcik, "Permitting updates through views of data bases", to appear 79.

[Paolini and Pelagatti 77] Paolini P., and G. Pelagatti, "Formal definitions of mappings in a data base", ACM SIGMOD, Proceedings of the Int. Conf. on Management of Data, Aug. 1977, pp. 40-46.

[Stonebraker 75] Stonebraker, M. "Implementation of integrity constraints and views by query modification", Proc. 1975 SIGMOD Conf., ACM, N.Y., pp. 65-78.

DATA BASE LANGUAGES

Data Base Architecture, Bracchi/Nijssen, eds.
North-Holland Publishing Company

CSL: A Language for Defining Conceptual Schemas

B. Breutmann, E. Falkenberg and R. Mauer

Siemens AG - ZT ZFE FL INF
Otto-Hahn-Ring 6
D-8000 München 83
Fed. Rep. of Germany

This paper describes a high level data definition language, CSL, which provides powerful capabilities for defining conceptual schemas within the three level architecture of DBMS. The language includes both descriptive and procedural elements in a well-balanced proportion providing a notation of the conceptual schema easy to survey. CSL provides a general solution to the naming and identification problem and the option of introducing time frames and calendar systems. Aiming at the central interface of the three level architecture CSL lends itself for expressing both the static and the dynamic aspects of conceptual data.

1. Introduction

The three level architecture of DBMS has been widely accepted as a good tool for managing large and complex data bases (/NIJSSEN 77/).
Much work has been invested to develop concepts for the central interface of this architecture.
Particularly conceptual data models are considered to be the best suited method for describing data at the central interface.
This paper deals with a language for defining conceptual schemas. CSL (Conceptual Schema Language) is based on the object-role model (/FALKENBERG 75/, /FALKENBERG 76/). The language lends itself to describe both the static aspects and the dynamic behaviour of data.

Solutions of special problems which have to be considered at the central interface, i.e. privacy, concurrency etc., are beyond the scope of our current language.
The purpose of this paper is to outline concepts which were designed to meet conceptual schema requirements and to describe the basic constructs of CSL developped in order to formulate these concepts.
In section 2 constructs for the conceptual schema are sketched. Section 3 deals with design criteria and design decisions taken in order to meet these criteria. Finally section 4 contains a detailed description of the most important CSL constructs.

2. Constructs for the Conceptual Schema

The conceptual schema formally defines the possible states and events of the data base universe (universe of discourse, information sphere). For reasons of better data base design, better stability and evolvability of the information system and better transformability of the various interfaces within the three level architecture, the conceptual schema should contain no aspects of how to represent the information in order to gain efficient physical storage and access or high user convenience. Only and all semantically relevant aspects should be considered within the conceptual schema (/FALKENBERG 77/).

These conditions are helpful in finding adequate constructs for the conceptual schema. In this paper the question of what are the most adequate constructs is not discussed. This was already done in earlier papers (e.g. /FALKENBERG 76/, /FALKENBERG 77/). However, since these constructs are the fundament of the conceptual schema language we list them in the following sections.

a) Atomic States and Events; Time
The conceptual schema should define not only the static, but also the dynamic aspects of the data base universe (short notation: DB universe). Thus we do not only use the construct of an atomic state which means a single elementary fact or association, but also the construct of an atomic event which means the begin, end or change of an atomic state. Furthermore, we provide the option to introduce time frames and calendar systems (/FALKENBERG 74/). While an atomic state is valid within a specific time period, an atomic event occurs at a specific point of time. To speak in conventional terms, by aid of this option we are able to define not only the "present state of the data base", but also its "history". Updating in a conventional static data base means, in our terms, to insert a set of atomic events and to forget the corresponding old states immediately afterwards. Thus, a conventional data base is a special "borderline case" of those data bases designed according to our method.

b) Components of Atomic States: Objects and Roles
The inner structure of an atomic state (association) is determined by a sequence of associated objects and by the roles these objects play within the association. Atomic means that the association cannot be split into smaller parts without loosing information. This criterion of irreducibility restricts the number of object-role pairs within an association. However, there does not exist a global restriction on this number, like the restriction on binary associations (see e.g. /SENKO 76/.)

c) Objects and their Identification
We have to face the problem that there might be DB universes where the unique signification (i.e. identification) of an object cannot be handled in the simple way by using a unique name for an object (i.e. a single referred object).

For an object there may be several names, or several objects may have the same name, or even not only the names but additional information is necessary to identify an object (i.e. a multiple referred object). In order to guarantee that nevertheless an object can be identified we distinguish between the names and the object they stand for and define explicit associations between the object and its names. These name associations and, if necessary, other associations addressing further needed information are used to identify the object. Names are strings over some alphabet.

d) Instances, Types and Populations
So far we have spoken about instances of constructs. Those instances which have certain "properties" in common are said to be of a certain type. There are object types which can be characterized for example by roles their object instances play within the associations in which they occur. For each object one can decide which object type it belongs to. There are association types, i.e. types of atomic states which are characterized by all participating object types and the roles which the object instances play in association instances of these types.

The set of instances belonging to a certain type X at a specific instance of time t is called a population of type X at time t (denoted by X_t).

Finally types of atomic events are characterized by association types. The events represent the begins or ends of the instances of these association types.

e) Characteristics of Types
A single type may possess a lot of characteristics which are relevant to be defined in the conceptual schema. We list some of those characteristics in the following:
- Characteristics of object types:
  format of names, standard type of names, operations applicable to objects, identification method for objects;
- characteristics of association types:
  occurrence frequencies of objects within association types, identifier of association types;
  transitivity, symmetry, reflexivity;
- characteristics of types of events:
  distance of time between atomic events of a certain type, frequency of atomic events within a period of time.

f) Interdependencies between Types
The population of a single type may be dependent on the population of another type or even on the population of several other types. In particular, most important are interdependencies between association types and interdependencies between event types.

With the above considerations in mind we can define more concretely what we unterstand by a conceptual schema:
A conceptual schema is the definition of all types relevant to a particular data base universe, together with their characteristics and interdependencies.

Specifications of characteristics and interdependencies we call semantical rules.

3. Design criteria and Design decisions

This chapter deals with the most important design criteria we had to consider when designing CSL, and outlines the design decisions we took in order to meet these criteria.

Self-evidently, CSL must be able to describe the conceptual schema constructs completely and explicitly.
Considering these requirements we decided that CSL should include both descriptive and procedural elements:
Object types and association types and some of their characteristics are described by descriptive language elements.
Types of atomic events and their characteristics as well as all the interdependencies are described in a half-procedural and half-descriptive way. This is done by signifying sets of objects, associations, and events and embedding these significations into procedures.

Referring to completeness and explicitness CSL particularly has to describe two conceptual schema constructs not yet in common use but attracting attention increasingly: the time concept and the identification concept.

Being a common denominator for a large variety of users and user types, CSL programs, even representing complex information structures, should be readable for all those different users. Particulary CSL provides constructs which lend themselves to good structured CSL programs.

Referring to a fixed conceptual schema, we are faced with the problem of preserving semantic integrity, i.e. guaranteeing that the data base instances do not violate the semantical rules. In order to solve this problem in a user-convenient way CSL offers a particular concept: the event-procedure concept.

3.1 Time handling facilities

CSL offers the possibility of optionally using time handling facilities.
In order to embed the data base history into the historical time axis, these facilities include the definition of an application-specific calendar system.
In CSL a calendar system is a n-tuple $(TT_1, \ldots, TT_n)$, consisting of time segment types TT_i, $1 \le i \le n$, where:

(C1) The time segment types are sets linearly ordered by the relation $\le$. Their elements are called time segments.

(C2) For $1 \le i \le n$ holds: There exists a time period such that each $TS \in TT_i$ represents this time period.

For $2 \le i \le n$ holds:
This time period is an integer multiple of the time period represented by the elements of TT_{i-1}.
For each $TS \in TT_i$ there exists $T_{FIRST} \in TT_{i-1}$ and $T_{LAST} \in TT_{i-1}$ where T_{FIRST} denotes the "begin" of TS and T_{LAST} the "end" of TS.

(C3) A fixed point has to be established on the time axis and the elements of TT_n have to refer to that fixed point.
This definition allows, for example, calendar systems like (DAY, MONTH, YEAR) or (SECOND, MINUTE, HOUR, DAY, MONTH, YEAR) based on the Christian era.
Starting from the definition of a calendar system we define a <u>point of time</u> to be a (n-i+1)-tuple $(D_i,\ldots,D_n)$, where

(T1) $D_j \in TT_j$, $i \leq j \leq n$

(T2) For $i \leq j \leq n-1$ holds:

$D_j \geqslant$ "begin" of D_{j+1} and

$D_j \leqslant$ "end" of D_{j+1}.

TT_i specifies the <u>duration</u> of the point of time $(D_i,\ldots,D_n)$.
Thus referring to the calendar systems mentioned above, (14,01,1950) and (09,1978) are points of time, denoting January 14-th 1950 resp. September 1978.
After having fixed the calendar system, CSL enables the DB administrator to declare for each association type, whether the history of its instances has to be recorded or not.
For each time-provided association type the DB administrator has to specify how long the begin or end of its instances can last.

3.2 Identification concept

According to the problem of identifying objects in DB universes there can occur single referred objects and multiple referred objects. For the sake of user-convenience, CSL offers the possibility to handle single referred objects in a straight forward manner. Therefore in CSL we distinguish between two kinds of object types, namely:

a) <u>Object type consisting of single referred objects</u>
Let T be the time-interval the conceptual schema description is valid within. Given a set of names (considered as strings over some alphabet), we call an object type 0 <u>self-identified</u> if within T either condition S1 or S2 holds:
(S1) Each object belonging to 0 possesses exactly one name and at most one object is assigned to a certain name.
(S2) Each object belonging to 0 is a string over some alphabet.

CSL facilitates the identification of single referred objects by not explicitly defining associations between single referred objects and their names. That means any single referred object is directly populated by its name.

b) <u>Object type consisting of multiple referred objects</u>
If an object type does not satisfy the condition for self-identified object types its objects are identified by means of one or more associations, i.e. they are multiple referred objects.

A set of association types $I = (A_1, \ldots, A_m)$ is called an <u>identifier for object type 0</u> (0 being non-self-identified), if the following conditions hold and if there is no $I' \subset I$ satisfying these conditions:

(I1) Within each association type $A \in I$ the object type 0 plays exactly one role.

(I2) For each time instance $t \in T$ holds:
o_1, o_2 being arbitrary but different objects $\in O_t$, implies the following:
There exists at least one association type $A \in I$ and one association instance $\alpha \in A_t$, o_1 playing a role in α, such that there exists no association instance $\beta \in A_t$, o_2 playing a role in β, which differs from α only with respect to the objects o_1 and o_2.

(I3) In the case of hierarchical identification of 0 the identifiers of object types which can be reached stepwise by the identifying association types of 0 must not lead to the object type 0.

Remarks:
- The association types $A_1, \ldots, A_m$ are called identifying association types for O.
- All association types in the DB universe may be used as identifying association types.
- Condition I3 ensures that recursive situations cannot occur.

For example, let the object type PERSON be identified by the association types FAMILY-NAME, FIRST-NAME and BIRTHDAY.

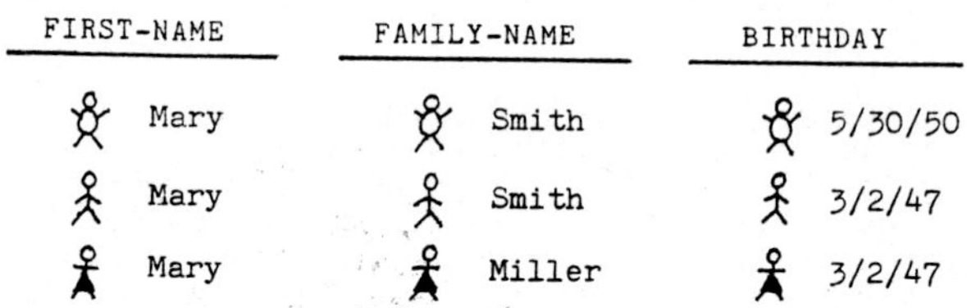

<u>Fig.</u> 1 Identifying associations for objects of type PERSON

In order to clear up the condition I2 let us check the condition in the example of Fig. 1. In order to distinguish between  and  choose A equal to BIRTHDAY; for distinguishing between  and  choose A equal to FAMILY-NAME.

Objects of non-self-identified object types are uniquely referred to by the objects associated by the identifying associations, e.g.  is referred to by (Mary, Smith, 5/30/50).
This concept of identifying objects is parallel to the concept of the identifying set of a type in /BILLER 78/.

3.3 Language divisions

For the sake of readability we introduce language constructs which lend themselves to good structured CSL programs.
In particular, CSL programs are divided into five divisions:

(D1) Within the standard type division the standard types provided by the DBMS are listed together with operations defined on and among these types.

(D2) The calendar division is optional. It includes the definition of the application specific calendar system.

(D3) The object type division includes the specification of the object types and their characteristics relevant to the DB universe. Particularly the identification of objects is specified.
Operations on object types are traced to operations on standard types.

(D4) The association type division consists of the specification of association types together with some of their characteristics.

(D5) Within the fifth division event types and their characteristics and interdependencies as well as interdependencies between association types and some of the association type characteristics are described. This division is called "semantical rule division".

Divisions D1, D2, D4 are formulated only by descriptive language elements. D3 is mainly formulated by descriptive language elements whereas D5 is formulated in a half-descriptive and half-procedural way.

3.4 The event-procedure concept

Due to papers dealing with the problem of preserving semantic integrity (/HAMMER 74/, /ESWARAN 75/, /NIJSSEN 78/) we have to solve the following three subproblems:

(P1) Construction of sequences of update statements in order to transfer the data base from an old valid state into a new valid state (i.e. construction of a conceptual transaction /NIJSSEN 78/; an update statement designates an atomic event, i.e. the insertion, deletion, or modification of a single elementary fact).

(P2) Assigning to the update statements those semantical rules which have to be checked when these update statements occur.

(P3) Providing good error handling facilities to handle violations against semantical rules.

Usually, the update program or the user is charged with the solution of problems P1 and P2. Designing CSL, we developed concepts taking this tasks off the user´s shoulder.

The main concept is the <u>event-procedure concept</u>.
As mentioned above, an atomic event is the insertion, the deletion, or the modification of an association of a certain type.
Since semantical rules can be violated only when events occur, the structure of the semantical rules within the semantical rule division is imposed by events:

All events corresponding to either the insertion, the deletion, or the modification of association instances of a particular type set up an <u>event procedure</u>.
The procedure head specifies the update operation and the association type considered. The formal parameters are substitutes for object instances. The procedure body contains the semantical rules to be checked when the event procedure is invoked.
In order to preserve semantic integrity, some of these rules require additional associations to be inserted or existing associations to be deleted or modified. In this case, further event procedures are invoked by the procedure body. These invocations cause the execution of the semantical rules relevant to the corresponding events.

Thus an update operation initialized by the user generally leads to an invocation hierarchy of event-procedures (Fig. 2).

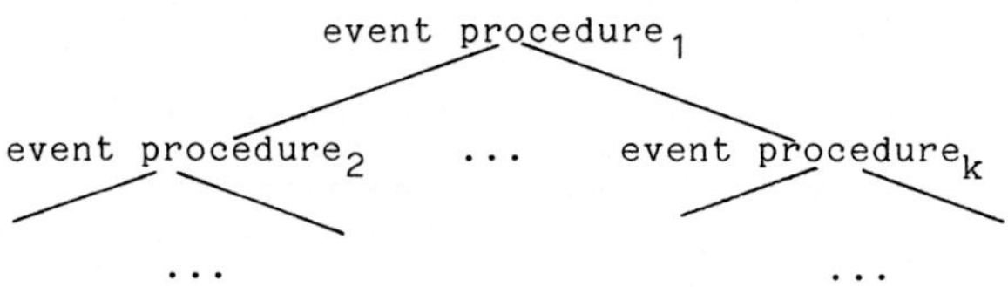

<u>Fig. 2</u> Hierarchy of event procedures

Traversing the tree illustrated in Fig. 2 means:
a) Building up the transaction transferring the old valid state into a new one (i.e. solving problem P1).
b) Checking all semantical rules relevant to the event procedure on top of the tree while the transaction is performed (i.e. solving problem P2).

The point is that the transactions need not be known in advance. They are built by the DBMS in an interactive way.

Moreover, the event-procedure concept makes the following error handling facilities possible:
a) The violation of a semantical rule ist detected at the first opportunity.
b) In the case of violation the following information is available:
   - the violated rule
   - the event procedure the rule is part of
   - the predecessors of the event procedure.

Finally, CSL offers the possibility of defining rules either to be laws or to be plausibility rules. The violation of a plausibility rule causes a warning instead of a rejection of the update statement.

4. <u>Language description</u>

We now describe the basic CSL constructs outlining their meaning and their use. By means of an example DB universe we first describe the definition of object types and association types, secondly how semantical rules are modelled and finally how the time frames are handled.

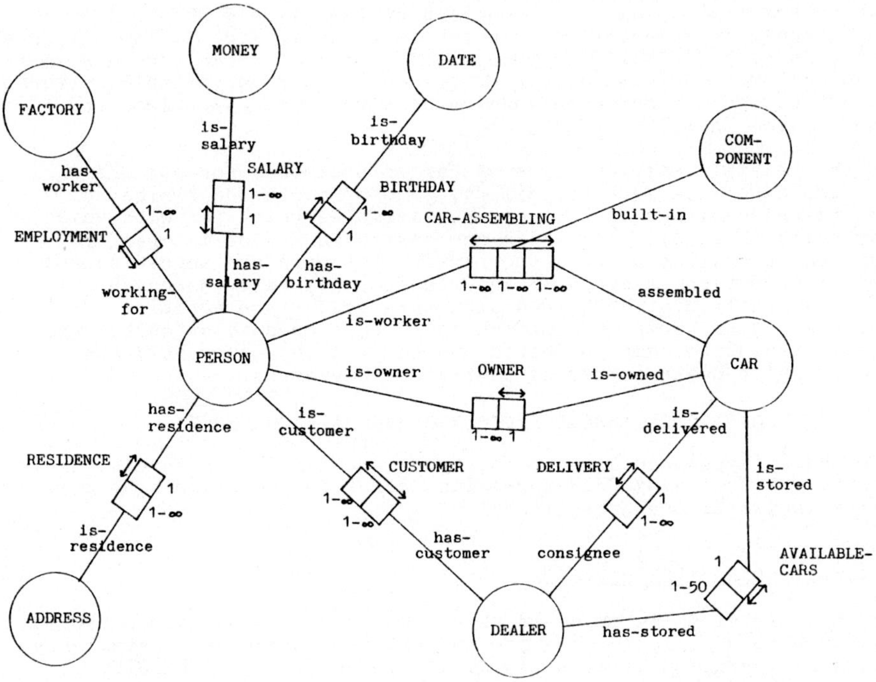

Explanation of the symbols used in the graphic representation (see /NIJSSEN 77/):

(OBJ)	object type
ASSOCIATION role1 [|] role2	association type with roles (the boxes correspond to the roles and may contain additional information)
⟷	identifier of an association type
m-n	simple occurrence frequencies

Fig. 3 An example DB universe

An Example Data Base Universe

Let us briefly explain the semantics of the example DB universe the graphic representation of which is given in Fig. 3. The universe contains both a simplified production process for cars and a simplified customer administration. Up to section 4.3 our example universe is not embedded into the dimension of time. Naming problems are encompassed in section 4.1.3.

In this example only one type of car is produced. For persons who are employed in a factory, salary, date of birth and residence are to be specified as well as who assembles which car with which car components. All cars which are assembled are of interest in this universe. The dealers who receive the cars are specified and this information is again of interest for all cars. Moreover the cars currently available from a certain dealer are notified. On the other side, some information is to be stored about customers, namely residence, date of birth, which cars they currently own, and of which dealers they currently are customers.

4.1 Definition of object types and association types

The object types and association types are defined in several divisions. The following CSL expressions refer to the example DB universe (keywords are underlined).

4.1.1 STANDARD TYPE DIVISION

In this division the standard types and standard operations provided by the DBMS are listed in order to tell the user what is available. Standard operations like =, ≠, ≤, <, ... and +, -, *, LENGTH, ... are defined for operands of the same standard types or different standard types like INTEGER, REAL, CHAR, STRING, DIGIT.

4.1.2 OBJECT TYPE DIVISION

The object types relevant to the DB universe must have unique names. Within the object type division only those characteristics can be described which hold for all objects of a certain type.

a) Self-identified object types are defined using the following rough syntax expressed in BNF:

<self-id object type>::= OBJECT TYPE <object type name>
{TYPE <standard type>}$_0^1$
{FORMAT <format description>}$_0^1$
{OPERATIONS <operation list>}$_0^1$

Generally speaking, objects of self-identified object types are considered as strings over some alphabet in the widest sense which gives the possibility to formulate manipulations on these strings. This enables us to describe the following characteristics of object types:

a1) First we can define of which standard type the objects of an object type are. The standard type determines implicitly the operations applicable to the objects. Objects occurring as operands of standard operations are handled like constants of the corresponding standard types.
Thus, the DB administrator does not have to define various operations between and among object types (/BILLER 78/) or compatibility sets of data domains (/ESWARAN 75/) himself.

a2) Format descriptions are used to describe objects of a certain type in a more precise way. In particular, they are necessary to formulate semantical rules like special operations. Format descriptions can be defined using standard operations, boolean expressions and conditional statements.
Examples are:

```
OBJECT TYPE DEALER TYPE STRING
  FORMAT LENGTH x = 25

OBJECT TYPE CAR TYPE STRING
  *car is denoted by its chassis-number*
  FORMAT x.1 ..  x.3 TYPE DIGIT
         x.4 = SPACE
         x.5 TYPE CHAR
         x.6 = SPACE
         x.7 ..  x.13 TYPE DIGIT
```

Remarks: - A comment is included by *.
- x.i selects the i-th character of string x.
- x.i .. x.j TYPE DIGIT means: every character x.l, $i \leq l \leq j$, is of type DIGIT.

a3) CSL offers the possibility to define special operations for an object type in order to gain a user-convenient notation for formulating semantical rules as well as for retrieval purposes. The operations are defined in the operation list in an ALGOL-like procedure concept.

Another possibility for characterizing self-identified object types is given by listing the objects explicitly, based on the following syntax:

```
<self-id object type>::= OBJECT TYPE <object type name>
                         {TYPE <standard type>}^1_0
                          OBJECTS <object list>
```

This concept lends itself to the definition of object types containing objects which are known in advance and do not change within T.
An example is:

```
OBJECT TYPE COMPONENT
   OBJECTS CHASSIS, TYRES, ENGINE, BODY,
           ELECTRIC EQUIPMENT, PAINTING
```

In this case, no standard type is specified. This may also be the case defining a self-identified object type without any characteristic specification. If this holds the objects of those types are considered to be strings. The only operation applicable to them is the comparison between strings.

b) Non-self-identified object types are declared by:

<non-self-id object type>::= <u>OBJECT TYPE</u> <object type name>
<u>IDENTIFIER</u> <identifier list>
$\{$<u>OPERATIONS</u> <operation list>$\}_0^1$

The <u>IDENTIFIER</u> clause of a non-self-identified object type specifies the identification method. The identifier list consists of the set of identifying association types. Assume that in the example universe objects of object type PERSON cannot be identified only by the family name, but in addition by the date of birth, whereby an object of type DATE is identified by its year, month and day. The identifier of object type PERSON is specified in Fig. 5.
Within the conceptual schema objects of non-self-identified object types are referred to by tuples, in the more general case (hierarchical identification) by trees. In our universe a particular object of type PERSON is referred to e.g. by (Smith, (50,5,30)).
Other characteristics like format or type specification must not be specified because the identifying associations lead to object types which have already such characteristics specified.

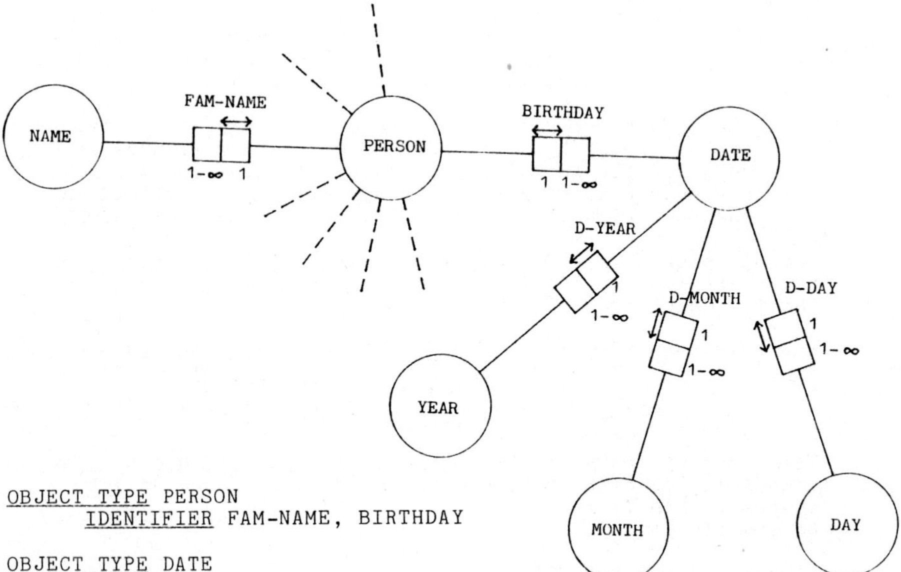

<u>OBJECT TYPE</u> PERSON
<u>IDENTIFIER</u> FAM-NAME, BIRTHDAY

<u>OBJECT TYPE</u> DATE
<u>IDENTIFIER</u> D-YEAR, D-MONTH, D-DAY

<u>Fig. 4</u> Identifiers of object types

4.1.3 ASSOCIATION TYPE DIVISION

The obligatory part of an association type definition consists of the unique association type name, the participating object types together with their roles and simple occurrence frequencies and the identifier of the association type together with the candidate identifiers.

Examples are:

```
ASSOCIATION TYPE SALARY
  OBJECT TYPE PERSON, ROLE HAS-SALARY, OCCURRENCE 1
  OBJECT TYPE MONEY,  ROLE IS-SALARY,  OCCURRENCE 1-ARB
    *currency of money in salary is DM*
  IDENTIFIER HAS-SALARY

ASSOCIATION TYPE AVAILABLE-CARS
  OBJECT TYPE CAR,    ROLE IS-STORED,  OCCURRENCE 1
  OBJECT TYPE DEALER, ROLE HAS-STORED, OCCURRENCE 1-50
  IDENTIFIER IS-STORED
```

The characteristics of association types are explained in the following:

a) Let O_i be object types, r_i be roles, $i=1,\ldots,n$ and $A = ((O_1,r_1),\ldots,(O_n,r_n))$ an association type associating the object types O_i by roles r_i (O_i resp. r_i not pairwise distinct).
A list of roles $I = (r_{p1},\ldots,r_{pm})$, $\{p_1,\ldots,p_m\} \subset \{1,\ldots,n\}$, is called an identifier of association type A, if the following holds:
   - I is minimal and
   - for each time instance $t \in T$ there exists only one association instance of A with a certain value combination of object instances of the object types $O_{p1},\ldots,O_{pm}$.

b) The <u>simple occurrence frequencies</u> connected to an object type and its role within an association type define that for each time instance $t \in T$ one object instance may occur in a certain number of association instances, whereby the possible numbers may be defined by sequences or ranges.
For example, the occurrence frequencies in the association type AVAILABLE-CARS state that a car, when it is delivered to a dealer, can only be delivered to one dealer and that a dealer cannot currently store more then fifty cars.
The occurrence frequencies refer only to such object instances which really occur in association instances. They do not express the characteristic that each object of the object type has to occur in an instance of the association type. This characteristic can be expressed within the semantical rule division.

Following characteristics may be defined optionally:

c) <u>Extended occurrence frequencies</u>
These characteristics, holding for each time instance $t \in$ T, are only relevant for n-ary association types, n>2.

c1) The projected occurrence frequencies are defined as simple occurrence frequencies in projections of association types. Such a projection contains only a part of the object types and their roles belonging to the original association type.

c2) The combined occurrence frequencies describe how often a combination of object instances may occur in the population of an association type.

4.1.4 Transitivity, symmetry, reflexivity

These features defined for mathematical relations can be used analogously for association types associating objects of the same object type. Such association types are called homogeneous association types. In this paper these features are defined for binary homogeneous association types, but the resulting concepts can be applied to n-aries.

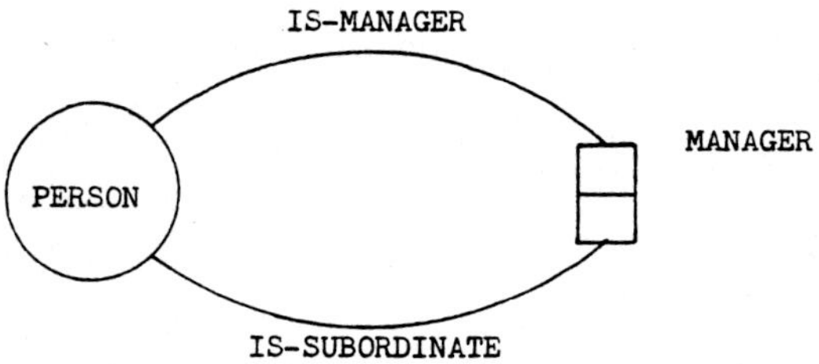

Fig. 5 A binary homogeneous association type

The association type described in Fig. 5 contains the two mathematical relations IS-MANAGER and IS-SUBORDINATE inverse to one another. Since the relations are inverse, they always have the same relational features and therefore the mathematical features of relations can be applied to such association types.

Let $A = ((O,r_1),(O,r_2))$ be a binary homogeneous association type. A is transitive, if for each $t \in T$ and for arbitrary o_1, o_2, o_3 being objects of type O and occurring in association instances of A holds:
If the association instances $((o_1,r_1),(o_2,r_2))$ and $((o_2,r_1),(o_3,r_2))$ exist, then the instance $((o_1,r_1),(o_3,r_2))$ must also exist.

A is reflexive, if for each $t \in T$ and for all objects o of type O occurring in association instances of A the association instance $((o,r_1),(o,r_2))$ exists.

A is symmetrical, if the two mathematical relations given by the roles are identical.
Therefore A should have identical roles like $A=((O,r),(O,r))$ in order to model symmetry without redundancy.

These characteristics are defined in CSL by the keyword FEATURE followed by the list of the corresponding characterstics, for example:

```
ASSOCIATION TYPE MANAGER
 FEATURE TRANSITIVE
         :
```

4.2 Modelling semantical rules

Semantical rules expressing interdependencies between association types or event types as well as several characteristics of types cannot be formulated by the language constructs introduced in section 4.1.
Referring to our particular data base universe, some of these rules are

(R1) An employee has always a salary.
(R2) The salary of an employee is more than 10.000 DM and less than 180.000 DM.
(R3) An employee has always a residence.
(R4) Changing the salary implies that the new salary is higher than the old salary.

Rules like these are placed in the SEMANTICAL RULE DIVISION.

In order to formulate semantical rules we first of all need a language for signifying sets of instances. CSL contains a descriptive and predicate logic oriented signification language handling this task.

4.2.1 The signification language

We now outline the basic constructs of the signification language.

Objects and populations of object types as well as populations of association types and roles are denoted by names.

- Names identifying objects:
  MONEY ´20.000´, COMPONENT ´CHASSIS´ etc.
- Names identifying populations of object types:
  PERSON, MONEY, CAR etc.
- Names identifying populations of association types:
  SALARY, BIRTH, OWNER etc.
- Names identifying roles:
  IS-SALARY, HAS-SALARY, IS-OWNER etc.

Subsets of populations of object types or association types are signified

- either by listing the elements of the subset:
  MONEY {´15.000´, ´20.000´, ´18.000´}
- or by adding a qualification clause to the type name:
  MONEY (WHERE <qualification expression>)

The qualification expression generally looks like a logical expression consisting of

- logical operators:
  IS-EQUIVALENT-TO, IMPLIES, OR, AND, NOT
- arithmetical operators: $=$, $\leq$, $\geq$, $<$, $>$, $\neq$
- set operators: ELEMENT-OF
- special operators handling relationships between conceptual schema constructs. They are called conceptual operators and

look as follows:

. objectsign OBJECT IN assocsign
. objectsign HAS ROLE rolesign $\{$IN assocsign$\}_0^1$
. objectsign ASSOCIATED $\{$ VIA assocsign$\}_0^1$ $\{$BY ROLE rolesign$\}_0^1$
  WITH objectsign
. assocsign INCLUDES OBJECT objectrolesign
. assocsign INCLUDES ROLE rolesign
. assocsign ASSOCIATES OBJECT objectrolesign
. rolesign ROLE OF objectsign
. rolesign ROLE IN assocsign

"objectsign", "assocsign", and "rolesign" denote sets of objects, associations and roles. "objectrolesign" denotes a set of objects to each object optionally a corresponding role being assigned.

- operands like
  . Sets of objects, associations and roles (i.e. significations)
  . function identifiers like NUMBER-OF [significations]

The following examples are intended to give a brief impression of the signification expressions:

. Signification of all persons owning a car:
  PERSON (WHERE PERSON HAS ROLE IS-OWNER)
  The qualification clause can be shortened:
  PERSON (HAS ROLE IS-OWNER).
. Signification of all roles which objects of type PERSON can play:
  ROLE (ROLE OF PERSON)
. Signification of all associations of type BIRTH:
  ASSOCIATION BIRTH
. Signification of all associations of type BIRTH where the year of the date of birth is less than 1975:
  ASSOCIATION BIRTH (INCLUDES OBJECT
  DATE (ASSOCIATED WITH
  YEAR(< 1975)))

4.2.2 The event-procedure constructs

On the basis of the signification language we are now able to formulate the semantical rules by means of event procedures. Event procedures are set up using the following rough syntax:

<eventproc> ::= <procedure head> <procedure body>
<procedure head>::={EVENT BEGIN|EVENT END|EVENT MODIFY}
<assoc type name> WITH <parameter list>
<procedure body>::= BEGIN{<rule part>|NO RULES } END

Remarks:

- An invocation of an event procedure results in checking whether the actual parameters meet the requirements stated within the object or association type division (i.e. checking the format, the identification, the occurrence frequencies etc.). Thus it is useful to invoke event procedures even if no rules are stated within the procedure body.
- The operators and operands, extended by formal parameters, listed in section 4.2.1 are used to express the semantical rules within the procedure body.

The following event procedures refer to the semantical rules R1 to R5:

```
EVENT BEGIN SALARY
      WITH PERSON X, MONEY Y
  BEGIN
      *The only rule to be checked is R2*
      10.000 < Y < 180.000
  END;
EVENT BEGIN RESIDENCE
      WITH PERSON X, ADDRESS Y
  BEGIN
      *No rule has to be checked*
      NO RULES
  END;
EVENT BEGIN EMPLOYMENT
      WITH PERSON X, FIRM Y
  BEGIN
      *Rules R1 and R3 have to be checked. Both rules set up inter-
      dependencies between associations and therefore involve calls
      of other event procedures*
    IF NOT X OBJECT IN SALARY
    THEN CALL EVENT BEGIN SALARY
                   WITH PERSON X, MONEY ? ;
    IF NOT X OBJECT IN RESIDENCE
    THEN CALL EVENT BEGIN RESIDENCE
                   WITH PERSON X, ADDRESS ?
  END;
```

Remark:
The procedure calls involved in rules R2, R3 are not fully specified: ´?´ denotes a missing parameter. In this case the user or the update program is asked for the parameter not yet specified. ´?´ is replaced by this parameter and the event procedure can be invoked.

Rule R4 requires the following special event procedure:

```
EVENT MODIFY SALARY
        WITH PERSON X,
             MONEY OLD Y  NEW Z
        BEGIN
             *Rule R4 has to be checked*
                   Y < Z
        END
```

4.3 Time Handling

Including the dimension of time into the DB universe requires some extensions of CSL constructs.

4.3.1 Introduction of a calendar system

Let us introduce the calendar system (DAY, MONTH, YEAR) based on the Christian era into our example universe.

```
CALENDAR DIVISION
  FIXPOINT = *Christ´s birth*;
  CALENDAR SYSTEM = (DAY, MONTH, YEAR)
  VALID-POINTS-OF-TIME (D1, D2, D3)
```

```
D1 ELOF DAY   {01 .. 31}
D2 ELOF MONTH {01 .. 12}
            COMPONENTS DAY
            (FOREACH M IN {01, 03, 05, 07, 08, 10, 12} DO
               FIRST M := DAY 01,
               LAST  M := DAY 31;

             FOREACH M IN {04, 06, 09, 11}  DO
               FIRST M := DAY 01,
               LAST  M := DAY 30;

               FIRST 02 := DAY 01,
               LAST 02  := DAY IF D3 = 0 MOD 4
                               THEN 29 ELSE 28)

D3 ELOF  YEAR {1950 .. CURRENT YEAR}
            COMPONENTS MONTH
```

Remarks:

- The segments of type DAY are considered to be atomar, i.e. they are not dividable into components.
- The segments of type MONTH consist of segments of type DAY.

  For each segment of type MONTH we specify the day it begins with and the day it ends with. Particulary we have to take care that the day ending February depends on leap years. If this kind of specification is missing the system implicitly assumes that all segments of a certain type begin with the minimum of the component segment type and end with the maximum (see, for instance, YEAR).
- CURRENT YEAR is a variable provided by the DBMS. It contains the number of the current year.

4.3.2 Further Extensions

The association type division has to be extended by declaring time-provided association types.
Referring to our example universe, the association type SALARY can be extended as follows:

```
ASSOCIATION TYPE SALARY
             :
IDENTIFIER HAS-SALARY
HISTORY REQUIRED
TEMPORAL CHANGE UNIT = MONTH
```

Remarks:

- HISTORY REQUIRED declares the type SALARY to be time- provided.
- TEMPORAL CHANGE UNIT = MONTH means, that events referring to associations of type SALARY can only occur monthly.

Within the object type division we have to restrict the definition of object types referring to the time axis. The object type DATE, for instance, has to meet the requirements imposed by the calendar system: The object types associated with DATE via identifying associations (see section 4.1.2) have to be segment types defined in the time division.

In order to embed the semantical rule constructs into the time axis the signification language and the event-procedure constructs have to be extended. In particular we introduce significations of points of time, time intervals, and events as well as operators between points of time and time intervals into the signification language.

The procedure bodies of event procedures can be extended by additional semantical rules, in particular characteristic of events and interdependencies between events.

5. Conclusions

We have described the main features of CSL. Above all we have outlined a time handling and an identification concept as well as a particular method for preserving data base integrity.

Using CSL we have the option of embedding the data base instances into the "historical" time axis. This requires the definition of an application-specific calendar system and the extension of several language constructs.
Based on the CSL time handling facilities, not only the static properties of the conceptual schema instances but also their dynamic behaviour can be expressed.
The identification concept used in CSL provides a general method for assigning names to the objects relevant to the data base universe. Particularly objects can be identified by sets of associations satisfying several identification conditions.

CSL provides constructs for solving the problem of preserving semantic integrity in a user-convenient manner. The event-procedure concept enables the DBMS to assign to each update operation the specific set of semantical rules to be checked. Sequences of update statements are built in an interactive way in order to transform an old valid data base state into a new one.

Acknowledgements

The authors want to thank Shamkant Navathe, University of New York, Sjir Nijssen, Control Data, Brussels, Esen Ozkarahan, METU Ankara, as well as Horst Biller, Klaus Hahne and Johann Lemke, Siemens AG, Munich, for valuable suggestions of improvement.

References

/BILLER 78/
Biller,H., Neuhold,E.J., "Semantics of Data Bases: The Semantics of Data Models", Information Systems, Vol.3, No.1, 1978
/ESWARAN 75/
Eswaran,K.P., Chamberlin,D.D., "Functional Specifications of a Subsystem for Data Base Integrity", Proc. Int. Conf. on VLDB, Framingham, Mass., Sept. 75
/FALKENBERG 74/
Falkenberg,E., "Time Handling in Data Base Management Systems" University of Stuttgart, Report 07/1974, 1974

/FALKENBERG 75/
Falkenberg,E., "Structuring and Representation of Information at the Interface between Data Base User and Data Base Management System", Doctoral thesis, University of Stuttgart, June 1975
/FALKENBERG 76/
Falkenberg,E., "Concepts for Modelling Information" in Nijssen (ed.): Modelling in Data Base Management Systems, North-Holland, Amsterdam 1976
/FALKENBERG 77/
Falkenberg,E., "Concepts for the Coexistence approach to Data Base Management" in: Morlet,E., Ribbens,D. (eds.), International Computing Symposium, Liege, Belgium, North-Holland, Amsterdam, 1977
/HAMMER 74/
Hammer,M.M., McLeod,D.J., "Semantic Integrity in a Relational Data Base System" in Kerr,D.S., Koffeman,K.L. (eds.), Data Base Management, IFIP 74, 1974
/NIJSSEN 76/
Nijssen,G.M., "A Gross Architecture for the Next Generation Data Base Management Systems", in: Nijssen,G.M. (ed.), Modelling in Data Base Management Systems, IFIP 1976, North- Holland, Amsterdam, 1976
/NIJSSEN 77/
Nijssen,G.M., "On the Gross Architecture for the Next Generation Data Base Management Systems" in: Gilchrist,B. (ed.), Information processing 77, IFIP 77, North-Holland, Amsterdam, 1977
/NIJSSEN 78/
Nijssen,G.M., "A Framework for Evaluating ANSI, CODASYL and other Data Base Approaches", Advanced Course on Data Base Management Systems, Milano, Course Notes, June 1978
/SENKO 76/
Senko,M.E., "DIAM as a Detailled Example of the ANSI/SPARC Architecture", in: Nijssen,G.M. (ed.), Modelling in Data Base Management Systems, IFIP 76, North-Holland, Amsterdam, 1976

Data Base Architecture, Bracchi/Nijssen, eds.
North-Holland Publishing Company

ASTRAL
A Structured and Unified Approach to Data Base Design and Manipulation

Tore Amble, Kjell Bratbergsengen and Oddvar Risnes
Division of Computer Science
University of Trondheim
N-7034 Trondheim-NTH

ASTRAL is a programming language based on PASCAL, designed for definition and manipulation of relatonal data bases.

The language suggests a new definition method of data bases realized as a hierarchy of blocks. EXPORT and IMPORT statements are introduced for defining the interface between the different blocks.

Operations towards the data base are expressed as assignments of table variables and table expressions. Data base objects are manipulated by the same means as objects local to an application program. Some nice language constructs for combining the relational operations select, join and projection are proposed.

Language constructs for handling concurrency problems of data base application programs are embedded in ASTRAL.

1. INTRODUCTION

ASTRAL is a programming language designed primarily to aid users in their effort of programming data base applications. The extended use of structured types and variables has made the relational model of data expressible in the language. Thus, the name: A STructured Relational Application Language.

When the design of the language commenced in 1976, we were especially concerned with the following design objectives:

- The language should be a language for the professional programmer. The task of writing application-programs should be easier and less expensive.

- Data base objects should be manipulated with the same ease and flexibility as other logical data objects. The language should not distinguish between variables local to the program and variables based on the content of the data base, at least not logically.

The first design resulted in a SIMULA like language [1,2,3]. However, we didn't feel quite content with this approach, mainly because we didn't find the data types of SIMULA sufficient. The class concept of SIMULA may be useful defining data structures, but we wanted a stronger type-oriented language with user-defined types. For instance, the standard types integer and real do not give the desired exactness for defining value ranges of data base items.

Such considerations lead us to the programming language PASCAL [4]. During 1978 the 'old version' of the language ASTRAL has been evaluated [5,6]. Based on the results of this evaluation, and our new design objective of a PASCAL like language, we have redesigned the language ASTRAL. The result is given in a draft report [7].

We have found the data type features of PASCAL sufficient for ASTRAL. The only main extension is the data type 'TABLE'. The decision of minimizing the number of new features added to the language, gives us the benefits of:

- higher possibility for acceptance of the language.

- reducing the problems of learning a new language.

- reducing the implementation cost of a compiler by utilizing existing PASCAL compilers.

The language is a part of the Relational DBMS ASTRA. In System ASTRA we are not only developing a new language, but also a new storage system to provide efficient relational data storage facilities for the language. System ASTRA also contains a query language and a data dictionary system maintained either from ASTRAL or the query language.

Since the introduction of the relational model of data [8,9], a large number of languages based on the relational model have been proposed [9-22]. Such languages may be classified as:

- data sublanguages vs. general purpose languages.
- calculus vs. algebra languages.

Most of the proposals are data sublanguages or query languages, some of them have been embedded in a host language such as PL/1. Common to all these languages is that they don't improve application programming. For this purpose a general language such as ASTRAL is needed. "While a given programming language and a given query language may be satisfactory in isolation, their combination may be less than satisfactory because neither one was designed for this more general setting" [23].

ASTRAL contains relational operators typical for both a calculus and an algebra oriented language. ASTRAL operates on table variables consisting of a table name followed by an associative index which is optional. This index is a first order predicate, and the operators select and join may be expressed by this index. The projection operation may be expressed by a table constructor.

In addition, ASTRAL deals with the set operators of the relational algebra. Actually - the set operators provided by PASCAL, are defined for table variables as well.

There has been some effort along the same general line as that taken by ASTRAL, of which the PLAIN language [19] by Wasserman and the RIGEL language [22] by Rowe are most similar. Schmidt's Relational Pascal [14] and Merret's language ALDAT [20] have also some ideas in common with ASTRAL.

This report describes the data management facilities of ASTRAL, both as a language for data base definition and manipulation. The paper also contains a discussion on concurrency and appropriate language constructs for definition of transactions and reservation of data base objects. For a more formal description of the language, the reader is referred to [7].

2. AN OUTLINE OF THE DATA BASE AND PROGRAM STRUCTURE

ASTRAL is a block structured language. This is also reflected in the manner a data base is declared. All variables, whether they designate permanent data of a data base or temporary data local to an application program, are described and handled in the same way.

Figure 1 gives an idea of how the data base and its application programs are structured. We have left the concept of data model and data submodel. It is, however, convenient to use the same terms even though their meaning are extended. The data base description is based on the usual declaration of types, variables and procedures at different block levels. The accessability of variables is determined by ordinary scope rules.

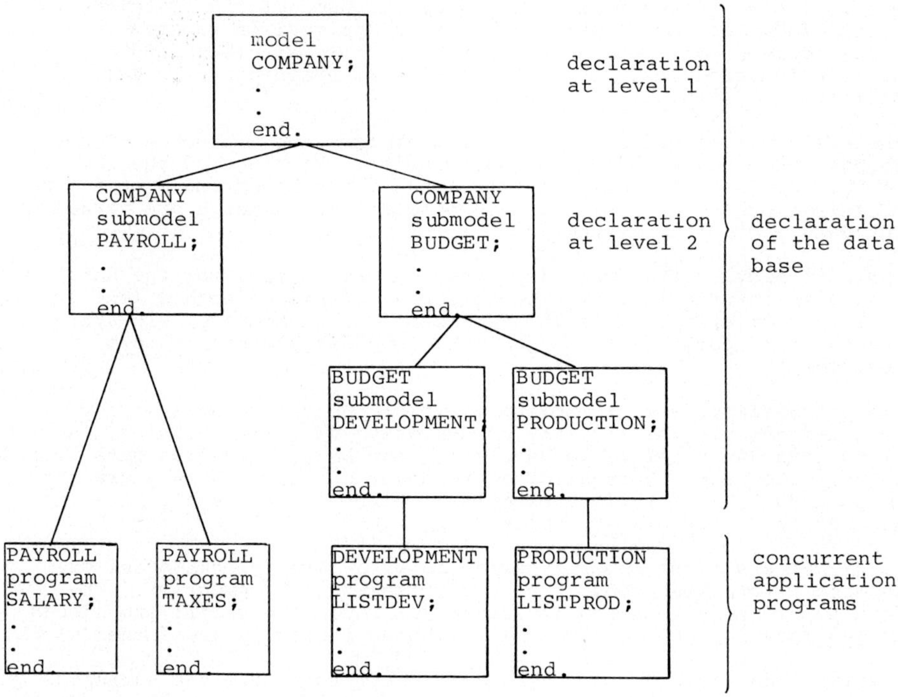

Fig. 1. The block structure of an ASTRAL data base and its application programs.

All variables declared at outer levels are available to the application program. For example, variables available to the program SALARY in Figure 1, are all the variables at the blocks: SALARY, PAYROLL, and COMPANY. Variables in the BUDGET block are not accessible for this program.

The data base definition method is strictly hierarchical, and the structure may be useful in several ways. One is data integrity.

Data common to a group of application programs are declared at the lowest possible level, and are thus hidden for other applications. Similar, subroutines and functions common to a group of applications, are declared at the lowest common level. A function used both by the LISTDEV and LISTPROD programs in Figure 1, has to be declared in the BUDGET block (or an outer block - in this case COMPANY).

An application program or a data base block is given a name (unique within its scope), and is prefixed by the name of the immediate outer block (father block). A block or application program is compiled separately and added to the assembly of blocks and application programs. This assembly is maintained by the data dictionary system.

The hierarchical definition method minimizes the influence of any changes made to the data base description. A change of the description of a block only effects the current block and blocks inner to this block level. Blocks made obsolete by a change are marked by the data dictionary system.

The data dictionary system is a very important tool for the data base administrator(s). The rather open definition method lend itself to a distribution of the data base responsibility. To avoid anarchy, the possibility of defining new data blocks has to be restricted.

The possibility of constructing views of the data base is fully retained through the facility of declaring virtual variables. A virtual variable refers to data which can be derived from data stored in the data base. Virtual data are never stored, and they are not to be updated. A typical example of virtual data is a table defined as a join of two tables.

An EXPORT statement exports variables of a given block (model or submodel) to a specified inner block (submodel or program). The data types are automatically exported. Thus, the underlying blocks or programs may only access the variables issued by the father block.

Similar, the blocks using these data, have to import the variables they are going to use. Only exported variables may be imported. An example of EXPORT and IMPORT statements is given in Section 3.2.

The use of functions and subroutines combined with the EXPORT and IMPORT restrictions may be an effective tool securing data base integrity. EXPORT and IMPORT statements are used to protect sensitive data from unauthorized access.

Besides securing the data base integrity, the EXPORT and IMPORT statements give an exact interface between blocks. If any changes are made to a father block, the data dictionary system will tell exactly which of the underlying blocks that has to be changed in order to be consistent with the father block.

3. DATA DEFINITION FACILITIES

The data definition facilities enable the data base administrator to design data bases, and the users to write well-structured application programs.

3.1. Definition of Data Types

The basic type concept of PASCAL is used, only with the extensions of the types FIXED(n) and STRING(n). The relational terms are expressed by the new structured type TABLE. A table type is similar to the file type of PASCAL in the sense that they both consist of records. The syntax[1] of a table type is:

```
<table type> ::= TABLE OF <record type>;
                 <unique specification>?*
                 <local routine declaration>?*
                 END
<unique specification> ::= UNIQUE <field identifier>**, ;
```

Example:

```
type EMPTYPE = table of
               record NAME  : NAMES ;
                      SAL   : 50000..200000 ;
                      MGR   : NAMES ;
                      DNO   : 1..100 ;
               end ;
               unique NAME ;
               end ;
```

The record type must not contain any variant part or pointers. The reason is found in the relational theory and the demand for tables on Third Normal Form.

The table type has some additional properties. Each table has an identifier (key) selecting a unique tuple from the table. The key is a logical key (hence, a unique identifier), and not any kind of a search or access key. The term 'physical key' is unknown in System ASTRA.

Each UNIQUE-specification specifies a set of fields (attributes) as one identifier. There may exist several identifier to a table depending on the functional dependencies of the attributes. If the UNIQUE-specification is missing, all the fields of the record type are regarded as one identifier.

---

1 *The syntax is an extended BNF.*
Explanation of the meta symbols used:

<A>?	- *zero or one A (Option)*
<A>*	- *one or several A (Repetition)*
<A>?*	- *zero or several A*
<A>**<B>	- *a list of A separated by B*

A table type has a set of standard routines associated (MAX, MIN, AVG, etc.). In addition, routines may be declared local to the table type, giving the same data abstraction facility as the CLASS concept in SIMULA. The routines may be accessed by prefixing them with the table variable.

3.2. Declaration of Variables and Specification of Access Control

A variable is declared being of a given type. A table variable is then defined as:

<u>var</u> EMPLOYEE : EMPTYPE ;

For tables there may be a need for specifying integrity constraints. For instance, we want to restrict the legal departmentnumbers of the employee table to those existing in the department table. Such constraints or assertions are defined in an access control statement.

<access control statement> ::=
<u>on</u> <u>access</u> <table identifier> <u>do</u> <statement>

An access control statement may be specified for each table, and will be executed prior to each access of the table. The statement is executed within the scope of the current record(s). Within this scope, there is also defined two variables:

- <u>var</u> OPERATION : (RETRIEVE,INSERT,DELETE,UPDATE)

  This variable is initialized to the corresponding type of the operation. A convenient way of using this variable may be in a case statement:

  <u>case</u> OPERATION <u>of</u> ..... <u>end</u>

- <u>var</u> OLD : <the record type of the table>

  This variable is assigned the value of the old record in case of UPDATE.

Examples of access control statements are given in the following example of a model definition where the tables EMPLOYEE and DEPARTMENT are formally described:

```
model COMPANY ;

      type NAMES    = string(20) ;
           DEPTS    = string(20) ;
           DNOS     = 1..100 ;
           SALARIES = 50000..200000 ;

           EMPREC = record NAME : NAMES ;
                           SAL  : SALARIES ;
                           MGR  : NAMES ;
                           DNO  : DNOS
                    end ;
           DEPREC = record DNO  : DNOS ;
                           NAME : DEPTS
                    end ;

           EMPTYPE = table of EMPREC ;
                     unique NAME ;
                     end ;
           DEPTYPE = table of DEPREC ;
                     unique DNO ;
                     end ;

      var  EMPLOYEE : EMPTYPE ;
           DEPARTMENT : DEPTYPE ;

      on access EMPLOYEE do
      case OPERATION of

      INSERT : (* The department and the manager
                  should exist. *)
               if no[ DEP in DEPARTMENT,
                      MANAGER in EMPLOYEE:
                      DEP.DNO = DNO and MANAGER.NAME = MGR ]
                  then signal ERROR ;

      UPDATE : (* New salary should be larger
                  than old salary. *)
               if SAL < OLD.SAL then signal ERROR ;

      DELETE : (* Managers deleted should not
                  have any slaves. *)
               if some[ SLAVE in EMPLOYEE:
                        SLAVE.MGR = NAME ]
                  then signal ERROR
      end ;

      on access DEPARTMENT do
      case OPERATION of

      DELETE : (* Departments having some employed,
                  should not be deleted. *)
               if some[  EMP in EMPLOYEE:
                         EMP.DNO = DNO  ]
                  then signal ERROR
      end ;

      export EMPLOYEE to PAYROLL ;
      export EMPLOYEE,
             DEPARTMENT to BUDGET

end.
```

The SIGNAL statement signals an exception condition, and the program control will return to an exception handler, see Chapter 5.

The data base will not only be accessed by an application program written in ASTRAL. A query language is also given access to the data base in the same way as ASTRAL programs, i.e. by access to a data base block as described in Chapter 2. It is therefore important to define the access control of tables in the data model formally to avoid query languages to omit the restrictions. Assertions should not be written in the programs [11,12,16,19].

4. DATA MANIPULATION

Conventionally, the basic operations on data bases are known as insertion, deletion, updating and retrieval of records. This approach is also taken by several relational languages. In our opinion, it is unnatural to group the basic table operations of a language into these four classes. For instance, a retrieval operation is also an insertion - into the resulting table.

A language for data base applications should provide the same mechanisms for data base objects and language objects, i.e. data base tables and temporary tables should be manipulated by the same operators.

In ASTRAL, operations towards the data base are basically carried out using assignments of table variables and table expressions. The table variable is described by the syntax:

```
<table variable> ::= <table identifier><[<predicate>]>?
```

A table variable consists of a table name followed by an associative index which is optional. This associative index may be a simple predicate or a join predicate. In the following examples simple predicates are used.

Examples of table variables:

```
DEPARTMENT
EMPLOYEE[ SAL > 50000 ]
```

A table variable denotes the set of records (tuples) that belongs to the table and satisfies the predicate, if present.

Examples of table assignments:

Example 1. "Get the underpaid employees".

```
UNDERPAID := EMPLOYEE[ SAL < 90000 ] ;
```

This example may be considered as a retrieval operation. However, we prefer to describe it as an assignment where the table variable UNDERPAID is given the result of the table expression.

When the table variable consists of the table identifier only, the predicate is assumed to be TRUE, i.e.

```
UNDERPAID[ true ] is equivalent to
UNDERPAID
```

If the table predicate is FALSE, a copy of the records of the table expression will be added to the table variable. For better readability, the Boolean constant NONE (equal to FALSE) is defined.

Example 2. "Insert new employees in the data base".

```
var NEWEMPS : EMPTYPE ;
...
EMPLOYEE[ none ] := NEWEMPS ;
```

The empty table subset is now replaced by NEWEMPS.

A record type may be converted to a table type as shown in the next example.

Example 3. "Insert a new employee Blake".

```
var  BLAKE : EMPREC ;
with BLAKE do begin  NAME := 'BLAKE' ;
                     SAL  := 96000 ;
                     MGR  := 'SMITH' ;
                     DNO  := 20
               end ;
EMPLOYEE[ none ] := BLAKE ;
```

Deletion of tuples is done by replacing the table subset with no tuples.

Example 4. "Delete employees working in department 20".

```
EMPLOYEE[ DNO = 20 ] := EMPLOYEE[ none ] ;
```

Generalized, a table or a table subset may be replaced by a table expression. For example, the employees of department 20 may be fired and replaced by new employees:

```
EMPLOYEE[ DNO = 20 ] := NEWEMPS ;
```

As these examples hopefully shows, the relational model is completely embedded in the language ASTRAL. The introduction of table variables presents the user with a homogenous view of data. Unlike the data sublanguages, results from a query to the data base is manipulated by the same means as the query operation itself. The interface becomes awkward in data sublanguages, and is often solved by using workspace and binding variables [12,23,24,25].

The smooth interface between data base variables and program variables in ASTRAL may be further demonstrated by the following example.

Example 5. "Find the highest wages in the employee table".

```
var WAGES : SALARIES ;
WAGES := EMPLOYEE.MAX(SAL) ;
```

So far, only simple predicates have been shown in the associative index. ASTRAL also operates on join and quantified predicates.

A join predicate contains one or several selectors or range variables ranging over other tables. A range variable is an inline declared record variable of same type as the record of the ranged table.

Example 6. "Get the employees earning more than their managers".

```
OVERPAID := EMPLOYEE[ MANAGER in EMPLOYEE:
                      SAL > MANAGER.SAL and
                      MGR = MANAGER.NAME ] ;
```

Join predicates express a join between tables, and may be used wherever a simple predicate may occur.

A quantified predicate consists of one of the quantifiers SOME, NO, ALL and a join predicate. A quantified predicate yields a Boolean value. Such predicates are used especially in access control statements, see Section 3.2.

As mentioned in the introduction, the set operators of PASCAL is extended to be defined for table variables giving the language some algebraic properties.

Example 7. "Employees except those in department 10 are fired, and new employees are employed".

```
EMPLOYEE : = EMPLOYEE[  DNO = 10  ] + NEWEMPS ;
```

A table constructor is a generalization of the table variable, unifying the concepts of projection, join and selection. This approach is also proposed by the ALDAT language [20]. The syntax of the table constructor is:

```
<table constructor> ::= <<attribute sequence>>
                        [ <join predicate> ]
<attribute sequence> ::= <<record identifier>.
                           <field identifier>>**,
```

The result of the table constructor is a new table of records satisfying the join predicate. The field identifiers and types are taken from the attribute sequence.

Example 8. "Get the name and the salary for employees earning more than their manager".

```
var OVERPAID : table of record NAME : NAMES ;
                               SAL  : SALARIES
                         end ;
               unique NAME ;
               end ;

OVERPAID : = <E.NAME,E.SAL>[ E in EMPLOYEE,
                             MANAGER in EMPLOYEE:
                             E.SAL > MANAGER.SAL and
                             E.MGR = MANAGER.NAME ] ;
```

Join predicates and table constructors give a more non-procedural manner of writing statements towards the data base. The same facilities are achieved by the procedural language primitives FOR and IN.

The above example expressed by the FOR statement in ASTRAL:

```
for E in EMPLOYEE do
for MANAGER in EMPLOYEE do
begin
      if E.MGR = MANAGER.NAME and E.SAL > MANAGER.SAL
      then OVERPAID[  none ]  := E ;
end ;
```

The record variables E and MANAGER are implicit declared.

Often, there is no need for the record variable:

Example 9. "Update the salaries for department 20 workers".

```
in EMPLOYEE[  DNO = 20 ] do SAL : = SAL*1.1 ;
```

We will recommend to use the more general table constructor and join predicates if possible, as the compiler is more likely to optimize such expressions rather than the procedural FOR-statements. Even if nothing is said of how a table is scanned in a FOR statement, the use of nested loops state that the inner table is scanned for each tuple of the outer one.

5. CONCURRENT ASTRAL

Being a language operating towards a data base, there is a need for concurrency constructs. The terms 'transaction' and 'reservation of data' are new in the sense that they are not treated in PASCAL.

The protection and synchronization of users access to common data is a simple problem, and is solved within system ASTRA. However, it is not sufficient only to synchronize accesses. A meaningful operation towards a data base usually consists of several ASTRAL statements each giving a number of accesses to the data base. Such operations need to be performed in such a manner that the data base remains consistent after the transaction has been executed.

We may call this a problem of synchronizing user accesses to the data base. This problem is solved by introducing the term transaction in the language. A transaction, or REGION, is a block of statements defined as one logical operation towards the data base.

In the relational storage of System ASTRA, a tuple is the smallest resource being synchronized. Within a transaction, updated tuples of data base tables will be reserved to the transaction performed, and will remain reserved until the end of the transaction. Thus, updates to the data base are kept reserved until all updates are confirmed. If the user decide to break the transaction, or the user is forced back to the start of the transaction because of deadlock, the updates to the data base may easily be undone.

In most transactions it is sufficient to reserve only updated tuples. This is done by the relational storage system, so will deadlock detection. The runtime system will take care of rollbacks whenever a deadlock occurs.

For some transactions we need to lock data base tuples before making any updates in order to obtain consistent transactions. This reservation has to be done explicit in the language.

A transaction in ASTRAL is defined as a REGION where the reservation of table subsets is done in a RESERVE clause, and the transaction itself follows DO:

```
<region statement> ::= REGION <reservation part>?
                       DO <compound statement>
                       <exception handling part>?

<reservation part> ::= RESERVE <var-synonym>**,
<var-synonym>::= <table variable>/
                 <table synonym identifier>=<table variable>

<exception handling part>::= EXCEPTION
                             <exception handler>**;
                             END
<exception handler> ::= <case list element>
```

The variables listed in the reservation part are locked for other users while this program is inside the region. If a table synonym identifier is used, this denotes the set of reserved tuples (textual substitution).

The EXCEPTION clause is performed whenever the transaction is interrupted for some reason. Such interrupts are initiated by a SIGNAL statement, and the program control is then returned to the dynamically closest block or region statement which has an exception handler for the exception condition signalled.

The following example will illustrate the need of both a transaction and the reservation facility.

In a booking system at an airline travel agent, there exists a table BOOKING giving the number of vacant seats on particular flights at a particular date. The definition of BOOKING is given in a model like:

```
type FLIGHTNOS = string(6) ;
     DATES     = 770101..991231 ;
     QUANTITY  = 0..400 ;
     BOOKINGTYPE = table of
                   record FLIGHTNO : FLIGHTNOS ;
                          DATE : DATES ;
                          CAPACITY,
                          VACANCY : QUANTITY
                   end ;
                   unique FLIGHTNO,DATE ;
                   end ;
var  BOOKING : BOOKINGTYPE ;
```

Customers ask for one or several flights, and they order the tour only if they may get on all the flights. If not, they change their plans and ask for a new tour. Note that the same customer may want more than one seat: He might bring his family with.

The program will:

1. Read the desired TOUR from the customer.
2. Check if the complete TOUR may be met.
3. If OK, confirm the TOUR.

```
var TOUR : table of record FLIGHTNO : FLIGHTNOS ;
                           DATE : DATES ;
                           QTY  : QUANTITY
                    end ;
           unique FLIGHTNO,DATE ;
           end ;

    FULLBOOKED : BOOKINGTYPE ;

    procedure READTOUR ; ...;
:
READTOUR ;  (* Reads the TOUR table *)
region reserve BOOKING[    T in TOUR:
                           FLIGHTNO = T.FLIGHTNO and
                           DATE = T.DATE  ]            do
begin
    FULLBOOKED := BOOKING[  T in TOUR :
                            FLIGHTNO = T.FLIGHTNO and
                            DATE = T.DATE and
                            VACANCY < T.QTY ] ;

    if some[ F in FULLBOOKED ] then
    begin
         for FLIGHT in FULLBOOKED do
         WRITELN(FLIGHT.FLIGHTNO:6,' at ',
                 FLIGHT.DATE:6,' is fully booked ')
    end
    else
    begin
         for T in TOUR do
         in BOOKING[  FLIGHTNO = T.FLIGHTNO and
                      DATE = T.DATE ]
         do VACANCY := VACANCY - T.QTY ;

         WRITELN('Booking confirmed')
    end
end
exception
    ERROR: exit region
end ;
```

If the reservation at the start of the transaction was missing, the answer from the check for a complete tour could be positive. Trying to confirm the tour may, however, result in a overbooking of a flight as others may have updated the BOOKING table between the check and the confirmation. The customer would, no doubt, be extremely upset arriving at the airport just to find a full plane.

As the example shows, an associative index is used for the reservation of a logical subset of tuples. Thus, the reservation made is the smallest possible, and the possibility that two users are attempting to reserve the same table subset, is minimal.

The reservation facility will have the effect of preventing deadlock situations within a transaction, as all relevant resources may be reserved before any of them are accessed.

The concurrency features described above, should be embedded completely in the data base language, and not be given as a set of procedure primitives [24]. Some ideas of locking in relational data bases are also given in [22] and [26].

The exception handling problem needs further investigation in ASTRAL. At present, this is suggested implemented by the exception clause in the region statement. This approach is not acceptable from a query language point of view. The exception handling should be done by the runtime system, and defined as violation actions in the model description like the integrity constraints, as proposed by Hammer and McLeod [27]. It's important to give the query and the application programs the same interface, not only to the logical data, but also in the operation on them.

6. IMPLEMENTATION

ASTRAL and the System ASTRA is currently being implemented for NORD Computers. This work is a joint project with the Computer Centre and the Division of Computer Science at the University of Trondheim and Norsk Data A/S as participants. The work is partially supported by the Royal Norwegian Institute of Scientific and Industrial Research (NTNF).

The ASTRAL compiler will be written in PASCAL. The table operations of ASTRAL will be translated into a code for the ASTRA Data Base Computer. This code is an extended relational algebra, designed to meet the ASTRAL language demands for a powerful and efficient relational storage.

The ASTRA Data Base Computer provides a complete Relational DBMS. Programs - ASTRAL programs or query applications - running on the host-computer, will communicate with the data base computer through the extended relational algebra.

The ASTRAL compiler will optimize the code generated for the data base computer. We have experience in generation and optimization of data base code from an earlier work using a conventional hierarchical data base system RA2 [1,28]. A RA2 data base was defined as a relational model, and ASTRAL-statements was translated into SIMULA code and appropriate DML procedure statements.

In System ASTRA, the lastest developments in computer hardware are used to increase the execution speed of relational operations. The main complaint against the relational model has been the lack of efficiency, but we hope to overcome this problem.

The software solution to the performance problem has been based on traditional storage systems (disk), common access methods and inverted lists on non-key attributes. The main effort in this approach has been put into optimization. The most known approaches are System R [24] and INGRES [12].

The other solution has emerged from the development in integrated circuit technology. Processing capability based on cheap LSI (VLSI) chips is moved to the secondary storage where the data resides. Several approaches that fall into this category are CAFS [29], CASSM [30], Hsiao's Data Base Computer [31], RAP [32] and RARES [33].

Evidently, the most demanding and complex data base operations can not be handled satisfactory by ordenary data base systems and storage technology. The reason for this, we believe, is that the software and the hardware solution has not been integrated. By using new storage technology and tuning this to the high level language ASTRAL, we hope to be much better off than any of the above mentioned approaches.

The approach taken in the design of the ASTRA Data Base Computer is similar to the one proposed by RAP. The storage and processing capability is partitioned into a number of equal cells, organized as a loosely coupled network.

7. CONCLUSION

The language ASTRAL unifies the approach to data base definiton and manipulation. This is achieved by introducing a new storage system combined with several benefits of the relational model.

No physical implementation of a data base has to be considered by the ASTRAL approach. The data base needs to be declared logical - if you have an ASTRA data base computer. Definition of tables and table types give the same features as the CODASYL definitions of records and sets. In addition, semantic integrity may be defined by the access control statement in ASTRAL. We have also intended to define the exception handling in the data base description. This is currently being investigated.

The data base definition method taken by ASTRAL, suggests a distribution of the data base definition and responsibility. The fact that the data base may grow in number of information sets by the depth of data block levels, gives us new possibilities.

With a few extensions to the original language PASCAL, ASTRAL has become a powerful language for data base applications. More important, the difference between data base objects and conventional language objects is made invisible to the user.

8. ACKNOWLEDGEMENTS

The authors wish to acknowledge work on an earlier version of the language by V. Brenna, R. Larsen and O.J. Hansen. The work on the language ASTRAL is a part of the ASTRA project. Participants in the project are, in addition to the authors, P. Kongshaug, S.H. Kvitsand, R. Larsen and T. Stålhane.

9. REFERENCES

[1] V. Brenna, O. Risnes
"ASTRA - A DBMS based on a high level, relational DML with access via a hierarchical DDL"
Thesis for M.Sc. in Computer Science, January 1977
Division of Computer Science
University of Trondheim, N-7034 Trondheim-NTH

[2] K. Bratbergsengen, O. Risnes
"ASTRA - A Relational DBMS with a SIMULA-like DML ASTRAL"
Proceedings SIMULA Users Conference, September 1977

[3] K. Bratbergsengen, O. Risnes
"ASTRAL - A Structured Relational Applications Language"
Technical Report 5/78, June 1978
Division of Computer Science
University of Trondheim, N-7034 Trondheim-NTH

[4] K. Jensen, N. Wirth
"Pascal - User Manual and Report"
Lecture Notes in computer science 18,
Springer-Verlag, New York, 1974

[5] Ø.O. Jensen
"Vurdering av ASTRA/ASTRAL" (Norwegian)
ASTRA Report 15, April 1978
The Computing Centre at the University of Trondheim

[6] O. Risnes
"Oppsummering av ASTRA/ASTRAL-vurderinga" (Norwegian)
ASTRA Report 18, June 1978
Division of Computer Science
University of Trondheim, N-7034 Trondheim-NTH

[7] T. Amble, K. Bratbergsengen, P. Kongshaug, S.H. Kvitsand,
R. Larsen, O. Risnes, T. Stålhane
"Draft Report of the Programming Language ASTRAL"
ASTRA Report 27, January 1979
Division of Computer Science
University of Trondheim, N-7034 Trondheim NTH

[8] E.F. Codd
"A Relational Model of Data for Large Shared Data Banks"
CACM Volume 13, no. 6, June 1970

[9] C.J. Date
"An Introduction to Database Systems"
Addison Wesley, Second edition 1977

[10] M.M. Astrahan, D.D. Chamberlin
"Implementation of a Structured English Query Language"
CACM Volume 18, no. 10, October 1975

[11] D.D. Chamberlin & al.
"SEQUEL 2: A Unified Approach to Data Definition,
Manipulation, and Control"
IBM Journal of Research and Development,
Volume 20, no. 6, November 1976

[12] M. Stonebraker & al.
"The Design and Implementation of INGRES"
ACM TODS Volume 1, no. 3, September 1976

[13] M. Lacroix, A. Pirotte
"ILL: An English Structured Query Language for
Relational Data Bases"
MBLE Brucelles Report R334, August 1976

[14] J.W. Schmidt
"Some High Level Language Constructs for Data
of Type Relation"
ACM TODS Volume 2, no. 3, September 1977

[15] R.F. Boyce & al.
"Specifying Queries as Relational Expressions"
ACM SIGPLAN - SIGIR Interface Meeting, November 1973

[16] M.M. Zloof
"Query-by-Example: a data base language"
IBM System Journal no. 4 - 1977

[17] N. McDonald, M. Stonebraker
"Cupid: the friendly query language"
Proc ACM Pacific 75 Regional Conference, April 1975

[18] E.F. Codd
"Seven steps to rendezvous with the casual user"
Conference on Data Base Management Systems, 1974.
North-Holland Publishing Company

[19] Wasserman & al.
"Report on the Programming Language PLAIN"
Technical Report no. 34
Laboratory of Medical Information Science,
University of California San Francisco, June 1978

[20] T.H. Merrett
"Aldat - Augmenting the Relational Algebra for Programmers"
Technical Report SOCS - 78.1, November 1977
School of Computer Science
McGill University, Montreal

[21] J. Mylopoulos, P.A. Bernstein, H.K.T. Wong
"A Preliminary Specification of TAXIS:
A Language for Designing Interactive Information Systems"
Technical Report CCA-78-02, Januar 1978
Aiken Computer Laboratory
Harvard University, Cambridge, MA 02138

[22] L.A. Rowe, K.A. Shoens
"Data Abstraction, Views and Updates in RIGEL"
ERL Memorandum 79/5, January 1979
Electronics Research Laboratory
University of California, Berkeley,CA 94720

[23] C.J. Prenner, L.A. Rowe
"Programming Languages for Relational Database Management"
Proc AFIPS 1978 NCC, Volume 47, pp. 849-855

[24] M.M. Astrahan & al.
"System R: Relational Approach to Data Base Management"
ACM TODS Volume 1, no. 3, September 1976

[25] M. Stonebraker, L.A. Rowe
"Observations on Data Manipulation Languages and their
Embedding in General Purpose Programming Languages"
Proc Very Large Data Bases, Tokyo, October 1977,
pp. 128-143

[26] D.D. Chamberlin, J.N. Gray, I.L. Traiger
"Views, Authorization, and Locking in a
Relational Data Base System"
Proc AFIPS 1975 NCC, Volume 44, pp. 425-430

[27] M.M. Hammer, D.J. McLeod
"Semantic Integrity in a Relational Data Base System"
Proc Very Large Data Bases, Framingham, September 1975,
pp. 25-47

[28] O.J. Hansen
"ASTRAL - Implementering av kompilator mot databasesystemet RA2" (Norwegian)
Thesis for M.Sc. in Computer Science, December 1978
Division of Computer Science
University of Trondheim, N-7034 Trondheim-NTH

[29] E. Babb
"Implementing a Relational Database by means of Specialized Hardware"
ACM TODS Volume 4, no. 1, March 1979

[30] S.Y.W. Su, G.J. Lipovski
"CASSM: A Celluar System for Very Large Data Bases"
Proc Very Large Data Bases, Framingham, September 1975
pp. 456-472

[31] D.K. Hsiao, K. Kannan
"The Architecture of a Data Base Computer"
Third Workshop on Computer Architecture for Non-Numeric Processing, Syracuse, May 1977

[32] E.A. Ozkarahan, S.A. Schuster, K.C. Smith,
"RAP - An Associative Processor for Data Base Management"
Proc AFIPS 1975 NCC, Volume 44, pp. 379-387

[33] C.S. Lin, D.C.P. Smith
"The Design of a Rotating Associative Array Memory for a Relational Data Base"
Proc Very Large Data Bases, Framingham, September 1975
pp. 453-455

MODELS FOR THE CONCEPTUAL SCHEMA

Data Base Architecture, Bracchi/Nijssen, eds.
North-Holland Publishing Company

ON THE NOTION OF IRREDUCIBLE RELATIONS

Horst Biller
Siemens AG
D AP S DB 2
Otto-Hahn-Ring 6
D-8000 München 83

Irreducible relations play an important role for the design of a conceptual schema. However, a precise and satisfying definition of irreducibility is still missing. The definitions given in the literature are discussed and a definition based on the semantics is given. The consequences of this definition to Codd's relational model are shown and some modifications suggested.

0. Introduction

The conceptual schema as introduced in the ANSI/SPARC report is the "enterprise's description of the information as modelled in the database" [1]. In the ANSI/SPARC framework the conceptual schema level is important not only to precisely describe the contents of the database. It also is the basic concept to achieve data independence.

Since the first publication of the ANSI/SPARC interim report [2] a lot of work has been done to develop a data model which is suitable for the conceptual schema (see [3]). The only general agreement achieved as far seems to be that several candidates for the conceptual model exist and that at the present state of the art it is impossible to decide which one of these models is the best, since no formal criteria exist on which an evaluation of conceptual data models could be based.

This seems to be a very pessimistic view. But if one compares the different candidates it might be rather surprising that there are several important points on which an agreement has been achieved. One of these points is that at the conceptual level one should deal with things called "entities" or "abstract objects", which model "real world objects" rather than with records, data-entries or groups. Another is that one has to deal with relations modelling relationships or associations between the real world objects. However, with respect to the degree of the relations two different positions exist. Some authors propose binary relations ([12], [13], [14]), others n-ary relations. Most authors proposing n-ary relations in the conceptual schema request them to be "irreducible" (cf. [4], [5], [7], [8], [9], [10], [11]).

In this paper we discuss the nature of irreducible relations. Currently, no satisfying, formal definition exists. Such a definition however is essential to the development of a conceptual schema model. To be useful in the design process of a conceptual schema it should also be easy to check, if the relations in a schema are irreducible or not. It should either be possible to develop algorithms which prove, based on consistency conditions like functional dependencies or multivalued dependencies, that the relations are irreducible or the definition itsself should be so that the data base designer can it easily apply to the relations.

There are two main definitions of irreducibility. The first one stems out of the (Codd's) relational data base theory and is based on the relational algebra. A relation is irreducible, if it is not possible to replace the relation by two or more projections in such a way, that the original relation may be recovered via suitable joins ([7], [29]). The second definition has been developed in the discussion on the concepts for the conceptual schema. It is based on the semantics of the relation. A relation is irreducible, if it models elementary facts.

First, we will discuss the relationship between the definitions (see also [30]). Then we will discuss some problems which arise if the notion of irreducibility is applied to relations of the relational model 19. These problems arise from the semantic ambiguity of Codd's relations, which has been described by several authors ([8], [11]). Finally, we propose a clarification of Codd's relational model which resolves these ambiguities.

1. Irreducible Relations

In this section we define the notion of irreducibility. First, we must clarify our meaning of the term relation which has been separately applied to different concepts.

A relation is an abstract concept, which is used to model a relationship (sometimes called association) between several (i. e. two or more) real world objects. A relation (or relation type [28]) is a set of relation occurrences.

In the following, we will denote relations by italics and relation occurrences by capital letters. So R denotes an occurrence of the relation *R*. Occurrences of relations model states of the "real world", and relations model the set of all possible real world states (see [4]). A relation occurrence consists of a set of tuples of abstract objects (sometimes called entities). Abstract objects model real world objects. A relation occurrence R models the state of a real world relationship if for all tuples of R the relationship modelled by $\mathcal{R}$ holds between the corresponding real world objects. In other words, a tuple of a relation occurrence models the fact, that a relationship holds between some objects.

This concept of a relation is used in a similar way in several papers, in which data models are introduced. For example, P. Chen uses the term "relationship relation" [21], P. Hall, J. Owlett and S. Todd use the term "relation" [7], H. A. Schmid and J. R. Swenson the term "association" [11] and D. Smith and J. Smith the term "aggregation" [22]. A comparison of these concepts may be found in [3].

Since tuples in relation occurrences model real world facts, and facts may be expressed by natural language sentences, a close correspondence between relations and sentences exists. A tuple of a relation may be represented by a natural language sentence. The other way around, we can say that a tuple of a relation occurrence is a formal and abstract model of a natural language sentence (see also [4]). Therefore, there exists a correspondence between predicates of natural language sentences and relations. This means that concording to our usage relations are always "well defined", i.e., they correspond to natural language predicative clauses. Similarily, aggregations are tied to natural language nouns in [22].

In Codd's relational model [19] the term relation is used in a different way. In the relational model relations (henceforth called RM-relations) do not possess such well defined semantics. RM-relations are defined to be a subset of the cartesian product of several simple domains which correspond to real world objects. In general, one does not know which domains of an RM-relation represent entities and which are part of composite names (compare [8], [11]), even if one only considers RM-relations in Boyce Codd normal form [25]. In general, in a relational database the names of RM-relations may not be semantically meaningful (cf [22]). Therefore, the meaning of a relational database schema is not known without further rules of interpretation. I.e., it is not known in general, which facts are to be represented in the database. This does not mean, that a set of RM-relations could not be a good and precise representation of an enterprise and therefore a good conceptual schema. In this case, there would be a direct correspondence between RM-relations and relations as defined in the foregoing paragraph.

The difference between RM-relations and relations is shown in the following example. Figure 1 represents the schema of a relation "HAS AGE".
The entity-types which are the domains of the relation are represented by rectangles, and the relation is represented by a label connecting the boxes.

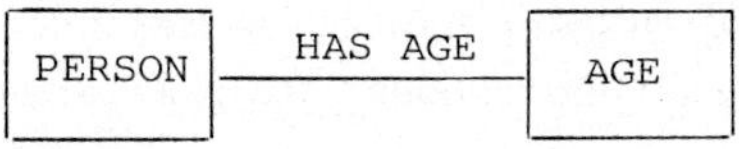

Figure 1: A graphic representation of the relation "HAS AGE"

To represent this relation by an RM-relation, we must choose a representation for the two domains on which the relation is defined. In figure 2a, the type PERSON is represented by the domains NAME, FIRST NAME, BIRTHDAY (with the assumption that within the relevant slice of reality [16], persons can be uniquely identified by one first name, the family name and their birthday), whereas in figure 2b, the type person is represented by a social security number.

a) AGE (NAME, FIRST NAME, BIRTHDAY, AGE)

b) HAS AGE (SOC-SEC#, AGE)

Figure 2: Two RM-relations representing the relation "HAS AGE"

Without having irreducibility precisely defined we make the following informal observations:

1. The relation HAS AGE certainly is irreducible, since it is a binary relation, and every Person can have at most one age.

2. The RM-relation HAS AGE also is irreducible.

3. The RM-relation AGE is not irreducible according to the algebraic definition, since the domain AGE is functionally dependent on the domain BIRTHDAY. It therefore can be split into two RM-relations, so that the (natural) Join of these relations is equal to the RM-relation AGE.

The third observation is a consequence of the introduction of a composite name for the type PERSON. A definition of irreducibility based on RM-relations would be representation dependent, i.e., dependent on the naming structure chosen. Similar arguments are given in [8].
To avoid this dependency, we will only deal with relations existing in an abstract model in the following.

The choice of the naming structure is a design decision which will be influenced by several aspects. With respect to the following it is only important, that the representation of Figure 2.a is possible within the relational theory.

Another observation can be made looking at the two RM-relations AGE and HAS AGE. In the RM-relation AGE also relations between first names, family names, birthdays, and ages are represented (i.e. for example the relation between a person's age and family name), so that queries like "Get the first names of persons 55 years old" could be directly answered by a restriction and a projection of the relation AGE.
To answer this question in the second case, we would have to have a second RM-relation representing the relation between a person's social security number and first names, and to join this RM-relation HAS AGE. But this difference between the two RM-relations of figure 2 is not important with respect to the problem discussed in this paper.

Two different definitions of irreducibility can be found in the literature. We distinguish them as algebraically irreducible or a-irreducible and semantically irreducible or s-irreducible.

The algebraic definition is based on the notion of decomposition of relations which was developed in the relational data base theory [29]:

Def. 1.1: A relation $\mathcal{R}$ is a-irreducible (undecomposable), if at least one occurrence R of the relation $\mathcal{R}$ exists, that cannot be broken down by means of projections into a series of relation occurrences $R_1, \ldots, R_n$ so that R is equal to the join of $R_1, \ldots, R_n$.

Two points are worth emphasizing with respect to this definition. Firstly, a-irreducibility must be specified as a consistency condition for a relation, since to decide, if a relation is a-irreducible, we must know all occurrences of the relation. This means that we cannot decide a-irreducibility by analyzing the data contained in a given data base. Secondly, it is required that the join of the relation occurrences $R_1, \ldots, R_n$ is equal to R. If condition 1.1 holds, by the decomposition of a relation no information is lost, according to the relational theory (cf. [24]), since all tuples of the original relation can be restored. We will come back to this point later on.

In the design of a conceptual schema, it is important to be able to detect contradictions within the set of consistency conditions specified for the schema. In this sense, the following theorem gives a tool to the data base designer.

Theorem 1.1:
An a-irrecucible relation is in fourth normal form [24].

One should notice again the difference between relations and RM-relations. As a consequence of this proposition, an a-irreducible relation also is in third normal form, as has been shown by Fagin. It should be noticed by the reader, that the converse of proposition 1.1 does not hold.

The semantic definition of irreducibility is based on the correspondence between relations and natural language sentences ([3], [8], [10]).

Def. 1.2: A relation is s-irreducible, if it models an elementary (atomic) predicative clause resp. sentence type.

Now the notion of elementary sentence type must be defined.

Def. 1.3: A sentence type S, represented by a predicate P with degree n 2, is elementary, if it cannot be split up into other sentence types $S_1, \ldots, S_m$ represented by predicates $P_1, \ldots, P_m$ so that for all (relevant) states of the real world

$$P(x_1,\ldots,x_n) \Leftrightarrow P_1(x_{i_1},\ldots,x_{i_k}) \wedge \ldots \wedge P_m(x_{j_1},\ldots,x_{j_1}) \text{ with}$$

$$\{x_{i_1},\ldots,x_{i_k}\} \subset \{x_1,\ldots,x_n\}$$

$$\{x_{j_1},\ldots,x_{j_1}\} \subset \{x_1,\ldots,x_n\}$$

$$i_m \neq i_1 \quad \text{for } m \neq 1$$

$$j_m \neq j_k \quad \text{for } m \neq k$$

A sentence type S is atomic, if no sentences $s_1,\ldots,s_m$ of the sentences types $S_1,\ldots,S_m$ and one state of the real world exists so that the sentences $s_1,\ldots,s_m$ are true but the sentence s of type S is not true or vice versa.

The semantic notion of irreducibility means, that anly those relations that model elementary sentences should be contained in a conceptual schema. Information would be lost splitting elementary sentences.
In terms of relations it means, that by the join of the projections of s-irreducible relations one would generate tuples which model facts which were not modelled by the original relation. In other words, one would create false sentences.

It is important that the definition of s-irreducibility is based on sentences and not on relations modelling sentences. It is possible, that by the join of the projections of a relation modelling a s-irreducible sentence type tuples are generated which are not contained in the original relation. But as long as these tuples model facts which were already modelled in the original relation, this is in accordance to the definition. Whereas the a-irreducibility only excludes the loss of tuples, is the generation of redundant tuples also covered by the s-irreducibility.

To discuss the interrelationship of s-irreducible relations and a-irreducible relations, we introduce an example. Figure 3 represents a relation SUPPLIES, which is defined on the domains SUPPLIER, PART, CUSTOMER.

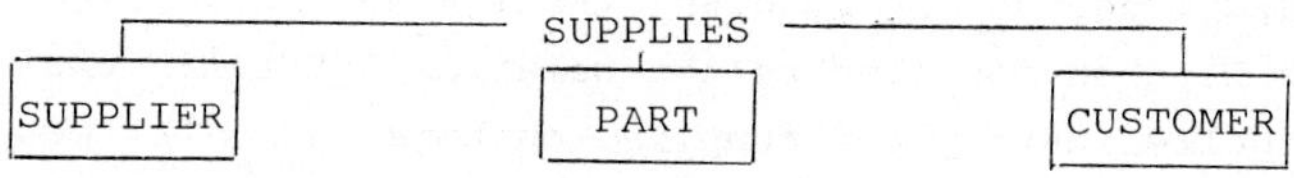

Figure 3: The relation SUPPLIES

Let the meaning of this relation be, that a tuple (x, y, z) is an element of an occurrence of this relation, if supplier x supplies the part y to the customer z. Let us assume that no consistency conditions (like functional dependencies or multivalued dependencies) exist. It is well known, that the relation SUPPLIES then is a-irreducible. In figure 4 all possible decompositions of the relation SUPPLIES are shown.

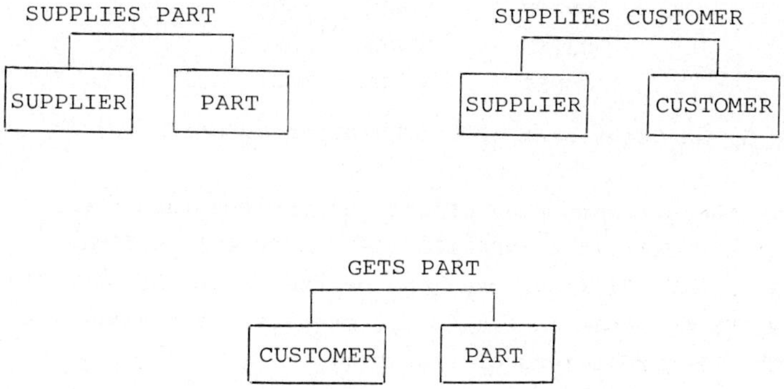

Figure 4: Decomposition of the relation SUPPLIES

The relation SUPPLIES is also s-irreducible, since neither from (x, y) ∈ SUPPLIES PART and (x, z) ∈ SUPPLIES CUSTOMER nor from (x, y) ∈ SUPPLIES PART and (z, y) ∈ GETS PART follows (x, y, z) ∈ SUPPLIES.

To show the difference we introduce now a relation SUPPLIES' with the meaning that, if a tuple (x, y, z) is an element of an occurrence of this relation, then holds supplier x supplies the part y (to any customer and not necessarily to customer z) and supplier x supplies customer z (with any part but not necessarily with part y). Furthermore, we do not request, that any consistency condition, like a multivalued dependency between SUPPLIER and PART holds. The sentence which is then modelled by the relation SUPPLIES' could be "supplier x supplies part y and supplies customer z". That means a tuple (x, y, z) ∈ SUPPLIES' implies, that the facts supplier x supplies part y and customer z hold. On the other hand, if the facts that supplier x supplies part y and customer z hold, the tuple (x, y, z) must not necessarily be an element of the relation SUPPLIES', since it is possible that tuples (x, y, z_1) and (x, y_1, z) are elements of the relation SUPPLIES', and so these facts are already modelled. An occurence of the relation SUPPLIES' is shown in figure 5.

SUPPLIES'	SUPPLIER	PART	CUSTOMER
	SMITH	WHEEL	JONES
	SMITH	SCREW	DOE
	JONES	WHEEL	DOE

Figure 5: An Occurrence of the Relation SUPPLIES

Figure 6 shows the decomposition of this occurrence into the occurrences of the relations SUPPLIES PART, SUPPLIES CUSTOMER, and PART CUSTOMER. Figure 7a shows the join of the relations SUPPLIES PART and SUPPLIES CUSTOMER on the domain supplier, and Figure 7b the join of the tree relations of Figure 6.

PART CUSTOMER	PART	CUSTOMER
	WHEEL	JONES
	SCREW	DOE
	WHEEL	DOE

SUPPLIES PART	SUPPLIER	PART
	SMITH	WHEEL
	SMITH	SCREW
	JONES	WHEEL

SUPPLIES CUSTOMER	SUPPLIER	CUSTOMER
	SMITH	JONES
	SMITH	DOE
	JONES	DOE

Figure 6: A Decomposition of the Relation of Figure 5.

SUPPLIES'	SUPPLIER	PART	CUSTOMER
	SMITH	WHEEL	JONES
	SMITH	SCREW	JONES
	SMITH	WHEEL	DOE
	SMITH	SCREW	DOE
	JONES	WHEEL	DOE

Figure 7a: The Join of the Relations SUPPLIES PART and SUPPLIES CUSTOMER

SUPPLIES'	SUPPLIER	PART	CUSTOMER
	SMITH	WHEEL	JONES
	SMITH	WHEEL	DOE
	SMITH	SCREW	DOE
	JONES	WHEEL	DOE

Figure 7b: The Join of the relations of Figure 6.

The occurrences of the relation SUPPLIES' in figure 7a and 7b are obviously not equal to that in figure 5, since the tuples (SMITH, SCREW, JONES) in Figure 7a, and (SMITH, WHEEL, DOE) in both Figures have been added.

The relation therefore is a-irreducible. On the other hand, if we look at these tuples, they do not contain any information which is not contained in the relation of figure 5 since it is already known that SMITH supplies the parts SCREW, and WHEEL and that SMITH supplies some parts to JONES and DOE.

Now we will investigate, whether the relation is s-irreducible. In an intuitive interpretation of the term irreducible we certainly would expect SUPPLIES' to be a reducible relation, since in one tuple of this relation two independent facts are modelled.

The sentences "supplier x supplies part y and supplies customer z" obviously can be split into the sentences s_1 = "supplier x supplies part y" and s_2 = "supplier x supplies customer z". Whenever s is true, then s_1 is true and s_2 is true and vice versa.
The reason is, that s is a conjunction of two independent sentences. According to definitions 1.2 and 1.3 the relation SUPPLIES' therefore is not s-irreducible. So the relation SUPPLIES' is an example, that a-irreducible relations need not be s-irreducible, too. s-irreducibility therefore is more restrictive than a-irreducibility, as stated in the following proposition.

Proposition 1.2:
A_n s-irreducible relation is a-irreducible.

The proof is given by deriving a contradiction, if we assume that the proposition does not hold. Let us assume, that there exists a relation $\mathcal{R}$ which is s-irreducible but not a-irreducible. If it is not a-irreducible, all occurrences R of can be decomposed into relation occurrences $R_1,\ldots,R_n$ so that the join of $R_1,\ldots,R_n$ is equal to R. The relations $\mathcal{R}_1,\ldots,\mathcal{R}_n$ are the models of sentence types $S_1,\ldots,S_2$ with the property that for all occurrences of these sentence types $s_1 \wedge \ldots \wedge s_n \Rightarrow s$, where $\mathcal{R}$ is the model of the sentence type S (see also 29). This is a contradiction to the definition 1.3, and we have proven the proposition 1.2.

The reason that the converse of this proposition does not hold is that the existence of an tuple of R implies the truth of the sentence s, but not vice versa, as the example shows.

It could be argued against the example, that the multivalued dependencies SUPPLIER $\twoheadrightarrow$ PART|CUSTOMER and SUPPLIER $\twoheadrightarrow$ CUSTOMER| PART must hold in the relation SUPPLIES' and that therefore the occurrence in Figure 5 would not be valid. However requiring for example the multivalued dependency SUPPLIER $\twoheadrightarrow$ PART|CUSTOMER to hold, e.g. "for any given customer which is supplied by a supplier the supplier supplies the same parts", would change the meaning of the relation. The MVD implies that a connection between the parts and customers supplied by a supplier exists, since in the definition of the MVD all three attributes of the relation SUPPLIES' play a role.

There is a semantic difference between the sentence represented by the relation SUPPLIES', e.g. "supplier x supplies part y and customer z" and the sentence type "supplier x supplies part y to customer z" together with above restriction. Since the meaning of these sentences is different, the set of extensions of the relation SUPPLIES' and a relation modelling the latter sentence cannot be the same. The difference between the two is that occurrences of SUPPLIES' like the one in Figure 5 cannot be occurrences of the other relation. If one argues that the above MVDs must hold for the relation SUPPLIES' one would not be able to express this difference.

For the data base designer the following proposition is important, to derive contradictions in the consistency conditions.

Proposition 1.3:
If a relation is not a-irreducible, it is not s-irreducible.

The proposition follows directly from proposition 5.2.
The interrelationship between s-irreducible relations, a-irreducible relations, fourth normal form relations, and third normal form relations is shown in Figure 8.

s-irreducible

$\Downarrow$

a-irreducible

$\Downarrow$

fourth normal form

$\Downarrow$

third normal form

Figure 8: The Interrelationship between the different Forms of Relations.

In the sequel we will use the term irreducible relations for s-irreducible relations.

2. Irreducible Relations and the Relational Model

In this section we return to the example given in Figures 1 and 2 and discuss in more detail the interrelationship between the notion of irreducible relations and RM-relations. In the relation AGE in Figure 2a, which ist a representation of the irreducible relation HAS AGE in Figure 1, the domain AGE is functional dependent on the domain BIRTHDAY. AGE is not in Boyce Codd normal form (abbr. 3NF) since it contains a partial dependency.

If we want to use the relational model as the conceptual schema data model, we must either introduce another definition of irreducibility or modify the relational model. In the following we will discuss three possible solutions.
In the first solution we do not distinguish between relations (of the abstract model) and RM-relations, and therefore define irreducibility of RM-relations according to the definitions 1.2 and 1.3. Hence, the RM-relation AGE would not be irreducible. Consequently, if we want to have only irreducible relations in our conceptual schema, we would have to split this RM-relation into two other ones, i.e. the RM-relations AGE' and AGE" as shown in Figure 9.

AGE' (NAME, FIRST NAME, BIRTHDAY)
AGE" (BIRTHDAY, INTEGER)

Figure 9: The decomposition of the RM-relation AGE into 3NF

But what would be the meaning of the RM-relation AGE'? If a tuple (x,y,z) is an element of this relation then there exists a person with name x, first name y, and birthday z. In other words tuples of this relation would not represent facts, which are either the existence of relationships between several objects or the existence of a property of an object [4] . We have avoided the update, deletion, and insertion anomalies of the original relation, but introduced another anomaly, which we call retrieval anomaly. If a user wants to know the age of a certain person, he would ask: What is the age of the person which has name x, first name y and birthday z? But using the decomposition of Figure 9, he first has to join the RM-relations AGE' and AGE" or he must modify his query to: What is the age of birthday z? In both cases he cannot formulate his question in the most natural way according to his view of the reality!

The second solution is simply to ignore those functional dependencies which do not exist in the corresponding abstract relations. This would mean that we would introduce two different classes of functional dependencies. The one containing those dependencies of relevance to the conceptual schema design and the other, containing those not of relevance. To achieve this separation, we start by introducing compound domains, so that each domain of an abstract relation is represented by a simple or a compound domain (depending on the naming structure chosen). A value of a compound domain represents an "real world object". In our example this would lead to the relations shown in Figure 10.

a) HAS AGE' (PERSON (SOC SEC#), INTEGER)

b) AGE' (PERSON (NAME, FIRST NAME, BIRTHDAY), AGE)

Figure 10: Representations of the relation HAS AGE using compound domains

In the conceptual schema the dependencies would only be defined between compound domains. The advantage of this solution is that we have a greater similarity between the abstract relations and the relational schema so that the semantic ambiguities of the relational model disappear. The RM-relations correspond to relations and the domains to entities. Furthermore, the relational operations could be extended in an obvious way to dealing with compound domains.

But there is one objection against this solution. If we know that the functional dependency between the domains BIRTHDAY and AGE in the RM-relation AGE' must hold we can use this knowledge, to reject a tuple which would violate the dependency.

Since we should use as much semantic knowledge as possible to assure the consistency of our data base, we therefore propose the following third solution.

This solution is to distinguish between the functional dependencies as in the second solution. Functional dependencies which do not exist in the corresponding abstract relation, are used for consistency checks only, and are not used to normalize a relation. We give the following definition for the irreducibility of RM-relations:

<u>Def. 2.1</u>: An RM-relation is (semantically) irreducible, if it represents an irreducible abstract relation.

The advantage of this solution compared to the first one is that we have a definition of irreducibility based on the semantics. A further advantage is, that the problems of semantic ambiguities of RM-relations is solved. One argument against this solution could be, that the update, deletion, and insertion anomalies still would exist. But as will be shown immediately, these anomalies are not very important for a semantically based relational schema.

In the following discussion, we will use the RM-relation INCOME (PERSON (NAME, PROFESSION), SALARY). A tuple of this relation represents the fact, that a person, which is identified by name and profession, makes a certain salary. Let us also assume, that a functional dependency from PROFESSION to SALARY holds, which means, that all persons having the same profession get the same salary.

Let us first look at the update anomaly. This anomaly arises when we want to change the salary of one person, since we must also change the salary of all other persons, having the same profession. On the other hand, this can be done automatically by the system without any inconvenience to an user.

The deletion and insertion anomalies, however, do not exist in this relation, since this relation does represent only the relationship between persons and salaries, and not the relationship between professions and salaries. If we want to represent this relationship in the conceptual schema, we must introduce a separate RM-relation (for example RATING (PROFESSION, SALARY) to represent this information explicitly.

These two relations of course are connected via some consistency conditions (e.g. "a tuple ((x, y), z) in the relation INCOME may only exist, if the tuple (y, z) is element of the relation RATING). This condition again can be validated automatically by the system. If we are not interested in the relationship between salaries and professions, we would not introduce the RATING relation. In this case we would not lose relevant information through the deletion anomalies. The corresponding argumentation holds with respect to the insertion anomalies.

3. Conclusion

Irreducible relations play a major role in the discussion about conceptual data models as well as for the logical design of data base schemas. The notion of irreducibility however is still quite fuzzy. To our opinion, the reason for this lack of precision is, that irreducibility is a semantic notion which cannot be covered completely by the algebraic definition developed in the relational theory.

We have introduced a definition of irreducibility based on a notion of the semantics of data. This definition has been compared with the algebraic definition and it has been shown, that relations exist, which are algebraicly irreducible but semanticly reducible. In the second part of the paper, we have discussed some problems which arise, if our definition is applied to Codds's relational model. It is possible, that relations, which are semanticly irreducible, are not in third normal form.

We have shown, how by the use of compound domains these problems can be avoided, so that the semantic definition of irreducibility can be transferred to the relational model.

In the discussion of the relational model we have only given examples in which functional dependencies were involved. We do not see, however, any difficulties, arising from the possible existence of multivalued dependencies or mutual dependencies to keep our definition of irreducibility of RM-relations.

4. Acknowledgement

I would like to thank M. Brodie, R. Demolombe, W. Kleefstra, and B. Meyer for their careful reading of an earlier version of this paper and their valuable comments.

5. References

[1] D. Tsichritzis, A. Klug (ed.): THE ANSI/X3/SPARC DBMS Framework - Report of the Study Group on Data Base Management systems. Technical Note 12, CSRG, University of Toronto, July 1977

[2] ANSI/X3/SPARC Study Group on Data Base Management Systems. Interim Report. In: ACM SIGMOD Newsletters, FDT. 7, 2, 1975

[3] H. Biller, E.J. Neuhold: Concepts for the Conceptual Schema. In: G.M. Nijssen (ed.): Architecture and Models in Data Base Management Systems, North Holland, Amsterdam, 1977

[4] H. Biller, E.J. Neuhold: On the Semantics of Data Bases: The Semantics of Data Models. Information Systems, Vol. 3, No. 1, 1978

[5] E. Falkenberg: Concepts for Modelling Information. In [6]

[6] G.M. Nijssen (ed.): Modelling in Data Base Management. North Holland, Amsterdam, 1976

[7] P. Hall, J. Owlett, S. Todd: Relations and Entities. In [6]

[8] W. Kent: Limitations of Record-Oriented Information Models, IBM Technical Report TR 03.028, San Jose, California, May 1977

[9] P. Moulin et al.: Conceptual Model as a Data Base Design Tool. In [6]

[10] G.M. Nijssen: On the Gross Architecture for the Next Generation Database Management Systems. In: Proc. IFIP Congress 1977, North Holland, Amsterdam, 1977

[11] H.A. Schmid, J.R. Swenson: On the Semantics of the Relational Data Model. Proc. ACM SIGMOD Conf. 1975

[12] J.R. Abrial: Data Semantics. In: J.W. Klimbie, K.L. Koffemann (eds.): Data Base Management, North Holland, Amsterdam, 1974

[13] G. Bracchi, P. Paolini, G. Pelagatti: Binary Logical Associations in Data Modelling. In [6]

[14] M.E. Senko: DIAM as a Detailed Example of the ANSI/SPARC Architecture. In [6]

[15] B. Langefors: Theoretical Analysis of Information Systems. Studentliteratur 1966

[16] B. Sundgren: An Infological Approach to Data Bases. Urval Nr. 7, Statistika Centralbyran, Stockholm, 1973

[17] S. Berild, S. Nachmens: Some practical Applications of CS4 - a DBMS for Associative Databases. In [6]

[18] N. Raver, G.U. Hubbard: Automated Data Base Design: Concepts and Applications. IBM Systems Journal No. 3, 1977

[19] E.F. Codd: A Relational Model for Large Shared Data Banks, Comm. ACM, Vol. 13, 6, 1970

[20] R. Carnap: Meaning and Necessity, 2nd Ed., University of Chicago Press, Chicago, 1956

[21] P.P. Chen: The Entity-Relationship Model. ACM TODS, Vol. 1, 1, 1976

[22] J.M. Smith, D.P. Smith: Database Abstractions: Aggregation. Comm. ACM, Vol. 20, 6, 1977

[23] C. Delobel, R.G. Casey: Decomposition of a Data Base and the Theory of Boolean Switching Functions. IBM Journal of Research and Development, Vol. 12, 5, Sept. 1973

[24] R. Fagin: Multivalued Dependencies and a new Normal Form for Relational Databases. ACM TODS, Vol. 2, 3, 1977

[25] E.F. Codd: Recent Investigations in Relational Data Base Systems. Proc. IFIP Congress 1974

[26] E.F. Codd: Further Normalization of the Data Base Relational Model. In: R. Rustin (ed.): Data Base Systems, Prentice Hall, New York, 1971

[27] E.F. Codd: Relational Completeness of Data Base Sublanguages. Same as [26]

[28] R. Durchholz, G. Richter: Concepts for Data Base Management Systems. Same as [12]

[29] J.M. Nicolas: Mutual Dependencies and some Results on Undecomposable Relations. Proc. 4th VLDB Conference, Berlin 1978

[30] R. Demolombe, J.M. Nicolas: Normal Form and Irreducible Relations. Atomic Relations: A New Proposal. Techn. Rep. CERT-LBD-77/2, Toulouse, Sept. 1977

Data Base Architecture, Bracchi/Nijssen, eds.
North-Holland Publishing Company

LOGICAL DESIGN OF A RELATIONAL SCHEMA AND INTEGRITY OF A DATA BASE

Yuzuru TANAKA

Graduate School of Information Engineering
Hokkaido University
Sapporo, 060 Japan

A class of 4NF schemata with a tree structure among constituent relations are considered. Such a schema is called a 4NF decomposition tree (4NF D*-tree) schema. A 4NF D*-tree schema is an extension of a BCNF dependency tree (BCNF D-tree) schema previously proposed and reviewed in this paper with some modifications since both types of schemata are commonly based on a dependency diagram of an object data base. However, it is shown that BCNF D-tree schema is better than BCNF D*-tree schema when there exists no MVD. We show an algorithm for the design of a 4NF D*-tree schema that is proved to construct an irredundant 4NF schema in a weak sense.

1. INTRODUCTION

The design methodology of a sound schema that consistently reflects semantic structures of a real world is acquiring a greater importance to cope with both the increasing size and the versatile utilization of data bases. Without the establishment of a method to describe and to analyze semantic structures of information, it will become almost impossible in the near future to construct a sound schema.

It is the purpose of various studies on schema design based on the relational framework [CODD70] to establish a theoretical basis necessary to cope with the difficulties of the design of a sound schema [DELO72][ZANI76][BERN76][FAGI77][TANA77].

The goal of the schema design is to separate the complicated dependency structures among attributes into simple substructures. However, it is well known that their total separation can not always be achieved without abandonment of some dependencies to be embodied in a constituent relation of a designed schema [BEER78]. Two alternative approaches are well known, i.e., synthesis and decomposition approaches. Synthesis approaches strive for total embodiment of fundamental dependencies with as simple relations as possible. While decomposition approaches strive for total separation of dependencies.

Our approach is classified in decomposition approaches. However, different from others, we consider a schema as a structured set of relations rather than a non-structured set of relations. As an interrelational structure, we consider two types of tree structures, i.e., a dependency tree (D-tree) structure and a decomposition tree (D*-tree) structure. BCNF D-tree schemata were introduced in [TANA77]. While, in this paper, we introduce 4NF D*-tree schemata. These interrelational structures increase integrity and handleability of a data base when described in a schema.

A 4NF D*-tree schema designed by our algorithm proposed in this paper is proved to be irredundant in a weak sense. BCNF D-tree schemata are also reviewed in this paper with significant modifications and compared with BCNF D*-tree schemata. The comparison shows the optimality of BCNF D-tree schemata when MVD's are not concerned.

2. PRELIMINARIES

2.1. Relational Model

A relation R(X) over an attribute set X={A1,A2,...,An} is a subset of the cartesian product Dom(A1)×Dom(A2)×...×Dom(An), where Dom(Ai) is the domain of Ai. The projection of R(X) to a subset Y of X is defined as R(X)[Y]={<y>|<y,z> ε R(X)}, where Z=X-Y. When Y is not a subset of X, R(X)[Y] is defined as R(X)[X$\cap$Y]. The set of all the attributes of a data base Δ is denoted by Ω0. In this paper, we assume that the uniqueness assumption holds in Ω0, i.e., R(X)[Y]=R(X$\cap$Y) for any subsets X and Y of Ω0. This condition is not always satisfied by a set of attributes of an object data base. However, we believe that we can design a family of attribute sets satisfying the uniqueness assumption for general data bases. This phase of design called attribute design of a data base is not treated in this paper. The natural join of two relations R(X,Y) and S(Y,Z) is a relation {<x,y,z>| <x,y> ε R(X,Y) and <y,z> ε R(Y,Z)} denoted by R*S, where X,Y,Z are disjoint. Since natural join is commutative and associative, the natural join of m relations R1,R2, ...,Rm can be defined. This is denoted by $\Pi_{i=1}^{m}$ Ri.

If each value of X in R(X,Y,Z) is associated with only one value of Y, it is said that there is a functional dependency (FD):X$\rightarrow$Y. If X,Y$\subset$Z and R(Z)=R(X,Y')*R(X,Y") where Y'=Y-X and Y"=Z-X-Y, then it is said that there is a multivalued dependency (MVD):X$\twoheadrightarrow$Y in Z. Three sets X,Y, and Z are respectively called the MVD-determinant, the MVD-dependant, and the context. If X$\twoheadrightarrow$Y1 in Z and X$\twoheadrightarrow$Y2 in Z then we use an abbriviated representation X$\twoheadrightarrow$Y1|Y2 in Z. The definition of MVD in this paper includes both MVD and embedded MVD(EMVD) defined by R.Fagin[FAGI77]. For any subset Ω of Ω0, an MVD is said to be global in Ω if its context includes Ω and the union of its MVD-determinant and its MVD-dependant is a subset of Ω. Otherwise an MVD is said to be local. A global MVD in Ω is nontrivial in Ω if the union of its MVD-determinant and its MVD-dependant is a proper subset of Ω.

2.2. Axioms for FD's and MVD's

For the design theory of 4NF schema, we need a complete set of axioms for FD's and MVD's as inference rules to calculate all dependencies. We conjecture the following set of axioms forms a complete set of axioms for FD's and MVD's. The set of axioms FD1-3, MVD0-3, FD-MVD1-2 is well known as a complete set of axioms for FD's and MVD's global in Ω0 [BEER77]. However, the completeness of the following axioms is unfortunately not proved yet.

FD1 (Reflexivity)	If Y $\subseteq$ X then X$\rightarrow$Y.
FD2 (Augmentation)	If Z $\subseteq$ W and X$\rightarrow$Y then XW$\rightarrow$YZ.
FD3 (Transitivity)	If X$\rightarrow$Y and Y$\rightarrow$Z then X$\rightarrow$Z.
MVD0 (Complementation)	If X$\twoheadrightarrow$Y in Z then X$\twoheadrightarrow$Z-Y in Z.
MVD1 (Reflexivity)	If Y $\subseteq$ X $\subseteq$ Z then X$\twoheadrightarrow$Y in Z.
MVD2 (Augmentation)	If V $\subseteq$ W $\subseteq$ Z and X$\twoheadrightarrow$Y in Z then XW$\twoheadrightarrow$YV in Z.
MVD3 (Transitivity)	If X$\twoheadrightarrow$Y in Z and Y$\twoheadrightarrow$W in Z then X$\twoheadrightarrow$W-Y in Z.
MVD4 (Embedding)	If X $\subseteq$ W $\subseteq$ Z and X$\twoheadrightarrow$Y in Z then X$\twoheadrightarrow$Y$\cap$W in W.
MVD5 (Extension)	If X$\twoheadrightarrow$Y in Z and (Z-Y)$\twoheadrightarrow$Y in W, where W $\supseteq$ Z then X$\twoheadrightarrow$Y in W.
MVD6 (Reconnection)	If X$\twoheadrightarrow$Y in Z, V$\twoheadrightarrow$Y in W, and Z$\cap$W$\twoheadrightarrow$X in XV(Z$\cap$W) then XV$\twoheadrightarrow$Y in XV(Z$\cap$W).
FD-MVD1	If X$\rightarrow$Y and X,Y $\subseteq$ Z then X$\twoheadrightarrow$Y in Z.
FD-MVD2	If X$\twoheadrightarrow$Y in Z and (Z-Y)$\rightarrow$Y then X$\rightarrow$Y.

For the proofs of MVD4-6, see [TANA79]. MVD6 may need some explanation. Fig.1 shows an example data base ({A,B,C,D},{A$\twoheadrightarrow$B|C in ABC,D$\twoheadrightarrow$B|C in DBC,BC$\twoheadrightarrow$A|D in ABCD}). This data base has two alternative decompositions. However, the decomposition (d) can not be inferred without MVD6.

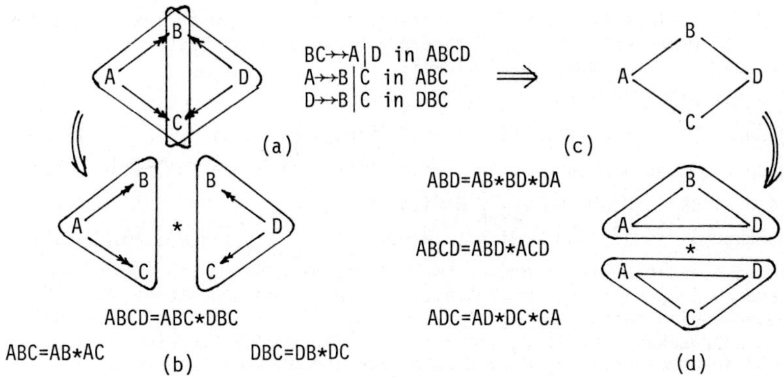

Fig. 1. Explanation of MVD6.

2.3. Closure of Dependencies

For the design of a schema, it is necessary to know the closure of FD's and MVD's, i.e., all the dependencies inferable from a given set of FD's and MVD's. Let F and M denote respectively a given set of FD's and that of MVD's. We denote $F \cup M$ by Γ. The closure of Γ is denoted by $\Gamma^\dagger$. For the convenience of computation, we introduce MVD7 and FD-MVD3 to replace respectively MVD3-5 and FD-MVD2.

MVD7 (MVD interaction)
If $X \twoheadrightarrow Y$ in Z, $U \twoheadrightarrow V$ in W, $X \subset W$ and $U \subset Z$
then $X(Y \cap U) \twoheadrightarrow Y \cap V$ in Z-(Y-W), and
$U(V \cap X) \twoheadrightarrow Y \cap V$ in Z-(Y-W).

FD-MVD3 (FD-MVD interaction)
If $X \rightarrow Y$, $U \twoheadrightarrow V$ in W and $X \subset W$ then $U(V \cap X) \rightarrow Y \cap V$.

The following Lemma holds with respect to these replacement.

Lemma 2.1.
A set A of axioms FD1-3, MVD0-6, and FD-MVD1-2 is equivalent to a set B of axioms FD1-3, MVD0-2, MVD6-7, and FD-MVD1,3 [TANA79].

In a strict sense, we can not calculate $\Gamma^\dagger$ unless the completeness of the axiom set A is proved. For an arbitrary set I of inference rules, we denote by Γ:I a set of all the dependencies inferable from Γ by I. In this paper, we approximate $\Gamma^\dagger$ by Γ:A. If A is complete, Γ:A is equal to $\Gamma^\dagger$.

In most of the practical situations, the dependency structure is not so complicated that MVD6 is necessary to compute the closure. If it is, we would not be able even to list up a sufficient set of dependencies from which all dependencies are inferable. Therefore, in a practical application, $\Gamma^\dagger$ can be approximated by Γ:C where C=B-{MVD6}.

Let FD($\Gamma^\dagger$) denote the FD part of $\Gamma^\dagger$. The following Lemma holds with respect to Γ:C.

Lemma 2.2.
Let D be {FD1-3, MVD0, FD-MVD3}, i.e., D has no rules about MVD interaction. Then the following relation holds true [TANA79];

$$FD(\Gamma:D) = FD(\Gamma:C).$$

3. SCHEMA OF A DATA BASE

3.1. Decomposition vs. Synthesis

A pair (Ω,Γ), where Ω is an attribute set and Γ is a dependency structure in Ω, is called a scheme over Ω. A schema of a data base $(\Omega 0,\Gamma)$ is a set of schemes over subsets of $\Omega 0$, i.e., $\{(\Omega i,\Gamma i) \mid 1 \le i \le k\}$, that represents $(\Omega 0,\Gamma)$ with least redundancy. The definition of representation and redundancy differs among researchers. In synthesis approaches, they mean the followig;

(Representation) $\Gamma\dagger = (\cup_{1\le i\le k} \Gamma i)\dagger$,

(Irredundancy) $\neg\exists i, \exists f \in \Gamma i$ s.t. $\Gamma\dagger = ((\cup_{1\le j\le k, j\ne i} \Gamma j) \cup (\Gamma i-\{f\}))\dagger$.

While, in decomposition approaches, they respectively mean the following [BEER78];

(Representation) $R(\Omega 0) = \Pi_{1\le i\le k} R(\Omega i)$,

(Irredundancy) $\neg\exists i, \exists A \in \Omega i$ s.t. $R(\Omega 0) = (\Pi_{1\le j\le k, j\ne i} R(\Omega j)) * R(\Omega i-\{A\})$.

Our approach is classified in decomposition approaches. Since the equivalence between $\Gamma\dagger$ and $(\cup_{1\le i\le k} \Gamma i)\dagger$ does not hold in decomposition approaches, a minimal set Γr of dependencies satisfying $\Gamma\dagger=((\cup_{1\le i\le k} \Gamma i)\cup \Gamma r)\dagger$ should be considered in decomposition approaches. Γr is called a residue dependency structure and plays an important role in procedural validity checks upon inconsistent updates.

Therefore, a schema is characterized by $(\{(\Omega i,\Gamma i)\}, \Gamma r)$.

3.2. Normal Forms

As to the decomposition of $(\Omega 0,\Gamma)$ into a set of $(\Omega i,\Gamma i)$'s, various normal forms of constituent schemes are proposed [CODD72][KENT73][CODD74][BERN76][FAGI77][BEER78]. We define two of them considered in this paper.

1. <u>Boyce-Codd normal form (BCNF)</u>
   (Ω,Γ) is in BCNF if, for any Y and A such that $Y \subset \Omega$, $A \in \Omega$, and $A \notin Y$, an FD: $Y \dashrightarrow A \in \Gamma\dagger$ implies that $Y \dashrightarrow \Omega \in \Gamma\dagger$.

2. <u>Fourth normal form (4NF)</u>
   (Ω,Γ) is in 4NF if a nontrivial MVD:$Y \twoheadrightarrow Z$ in $\Omega \in \Gamma\dagger$ implies that an FD:$Y \dashrightarrow Z$ is in $\Gamma\dagger$.

A schema $\{(\Omega i,\Gamma i)\}$ is in BCNF (4NF) if each constituent scheme is in BCNF (4NF) and $\Omega i \dashrightarrow \Omega j$ and $\Omega j \dashrightarrow \Omega i$ do not simultaneously hold if $i\ne j$. The latter condition is necessary to exclude such a schema as $\{(\{A,B\},\{A \dashrightarrow B\}), (\{A,C\},\{A \dashrightarrow C\})\}$ for a data base $(\{A,B,C\}, \{A \dashrightarrow B, B \dashrightarrow C\})$.

3.3. Decomposition Tree Schema (D*-tree Schema)

The process of decomposition of $(\Omega 0,\Gamma)$ into $\{(\Omega i,\Gamma i)\}$ by repetitive application of a proper MVD in $\Gamma\dagger$ is representable by a decomposition tree. Such decomposition is called MVD-decomposition. As shown by J.M.Nicolas, there exists non MVD-decomposition like that by a mutual dependency [NICO78]. However, in this paper, we only consider MVD-decomposition. A subtree T' of a decomposition tree T is a son of T if the root of T' is a son node of the root of T. A set of son trees of T is denoted by son(T).

A decomposition tree T for (Ω,Γ) is formally defined as follows, where $\Omega(T)$ is a set of attributes appearing in T.

<u>Definition 3.1.</u>
T is a decomposition tree of (Ω,Γ) if it has one of the following three forms; Ω, or (T0;T1,T2,...,Tn), or (T1,T2,...,Tn),
where
1. Ti is a decomposition tree of $(\Omega(Ti),\Gamma)$,
2. $\Omega = \cup_i \Omega(Ti)$,
3. $\forall i,j \in [0,n]$ $\Omega(Ti) \cap \Omega(Tj) = \cap_k \Omega(Tk)$,
4. $(\cap_k \Omega(Tk) \dashrightarrow \Omega(T0)) \in \Gamma\dagger$,
5. $\forall i \in [1,n]$ $(\cap_k \Omega(Tk) \twoheadrightarrow \Omega(Ti)$ in $\Omega) \in \Gamma\dagger$.

A subtree T' of T is a leaf node of T if $T'=\Omega(T')$. Fig.2 shows an example of a decomposition tree. For explanation, $\Omega(T')$ of a non leaf subtree of T is shown at the root of T' enclosed in parentheses.

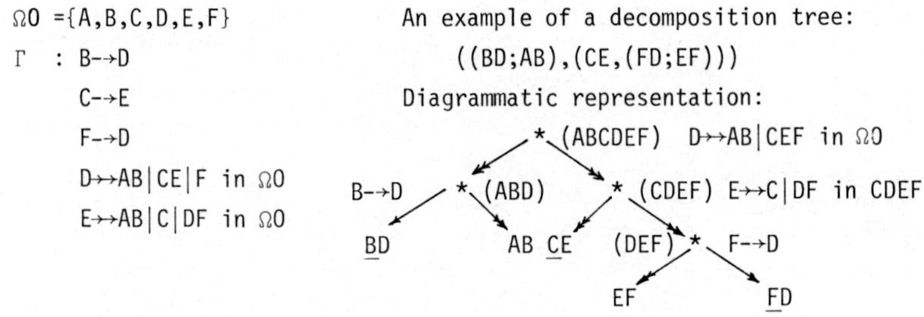

Fig. 2. An example of a decomposition tree.

For a scheme (Ω,Γ), a projection of Γ to $\Omega' \subset \Omega$ is defined as $\{f \mid f \in \Gamma\dagger$, f is nontrivial or local in $\Omega'\}$ and denoted by $\Gamma(\Omega')$. We denote by S(T) a set of schemes for a decomposition tree T of $(\Omega 0,\Gamma)$ defined as follows;

$$S(T) = \{(\Omega(T'),\Gamma(\Omega(T'))) \mid T' \text{ is a leaf of } T\}.$$

A tree T is called an X-NF D*-tree schema if S(T) is an X-NF schema. If we denote by $\Gamma(T)$ a set of MVD's in $\Gamma\dagger$ that is used to decompose $(\Omega 0,\Gamma)$ to construct T, the following relation holds;

$$(\cup_{(\Omega i,\Gamma i) \in S(T)} \Gamma i)\dagger \subsetneq ((\cup_{(\Omega i,\Gamma i) \in S(T)} \Gamma i) \cup \Gamma(T))\dagger.$$

Therefore we redefine a residue dependency structure Γr as a minimal set of dependencies satisfying

$$\Gamma\dagger = ((\cup_{(\Omega i,\Gamma i) \in S(T)} \Gamma i) \cup \Gamma(T) \cup \Gamma r)\dagger.$$

In the next chapter, we show an algorithm to design an 4NF D*-tree schema from a given scheme $(\Omega 0,\Gamma)$.

4. 4NF D*-tree SCHEMA

4.1. Some Considerations on 4NF D*-tree Schema Design

Before presenting an algorithm for 4NF D*-tree schema design in a "pulled-out-of-a-hat" manner, we show some observations on the appropriate order of MVD-decompositions. One might suppose that decomposition by FD's should precede that by MVD's or vice versa. However, that is not the case as shown in Fig.3 and Fig.4.

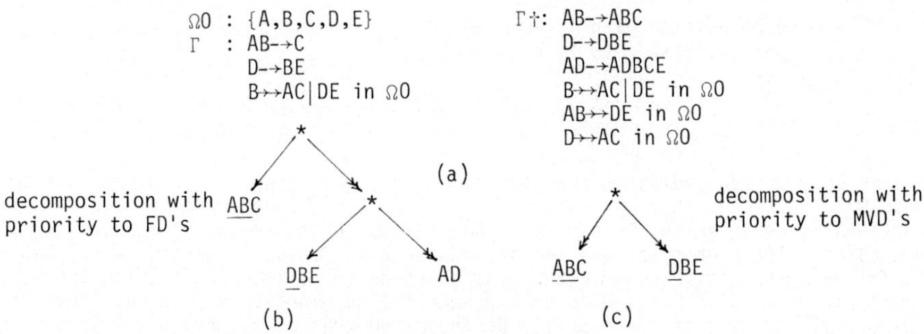

Fig. 3. An example of a data base in which the decomposition with priority to FD's causes redundancy.

$\Omega 0$: $\{A,B,C,D,E\}$
Γ : $B \to C$
$AB \twoheadrightarrow CD|E$ in $\Omega 0$

$\Gamma^{\dagger}$: $B \to BC$
$AB \twoheadrightarrow C|D|E$ in $\Omega 0$

(a)

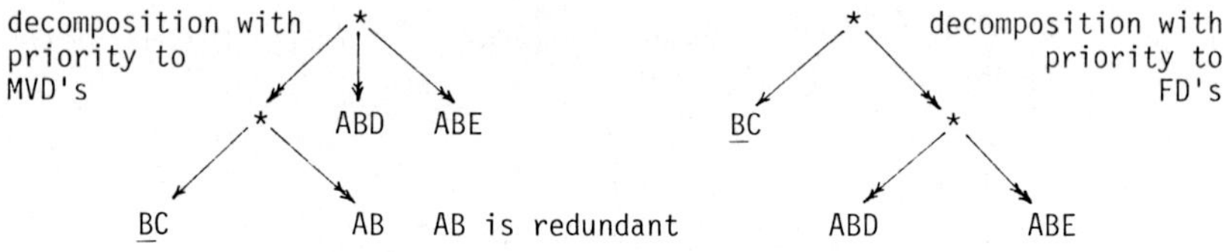

(b) (c)

Fig. 4. An example of a data base in which the decomposition with priority to MVD's causes redundancy.

In Fig.3, priority given to FD's causes redundancy, while, in Fig.4, the opposite situation occurs.

Fig.5 shows two alternative decomposition order between two MVD's. The redundancy occurs when the MVD with an MVD-determinant including that of the other is applied first to decompose the data base.

$\Omega 0$: $\{A,B,C,D\}$
$\Gamma^{\dagger}$: $AB \twoheadrightarrow C|D$ in $\Omega 0$
$A \twoheadrightarrow B|C|D$ in $\Omega 0$ (a)

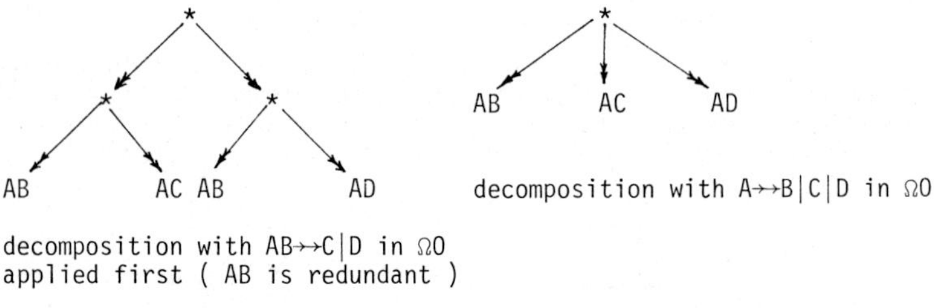

Fig. 5. Decomposition order and redundancy.

Further observation indicates that the redundancy may occur if the decomposition by an MVD f precedes that by another g such that the MVD-determinant of g is functionally dependent on that of f. The previous examples in Fig.3 and Fig.4 are such cases. These observations are proved their validness in Section 4.4. Besides, the following heuristic observation also approves the criterion in which the decomposition by an MVD f should not precede the decomposition by g such that the MVD-determinant of g is functionally dependent on that of f. Fig.6 (b), (c) show two alternative decomposition orders for a data base in Fig.6 (a), where (b) contradicts the criterion. Although it causes no redundancy in this case, the table R(<Employee>, <Item>, <Supplyer>) in Fig.6 (b) seems generally much larger than R(<Department>, <Item>, <Supplyer>) in Fig.6 (c). This is a different type of redundancy.

Ω0 = {<Employee>, <Salary>, <Department>, <Item>, <Supplyer>, <Skill>}

Γ : <Employee> → <Salary><Department>
<Department> ↠ <Employee><Salary><Skill> | <Item><Supplyer> in Ω0
<Employee> ↠ <Skill> in Ω0

an example scheme (Ω0,Γ)

Γ† : <Employee> → <Employee><Salary><Department>
<Department> ↠ <Employee><Salary><Skill> | <Item><Supplyer> in Ω0
<Employee> ↠ <Skill> | <Item><Supplyer> in Ω0

the closure

(a)

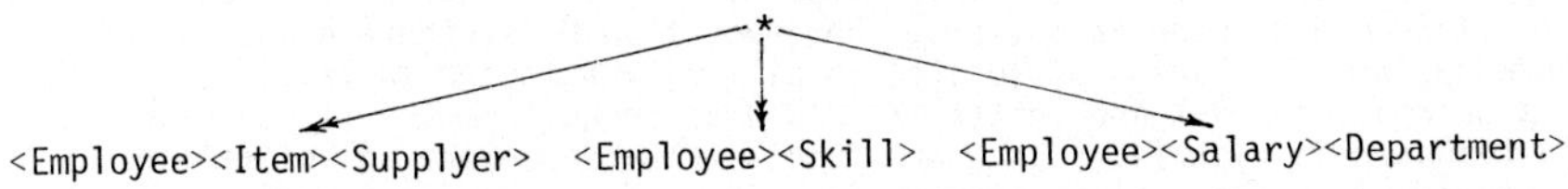

(b) decomposition with <Employee>↠<Skill>|<Item><Supplyer> applied first

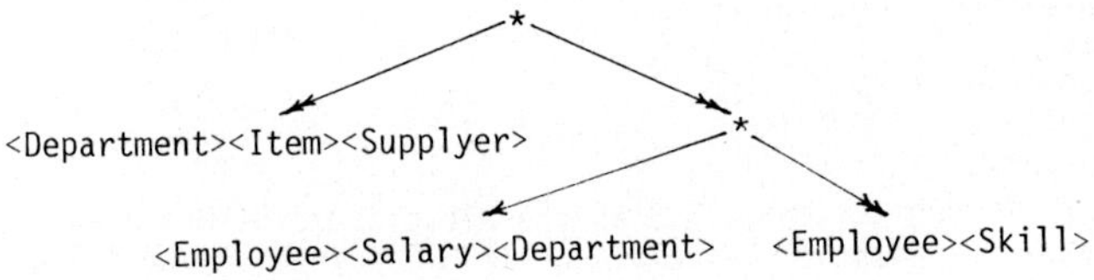

(c) decomposition with <Department>↠<Employee><Salary><Skill>| <Item><Supplyer> applied first

Fig. 6. Comparison of two decompositions.

4.2. Computation of Closure of Dependencies

For the convenience of computation of a dependency closure, we introduce a standard representation of an MVD and/or an FD. The standard representation of a dependency f with a context Z has a form:

$$X : [Y0]\ Y1 \mid Y2 \mid \dots \mid Yn,$$

where {X, Y0, Y1, Y2, ... , Yn} is a partition of Z, X→Y0, and X↠Yi in Z for any i. Three functions are defined for a standard representation;

context(f) = Z,
left(f) = X,
right(i, f) = if i>n then ϕ else Yi.

By Lemma 2.1, Γ:A can be calculated as Γ:B. Instead of calculating all the dependencies in Γ:B, we calculate a subset of Γ:B satisfying the following.

Definition 4.1.
For the I-closure of Γ with all the elements in standard representation, we define a set of base dependencies denoted by (Γ:I)* as follows;

$\forall f \in \Gamma:I,\ \exists^1 g \in (\Gamma:I)^*$
such that

1. left(g) ⊂ left(f)   (minimality of left(g)),
2. right(0,g) ⊃ right(0,f)   (maximality of right(0,g)),
3. ∀i≠0, ∃j≠0 s.t. left(g) ∪ right(j,g) ⊂ left(f) ∪ right(i,f) (minimality of left(g) ∪ right(j,g) (j≠0)),
4. context(g) ⊃ context(f)   (maximality of context(g)).

Since the calculation of (Γ:B)* is a direct application of axioms in B except the difficulty to efficiently find out applicability of MVD6, we do not show the detail how to calculate (Γ:B)*. Some considerations to speed up this process will be shown elsewhere.

As it has been pointed out in section 2.3, MVD6 is reasonably neglectable in most of the practical applications. The calculation of Γ:C becomes much easier than that of Γ:B. Let F' and M" respectively denote FD part and MVD part of Γ:C. By Lemma 2.2, we can calculate F' independently from MVD interactions, i.e., F'=FD(Γ:C) =FD(Γ:D).

If Γ is initially represented in standard form, MVD0 can be deleted from inference rules D. By removing FD's in FD(Γ:D) from M, we obtain the intermediate set M' of MVD's. This can be done as follows. For each f in M, if there exists a functional dependency from a subset X of left(f) to all the attributes in left(f), left(f) should be replaced by X and left(f)-X should be moved from left(f) to right(0,f). All attributes in right(i,f) that are functionally dependent on left(f) should be also moved from right(i,f) to right(0,f). Then, for each functional dependency f: X-→Y satisfying that Y is a maximum set dependent on X and X is a minimal set that determines X∪Y, we add an MVD g to M' that is defined as follows;

context(g) = Ω0,
left(g) = X,
right(0,g) = Y,
right(1,g) = Ω0-X-Y,
right(i,g) = φ (i>1).

The closure of all MVD's is obtained as the MVD-closure of M', i.e., M':E, where E={MVD0-2, MVD7}. Instead of calculating all MVD's in M':E, we calculate a set (M':E)*, which is denoted by M" in the sequel. The computation of M" is the direct application of MVD7 on M' in standard representation with some modification to the resultant MVD's by MVD0-2. Fig.7 shows example sets of F and M. The FD part F' of the closure and intermediate set M' of MVD's are calculated in Fig.8. The MVD-closure M" of M' is shown in Fig.9.

```
Ω0= {A,B,C,D,E,F,G,H,I,J,K,
     L,M,N,O,P,Q}

F : G-→DKLM
    AC-→OPQ
    H-→ABN

M : AB→→CDEFKLM|GHIJNOPQ
    C→→AELM|BFOP
    D→→AHL|BIJMOPN
    F→→ABG|HIJLM
    HC→→AD|BEF
    K→→LM|QPAB
    L→→QP|C
    M→→ON|C
```

Fig. 7. An example scheme (Ω0,Γ).

```
F' : G-→DGKLMOP         M' : G:[BDKLMNOP] ACEFHIJQ
     AC-→ACLMOPQ             AC:[LMOPQ] BDEFGHIJKN
     H-→ABDHKLMNOPQ          H:[ABDKLMNOPQ] CEFGIJ
     AB-→ABDKLMNOPQ          AB:[DKLMNOPQ] CEF|GHIJ
     C-→ACLMOP               C:[ALMOP] E|BF
     D-→DBMNOP               D:[BMNOP] AHL|IJ
     AD-→ADBKLMNOPQ          F:[ABDKLMNOPQ] G|HIJ
     F-→ABDFKLMNOPQ          K:[LMOP] ABCDEFGHIJNQ
     K-→KLMOP                L:[p] ABCDEFGHIJKMNOQ
     L-→LP                   L:[P] Q|C
     M-→MO                   M:[O] ABCDEFGHIJKLNPQ
                             M:[O] N|C
                             C:[ALMOP] BDEFGHIJKNQ
                             D:[BMNOP] ACEFGHIJKLQ
                             F:[ABDKLMNOPQ] CEGHIJ
                             AD:[BKLMNOPQ] CEFGHIJ
```

Fig. 8. Calculation of F' and M' of the data base in Fig.7.

```
M" : G : [BDKLMNOP] ACEFHQ | IJ
     H : [ABDKLMNOPQ] CEF | G | IJ
     AB : [DKLMNOPQ] CEF | G | H | IJ
     F : [ABDKLMOPQ] G | H | IJ | CE
     C : [ALMOP] E | BDFGHIJKLMNQ
     D : [BMNOP] IJ | ACEFGHKLQ
     CB : [ADKLMNOPQ] E | F | G | H | IJ
     DA : [BKLMNOPQ] IJ | CEF | G | H
     L : [P] Q | C
     M : [O] N | C
```

Fig. 9. Calculation of M" of the data base in Fig.7.

4.3. Dependency Diagram

Since we have to know functional dependencies among MVD-determinants of MVD's in (Γ:B)* to design an irredundant schema, we introduce a dependency diagram of a data base in this section.

For a dependency f in (Γ:B)*, let ε(f) denote the set of all the attributes that are functionally dependent on the MVD-determinant of f. This can be calculated with FD(Γ:B), or with FD(Γ:D) if MVD6 can be neglected. We define an equivalence relation f≡g in (Γ:B)* as

$$f \equiv g \quad \text{iff} \quad \varepsilon(f) = \varepsilon(g).$$

The classification of (Γ:B)* by ε is a set of equivalence classes with respect to '≡'. This is denoted by (Γ:B)*/ε. For each g in (Γ:B)*/ε, ε(g) is defined as ε(f) where f is a member of g, i.e., g=[f].

We define a partial order '>' in (Γ:B)*/ε as

$$f > g \quad \text{iff} \quad \varepsilon(f) \supset \varepsilon(g).$$

The partial order '>' uniquely defines a Hasse diagram ((Γ:B)*/ε, >) for a given scheme (Ω0,Γ) of a data base. This is called a dependency diagram of this data base. Fig.10 shows a dependency diagram of a data base in Fig.7, (Γ:B)* of which is given in Fig.8 (F') and Fig.9 (M").

(Γ:B)*:

```
f1 :  G:[BDKLMNOP] ACEFHQ|IJ
f2 :  AC:[LMOPQ] BDEFGHIJKN
f3 :  H:[ABDKLMNOPQ] CEF|G|IJ
f4 :  AB:[DKLMNOPQ] CEF|G|H|IJ
f5 :  C:[ALMOP] E|BDFGHIJKLMNQ
f6 :  D:[BMNOP] IJ|ACEFGHKLQ
f7 :  AD:[BKLMNOPQ] IJ|CEF|G|H
f8 :  F:[ABDKLMNOPQ] G|H|IJ|CE
f9 :  K:[LMOP] ABCDEFGHIJNQ
f10:  L:[P] ABCDEFGHIJKMNOQ
f11:  L:[P] Q|C
f12:  M:[O] ABCDEFGHIJKLNPQ
f13:  M:[O] N|C
f14:  CB:[ADKLMNOPQ] E|F|G|H|IJ
```

(a) (Γ:B)*

(Γ:B)*/ε:

g1 = {f8} g2 = {f3}
g3 = {f14} g4 = {f2}
g5 = {f1} g6 = {f7, f4}
g7 = {f5} g8 = {f6}
g9 = {f9} g10= {f10, f11}
g11= {f12, f13}

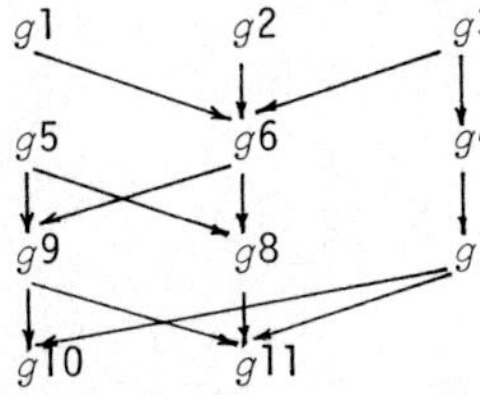

(b) dependency diagram

Fig. 10. (Γ:B)* and a dependency diagram of a scheme in Fig.7.

4.4. 4NF D*-tree Schema Design

Now we describe an algorithm that designs a 4NF D*-tree schema T0 from $(\Omega 0,\Gamma)$. The execution of Decomp(X,Λ) with X, Λ set to Ω0 and $(\Gamma:B)^*$ gives a 4NF D*-tree schema T0.

```
recursive procedure  Decomp(X,Λ);
  begin
    find a minimal node g in ((Λ:B)*/ε, >) such that there exists f in g that
    is global and nontrivial in X.
    if there is no such node
      then
        begin
          Decomp:=X;
          exit;
        end;
    if right(0,f)∩ X≠φ
      then
        T0':=left(f)∪(right(0,f)∩X)
      else
        T0':=φ;
    let {i1, i2, ... ,ik} be a set of indices such that ij≠0 and
    right(ij,f)∩X≠φ;
    for j=1 to k do
      Tj:=Decomp(left(f)∪right(ij,f)∩X, Λ);
    if T0'≠φ then
        Decomp:=(T0'; T1, T2,..., Tn)
      else
        Decomp:=(T1, T2,..., Tn);
  end;
```

Fig.11 shows a 4NF D*-tree schema of a data base in Fig.7.

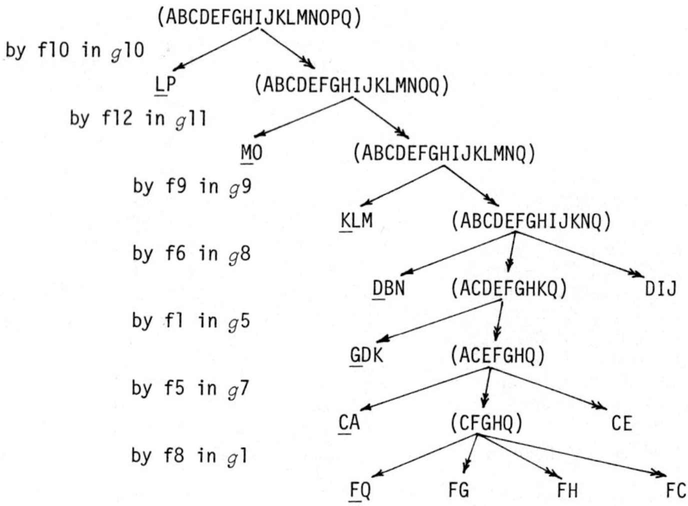

Fig. 11. A 4NF D*-tree schema of a data base in Fig. 7.

Theorem 4.1.

A schema S(T0) where T0 is a decomposition tree obtained by Decomp($\Omega 0,\Gamma$) is a 4NF schema of ($\Omega 0,\Gamma$).

proof

Obviously, each constituent relation is in 4NF. Thus we show that if there exist ($\Omega i,\Gamma i$) and ($\Omega j,\Gamma j$) in S(T0) such that $\Omega i \dashrightarrow \Omega j$ and $\Omega j \dashrightarrow \Omega i$ simultaneously hold then i and j are equal. Assume that two leaves ($\Omega i,\Gamma i$) and ($\Omega j,\Gamma j$) appear in different subtrees of T0. Then we can find a pair of subtrees T1 and T2 such that T1 and T2 are both sons of another subtree T and that the i-th scheme is a leaf in T1 while the j-th scheme is in T2. Since $\Omega(T1) \cap \Omega(T2) \twoheadrightarrow \Omega(T1)|\Omega(T2)$ in $\Omega(T1) \cup \Omega(T2)$ holds and Ωi (Ωj) is a subset of Ω(T1) (Ω(T2)), we can conclude by FD-MVD3 that $\Omega(T1) \cap \Omega(T2) \dashrightarrow \Omega i \Omega j$. Therefore, Ωi and Ωj are in the left most son tree of T, i.e., in T0' where T0=(T0';T1,..., Tn). This contradicts the assumption.

We now prove the weak-irredundancy of this decomposition.

Theorem 4.2.

For any leaf Tki of a 4NF D*-tree schema T0 thus obtained, there exists no such subtree T of T0 satisfying that T=(T1; T2, ..., Tk, ...), Tk=(Tk1; Tk2, ..., Tki, ...), and Ω(Tki) is a subset of either $\cup_{j\neq k} \Omega(Tj)$ or $\cup_{j\neq i} \Omega(Tkj)$.

proof

Let Ωk, Ωk^*, Ωki^*, Ωki denote respectively Ω(Tk), $\cup_{j\neq k} \Omega(Tj)$, $\cup_{j\neq i} \Omega(Tkj)$, and Ω(Tki). Then it holds that $R(\Omega(T))=R(\Omega k^*)*R(\Omega ki^*)*R(\Omega ki)$. If $\Omega ki \subset \Omega k^*$ holds, it holds that $R(\Omega(T))=R(\Omega k^*)*R(\Omega ki^*)$. Thus $\Omega k^* \cap \Omega ki^* \twoheadrightarrow \Omega k^*|\Omega ki^*$ in Ω(T). Since, for any j, $\Omega(Tj) \cap \Omega(Tk) = \cap_h \Omega(Th)$ holds in decomposition trees, it holds that pivot(T)=$\Omega k^* \cap \Omega k$, where pivot(T) denotes the MVD-determinant of an MVD used to decompose T. If $\Omega k^* \cap \Omega ki^* \subset \Omega k^* \cap \Omega k$ holds, it contradicts the minimality of pivot(T) assured by the first part of the Decomp algorithm. Thus $\Omega k^* \cap \Omega ki^*$ should be equal to $\Omega k \cap \Omega k^*$, which is equal to $\Omega k^* \cap (\Omega ki \Omega ki^*)$. Hence it holds that $\Omega ki \subset \Omega ki^*$. Since it holds that pivot(Tk)=$\Omega ki \cap \Omega ki^* \supset \Omega ki$, Tk is decomposed as Tk=(Tk1; ...,Tk(i-1), Tk(i+1), ...) by our algorithm rather than (Tk1; ...,Tki, ...). This contradicts the assumption.

It should be noticed that irredundancy in the strict sense is not assured by this algorithm. Fig.12 shows two alternative decomposition trees of a data base. Both of them are obtained by our algorithm. However, a decomposition tree (b) causes redundancy. If non MVD-decomposition is allowed, the problem of redundancy becomes much more difficult to deal with. We have no solutions to these problems at present.

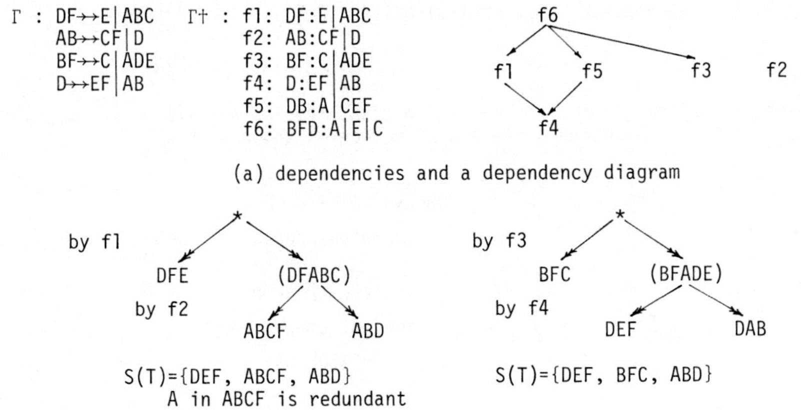

Fig. 12. redundancy that can not be removed by the Decomp algorithm.

5. SEMANTIC CONSTRAINT AND QUERY PROCESSING

5.1. Semantic Constraint

As noticed in section 3.1, a residue dependency structure Γr plays an important role in integrity checks and query processing. However, in this paper, we use $(\Gamma:B)^*$ itself as semantic constraints instead of calculating Γr. For each subtree T' in T, we label T' with a projection of $(\Gamma:B)^*$ to $\Omega(T')$ which is equal to $\Gamma(\Omega(T'))$ defined in section 3.3.

5.2. Query Processing

A query has a following general form if an object data base satisfies the uniqueness assumption:

<u>select</u> Q1

<u>where</u> Pred(Q2; C)

where Q1 and Q2 are attribute sets, Pred is a predicate, and C is a vector constant. The relational expression for this query is expressed as

$$R(Q1 \cup Q2)[Pred(Q2; C)][Q1],$$

where [Pred(Q2; C)] is a restriction and [Q1] denotes projection. It is not efficient to execute this expression directly. However, some optimization techniques are already known [SMIT75]. Therefore, if we can automate the process to compose a relational expression for R(Q1,Q2), we can design a highly non-procedural query language.

The following recursive procedure execute this process for $Q=Q1 \cup Q2$ when called with Ω, T respectively set to Q and a 4NF D*-tree schema T0, where pivot(T) denotes an MVD-determinant of the MVD used to decompose T.

```
recursive procedure  Rel(Ω,T);
  begin
    if T is a leaf
      then
        Rel:=R(Ω(T))[Ω]
      else
        if Ω-pivot(T)≠φ and there exists T' in son(T) s.t. Ω ⊂ Ω(T')
          then
            Rel:=Rel(Ω,T')
          else
            Rel:=(Π_{T' ε son(T), Ω(T')∩Ω≠φ} Rel(pivot(T) ∪ (Ω(T')∩Ω), T'))[Ω];
  end;
```

Although the algorithm gives a desired expression, this is not always the simplest expression for R(Q). An example of this situation is shown in Fig.13.

Γ : $AB \to\to C|D$
$B \to\to C|D$

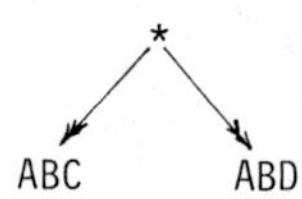

Query : Q = {C, D}

automated processing without any consideration for hidden MVD's

(ABC*ABD)[CD]

simplest expression

(BC*BD)[CD]

Fig. 13. The necessity of consideration for hidden MVD's to compose an irredundant relational expression for a given query.

Therefore, we have to replace the last line of the algorithm by

$$\min_{X \twoheadrightarrow W1|W2|\ldots|Wn \,\varepsilon\, \Gamma(\Omega(T))} \left(\Pi_{Wi \cap \Omega \neq \phi} \mathrm{Rel}(X(Wi \cap \Omega), T)\right)[\Omega],$$

where min(E) denotes the simplest expression in a set E of expressions. We do not know what measure should be used in general for simplicity of a relational expression.

6. BCNF D*-tree SCHEMA and BCNF D-tree SCHEMA

6.1. BCNF D-tree Schema

When only FD's are concerned, we can design a schema with another kind of tree structures called a BCNF dependency tree schema or a BCNF D-tree schema directly from a dependency diagram of a data base. This was shown in the previous paper [TANA77]. We review this type of schemata in this chapter with some modifications and compare this D-tree approach with D*-tree approach in the preceding sections.

A BCNF D-tree schema is formally defined as a septuple (N, n0, attr, α, τ, par, Ω0) satisfying:

(0) (N, n0, par) is a tree structure with a node set N and a root n0 ε N. A mapping par: N-{n0} $\rightarrow$ N maps n ε N-{n0} to its parent node in the tree.
(1) representability : $R(\Omega 0) = \Pi_{n \,\varepsilon\, N} R(attr(n))$.
(2) irredundancy
$\neg \exists n \,\varepsilon\, N, \exists A \,\varepsilon\, attr(n) \; (R(\Omega 0) = (\Pi_{n' \,\varepsilon\, N-\{n\}} R(attr(n'))) * R(attr(n)-\{A\}))$.
(3) existance of a key $\alpha : N \rightarrow 2^{\Omega}$
$\forall n \,\varepsilon\, N \; (\alpha(n) \neq \phi$ and $\alpha(n) \rightarrow attr(n))$
(4) existance of dependants
$\forall n \,\varepsilon\, N-\{n0\} \; (attr(n) \neq \alpha(n))$
(5) Boyce-Codd property
$\forall n \,\varepsilon\, N$ (if $\exists X \subset attr(n)$, $A \,\varepsilon\, attr(n)-X$ s.t. $\alpha(n) \rightarrow X$ and $X \rightarrow A$ then $X \rightarrow \alpha(n)$)
(6) Downward interrelational dependency
$\forall n \,\varepsilon\, N-\{n0\} \; (\alpha(par(n)) \rightarrow \alpha(n))$
(7) a list of determinants
$\forall n \,\varepsilon\, N \; (\tau(n) = ker(\tau(n)), \tau(n) \subset 2^{attr(n)}$, and $\forall X \,\varepsilon\, \tau(n) \; (X \rightarrow \alpha(n)))$,
where ker is a function from a class of attribute sets to another class defined as

$$ker(S) = \{s \mid s \,\varepsilon\, S, \nexists s' \,\varepsilon\, S \; (s \supset s') \}.$$

(8) BCNF schema
$\forall n, n' \,\varepsilon\, N$ (if $\alpha(n) \rightarrow \alpha(n')$ and $\alpha(n') \rightarrow \alpha(n)$ then n = n').

6.2. Algorithm for BCNF D-tree Schema Design

The algorithm uses a dependency diagram (F†/ε, >). We define $\tau(g)$ for any g in F†/ε as

$$\tau(g) = ker(\cup_{f \,\varepsilon\, g} \{left(f)\}).$$

If a node $g \varepsilon$F†/ε has no son nodes, R($\varepsilon(g)$) is already in BCNF. Let attr(g) be defined as $\varepsilon(g)$ for such a node g. The key of g is arbitrarily chosen among members of $\tau(g)$.

Suppose that a node g has son nodes $g1$, $g2$, ... , gn and that the values of attr and α at these son nodes are already calculated. We define the list $\omega(g)$ of attribute sets as a set

$$\{X \mid X \subset \varepsilon(f), X \twoheadrightarrow \varepsilon(f), R(X) \text{ is in BCNF, and } \nexists Y \supset X \text{ s.t. } Y \subset \varepsilon(f), Y \twoheadrightarrow X, \text{ and } R(Y) \text{ is in BCNF, where } f \,\varepsilon\, g \}.$$

The following program calculates $\omega(g)$.

```
procedure ω(g);
  begin
    ω:={ε(g)};
    while there exists gi for some σ in ω s.t. σ ∩ (ε(gi)-α(gi))≠ϕ
      do
        begin
          ω:=ker (ω ∪ {(σ-ε(gi))∪α(gi)});
        end;
  end;
```

Let attr(g) be an arbitrarily chosen attribute set in $\omega(g)$. Then R(attr(g)) has no transitive dependency and thus it is in BCNF. It should be noticed here that both attr(g) $\rightarrow \varepsilon(g)$ and $\varepsilon(g) \rightarrow$ attr(g) hold. As seen later, attr(g) is an attribute set of a relation exactly corresponding to the location of g in a dependency diagram. Corresponding to attributes attr(g), the list $\tau(g)$ of candidate determinants of $\varepsilon(g)$ should be modified so that each element of $\tau(g)$ becomes a candidate determinant of attr(g).

```
procedure τ(g);
  begin
    while there exists a son node gi of g for some σ s.t. σ ⊄ attr(g) and
    σ∩((ε(gi)-α(gi))≠ϕ
    do
      begin
        τ(g):=ker((τ(g)-{σ})∪{α(gi)∪(σ-ε(gi))})
      end;
    α(g):= an arbitrary element of τ(g);
  end;
```

We show an example data base in Fig.14, its dependency diagram in Fig.15, and the computation of attr, α, and τ for this data base in Fig.16, where f0 is a special functional dependency added for the completeness of computation (ε(f0)=Ω0).

F:	f1: ABC-→E	f2: AE-→CB	ε : ε(f0) = {A,B,C,D,E,F,G,H,I,J}
	f3: B-→DH	f4: D-→E	ε(f1) = {A,B,C,D,E,H}
	f5: G-→DFJ	f6: DF-→I	ε(f2) = {A,B,C,D,E,H}
	f7: H-→B		ε(f3) = {B,D,E,H}
			ε(f4) = {D,E}
			ε(f5) = {D,E,F,G,I,J}
			ε(f6) = {D,E,F,I}
			ε(f7) = {B,D,E,H}

Fig. 14. An example data base and its FD closure.

$g0$ = {f0}
$g1$ = {f1, f2}
$g2$ = {f3, f7}
$g3$ = {f4}
$g4$ = {f5}
$g5$ = {f6}

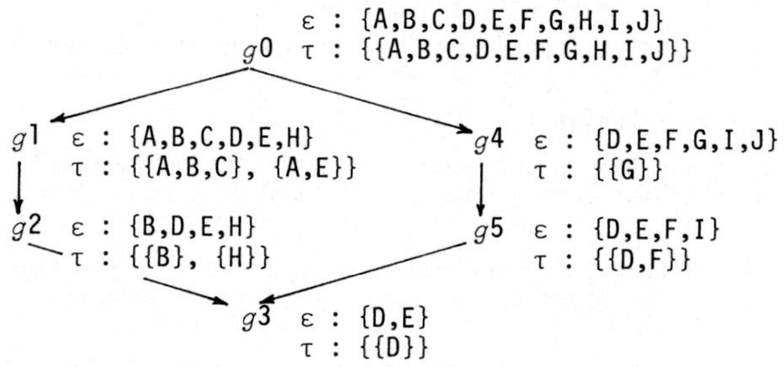

Fig. 15. A dependency diagram of a data base in Fig.14.

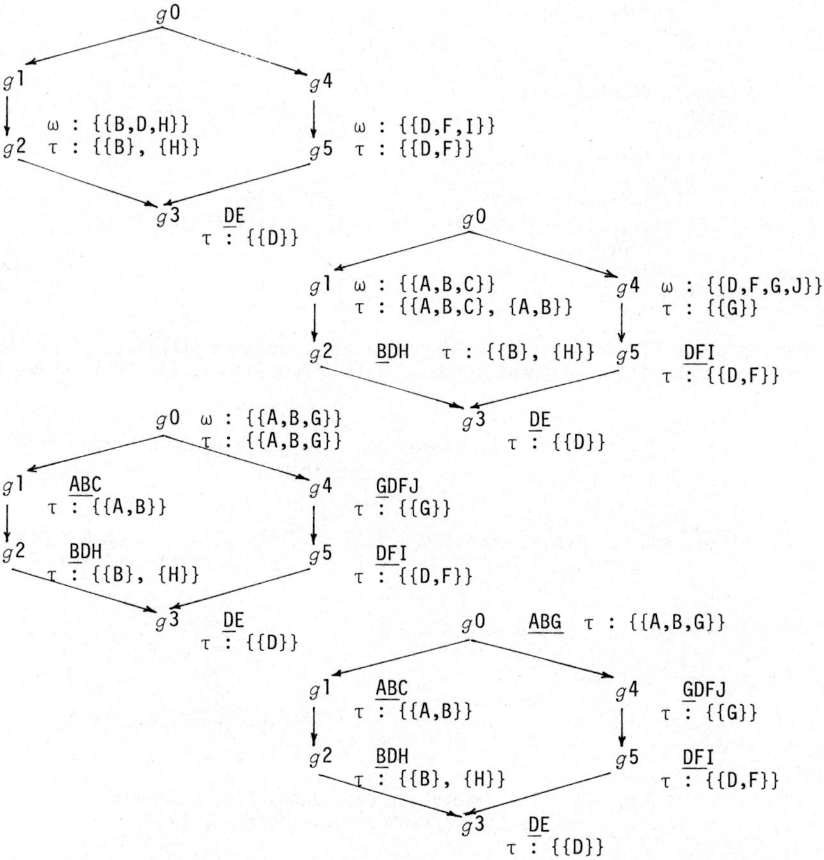

Fig. 16. Computation of attr, α, and τ of a data base in Fig.14.

The resultant diagram thus obtained is a kind of schemata, however, its irredundancy is not guaranteed. Let Mark(r,X) and Delete(S,X) be two procedures defined below, where ID(r) denotes a set of all the son nodes of r in F†/ε. We assume that, for each g, $\mu(g)$ is initially equal to ϕ.

```
procedure Mark(r,X);
  begin
    μ(r):=X;
    Y:=X;
    X:=X∩(ε(r)-α(r));
    S:=ID(r);
    while there exists r'ε S do
      begin
        Z:=Y;
        S:=S-{r'};
        Mark(r',Z);
        Y:=Y-Z;
```

```
            Delete(S,Z);
          end;
        end;

      procedure Delete(S,X);
        begin
          S':=S;
          while there exists r' ε S' do
            begin
              S':=S'-{r'};
              attr(r'):=α(r') ∪ (μ(r') ∩ attr(r')) ∪ (attr(r')-X);
              T:=ID(r');
              Delete(T,X);
            end;
        end;
```

The execution of Mark(g0, Ω0) will remove all redundant attributes from the previously obtained redundant schema. This execution for Fig.16 is shown in Fig.17.

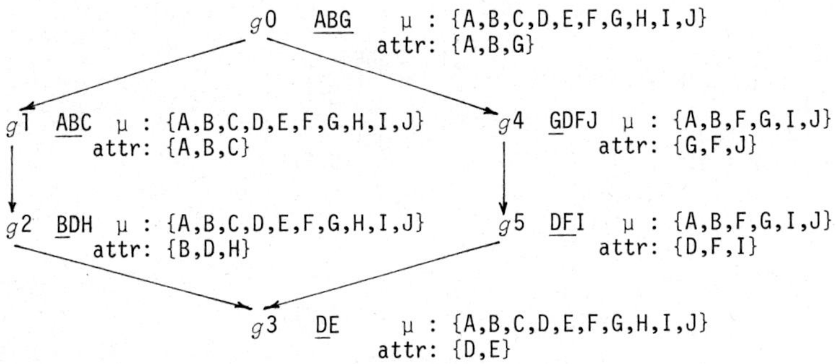

Fig. 17. The removal of redundancy from a schema by the marking process Mark(g0,Ω0).

The par function of a BCNF D-tree schema is defined as follows by truncating superfluous links in the diagram.

par(g) = if attr(g')≠α(g') or g'=g0 then g'
else par(g'), where g' is a parent node of g satisfying
that μ(g') ⊃ μ(g).

The irredundant BCNF D-tree schema can be obtained by deleting those nodes except g0 that have no dependant part, i.e., α(g)=attr(g). The conditions (3),(4),(5),(6) in section 6.1 hold from the definition of par, (1),(2) hold from the definition of μ, and (7),(8) hold from the construction method of (F†/ε,>). Fig.18 shows a resultant BCNF D-tree schema of the example data base in Fig.14.

Since the algorithm is nondeterministic at several steps, man machine interaction may be necessary to design a better schema.

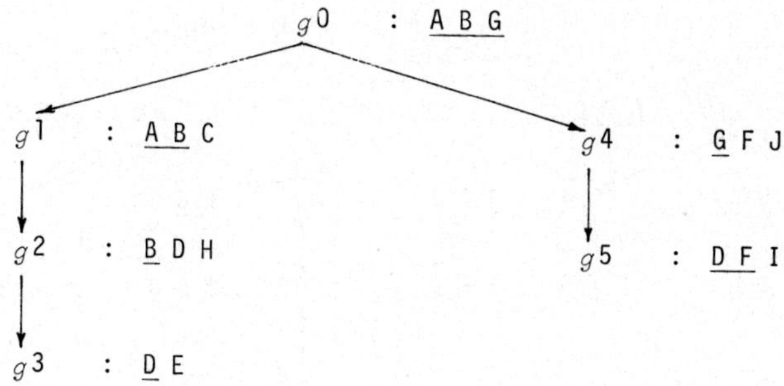

Fig. 18 A BCNF D-tree schema for a data base in Fig.14.

6.3. Query Processing with a BCNF D-tree Schema

When a BCNF D-tree schema is used, the most simplified relational expression that gives R(Q) is constructed by the following algorithm for arbitrarily given Q. For each A in $\Omega 0$, we define the node node(A) in N that is uniquely determined as

$$\text{node}(A) = \text{if } A \in \text{attr}(g0) \text{ then } g0 \text{ else } g \text{ s.t. } A \in \text{attr}(g)-\alpha(g).$$

Let des(g) denote all the descendant nodes of g including g itself, and Rel(g) denote R(attr(g)). We define a minimal node in a subset N' of N as a minimal element of N' with respect to the partial order ">". A relational expression for R(Q) is given by rel(Q) of the following procedure.

```
procedure rel(Q);
  begin
    rel:=11 ; ( 11 is the identity of join operation. )
    M:=N;
    while Q≠φ do
      begin
        Ωd:= ∪_{r ε M} (α(r)-μ(r));
         if Q-Ωd=φ
          then P:=Q
          else P:=Q-Ωd;
        r:=minimal node of {node(A) | A ε P};
        if Q-attr(r)=φ
          then
            begin
              rel:=rel*(Rel(r)[Q]);
              Q:=φ;
            end
          else
            begin
              rel:=rel*(Rel(r)[α(r)∪ Q]);
              Q:=(Q-attr(r))∪ α(r);
              M:=M-des(r);
            end;
      end;
  end;
```

In Fig.19, the composition process of a relational expression for Q={I, J} in the example data base Fig.14 is shown.

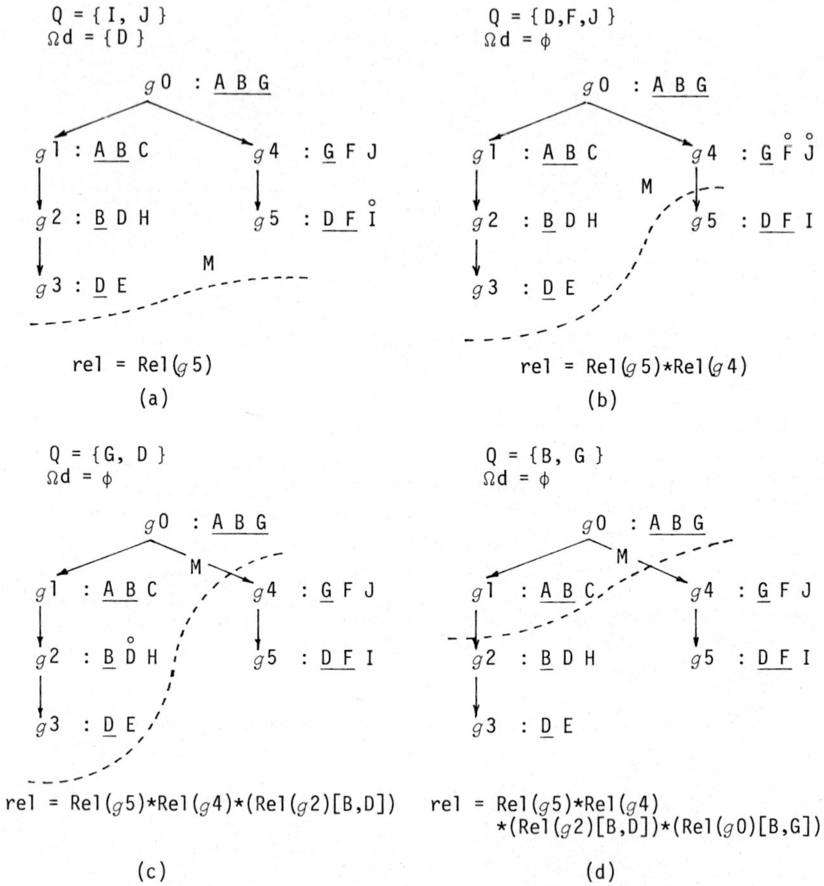

Fig. 19. The composition process of a relational expression for Q={I,J} in the example data base Fig.18.

6.4. Comparison between BCNF D-tree Schema and BCNF D*-tree Schema

If we apply the algorithm for D*-tree schema to the same example in section 6.2, we obtain a resultant BCNF D*-tree schema as shown in Fig.20 (a). Fig.20 (b) is the restructuring of (a) into a D-tree like form. The comparison shows that DFI in Fig.18 is replaced by ABFI in Fig.20, and that ABF-→DF holds but not DF-→ABF. In reality, from the properties of a dependency diagram, it can be proved that, in a BCNF D-tree schema, if A ε attr(n)-α(n), then there is no FD's X-→A such that α(n)-→X and A is nonprime in the set of all the attributes dependent on X. This property does not hold in a BCNF D*-tree schema. It is very difficult to modify the algorithm for 4NF D*-tree schema to 4NF D-tree schema theory.

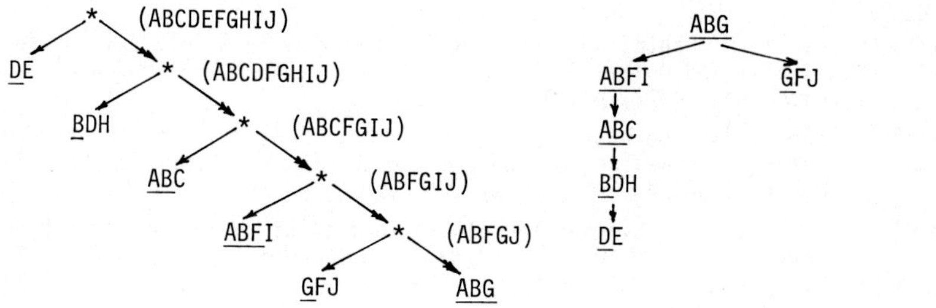

(a) BCNF D*-tree schema

(b) BCNF D*-tree schema in D-tree representation

Fig. 20. BCNF D*-tree schema corresponding to the BCNF D-tree schema in Fig.18.

7. CONCLUDING REMARKS

The D*-tree schema and D-tree schema approaches presented in this paper are useful to cope with the logical problems of data bases concerning data base integrity. We are implementing a relational query language based on these approaches that is similar to SEQUEL but has default facility to analyze the access path when FROM clause is omitted. The validity check of update operation can be also treated following this approach. We can find a set of relations necessary to check dependency structures with respect to the validity of update request. It should be noticed that the introduction of interrelational tree structure is not the complication of a schema but the simplification of it. Therefore, the handleability of a schema is increased significantly.

On the other hand, this simplification may cause various problems concerning a gap between the reality and its rather mathematical model [KENT78]. Further studies such as [SCHM75][SMIT77] may be necessary to fill up this gap. One of them may be a theoretical basis for a design of attribute sets each of which satisfies the uniqueness assumption.

Problems also exist among different interpretation of mathematical models. Although the concept of independent relations by J.Rissanen [RISS77] has suggested some theoretical orientation, we do not think this interpretation problem like the selection problem among synthesis and decomposition approaches may be tractable in mathematical formalizations. We believe some of the integrity checks must be done procedurally. Hence we think it is not absolutely necessary to make a schema to embody all dependencies. This is the reason we are standing on the basis of decomposition approaches.

As to the decomposability of a relation, the concept of mutual dependency [NICO78] may be interesting to consider in D-tree and D*-tree frameworks. However, much more studies may be necessary to know complete mathematical properties of relational structures.

Acknowledgements

This work is supported by the Grant-in-Aid from the Ministry of Education of Japan. The author wishes to express his thanks to Prof. T.Tsuda.

References

[BEER77] C. Beeri, R. Fagin, and J.H. Howard, "A Complete Axiomatization for Functional and Multivalued Dependencies," Proc. ACM-SIGMOD Conf., Toronto, Aug. 1977, pp. 47-61.

[BEER78] C. Beeri, P.A. Bernstein, and N. Goodman, "A Sophisticate's Introduction to Database Normalization Theory," Proc. 4th VLDB Conf., Berlin, Sept. 1978, pp. 113-124.

[BERN76] P.A. Bernstein, "Synthesizing Third Normal Form Relations from Functional Dependencies," *ACM Trans. on Database Sys.*, Vol. 1, No. 4 (Dec. 1976), pp. 277-298.

[CODD70] E.F. Codd, "A Relational Model for Large Shared Data Bases," *CACM*, Vol. 13, No. 6 (June, 1970), pp. 377-387.

[CODD72] E.F. Codd, "Further Normalization of the Data Base Relational Model," in *Data Base Systems* (R. Rustin, ed.), Prentice-Hall, Englewood Cliffs, N.J., 1972, pp. 33-64.

[CODD74] E.F. Codd, "Recent Investigations in Relational Data Base Systems," Proc. IFIP 74, North-Holland, 1974, pp. 1017-1021.

[DELO72] C. Delobel and R.C. Casey, "Decomposition of a Data Base and the Theory of Boolean Switching Functions," *IBM J. of Res. and Dev.*, Vol. 17, No. 5 (Sept. 1972), pp. 370-386.

[FAGI77] R. Fagin, "Multivalued Dependencies and a New Normal Form for Relational Data Bases," *ACM Trans. on Database Sys.*, Vol. 2, No. 3 (Sept. 1977), pp. 262-278.

[KENT73] W. Kent, "A Primer of Normal Forms," IBM Sys. Dev. Div., TR02.600, San Jose, Cal., 1973.

[KENT78] W. Kent, *Data and Reality*, North-Holland, Amsterdam, 1978.

[NICO78] J.M. Nicolas, "Mutual Dependencies and Some Results on Undecomposable Relations," Proc. 4th VLDB Conf., Berlin, Sept. 1978, pp. 360-367.

[RISS77] J. Rissanen, "Independent Components of Relations," *ACM Trans. on Database Sys.*, Vol. 2, No. 4 (Dec. 1977), pp. 317-325.

[SCHM75] H.A. Schmid and J.R. Swenson, "On the Semantics of the Relational Data Model," Proc. 1975 ACM-SIGMOD Conf., San Jose, Cal., pp.211-223.

[SMIT75] J.M. Smith and P.Y.T. Chang, "Optimizing the Performance of a Relational Algebra Database Interface," *CACM*, Vol. 18, No. 10 (Oct. 1975), pp. 568-579.

[SMIT77] J.M. Smith and D.C.P. Smith, "Database Abstractions: Aggregation and Generalization," *ACM Trans. on Database Sys.*, Vol. 2, No. 2 (June 1977), pp. 105-133.

[TANA77] Y. Tanaka and T. Tsuda, "Decomposition and Composition of a Relational Database," Proc. 3rd VLDB Conf., Tokyo, Oct. 1977, pp. 454-461.

[TANA79] Y. Tanaka, "The Design of a 4NF D*-tree schema," Tech. Rep. HU-ENZ-7900, (available from the author).

[ZANI76] C. Zaniolo, "Analysis and Design of Relational Schemata for Database Systems," Tech. Rep. UCLA-ENG-7769, Dept. of Computer Science, UCLA, July 1976.

Data Base Architecture, Bracchi/Nijssen, eds.
North-Holland Publishing Company
© SRC, SSRC (1979)

TOWARDS A SEMANTIC NORMAL FORM

R. K. Stamper
London School of Economics & Political Science
Houghton Street
London WC2A 2AE
United Kingdom

Abstract

Research on the LEGOL language for the formal expression of legislative rules draws attention to a new and fruitful approach to semantics. A data modelling technique is being evolved based on the operations which link data with ostensible reality (not concepts). It draws attention to many distinctions, not found in current techniques, that might constrain the form of the data model tightly enough to remove most if not all the arbitrariness of structure. The operational semantic model is described and illustrated by its application to some familiar examples. The potential benefits of the approach are reviewed. Some of the unsolved problems are indicated.

1. Introduction

1.1 Towards what?

The words of the title will be explained in order to provide an introduction. The research* we are doing is intended to produce techniques for specifying information systems by imitating, in a formal language (LEGOL), the techniques whereby administrative legislation specifies, in a non-procedural way, the tasks of a bureaucracy.

A person who reads, understands and applies legislation does so with the benefit of extensive knowledge of the world. A semantic model is required to hold that knowledge in the computer system which interprets LEGOL. The knowledge required by the law has to be public knowledge in the important sense that it can be supported ultimately by objective evidence wherever possible or otherwise related to known persons whose judgement it embodies. This criterion of meaningfulness is new for the database community and it leads towards a new kind of data model, as will be shown.

The goal has not been reached. Some of the outstanding problems will be mentioned later but enough progress has been made to cast doubt upon the adequacy of the data modelling ideas currently favoured.

1.2 Semantic - in what sense?

A semantic theory requires a criterion of meaning. Understanding on this point is normally taken for granted, but this time an unfamiliar criterion is being introduced which is crucial to the rest of the argument in the paper.

Suppose we take a legal prescription written in LEGOL, such as the first subsection of the Family Allowances Act 1965.

> 1. Subject to the provisions of this Act, there shall be paid by the Minister for every family which includes two or more children, and for the benefit of the family as a whole, an allowance in respect of each child in the family other than the elder or eldest at the rate of eight shillings

* LEGOL Project supported by U.K. Science & Social Science Research Councils.

a week in respect of the first child other than the elder or eldest and ten shillings a week in respect of each other such child.

This is written in LEGOL

ALLOWANCE(FAMILY) ⇐ RATE(NO. OF CHILDREN) * NO. OF CHILDREN(FAMILY)

or A(F) ⇐ R(N) * N(F).

The most common criterion of meaning is the linguistic based upon the idea of paraphrase judged to be correct by a competent user of the language. (Notice the apparent use of paraphrase in this example: the statute specifies an allowance "in respect of each child" but it also directs that the allowance should be for the family as a whole so that there is in practice no need to create separate allowances. The LEGOL version takes advantage of this and expresses not the statute but an obvious paraphrase.) The linguistic criterion of meaning is basic to most of the work on the machine understanding of language but it is not the appropriate criterion for database semantics, partly because it is too subtle.

The computational semantic criterion presents no problem; the operators have a meaning which can be expressed precisely by stating the transformations they are intended to produce given any valid arrangements of data which the operands can represent. The data administrator wants the manipulations of data to be well-defined, but he needs to know more.

The rearrangement of data without loss of meaning or the equivalence of arrangements under different kinds of DBMS schemata is important. The criteria for transformational semantics have received attention over recent years, in particular by Biller and Neuhold [1] who presented a logical data definition language, LDDL, to serve as a basis for proving semantic equivalence. The function of LDDL is to enable the schemata of different databases to be expressed as a logical schema (in LDDL) through which equivalence can be tested. The formal aspects of this mapping do not capture all the essentials of the desired semantic equivalence; Biller [2] notes that "One weak point with respect to a formal proof of equivalence is that the notion of a fact cannot be formalised. On the other hand a meaningful definition of equivalence of databases cannot be given without use of the semantics of data." LDDL is able to capture the semantic distinctions drawn by other data description languages and it provides a criterion for the equivalence of meaning between two databases in terms of the preservation of structures or distinctions when a transformation is made.

The data administrator must also be concerned with meanings based on the link between data and reality. This calls for a criterion distinct from the linguistic, computational or transformational criteria of meaning. Unfortunately, the literature on databases and information systems provides only a criterion based upon a purported link between data and mental constructs. In a long tradition of appealing to mentalistic criteria [5,9,11,13,14] ANSI-SPARC introduced the expression "conceptual schema" which has helped to foster an approach to semantics in the DBMS community. This was rejected in [21] in the following terms: "As designers of systems to handle and share data in the public domain, we should avoid a theory of data which needs access to the processes inside someone's head." The solution proposed* is an operational criterion of semantics and this paper shows some of its consequences.

An operational criterion of meaning arises naturally from a study of the law. Statements made in a court of law are ideally supported by first-hand observation. To say that the person in the dock is an "employee" leads to the identification of a "contract of employment", thence to the "company" which is the other party to the contract and perhaps to the persons and events which brought into being that fictitious person, the "company" and so on. The term EMPLOYEE so frequently used in data descriptions need not be regarded, lamely, as a concept but it can be treated as an abstraction or summary of a highly complex but concrete state of affiars both physical and social. The operational criterion of meaning asks for an account of the purported link between data and reality in

* See [15] for a modern philosophical view that tends to support our engineering approach to meaning. Hilary Putnam there concludes: "cut the pie any way you like, 'meanings' just ain't in the head" p.227.

terms of actions which can be performed to clarify and then refute or confirm a statement. The data model, which arises from the application of this criterion, serves as a road-map showing how one must travel to obtain ever more reliable evidence until ideally the routes terminate at commonplace objects which can be described and evaluated in reliable ways.

Just as a road-map needs ultimately to be interpreted as the movements of the traveller, so must the data model be interpreted in actions. In both cases we rely upon the interpreter having a repertoire of commonplace operations at his disposal so that the map or data model can be constructed from elementary components which correspond to these simple operations. The law relies upon the ordinary use of language and where that is not precise enough it builds definitions upon a few very simple terms. Thus, even the familiar notions of "family" or "child" are defined carefully in a series of rules in the Family Allowance Act.

Although the final leap from formal symbol to reality cannot be evaded, it can be made relatively safe. The safest way is to retrace our steps, through a formal analysis, from the organisational abstractions and legal fictions back to the commonplace observations and judgements from which they are derived. Then the only gaps between symbols and reality are filled by everyday usage of language; norms of language and behaviour which can easily be demonstrated or taught. The meanings of signs are ultimately rooted in social behaviour so this is the best we can do - better by far, I suggest, than having recourse to mentalistic constructs.

1.3 Normal form

The expression "normal form" has been chosen for the title because it has the required connotation. It suggests a data structure obtained by a series of transformations aimed at removing anomalies in the database. Codd's normalisation aimed at removing the update anomalies. Thus semantic normalisation may be regarded as aiming to lessen (or eliminate, at best) the anomalies that arise when the schema itself is updated.

The essential difference between the two kinds of normalisation is that the familiar normalisation is a formal process, given the functional dependencies that underlie the update anomalies, whereas semantic normalisation cannot be formalised. A database serves an organisation (or at least a group of people with a shared problem). Its schema is updated to account for shifts in the organisation (or problem), changes of view, scope, or detail, and the consequences of such changes cannot be examined solely by mathematical or formal techniques. Nonetheless, they can be examined systematically, and the touchstone is to ask for an operational account of the data's meanings as one might ask for evidence in a court of law.

Operational semantics draws attention to many essential distinctions that one is not obliged to make when preparing other schemata (even in LDDL). These distinctions, which are the equivalent of constraints on the schema, may be sufficiently numerous to force the data analyst towards a unique solution for a given problem. If that is so we should have a canonical form instead of the relatively arbitrary models we must be content with today. The quest for this canonical form is a reasonable ambition, as I hope to indicate. It cannot be a wholely mathematical construct, so perhaps 'normal form' is a better term to use.

2. Semantic Model*

2.1 Context

It should be borne in mind that we are developing a method of representing a formal organisation which is based upon general rules of conduct such as those found in legislation. The purpose of the rules will be to cause certain actions to be performed when certain states of the world come about. The emphasis is not on sharing information and answering questions, but upon performing actions, whether

* The decision to survey the semantic model before illustrating the 'normal form' in Section 3 may not suit some readers who may wish now to glance at that Section.

merely to observe and report upon the world or to change it. It may not matter who performs the actions or what he calls them, provided that they are done. The semantic model is a guide to action. This paper concentrates upon one part, the surrogate division, which is a navigational aid, to use a familiar analogy, not for navigating through storage media to find data, but instead, to navigate through the real world. The model has four divisions for

CONTEXTS LANGUAGES RULES SURROGATES

that will now be explained. (Echos of COBOL are unintended!)

Meanings are always relative to a context which may be subdivided into three parts:

CONTEXT: PROBLEM, JURISDICTION, LANGUAGE.

Even the simplest semantic analysis cannot be performed without regard for the PROBLEM (task or purpose). This was demonstrated in the case of the identification of physical objects in [20]. Just consider the EEC Commission's problem of defining a sausage. The English variety is totally different from the Continental variety and regulations relating to sausages have generated fierce disputes. The purpose of the regulations will largely determine what commodities are brought under their control.

Only a few of the entities with which the regulations are concerned will be so commonplace that they will need no legal definition. Meanings of all legal fictions will depend upon the JURISDICTION; in different jurisdictions expressions will have different meanings. This is especially important for the rules themselves because they will have no sanctions to make them effective (meaningful in terms of action) outside the jurisdiction that enacted them (UK, EEC).

The JURISDICTION is handled as a tree structure of the spheres of influence within which specific bodies have the competence to formulate rules and the power to invoke sanctions. Insofar as rules or legal fictions have a spatial dimension, it is provided by the jurisdiction. This is not a specialist legal idea because, on a small scale, it deals with the distribution of powers in an organisation and the "micro-jurisdictions" formed when people enter into contracts which consist of rules to govern some of their own actions.

The PROBLEM context* is readily introduced within a jurisdiction by grouping rules and their subject matter in a tree structure such as

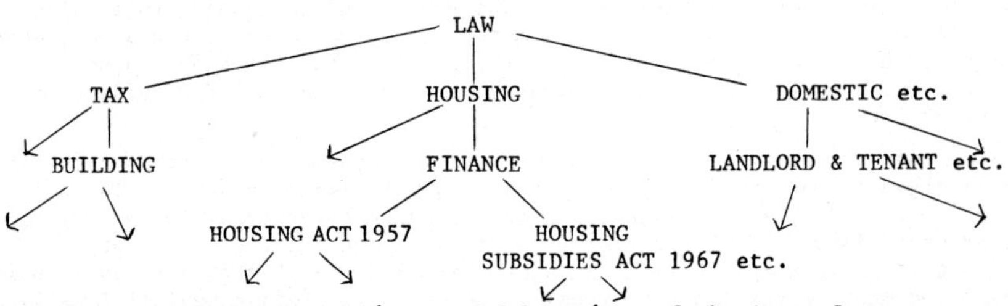

and so on through the Parts, Sections and Subsections of the Acts, Statutory Instruments and the Regulations derived from the Acts. Problem areas straddle across this tree structure and their components can be brought together so that the resulting structure will be a hierarchy or semi-lattice.

Normally LANGUAGE contexts will be mutually distinct, but some specialist, artificial "languages", such as the company codes mentioned below, may be shared by several main language contexts.

2.2 Language

Within a given language context, the language itself has to be specified. Imagine

* Putnam's hypothesis of the "division of linguistic labour" in [15] is closely related to the recognition that operational meanings depend upon the problem context [20].

that the semantic model has an internal code, each word representing some *operation* which helps the user to find a real entity. These code words are translated by the language division into expressions in each relevant language. It may be regarded as comprising records of the general form

<language> <operation code> <expression> <period> <reference>

for example,

ENGLISH	1234	SAUSAGE	——1956	p
ENGLISH	1234	SAUSAGE	1956-1978	q
ENGLISH	1234	SAUSAGE	1978——	r

The law will base the operational meaning of the expression upon common usage but subject to modification by courts which determine questions of interpretation. The references, p,q,r, could direct the user to informal definitions in dictionaries or to law reports. In the example, conceivably a 1956 UK court decision in a case under the Food & Drugs Act 1955 established a new meaning for 'sausage' and, in 1978, this was changed with the enactment of the EEC Regulations. Notice that the word 'sausage' remained unchanged but its operational meaning and that of the code '1234' was altered. Lest one imagine that this kind of facility is peculiar to systems concerned with the law, it is worth citing a database for motor car component designs. The *code* may represent a particular type of component which will be interpreted by an *expression* (i.e. another code) in the supplier's jargon or *language* (stretching the use of that term); there may be several suppliers, each with its own 'language' and any supplier may make that component for only a limited period in one precise way; changes in the suppliers' specifications must be recorded although the car design is unaffected.

2.3 Rules

Legislation consists of general rules of conduct capable of generating specific commands requiring well-defined actions. The commands are triggered by specific states of the world. Legal rules are constraints upon our behaviour. An organisational "law" such as

"Every department must have one and only one manager."

may be exploited by a database designer as a constraint enforceable on the data, but it is more relevant, more important and far more difficult to enforce the constraint on the real world. A semantic model must cope with the fact that a department for a time may have no manager or even two managers. The legal rule, if well-constructed, should be a step towards specific actions to remedy such real anomalies. The action may be formal, as when the death of a manager leads to his post being taken automatically by a previously designated successor, or it may require action such as the announcement of a vacancy and the convening of an appointment board; it might even be a legislative action such as the abolition of the department. Whatever the action, it is nonsense to regard it as constraining the database at the logical or semantic level; it *may* be expedient when implementing a database to introduce a constraint upon the data as a crude analogue of the legal constraint.

Scientific laws may also be regarded as constraints. They are 'enforceable' not within a jurisdiction, but within a problem context that determines their meanfulness and appropriateness. The universality of scientific laws is limited and they are obeyed only in strictly limited circumstances. For example, the Law of Conservation of Matter may serve well in a laboratory but not when applied, say, to international law on the exploitation of shared rivers and ground water, or in the construction of a database for monitoring of these water uses. Here it would be unwise to use the Conservation Law except to formulate hypotheses about water removed by evaporation or diverted into underground streams. Such scientific laws which predict cannot be used as constraints on the database, but they can serve as indicators of *possible* anomalies in the data or to suggest inferences which might be drawn from the data.

Much scientific and legal knowledge is not concerned with prediction but with taxonomy. This information does not belong in the rule division of the semantic model but in the surrogate division which uses our naming and describing conventions to form a substitute world for formal treatment.

The detailed treatment of rules in this paper is impossible for want of space but a version of the LEGOL language, LEGOL-2, is described in [8]. This limited version, however, does not use the semantics discussed below.

2.4 Surrogates

Much more will be said about the surrogate division, but it has to be understood in the context of the other divisions of the semantic model. It includes schema and data in DBMS terminology. The simplest introduction is to present the most straightforward of the structures it contains. These are classes of entities subdivided into some main types including particular 'things', 'conditions' and 'states'. All have the structure:

⟨sort of entity⟩ ⟨characteristic⟩ [{⟨identifier⟩}] ⟨period⟩

The period in each case is the period of the entity's existence, and the identifiers are references to other entities needed for the location of this entity. The variant forms are:

⟨sort of thing⟩ ⟨name⟩ [{⟨identifier⟩}] ⟨period⟩

⟨sort of condition⟩ ⟨criterion⟩ [{⟨identifier⟩}] ⟨period⟩

⟨sort of state⟩ ⟨value⟩ [{⟨identifier⟩}] ⟨period⟩

Before the reader jumps to the superficial and incorrect assumption that this is like the familiar data models, he should consider the following explanation carefully.

We are not concerned with defining a database, but with formalising patterns of behaviour specified in laws. Legal rules specify things in the world and we can interpret the references they make directly in the real world. However, the explication of the semantics of the law is difficult without making use of an intermediate structure. This intermediate structure consists of surrogate entities. The surrogates should be capable of embodying all the relevant facts about the world in order to overcome the problem noted by Biller [2]: "the notion of a fact cannot be formalised." Figure 1 shows how the meanings of abstractions are mediated through the surrogates and the laws which create the abstractions so that only the simplest notions require direct interpretation in the real world.

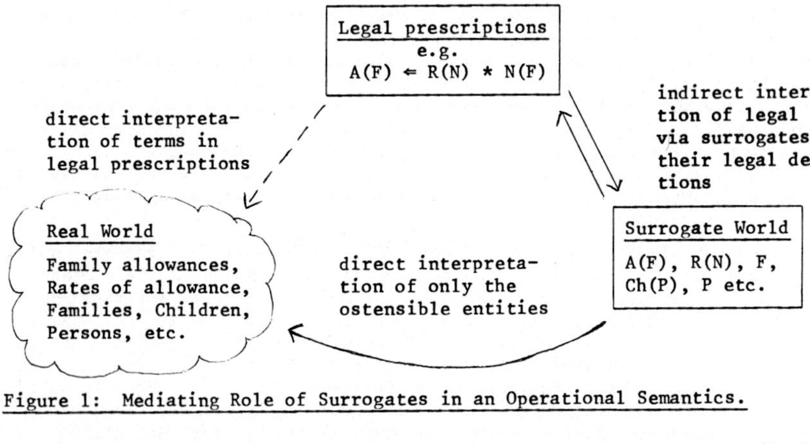

Figure 1: Mediating Role of Surrogates in an Operational Semantics.

As we are concerned with the study of information systems we must avoid the trap of confusing information about the world with the world itself. The idea of a surrogate helps. Surrogates are not statements but formal substitutes for the real world entities to which statements and legal prescriptions may make reference. The word 'fact' is used in this way but sometimes misleadingly to mean 'statement'. We avoid the word 'fact', preferring either 'entity' or 'surrogate' which embody the facts and are assumed to change in step with one another.

The notion of a 'surrogate' was introduced into DBMS vocabulary by Hall, Owlett & Todd [7], but in a rather different sense from ours, at least to judge by certain statements in their paper. They say "In a conceptual schema, it is desirable to hold only basic facts. That such and such a person has age 49 years and that he has a salary of £6900 are two separate facts." and later, "...when an employee retires, his surrogate may cease to exist in the company's information system although he himself may continue to exist." This DBMS interpretation treats the schema as a store of facts in the sense of statements (or kinds of statements) and the surrogate as a sign which refers to an individual employee, for example. In the world of legal or social reality the past employment of the person is a fact of potential importance. The surrogate world must retain this history so the surrogate for the employee would never be deleted in our model. They view a surrogate as a part of a record which can be updated or deleted. In our model the end of the period of the entity's existence would be represented. References to entities that no longer exist present semantic difficulties, but their continued social and legal significance means that in a legal sense they should not be removed. In their Postscript Hall, Owlett & Todd say: "...our surrogates are representatives where the real thing cannot represent itself." (i.e. inside the computer). Our view is different because the law refers directly to the real thing. The surrogates are a technical device that enables us to clarify the interpretation of a LEGOL version of the law in terms of the actions which give effect to it.

It is an incidental by-product of the solution to our problem of interpreting laws and specifying organisations that the resulting semantic model can be treated as a logical database and, hence, as a candidate for the conceptual schema. The DBMS proposals for the conceptual schema do not meet our needs, on the other hand. Besides their lack of an operational criterion of semantics, they fail on one principal score: they make the assumption that the contents of the database described by the schema are continually updated and over-written. This assumption is natural enough if one is concerned with storing records in a limited space; essentially it is a tacit recognition of an implementation problem. Our surrogate division has to accommodate the physical and socio-legal realities regardless of storage problems. Obviously, the conceptual schema embodied in a LEGOL semantic model would be richer than a practical DBMS could always accommodate. Cutting down the "semantic schema" to a shape which a DBMS could handle would entail the making of possibly crucial design decisions. Our approach forces them to be made explicitly and provides a means of assessing their effects.

The LEGOL treatment of time and changes is unorthodox from a DBMS point of view. Time is only referred to through the starting and ending of the periods of existence of entities. During its period of existence, an entity does not change; its surrogate is never 'updated' except to include the end time. Any other change is registered by the start or end of some other surrogate such as a state or a condition. Thus a surrogate embodies only the features which are semantically necessary to identify an entity plus, at most, one other feature such as a value of a state. A basic principle to bear in mind when performing the analysis that creates the surrogate model ("semantic normalisation" it might be called) is that any change, other than termination of an entity, points to the need for another surrogate to be defined (see Section 3 for examples).

The notions of truth and falsity have no place in describing surrogates: a real chair is neither true nor false, it simply exists for a period. Similarly, the surrogate chair should be treated logically, not as a proposition, but as the referent of a logical constant. The notion of truth-value is replaced by the more fundamental notion of existence at the surrogate level, which is the nearest one can get to reality within a formalism. Statements and rules may then be formulated on a different logical level, referring to the entities via their surrogates. Thus, truth or falsity would be a property of a statement and one that may be decided using the surrogate model. Truth or falsity is anyway not a property of a legal rule which must be judged valid or invalid by some quite different criteria that we shall explore using the surrogate model.

2.5 Universals and Particulars*

A distinction of major philosophic importance which has been recognised as fundamental in database design is that between universals such as 'red' and 'human' and particulars such as 'the pencil I am now holding' and 'Sijr Nijssen'. From a DBMS point of view a cogent treatment of this distinction has been given by Smith & Smith [17,18]. Their approach is via the definition of the data structures, aggregate, collection of aggregate and generic. The semantic distinctions which one associates with these structures appear in the LEGOL semantic model in the surrogate division. The fact that surrogates may look like data structures is incidental. Their major function as substitutes for reality is justified by the operational semantic criterion: given a surrogate (suitably formulated in words taken from the Language Division) a person should be able to find the corresponding physical reality. In this sense, the surrogate is a kind of navigational aid. To see how to use it consider the general structure:

⟨ sort of entity⟩ ⟨ characteristic⟩ [{⟨identifier⟩}] ⟨ period⟩

A person acquires social norms, or patterns, of behaviour that enable him to make practical use of universal terms. These are like the orientations that a navigator can select, the primary ones being sorts of entities which partition reality into classes of entities, these classes being defined intentionally by the patterns of behaviour of people, e.g. 'human', 'dog', 'vehicle', 'helicopter' which are sorts of things. In a given situation the person will use a sorting operation to select a set of particular things.** To locate those particulars one by one, he will need to learn the names*** of the individuals. These names are universals, in the sense of behaviour patterns, and they must not be confused with the surrogates of the things they name; this is clear if one considers the existence of the name which usually persists after the termination of the thing.

To be able to observe a condition such as 'happy' or 'together' one needs also to take bearings on particular entities being described, as a navigator does in order to find a particular place given the orientation. That is the usual function of the identifiers, although in some surrogates they can be universals as well as particulars. The final category of universals, values, which characterise states are semantically very complex and represent the operations performed**** in arranging and interrelating the members of an entity class.

There remains only the period to explain. This requires a brief account of the semantics of time. Essentially no assumptions are made about there being a continuous stream of time. Operationally all we can find in reality are events which we can treat with the commonplace notions of 'change' and 'before' and 'after'. Things are entities which we can locate independently of knowing their periods of existence so we can make their start and end events into the reference events. Using a chronometer, we can distinguish short periods which are named by the instrument's calibration. These 'times' in a conventional sense serve to complete the 'navigational' instructions for finding either a condition or a state. Thus

MARRIED	—	BURTON	TAYLOR	1964 - 1974
MARRIED	—	BURTON	TAYLOR	1975 - 1977

* This topic has been treated differently in [21] and the overlap has been kept to a minimum.

** Notice the careful use of 'sort' to mean a sorting action, 'class' to mean the entities which could be selected by this action and 'set' for the actual ones selected.

*** Note that 'name' is used here in a technical sense closer to the Hall, Owlett & Todd 'surrogate' than to the idea of a social security number, for example, which could conceivably change without necessarily changing the name's operational meaning.

**** A full discussion would include the examination of the semantics of measurement which is far beyond the scope of this paper, but see [23] and Ch.9 of [19].

is a condition clearly requiring the periods for the complete identification of its particular instances. There is a natural inbuilt constraint on the period of existence of a condition or state: it cannot extend beyond the period of existence of any of its identifiers because each of these is indispensible to tracing the condition or state in the world. In the case of thing this constraint is avoided enabling one to construct abstract, legal things such as a DOCTORATE awarded to a particular person which will exist in a legal sense even though its conferring and, therefore, identifying university should cease to exist either in fact or legally.

Thus we see that most of the information in the surrogate has a 'navigational' role: it enables us to link operationally the reality to its formal representative. The navigational items are underlined in the following:

⟨ sort of thing⟩ ⟨ name⟩ [{⟨identifier⟩}]⟨ period⟩*

⟨ sort of condition⟩ ⟨ criterion⟩ [{⟨identifier⟩}]⟨ period⟩

⟨ sort of state⟩ ⟨ value⟩* [{⟨identifier⟩}]⟨ period⟩

They have the appearance of compound keys for relations but note that they are not keys for the location of data, though the analogy is useful if we want to treat the semantic model as a candidate for the conceptual schema. There remain two asterisked items which are treated as semantically inseparable from the navigational items: the period of a thing and the value of a state. Each of these is functionally dependent upon the identity of the entity which embodies it. This can be translated into an analogy with relational functional dependencies if we choose to view the model as a conceptual schema. Conditions and states are two kinds of properties that differ in three important respects. Firstly, during the period of joint existence of their identifiers states are always meaningful, whereas conditions are not. (N.B. to treat a condition as either true or false would be to treat it as a statement not a surrogate; there must be a positive procedure for testing the existence of a condition and its failure does not necessarily guarantee that a kind of opposite condition exists.) Secondly, all the features of a condition are needed to identify it, whereas the value of a state is additional information. Thirdly, within a set of conditions no structure is supplied by the criterion, whereas the values of a state can tell one about a structure of relationships among the things it measures.

It may be noted that the semantically interesting distinctions which are drawn by Schmid & Swenson in [16] among "characteristic objects", "independent objects", "characteristic" [relationships] and "association" are all contained in the LEGOL semantic model, but quite differently arranged. There is also an interpretation of the irreducibility concept in the structure of a surrogate; this is not a mathematical but a semantic interpretation. The distinction between condition and state reflects the useful notions of contingent and necessary properties.

One distinction widely used in DBMS work which is not admitted by this semantic model is that of the so-called entity/relationship model [5]. Every entity in the LEGOL model has an independent existence, within certain constraints, and it can be involved in relationships with other entities. Many entities (those with two or more identifiers) would be regarded in DBMS terms as relationships whether things, conditions or states in our sense. There is also no arbitrariness in the choice of entity type as there may be in deciding what is an 'entity' and what a 'relation' in Chen's model.

2.6 Sorts*

Context determines meaning to a large extent and the meanings of the expressions we use to classify the world's entities often depend critically upon the purpose or problem which is the context for both our action and use of language. In this brief account of how sorts are handled in the model it is important to remember that the classification scheme is likely to be problem-specific.

Universals, as well as particulars, have surrogates; they will have periods of

* The term 'species' has been used in earlier papers but it seems slightly incongruous in some circumstances.

existence, the meaning of which may be obscure for such cases as 'human' or 'machine', but very clear for a class such as 'industrial use' which may be respecified from time to time by a Minister. The structure of a surrogate for a sort, in line with the general surrogate structure, is:

SORT OF ENTITY ⟨specific sort⟩⟨generic sort⟩⟨period⟩

in line with the standard entity structure, the generic class being required to identify the characteristic or specific class. The result of this is that we generate a hierarchy of generic-specific relationships with SORT OF THING, SORT OF CONDITION and SORT OF STATE as the maximal elements of three disjoint structures. For example, the problem of ownership may require the following:

THING: PERSON, OBJECT, INTEREST...

PERSON: INDIVIDUAL, CORPORATE BODY...

OBJECT: INDIVIDUAL PERSON, MOVEABLES, BUILDING...

INTEREST: COPYRIGHT, PATENT, RIGHT OF PASSAGE, LIMITED COMPANY...

CORPORATE BODY: CHARTERED CORPORATION, LIMITED COMPANY, PARTNERSHIP...

... and so on.

No attempt has been made to use strict legal terms nor to indicate the dates when these sorts became meaningful, although precise dates could be given for the legal constructs in specific jurisdictions. The sorts of things are not called upon to provide an exhaustive classification, they deal only with major distinctions that are intrinsic to the entities, invariant with time, necessary for identification and providing the general context within which unique names are assigned. In this, our sorts differ from the Smith & Smith generic objects. We do not attempt to include in the surrogate model their notion of a cluster which they define as "a mutually exclusive group of generic objects sharing a common parent". The only constraint implied by the hierarchy is that any specific sort must also be of the sort of its parent. The specific sorts are neither exhaustive nor mutually exclusive unless specified in rules that do not belong among the surrogates, but either to law or "science".

The classification hierarchy can be expanded by applying the calculus of classes to the given sorts. For example,

CORPORATE BODY ∪ INTEREST

might be called the class of OWNABLE PERSON, evidently

LIMITED COMPANY ⊂ OWNABLE PERSON.

There is no need to conjure up a name for every complex class; the expressions generating the classes are sufficient.

2.7 Roles

In a surrogate model a person should not be represented separately as EMPLOYEE, SHAREHOLDER and CUSTOMER because he plays these roles. Roles exist by virtue of the person's involvement in relationships that will be expressed by surrogates of other entities, usually conditions. The roles may be introduced in the surrogate definitions. For example,

Thing	PERSON	P
State	SEX(PERSON)	S(P)
Condition	ADULTHOOD(PERSON)	A(P)
Role	ADULTHOOD(ADULT)	
Definition:	A(P) ← P since (start of P+16)	
Condition	MANHOOD(PERSON)	M(P)
Role	MANHOOD(MAN)	
Definition:	M(P) ← A(P) while S"MALE"(P)	
Condition	WOMANHOOD(PERSON)	W(P)
Role	WOMANHOOD(WOMAN)	
Definition:	W(P) ← A(P) while S"FEMALE"(P)	

Condition	MARRIED(PERSON-1, PERSON-2)
Role	MARRIED(HUSBAND, WIFE)
Constraint:	Start of MARRIED(MAN, WOMAN)

This illustrates surrogates, their definitions in some cases, the role names which they introduce and a constraint* expressed using sorts and role names. The use of role names in expressions is fraught with potential ambiguities and the conventions for this aspect of the LEGOL language have not been resolved.

Roles appear in another way: as components of systems. A system is not a thing, rather it is a way of viewing a thing. Defining a system entails defining a set of system-roles, e.g.

sort of role	role	(sort of)thing	period
SUB-ASSEMBLY	BODY	CAR	
SUB-ASSEMBLY	PROPULSION	CAR	
SUB-ASSEMBLY	CONTROL	CAR	

gives the basic structure of the sort of thing. Sometimes role names are only meaningful for a particular system, as in the government of a sovereign state. (I doubt if any other than the UK government has a role of Lord Privy Seal.) The semantics of systems raises many questions which are still unresolved.

2.8 Substantive reality

The surrogates are representatives of the substantive reality to which the law refers. They are not statements, records or messages about the substantive reality. This can be seen by considering the above constraint that requires when a marriage begins that one partner, known as the husband, must be a man and the other, the wife, must be a woman. This legal constraint is satisfied in the sense that no marriage and no surrogate is formed if it does not hold. A message which says "X is married to Y" is a statement that may be false. If we wish to talk about and lay down regulations to deal with documents referring to a marriage then they will have to be given their own surrogates. Laws about marriage certificates are quite different from laws about marriages but this is not always clear in DBMS schemata, as will be demonstrated in the examples which follow.

3. Examples of Semantic Normalisation

This process of critical analysis will be illustrated using schemata found in papers which have relevant things to say about semantics of databases and the conceptual schema in particular. Often the authors are dealing with different problems from the ones that concern the LEGOL Project. Nevertheless, those who are familiar with our research tend to believe that our semantic problems have already been disposed of by these authors. Unfortunately, that is not the case. The purpose of these examples is not to refute the authors in their varied talks, but to show that our task is distinct in many respects especially in organisational terms.

DBMS research, quite correctly, emphasises computer system effectiveness. Our research is about information systems and concerns organisational effectiveness. The semantic/conceptual schema is a problem shared by these two fields, and we hope that our rather different point of view will be helpful to DBMS researchers.

3.1 Presidential database

There are many versions of this example which has been chosen in order to make a large number of basic points. The version used is from Chamberlin [4], a schema in 4NF:

Elections won (Year,Winner,Winner votes)
Presidents (Name,Party,Home state)
Elections lost (Year,Loser,Loser votes)
Losers (Name,Party)

---

* This belongs to the Rule Division, although it is conveniently introduced with the definition of the surrogates.

Consider some of the semantic anomalies. Firstly, we have

Elections won Elections lost

as distinct relations presenting different aspects of the same election but allowing no place for an abandoned election or one declared null and void. There is a tacit assumption:

not won ≡ lost

which may be valid fortuitously for the closed system of past presidential elections, but future events may not fit this limitation. Semantically, we want an entity

ELECTION

which is a legal construct with a period of existence over-lapping possibly two calendar years (notice another anomaly).

An election will be for an office and this is used to name a relation through which we can refer to some of the persons of interest to the database. The others are also known by their role. The roles are:

President Loser

One is a role in a government whilst the other is a role in an electoral process. The schema begs many semantic questions about the link between an election and someone holding an office. In addition to the election we shall need to identify the

ORGANISATION

in which there is a role or an

OFFICE

for which the election is taking place. Given this kind of analysis there is no problem about extending the DB without adjusting the schema to include elections for individual States of the Union and for governments in other countries and even for rather different sorts of organisations. Semantically, we cannot have these roles without the

PERSON

who occupies them. There is also a relatively concrete

STATE,

the geographic area designated as

HOME

by a person. Can he have several homestates? If so, the relational schema has no room for this politically valuable information. (Quite a different treatment would be required if it means "birthplace" but this will not be assumed. The semantic analysis would force us to pursue the question to a conclusion.) There is a legal fiction

PARTY

to which a person may be related by occupying one of its roles, the simplest being "member" but the relational schema implies that membership of a party is obligatory and fixed.

CANDIDATE

gives a person a special role in the election to which

VOTES

are cast to determine according to complex rules the

OFFICER-ELECT

before he has transferred upon him the

INCUMBANCY

of the President's office. By spelling out this legal process the surrogate model created yields a remarkably stable schema for a database, being able to accommodate even its extension to the reporting of elections whilst in progress, when the numbers of votes may be changing, and the further extension to the interregnum. Changes to the law may alter the model, after all, many of the entities are legal fictions. Nevertheless, only the most drastic revisions of the law will affect the entities involved. From another point of view, countries and states with quite different electoral rules may use analogous surrogates.

The "semantic normal form", as we might call the DBMS interpretation of the surrogate model is:

PERSON
PARTY
STATE
ORGANISATION
HOME(Person,State)
MEMBERSHIP(Person,Party)
OFFICE(Organisation)
ELECTION(Office)
CANDIDATURE(Person,Election)
VOTES(Candidature)
OFFICER-ELECT(Person,Office)
INCUMBANCY(Person,Office)

Upon this, some minor variations can be played depending upon whether one treats PARTY and ELECTION as systems of roles including MEMBER and CANDIDATE, for example. There may be some unavoidable arbitrariness where systems are involved. Systems represent views that need not be adopted unless one is making rules or statements about the relations of wholes to parts.

A graph may be drawn to exhibit the dependence of one legal abstraction upon another; see Figure 2.

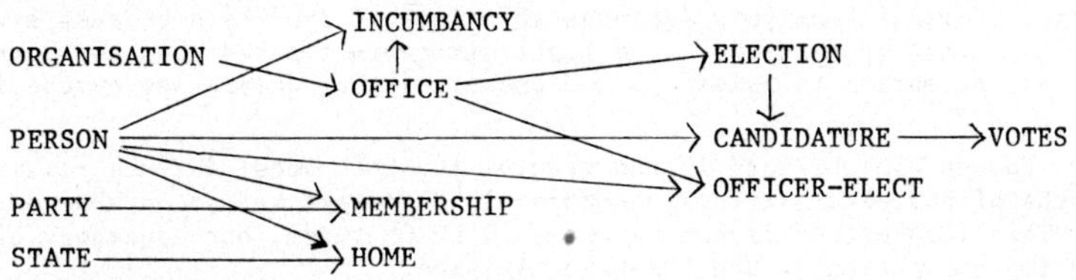

Figure 2: Abstraction Network

The way in which time is handled in the surrogate model and the semantic irreducibility of the surrogates makes it easier to handle what are now called "dynamic" constraints on the DB. The only events are the starts and ends of the entities. The interesting cycle is

INCUMBANCY
ELECTION
CANDIDATURE
VOTES
OFFICER-ELECT
INCUMBANCY

which is not a feature easily discernible in the orginal relational schema but potentially valuable to the DB Administrator.

A similar schema is analysed by Biller [2] when showing how LDDL can be used to demonstrate the equivalence of a CODASYL and a RELATIONAL schema. Space does not permit the reproduction of the example in full, but a summary will suffice to reveal how different is the approach we offer.

basic types are introduced: INTEGER, DIGIT, STRING;
types are defined as subsets of these: NAME, DATE, PARTY, OCCUPATION, NO-OF-CHILDREN, YEAR, VOTES;
intensionally defined types: CANDIDATE, ELECTION are specified by the

characteristic relations in which they are involved and an identifying set;

derived type: PRESIDENT is defined as a subset of CANDIDATE;

characteristic relations, with their domains in brackets are:

HAS NAME (Candidate, Name)
MEMBER OF (Candidate, Party)
HAS NUMBER OF OCCUPATIONS (President, Integer)
IS BORN ON (President, Date)
IN YEAR (Election, Year)
IS WINNER OF (President, Election)
GOT VOTES IN (Candidate, Election, Votes)
HAS OCCUPATION (President, Occupation)
MARRIED ON (President, Name, Dare)
HAS CHILDREN WITH (President, Name, No.-of-children)
MARRIED WITH (President, Name)

Notice firstly the choice of data types as the basis of the schema. In LEGOL the basis of the semantic analysis is a set of ostensible entities; what they are called is a matter for the Language Division of the semantic model, not the Surrogate Division which says nothing about data types unless a surrogate for a message and its syntactic components is required.

Secondly, time is treated as a domain on a par with others, whereas in LEGOL time is embedded in the model in a way that corresponds to a semantic theory of that concept. Historical information cannot always be accommodated readily, for example, party membership and marital history would require other characteristic relations to be defined.

Thirdly, roles are not fully distinguished from their occupants; for example, there is the assumption that a President is necessarily also a Candidate.

Fourthly, the logical analysis which Biller describes would not force the discovery of the full range of legal entities underlying the process of Electing the President. Semantic analysis includes this task of synthesis because its focus of attention is the organisation. The tight structure imposed upon the surrogate model draws attention to omissions and anomalies that only a new synthesis can remedy.

Fifthly, though not included in the precis, the LDDL model defines restrictions on lengths of character strings, numbers of characters and so on when defining types. This information is not semantic in LEGOL terms, but concerned either with DB implementation or the Language Division.

3.2 Expense Vouchers

In order to illustrate another of the basic semantic distinctions which are usually blurred, we may use an example adduced by P.J.H. King in [12]. The example was coined by Hitchcock. It is presented as follows.

"Three different designs, all with relations (files) in third normal form are available." They deal with expense vouchers and are as follows:

Model A: R1 (VOUCH-NO, MEALS, MILEAGE, TRAVEL)
Model B: R2 (VOUCH-NO, EXPENSE-TYPE, AMOUNT)
Model C: MEALS (VOUCH-NO, AMOUNT)
MILEAGE (VOUCH-NO, AMOUNT)
TRAVEL (VOUCH-NO, AMOUNT)

After showing their equivalence, allowing for MEALS, MILEAGE and TRAVEL being role names for the same AMOUNT domain, King says that

> "It does not seem ... that it is at all useful to attempt to identify the 'real world entities' with which the system is concerned",

and furthermore,

> "one can ... postulate that there is a 'real world activity' called a 'trip' which has attributes like 'amount spent on meals' or that there is an entity 'employee' which visits other entities called 'locations' and that an expense claim is an attribute of a rela-

> tionship between them called a 'visit', but it all does not seem very helpful. It certainly does not seem a good approach to make the identification of such entities and of the relationships among them a requirement in order to be able to specify a conceptual schema".

On the contrary! By using the notion of a surrogate it is possible to demonstrate not only that it seems to be desirable to arrive at a semantic model (conceptual schema) by identifying real world entities, but moreover, that it is necessary. I have italicised the word 'seem' throughout those quotations in order to draw attention to the evaluative quality of the argument. As that argument stands, it is reasonable and acceptable, but it has been formulated without regard for there being two layers of reality involved.

Earlier, the idea of a substantive reality was introduced (e.g. a marriage) to distinguish it from a message about that reality (e.g. a marriage certificate). The distinction is a clear one in the terms of semiotics (the theory of signs). Messages, such as expense vouchers, are procedural entities which are real enough but interest us not for their intrinsic or substantive properties so much as for their ability to refer to entities at the substantive level such as 'trips', 'employees', 'visits' and so on. When studying information problems, the point of view of semiotics helps us to maintain a clear distinction between signs and the things they represent. The surrogate model embodies this distinction: a 'trip', a 'visit', a 'location' or a 'marriage' would have quite distinct surrogates from a message stating "a trip was made to visit some location" or from a marriage certificate. The structure of the message could be specified by a syntax using terms such as 'trip', 'visit', 'location', but their real world interpretations remain unspecified.

To build a DB with the meanings of data elements left to intuition is one thing, but quite another is to say that a conceptual schema has been specified when all we have is a document or record design. The three Models, A, B and C, are different ways of arranging character strings on sets of documents or in files. King, on that basis, has demonstrated their equivalence. The only identifying information is a semantic sense is VOUCH-NO which in the real world would lead us to a document.

What is the significance of such an analysis for a rule-maker? If this schema contains the vocabulary he must use in drafting then he will only be able to write rules to control the procedures of filling in, moving around and storing the vouchers and character strings they contain. The schemas of Models A, B and C do not allow rules to be drafted referring to the substantive behaviour of employees spending money on business trips.

This illusion that we have made a semantic analysis when we have carefully defined the syntax of some records is commonplace in DBMS work. It is especially obvious in this example. The reason for the error is the conceptualist criterion of semantics which allows us to rely on the intuitive understanding of the reader, given the names of the syntactic categories. The distinction is clear when trying to specify an organisation: at the substantive level the rules say what the organisation should accomplish whilst rules about the messages only specify an intuitively related bureaucracy. Perhaps we could refer to this problem as the bureaucratic fallacy because it confuses documents with the reality they describe, a common sickness in our society.

In fact we need both procedural entities such as messages and substantive entities. In the semantic model they have distinct surrogates linked by a function which we might call content which maps the signs onto the fragments of the substantive semantic model for which they stand. (A document may refer to other documents, of course, as a batch-slip may refer to a set of vouchers.) The semantic normal form will have to make the distinction between the substantive and procedural.

King's example is not an easy one to analyse, but subject to further refinement, it would be like the following:

PERSON
MISSION

ASSIGNMENT(Person, Mission)
MEAL(Person)
COST(Meal)
JOURNEY(Person, Vehicle)
COST(Journey)
MILES(Journey)
PURPOSE(Journey, Mission)
PURPOSE(Meal, Mission)

where rules would be formulated to use COST when the vehicle is a form of public transport and MILES when the vehicle is a car belonging to the person. The procedural entity we need is

EXPENSE CLAIM

where

Content(EXPENSE CLAIM) = {COST(MEAL), COST(JOURNEY), MILES(JOURNEY)}

The expense claim itself may be treated as an object with this special property of being a sign and having an information content. All the Models A, B and C are covered by the one entity, EXPENSE CLAIM, as they all have the same content.

An important semantic difficulty arises in this problem. It concerns the notion of an action with an intention. The notion of a mission enables the purpose of the expense-generating activity to be specified but it has been dealt with in an artificaal way in this solution. Intention needs a distinct treatment which has not yet been worked out. Although crucial to the interpretation of certain kinds of law this issue is probably of minor concern in DBMS studies.

3.3 Generic structure

Smith & Smith [18] introduced a method of specifying generic structures and gave the example which is condensed into Figure 3. To indicate how the LEGOL surrogate model deals with generics this example will be put into a 'semantic normal form'.

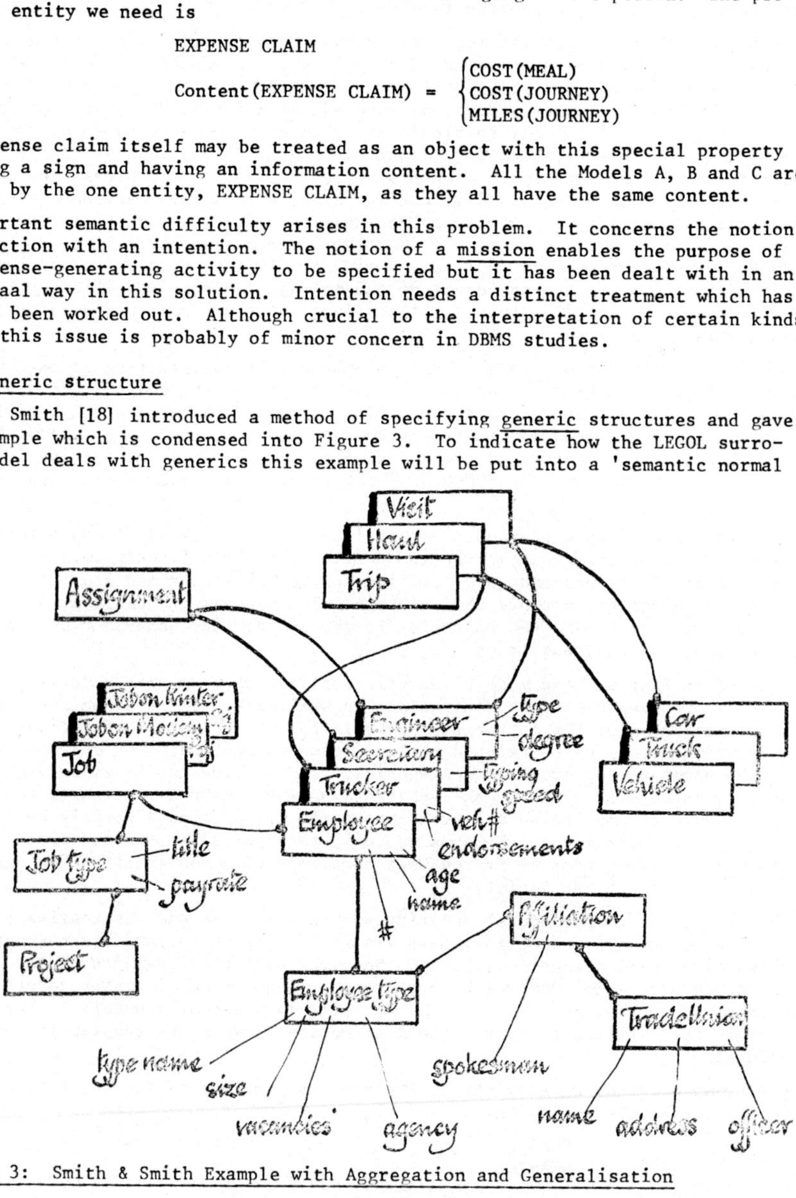

Figure 3: Smith & Smith Example with Aggregation and Generalisation

The generic of Smith & Smith, such as JOB or EMOLOYEE makes use of a common structure such as JOBTYPE or EMPLOYEETYPE to carry the attributes that all the specific forms have in addition to their special properties or "clusters". This is handled, along with some other features, by the use of sorts in the surrogate model, as will be demonstrated.

For the sake of brevity the surrogate model will be presented as a whole. Times are not specified but the periods of existence can always be taken as implicit in any definition. Similarly, characteristics such as names and values are assumed. Generics and aggregates in Smith & Smith terminology are related to, but not the same as, sorts and, more complex, surrogate classes.

	COMPANY	
	PERSON	
	SKILL(Person)	-(1)
	LICENCED(Driving)	-(2)
sorts SKILL:	TYPING, DRIVING, ENGINEERING	
	TRADE(Person) cf. "Employee type"	-(3)
sorts TRADE:	SECRETARIAL, TRUCKING, ENGINEERING	
role	TRADE(Tradesman)	
sorts TRADESMAN:	SECRETARY, TRUCKER, ENGINEER	
role	SECRETARIAL(Secretary)	-(4)
	... and so on	
	EMPLOYMENT(Person, Company)	
roles	EMPLOYMENT(Employee, Employer)	-(5)
	UNION	
system role	OFFICE(Union)	-(6)
	INCUMBENT(Person, Office)	-(7)
role	INCUMBENT(Officer, Office	
	STAFF GROUP(Sort of tradesman, Person)	-(8)
role	STAFF GROUP(Sort of tradesman, Spokesman)	
	AFFILIATION(Union, Staff group)	
	ADMIN-ASSIGNMENT(Secretary, Engineer)	
	TRANSPORT-ASSIGNMENT(Trucker, Engineer)	
	ASSIGNMENT RIGHT(Sort of tradesman, Post)	-(10)
system role	POST(Company)	-(6)
	PROJECT	
sorts PROJECT:	DESIGN, DEVELOPMENT, CONSTRUCTION	-(11)
system role	JOB(Project)	-(6)(11)
	SKILL REQUIREMENT(Job)	
	WORK PLAN(Sort of tradesman, Job)	-(10)
	WORK ALLOCATION(Tradesman, Job)	
	VEHICLE	
sort VEHICLE:	TRUCK, CAR...	
	TRIP(Person, Vehicle)	-(12)
sort TRIP:	HAUL, VISIT...	
	HAUL(Trucker, Truck)	
	VISIT(Engineer, Car)	
	ESTABLISHMENT(Sort of trade, Company)	-(9)
	SIZE(Establishment)	
	VACANCIES(Establishment)	
	SPEED(Typing)	
	ENDORSEMENTS(Licenced)	
	... and so on.	

Figure 4: Surrogate Analysis of the Smith & Smith Example

Some of the interesting features of this analysis are indicated in these notes relating to Figure 4:

(1) the treatment of skills, degrees of skill and trades should dovetail with a personnel DB if the analysis is thorough;
(2) being licensed to drive and having the skill to drive are different; for a trucker plying between UK and Saudi Arabia this may be important;

(3) the notions of tradesman and employee are not confused;
(4) strictly, the introduction of these role names belongs to the Language Division of the semantic model;
(5) by treating "employee" as a role, with strict regard for reality, there is no problem about introducing data on persons who are being considered for employment and we could handle the information for a group of companies as easily as for one;
(6) some systems are introduced to identify roles such as "office", "post" and "job", relating them to their wholes "union", "company" and "project";
(7) the union office and the office-holder, about both of which we may need information, are not confused;
(8) the "staff group" is a collective thing: notice that one of its identifiers is a sort of thing collected or convened, in this case, by a spokesman (the sort is also a role which complicates the example);
(9) the meaning of "affiliation" in the original example is confused because the notions of "employee" and "tradesman" are mixed, and also because the generic's sub-categories, which are classes of people, are confused with well-defined groups - consider the analogous case (see [21])

ANIMAL TYPE —— AFFILIATION —— FARM

which is replaced in the surrogate model by

COLLECTIVE(HERD,FLOCK...) —— AFFILIATION —— FARM;

"establishment" is another example of a collective;
(10) in addition to the assignments of individuals to individuals, as in the original, we have included a "legal" abstraction called an "assignment-right" which has a sort of tradesman as an identifier; this kind of abstract entity should perhaps be called "prescriptive" as its operational meaning rests upon someone's judgement about what should be done rather than upon anyone's observation of what is the case; "work plan" is a further illustration;
(11) the original analysis confuses the generic idea of a job with the need to identify jobs as components of the projects which are systems of activity; here sorts are used to provide a generic structure for projects whilst individual projects define specific jobs as system roles; it would be feasible to introduce the notion of a job sort identified by project sort;
(12) the Smith & Smith strategy of confining trips to haulage and visiting, depending upon the person and the vehicle has the danger of making miscellaneous trips unrecordable in their DB; here the notion of "trip" is unconstrained by roles of driver or sorts of vehicle.

3.4 Methodology

The above examples point towards, but do not adequately define a method for semantic analysis. There will never be an algorithm which can take us from, say, a relational model to a semantic normal form. This is not surprising because we are not dealing with a mathematical problem. It is a problem of observing the relevant physical and organisational (socio-legal) realities and providing a vocabulary in our formal system for describing what must and what we desire to happen.

In the first instance the LEGOL entity structure:

⟨sort⟩ ⟨characteristic⟩ [{⟨identifier⟩}] ⟨period⟩

provides a unique entry point for each universal as it is specified and forces each particular to be given a unique slot in the model without the risk of its existence being confounded with others. Nevertheless, each entity is linked to others by its identifiers insofar as they are operationally necessary for its location, observation, testing and so on. The operational criterion of meaning binds the signs in the database to the realities they represent, via an abstraction hierarchy.

Secondly, the entity types (e.g. things, conditions and states) impose tight constraints upon the existence of entities linked by the identifier structure. An abstract entity can only exist outside the period of joint existence of its underlying identifiers if there is an intervening abstract thing in the structure.

Thirdly, we have noticed that much of the shape of the semantic model is determined by having to build a time-augmenting surrogate world instead of an updating DB. Every possible change in the universe of discourse has a natural place to be recorded as the start or end time of the period of existence of an entity. These times are necessarily associated with each entity. This is often a difficult constraint to deal with when modelling legal or organisational fictions (abstractions) because it is frequently embarrassingly difficult to determine when they begin and cease their existence. Facing this difficulty has often been an important step in the semantic analysis.

Subsequent processes in the analysis depend upon recognising essential semantic distinctions such as

procedural vs substantive

universal vs particular

and removing the confusions of spurious distinctions, e.g.

role-1 vs role-2 (with the same occupant)

current vs historical entities.

Beyond that we have noticed the value of inspecting any assumptions and ensuring that they do not become implicit in the surrogate model because they are rules ('legal' or scientific) which belong in the Rule Division.

Further, distinctions of context are required. We have seen the value of being explicit about the jurisdiction within which the entities are meaningful, but there are other contexts. The problem area of application is important and so is the language context.

That is by no means the end of the list of semantic criteria to be used to structure the model. Space does not permit a discussion of the distinctions between

prescription & description

hypothetical & intentional use of signs

which can lead to new entities being distinguished. Lack of understanding prevents a useful discussion of the notions of causality and of intentional action in formulating a model although it is perceived that these are vital to the specification of an organisation. No apology is made for this inadequate knowledge!

4. Practical and theoretical benefits

4.1 Uniformity of analysis

Each of the above examples, and several that have been omitted for want of space, was intended, among other things, to show from an organisational point of view that surrogates can be characterised in ways that are irrelevant to an implemented DB. By recognising these distinctions and using them to constrain the surrogate model, we shall force any analyst to arrive at virtually the same solution given a problem. There will remain some arbitrariness, in all probability, but we should at least be able to approximate to a canonical form for the surrogate model, and hence for a conceptual schema.

The value of this for the DB Administrator should be significant. Agreement among a team of analysts should be easier to achieve. Packaged software solutions, if based on a careful semantic analysis of the problem area should be more portable. Specific software for the same problem area but for different organisations will tend to show more similarity if based on this kind of semantic analysis. As the next subsection indicates, semantic analyses can be treated as an investment, to be augmented and refined, but seldom discarded.

4.2 Reduction of anomalies in an evolving schema

Throughout the examples we noted features of the conventional data models that might cause practical problems to the data manager working in a constantly shifting organisational environment. Codd showed how the relational normal forms could progressively eliminate the manipulative anomalies of update, insertion and deletion. But his analysis tends to assume that the data model is stable and that only the data changes. The data management problems arise because the model also must change.

A conceptual schema based on a surrogate model would help to reduce the anomalies caused by the changes to the organisation. Time anomalies go because there is a place for each distinct change and history is a by-product of the model which does not call for new entities if it is decided to keep information. Down-dating anomalies which are built into the time-varying database are not encountered in the surrogate model; they arise because one cannot always keep all the data, but one decides which anomalies one can accept, as an explicit design decision following the semantic analysis. Over-writing or removal of data has to be determined by an explicit design decision, it is not a by-product of the surrogate model.

Extension anomalies occur when a data model cannot accept a new but closely related application without restructuring, as when a personnel application cannot use an exciting employee file because distinctions of job/skill/trade have not been recognised. Increase of scope can cause anomalies, e.g. when generic/specific structure is constrained by implicit rules (e.g. define a 'cluster' of mutually exclusive land and water vehicles, then add hovercraft). Greater detail cannot always be accommodated smoothly, but the surrogate model allows for this through sorts, system roles and the treatment of value domains (not discussed here).

Organisational/legal anomalies exist in data models that exploit what Date [6] and others call rather misleadingly "semantic assumptions" (e.g. "No employee manages more than one department at a time."). These are assumptions about the pattern of organisation which can be changed by fiat of the governing authority (legislature). What I shall call the bureaucratic anomaly exists in a data model which fails to deal with substantive entities because it can only be interpreted objectively in terms of message flows and record keeping. Meanings at the substantive level are then outside the data manager's control. Role anomalies can be reduced by distinguishing the occupant as an entity and treating role and incumbancy as other entities. Neutral terms should be chosen, thus "commodity" instead of "product" and "raw material" as the commodity may be either according to its role. Identifier anomalies involve a confusion of the notions of 'key' which is used to locate character strings or lists in a formal sign-structure and 'identifier' in the LEGOL sense which is a set of data elements which have an operational interpretation leading to a real world entity. Language anomalies arise from confusing an operation such as the characteristic of a thing for locating a unique individual with the words that can encode it (e.g. a name and aliases).

A more systematic study of data management in a changing organisation would probably reveal a better structured list of anomalies than this. Nevertheless, it suffices to make the point that a semantic data model has potentially large benefits despite the apparent added complexity caused by forcing neglected distinctions to the surface.

4.3 Theoretical relevance

The surrogate model closes the gap between sentences and the real world by providing an interpretation for the extra-logical constants in assertions and prescriptions. Surrogates are concerned with existence rather than the truth of assertions and the validity of prescriptions. Abstractions are linked to the real world via a ladder of interpretations leading down through surrogates of increasingly concrete entities until the operational interpretation of the basic entities can be accomplished with confidence.

The multitudinous semantic problems raised by Kent [10,11] can be structured and, in many cases, solved by using the framework proposed here. For example, many of the problems in [10] arise from confusion about contexts.

The conceptual schema could be based on the kind of surrogate model outlined above. The advantages would include a more stringent criterion of meaning, a richer and more informative structure in organisational terms, less arbitrariness in its specification and the disentangling of design decisions from semantic/conceptual analysis. Three examples of these advantages are worth giving. Linguistic 'objects' are treated separately from the encoding of operational meanings, so that the system can be analysed in terms of the business activities it should govern, leaving the choice of descriptors and identifiers as a separate design task. Next, it was shown that the schema for a time-varying database tends to pre-empt design decisions about the capacity of the data store and the strategy for deletion, whereas the surrogate model begs none of these questions. As a third example, we can cite the confusion between the substantive and the procedural levels of organisational specification; a sharp distinction between these enables the kernel of an organisation to be designed before a bureaucratic implementation [22].

Date [6] has provided some criteria by which a conceptual schema should be judged. The surrogate model meets these and it suggests some more. Take Date's first.

(1) It should be "simple", simplicity calling for
  a) a small number of basic constructs: this is met because there is only the entity which has a common structure for the types into which it is differentiated;
  b) distinct concepts cleanly separated: the identifier structure and the requirement of invariance of an entity during its existence lead to this criterion being met;
  c) symmetry should be preserved: the operational criterion of semantics shows that many symmetries are more apparent than real (the expense voucher example shows that symmetries at the procedural level of analysis cannot be sustained at the substantive level); the only symmetry within a surrogate specification which may be lost is in the order of the identifiers, and the use of role names or attribute descriptors preserves this symmetry;
  d) redundancy should be controlled: this is a strong feature of the surrogate model which provides a unique entry point for each feature of the real world, whether appertaining to a particular or to a universal.

Date also requires the schema to have

(2) a sound theoretical basis
  a) in logic: the surrogate model adds to logic a new structure that bears some resemblance to a many-sorted predicate calculus dealing not with the truth of statements, but with the existence of entities;
  b) with irreducible structures: the parts of a surrogate are either indispensible for finding the real entity it represents or for embodying a single feature necessarily associated with an entity which can be located; and
  c) with closure: the common structure of sort, characteristic, identifiers and period is generated by all the operators in the LEGOL language for expressing rules.

In addition to appearing to meet Date's criteria the surrogate model has drawn attention to other features that should perhaps be used to judge candidates for the conceptual schema. As the pivot linking the organisation and the database, the semantic shhema should serve both. They are

(3) to facilitate semantic analysis
  a) design decisions should not be forced upon the user of the method of analysis (e.g. time);
  b) separable aspects of analysis should be distinguished by the method (e.g. contexts, language, rules and surrogates);
  c) the modelling method should enforce all the necessary constraints (e.g. existence relationships); but
  d) no contingent constraints (e.g. organisational rules).

(4) to link data to reality securely:
  a) the ontology should be clear (e.g. an individual should not be confused with his roles);
  b) the epistemology should be clear (e.g. any abstraction should be linked via the schema to ostensible reality either of an objective kind or of a subjective kind where the judge is specifiable);
  c) different significations in organisational terms should be expressed in the schema (e.g. substantive versus procedural, descriptive versus prescriptive);

d) structures inherent in words should be differentiated from structures based in actions (e.g. the surrogate attribute of Hall, Owlett & Todd).

(5) to generate a schema which is unaffected except by profound organisational changes so that the new version of a schema may be derived by adding to or deleting from the old, but not by changing the surrogate structure:

a) whenever more detail is required;
b) when contexts change;
c) when further classes of atrributes are to be recognised;
d) when new abstractions, attributes or properties are introduced;
e) when individuals are subsequently decomposed as systems;
f) when historical or hypothetical realities are added or removed.

The extent to which the LEGOL semantic model can achieve these aims is not yet certain, but the interpretation of legislation, which is our proximate goal, requires a high degree of success.

5. Conclusions

This paper has indicated an approach to the conceptual schema from the field of information systems. It suggests some methods of analysis that should serve the database community.

An approach to a semantic normal form has been proposed. This adds many extra-mathematical, semantic constraints to those familiar in the theory of normalisation. If enough of these constraints can be found, it is suggested that an approximation to canonical form may result as the semantic analysis is improved. The model based upon the notion of a surrogate world within a formal system has so far shown how a schema can be created with the advantages of the models previously introduced in the literature plus a high degree of stability in the face of changing organisational requirements of the database.

The work outlined here is by no means complete. Severe semantic problems have yet to be resolved, especially those concerned with causation and with intention. The LEGOL language which operates upon the surrogate model is still in the course of development.

Acknowledgements

To my colleagues, Sandra Cook, Peter Mason and Clare Tagg, I am deeply in debt for many fruitful discussions, their positive criticisms and helpful suggestions. Buffy Gibson, secretary to the LEGOL Project has done a heroic job preparing this long typescript under great pressure; she has my most sincere thanks.

References

[1] Biller, H. and Neuhold, E.J. "Semantics of databases: the semantics of data models." Information Systems. 3(1), 35, 1978.

[2] Biller, H. "On the Equivalence of Data Base Schemas - A Semantic Approach to Data Translation." Information Systems. Vol.4 No.1, pp.35-47, 1979.

[3] Biller, H. "On the Notion of Irreducible Relations." Proceedings IFIP WG2.6 Working Conference, Venice, June 1979.

[4] Chamberlin, D.D. "Relational Database Management Systems." ACM Computing Surveys. Vol.8 No.1, March 1976.

[5] Chen, P.P-S. "Entity - Relationship Model - Toward a Unified View of Data." ACM - TODS. Vol.1 No.1, March 1976.

[6] Date, C. J. An Introduction to Database Systems. (Second Edition), Addison-Wesley, Reading, Mass., 1977.

[7] Hall, P., Owlett, J. and Todd, S. "Relations and Entities." in Modelling Database Management Systems. G.M. Nijssen, ed. North Holland, Amsterdam, 1976.

[8] Jones, S., Mason, P.J. and Stamper, R.K. "LEGOL-2: A Language Based on the Relational Algebra for specifying Legislation." Submitted for Publication, 1978.

[9] Kangassalo, H. "Logical & Semantical Properties of Evnironmental Situations for Stating Information Requirements." Formal Models & Practical Tools for Information System Design. H.J. Schneider, ed. North Holland, Amsterdam, 1979.

[10] Kent, W. "Entities & Relationships in Information." In Architecture & Models in Database Management Systems. G.M. Nijssen, ed. North Holland, Amsterdam, 1977.

[11] Kent, W. Data and Reality. North Holland, Amsterdam, 1978.

[12] King, P.J.H. "Information Analysis for Database Design." Proceedings On-Line, 1977.

[13] Langefors, B. and Samuelson, K. Information and Data in Systems. Petrocelli-Charter, New York, 1976.

[14] Nijssen, G.M. "One, Two or Three Conceptual Schemata." IFIP WG2.6 Working Paper, 1979.

[15] Putnam, H. "The Meaning of 'Meaning'." In Mind, Language and Reality. CUP, 1975.

[16] Schmid, H.A. and Swenson, J.R. "On the Semantics of the Relational Data Model." Proceedings ACM SIGMOD Conference, May 1975.

[17] Smith, J.M. and Smith, D.C.P. "Database Abstractions: Aggregation." Comm. ACM. Vol.20 No.6, pp.405-413, June 1977.

[18] Smith, J.M. and Smith, D.C.P. "Database Abstractions: Aggregation and Generalisation." ACM - TODS. Vol.2 No.2, pp.105-133, June 1977.

[19] Stamper, R.K. Information. Batsford, London and J. Wiley, New York, 1973.

[20] Stamper, R.K. "Physical Objects, Human Discourse and Formal Systems." In Architecture and Models in Data Base Management Systems. G.M. Nijssen, ed. North Holland, Amsterdam, 1977.

[21] Stamper, R.K. "Aspects of Data Semantics: Names, Species and Complex Physical Objects." In Information Systems Methodology. G. Bracchi and P.C. Lockemann, eds. Springer-Verlag, Berlin, 1978.

[22] Stamper, R.K. and Cook, S. "LEGOL as a Tool for the Study of Bureaucracy." Proceedings IFIP-TC8 Working Conference on the Interaction of Information Systems and the Organisation, Bonn, 1979.

[23] Suppes, P. and Zinnes, J.L. "Basic Measurement Theory." In Handbook of Mathematical Psychology - Vol.I. Luce, et.al., eds. J. Wiley, New York, London, 1963.

LIST OF AUTHORS